NOWHERE TO RUN
THE WILDERNESS, MAY 4TH & 5TH, 1864

by

John Michael Priest

WHITE MANE PUBLISHING COMPANY, INC.

31900472

This White Mane Publishing Company, Inc. publication
was printed by
Beidel Printing House, Inc.
63 West Burd Street
Shippensburg, PA 17257 USA

In respect for the scholarship contained herein, the acid-free paper used in this book meets the guidelines for permanence and durability of the Committee on Production Guidelines for Book Longevity of the Council on Library Resources.

For a complete list of available publications
please write
White Mane Publishing Company, Inc.
P.O. Box 152
Shippensburg, PA 17257 USA

Library of Congress Cataloging-in-Publication Data

Priest, John M., 1949-
    Nowhere to run / by John Michael Priest.
        p.   cm.
    Includes bibliographical references and index.
    ISBN 0-942597-74-5
        1. Wilderness, Battle of the, Va., 1864.   I. Title.
E476.52.P75   1995
973.7'36--dc20   95-2000
                                                               CIP

PRINTED IN THE UNITED STATES OF AMERICA

This book is most lovingly dedicated

to

my wife,

Rhonda,

whose love and support have made my life worth living,

and to

my parents,

Rita Marie (Tresselt) Priest,

who gave me my love of writing and of books,

and

Ira Lee Priest,

who taught me that wars do not end when the shooting stops.

Table of Contents

List of Maps

Photographs

Acknowledgements

My special thanks go out to the following individuals and institutions for their cooperation in making this book possible.

Mr. Donald Pfanz, Historian at Fredericksburg and Spotsylvania National Battlefield Park, read the first four chapters of the manuscript. His comments and advice were taken to heart. Mr. Pfanz also took my son and me on our first walking tour of the Wilderness. What a tremendous experience!

Paul Chiles, Historian at Antietam National Battlefield, let me use the park's microfilm copies of *The National Tribune* and provided me with valuable information on artillery projectiles.

Ted Alexander, Historian at Antietam National Battlefield, generously opened the park's library for my research.

Dr. Richard Sommers and his staff in the Manuscripts Department at USAMHI, as usual, were tremendously helpful in supplying me with manuscript material. Dr. Sommers also offered valuable advice on verifying information which I had some questions about and he also guided me to the *Grand Army Scout and Soldiers' Mail* where I found two excellent accounts about the Wilderness.

Mr. Mike Winey and Mr. Randy Hackenburg, photograph division at USAMHI, once again opened their archives for my use. Most of the pictures in this book came from the collection at USAMHI.

Mr. Bryce Suderow generously provided me with his primary material on the cavalry in the Wilderness and loaned me his monograph of the cavalry action there. He also provided me with nominal lists of the Federal cavalry's casualties and with their returns for April 1864.

Mr. Alfred Young, who has spent years working on the casualties and returns for the Army of Northern Virginia, shared troop strength estimates for the Army of Northern Virginia with me for use with the maps in this book.

Mr. Wilmer D. Martin graciously gave me permission to use the Diary of Thomas Alfred Martin, 38th North Carolina, as did Marjory G. Blubaugh in regard to the William Shaw Stewart reminiscences. Mr. Robert Trout, recognized expert on Jeb Stuart, provided me with information on Alexander Boteler. I am grateful to all of them.

As always, the staffs of the Special Collections Department at Duke University and the Southern Historical Collections at the University of North Carolina at Chapel Hill went out of their way to make my visits there comfortable and profitable. Their friendly cooperation has always made my days spent with them pleasant.

The following institutions have also provided me with primary documents: Alabama State Archives, Georgia Department of Archives and History, Eggleston Library, Hampden-Sydney College, Library of Congress, Michigan State University Press, The Museum of the Confederacy, The University of Georgia, The University of South Carolina, The University of Virginia, The Virginia Historical Society, and Virginia Military Institute, and Virginia State Archives.

Jim Kehoe, Antietam Gallery, Sharpsburg, Maryland, generously allowed me to work for him and write at the same time. Friends and employers like him are very rare indeed.

Bill Hilton, my longtime friend and colleague, who, as with my two previous battle books, loaned me any book I needed which he had in his personal library. (Bill passed away on August 8, 1993.)

None of this would have been possible without the assistance of Harold Collier, Duaine Collier, and Dr. Martin K. Gordon of White Mane Publishing. I would like to thank, in particular, Vicki Stouffer and Kimberly Shirley who so painstakingly produced the maps for this volume.

My wife and children deserve particular thanks for surrendering my time with them so that I could do the research and writing necessary for the completion of this book. The Lord has blessed me more than abundantly with the fine family which He has given me.

Introductory Remarks

In the early days of 1864 Lieutenant General Ulysses S. Grant, commanding the United States Armies, prepared to launch an all out offensive against the Confederate Armies. Major General William T. Sherman's Union Army in Tennessee was to leave Chattanooga and sweep into Georgia, intent upon destroying General Joseph Johnston's Army of the Tennessee before taking Atlanta. That would cut off troop movements and supply shipments intended to support the Confederate forces in Virginia and in the deep South. Major General Nathaniel Banks, commanding the Department of the Gulf, was to move north and besiege Mobile, Alabama. Major General Franz Sigel was to move his Federal army through the Shenandoah Valley of Virginia to destroy or capture General Robert E. Lee's major base of supply for his Army of Northern Virginia. Farther to the east, Major General Benjamin Butler and his Army of the James were to advance up the James River and invest Richmond and Petersburg. While this was going on, Grant, traveling with Major General George G. Meade, would take the Army of the Potomac across the Rapidan River along the Army of Northern Virginia's eastern flank in an effort to keep Lee away from Richmond. By positioning the Army of the Potomac between the Confederates and the east coast of Virginia, Grant could maintain a steady supply of materials moving to his army and keep Lee boxed in and on the offensive. That move across the Rapidan began the Overland Campaign - a series of bloody battles which would last from the first skirmish on May 4, 1864 through June 12, 1864. The names of the Wilderness, Spotsylvania Court House, and Cold Harbor conjure up bitter memories of relentless combat and butchery similar to those of World War I and rightfully so.

I have decided to reconstruct the fighting in the Wilderness (May 4 - 7, 1864) from the perspective of the front line soldiers. This is not a book about grand strategies or generals. For that type of study I would highly recommend Edward Steere, *The Wilderness Campaign* (Stackpole: 1960). To date, it has been the most detailed tactical work produced about the Wilderness. (For an excellent narrative on the Overland Campaign, see Noah Trudeau, *Bloody Roads South*).

Nevertheless, I believe that it is necessary to state both how the book is organized and the basic strategies involved in the fighting which took place on the battlefield. The book is written in chronological order so that the reader can see the battle unfolding as it occurred. Initially this means that the scenes of the opening actions will switch from one location to the next within each chapter until the different skirmishes develop into full scale actions in their own right. Once the several independent battles erupt then they are followed through until their conclusion.

Antietam: The Soldiers' Battle and *Before Antietam: The Battle for South Mountain* are filled with vivid (often gory) recollections of combat from the infantryman's and artilleryman's perspectives. *Nowhere to Run*, while written similar to the preceding books, is different. The soldiers' recollections of the Wilderness were not as lucid. By 1864 the armies on both sides had seen so much killing that the bloodshed and the carnage of the Wilderness had become too commonplace to pay any particular attention to them. The war had numbed their sensibilities. They had become veterans. They spoke more of maneuvers than feelings. They described their world in more concise terms. Wherever possible, I have identified lieutenants by their actual grades of 1st, 2nd or 3rd lieutenants. I could not get detailed information on the Mississippi regiments and therefore was not able to provide the company level information to which my readers have become accustomed. Unless otherwise stated in the primary sources, I did not list sergeants and corporals by their grades. Wherever possible I have identified individuals by their first and/or middle names rather than by their initials.

Battles were seldom fought as neatly as the generals' after-action reports tended to report them. I am convinced that Grant had no grand strategy for the Wilderness but that Lee precipitated the action and that Grant's strategy was to fend Lee off then to get out of that terrible battleground. I further contend that Grant did not have a good tactical grasp of the combat situation at the front lines and that he let his generals fight it out on their own.

The Federal cavalry crossed the Rapidan River on May 4 and threw out a protective screen from Chancellorsville to Piney Branch Church, from Todd's Tavern to Payte's Corner and from the Orange Turnpike to Parker's Store on the Orange Plank Road. On May 5, 1864 the Union army's headquarters ignored the reports from the V Corps' pickets in Saunders Field and started a flank march of the V Corps toward Parker's Store in an attempt to get past the Wilderness. When it became evident that a large part of the Army of Northern Virginia might be opposite Saunders Field, Grant suspended the flank movement and ordered a general attack along the line from Saunders Field to the Higgerson farm. The formation of the troops suggests that Grant possibly thought that he could envelop Lee's army with the V Corps. Army headquarters ignored reports from the extreme left of the V Corps at Chewning's that there was heavy cavalry action at Parker's Store which threatened the army's southern flank.

While the V Corps attempted to trap the Confederates on the northern end of the field, Getty's division of the VI Corps moved south on the Germanna Plank Road to the Brock Road intent upon backing up what appeared to be a minor cavalry skirmish at Parker's Store. That division encountered the advance units of A. P. Hill's Corps and became immersed in a major action at the Brock Road-Plank Road intersection. The Confederates had actually flanked the Army of the Potomac. That forced Grant to recall the II Corps which had already reached Todd's Tavern, a few miles south of Getty's division, and send them north to hold back Hill. While all that was going on, Confederate cavalry successfully harassed the extreme Federal left at Alsop's Gate and along the Catharpin Road west of Todd's Tavern, forcing Grant to constantly watch his line to the south. Once Grant developed Lee's army, he decided to hammer it out in the Wilderness. This is not a battle known for far sighted planning and brilliant strategy. It was a no-hold-barred Western fight on a scale of which the armies in the East had never seen before. Grant had men and munitions to spare. Lee did not. If there was a grand scheme behind the Wilderness and the battles which followed, it was one of attrition.

HAPTER ONE

"You have played hell!"

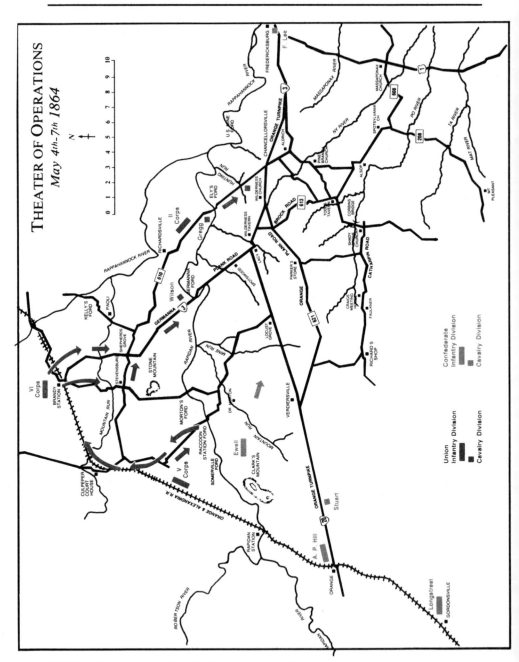

MAP 1: Federal and Confederate troop dispositions before noon on May 4, 1864.

May 4, 1864: The Army of the Potomac
The V Corps at Mitchell's Station

*(7.25 miles southwest of Culpeper Court House on the Orange and Alexandria Railroad. 12 miles west of Germanna Ford.)**

Sergeant Austin "Jim" Stearns (Company K, 13th Massachusetts) never forgot that exhausting day. Roused out at 1:00 A.M., his regiment struck their tents and within an hour and a half had left Mitchell's Station and headed toward Stevensburg by way of Culpeper Court House.[1] Along the route Colonel Samuel Leonard's brigade joined the rest of Brigadier General John C. Robinson's division.[2]

It had become unpleasantly warm. In squads, the veteran New Englanders began to "overhaul" their excess baggage. They threw away letters, stockings, drawers, overcoats, blankets, and knapsacks. Stearns wisely discarded his extra socks and drawers. He cut his blanket in half but kept his heavy overcoat, because he knew he would need it later. He ripped the cape off to lighten it some. Most of his comrades tossed aside everything but their rations.[3] Regimental adjutant, First Lieutenant Abner Small (16th Maine), concentrated upon the natural beauty which surrounded him. He studied the twinkling stars in the black sky, and reassured himself they would gradually yield to a gorgeous day.[4]

Captain Amos M. Judson (Company E, 83rd Pennsylvania) paid more attention to the division's route. About three and one fourths of a mile northeast of Mitchell's Station, the brigade turned southeast on the Raccoon Ford Road, rather than continue toward Culpeper Court House. Small fires lined the road south toward the crossing. After following this road a short distance, the brigade suddenly countermarched northwest back toward its original point of departure. Judson surmised the brigade had been part of a huge feint to draw the Confederates' attention five miles farther west than the V Corps' actual destination – Germanna Ford.[5] Trudging north through Culpeper Court House, the division followed the Orange and Alexandria Railroad to Brandy Station. The men, averaging a little under three miles per hour, marched almost sixteen miles since leaving their winter bivouacs.

The 88th Pennsylvania (Baxter's brigade), Captain George B. Rhoads (Company B) commanding, wheezed into Brandy Station at first light, where, without halting, it joined the lumbering wagon train, and sluggishly followed it south. Caked with the fine powdery dust churned up by the thousands of troops and the wagons, the men turned various shades of brown.

---

* These directional statements will appear periodically throughout the text to orient the reader to the geography of the region so that he/she can get a mental image of its location without necessarily referring back to the larger area maps.

Their mouths were dry and their bodies sweltering. Brandy Station, as Private John Vautier (Company I) complained, did not deserve its name. If there was any alcohol around, the officers had probably already secreted it away because the ever sensitive noses of the enlisted men could not find any of it as they shuffled through the place.[6] The brigade passed through the camps of the battle toughened VI Corps, and, Robinson's division did not catch up with the rest of the corps until it arrived at Germanna Ford.[7]

By morning, May 4, Robinson's division had reached Stevensburg, with Brigadier General James Wadsworth's Fourth Division on the road behind it. Wadsworth's men had already covered twenty miles before reaching Stevensburg and still they had to keep going.[8] A gentle breeze rustled the wild flowers along the roadside. They cheered up the sensitive Small as he marched down the road. When Leonard's brigade passed through the tiny village and crested an open ridge just beyond it, he beheld a spectacle which he would never forget. Below him thousands of infantrymen, marching with their weapons at the shoulder, followed by their supporting artillery, wove their way along the roads toward the Rapidan River. The sunlight, which bounced off their rifles and the burnished cannon barrels, danced in the morning light like so many little mirrors.[9]

The division halted to keep from crowding the lead brigades of the corps which had stalled near Germanna Ford, while the engineers feverishly worked to float two pontoon bridges across the river. The 83rd New York used the respite to enjoy breakfast. An hour later, the New Yorkers resumed the march with the division, somewhat refreshed and in a fairly good mood.[10] The Massachusetts men in Leonard's brigade were not relishing the idea of moving deeper into Virginia. They were heading for the Rapidan River again. The veterans mused over the river's quaint name. On some of the maps it appeared as the "Rapid Ann" – a name which they believed belonged to a fleet footed young lady of days past. The regiment waded through the thick dust kicked up by the huge army on the road. The men were glad to be away from the army's massive, slow moving wagon trains. Near the quartermaster's headquarters a number of them remembered seeing 500 wagons lined up as straight as soldiers on parade. They disliked the incessant racket of mules being shod, wheels being rimmed, and blacksmiths hammering away, and looked forward to being serenaded to sleep by snores rather than by the irritating braying of over 2,000 cantankerous mules.[11]

The VI Corps at Brandy Station

Reveille sounded at 2:30 A.M. in Brigadier General Thomas H. Neill's brigade.[12] Simultaneously, it blared throughout the VI Corps' bivouacs.[13] Nearby, the worried veterans of the 7th Massachusetts (Eustis' brigade) sadly ripped their tents from the roofs of their comfortable log huts. This was their last campaign and they did not want to take part in it.[14] In Brigadier General David A. Russell's brigade, Sergeant Alfred Thompson (Company A, 49th Pennsylvania) started his day with prayer and devotions. He was going to be right with God despite his evil surroundings.[15]

Lieutenant Colonel Thomas Hyde (7th Maine) began his morning with the customary ablutions – his servant pouring two canteens of water over his head followed by a rub down. After stuffing a hard cracker in his mouth, he set out with Major General John Sedgwick (VI Corps commanding) and the rest of the headquarters staff.[16]

The corps, according to the official itinerary, took the road toward Germanna Ford at 4:00 A.M.[17] The ever observant Captain Oliver Wendell Holmes, Jr., on the general's staff, awakened at 3:00 A.M. Three hours later, the corps was on the march. "At 4 A.M., nominally," he smirked, "we started on the Spring Campaign." At 6:00 A.M., he rode out in the cold air upon a newly purchased $150 mare.[18]

The 1st Battalion, 4th New York Heavy Artillery silently left its camp as infantry, detached from the rest of the VI Corps artillery. No drum taps rapped the men into a cadence as they headed south in column of fours. They hauled everything imaginable with them and it did not take long for the men to start shedding their extra baggage.

Wilson's Cavalry and the 50th New York Engineers at Germanna Ford

Brigadier General James H. Wilson's cavalry division, led by the 1st Vermont Cavalry (Chapman's brigade), contacted Captains James H. McDonald's and Martin Van Brocklin's companies of the 50th New York Engineers shortly before 3:00 A.M.[19] At 4:00 A.M., the four companies of engineers pulled their pontoon train into park on a hill about one thousand feet north of the Rapidan. The New Yorkers unloaded their boats and planking and carried them down to the river. McDonald's three companies (D, K, and M) worked a little faster than Van Brocklin's Company C.[20]

Lieutenant Colonel Addison W. Preston's 1st Vermont Cavalry guarded the operation from a position several rods north of the ford. The muzzle flashes which stabbed sporadically through the fading darkness from the southern side of the Rapidan startled Second Lieutenant Waldo J. Clark (Company G). Before he had time to react, his company, with the rest of the regiment in its wake, splashed into the dark waters to silence the Confederate skirmishers.[21] Private Charles Chapin (Company L) took a bath when his horse stumbled and completely immersed his feet and pants legs in the cold water. While he slogged ashore, Chapin glared at the first rays of sunlight which were poking over the tree tops. The skirmishers disappeared and the cavalrymen, having achieved their objective, dismounted to dry out and enjoy coffee. Chapin glanced at his watch. It was 5:30 A.M.[22] By the time the firing had stopped both McDonald's and Van Brocklin's men had finished their bridge work. It had taken the engineers one and one half hours to float and install two parallel pontoon bridges across the two hundred twenty foot wide Rapidan.[23]

The V Corps at Germanna Ford

Brigadier General Charles Griffin's division arrived at the ford at 6:00 A.M. An hour later Brigadier General Romeyn Ayres' brigade marched to the other side of the river.[24] At 8:00 A.M., the 22nd Massachusetts crossed with Colonel Jacob Sweitzer's brigade. Private Robert Carter (Company H, 22nd Massachusetts) felt elated. Grant's "go for the throat" Western attitude permeated the ranks. Carter and his friends believed the Army of the Potomac was not going to recross the Rapidan until that final push was over and the war was won.[25]

Private Theodore Gerrish (Company H, 20th Maine) studied the brilliant blue sky and breathed in a chest full of the balmy air. It offered some relief from the stifling march through the woods below Stevensburg.[26] Birds whistled and piped in the trees. It did not seem as if he were marching to battle. He stared blankly at the dark, swift water which surged under the swaying pontoon bridge, mesmerized.[27] Nearby, the Army Engineers with "volunteered" foot soldiers struggled to float another pontoon bridge across the rolling, rain swollen river.[28] At 10:00 A.M., Wadsworth's division, following an hour's rest, marched across the swaying pontoons to the other side.[29] The V Corps was entirely over the Rapidan by noon.[30] By then the Engineers had another bridge in operation, which increased the flow of troops to the southern bank.[31] The corps halted for an hour, waiting for the VI Corps and the IX Corps to catch up with it.[32] The soldiers crawled over and around the abandoned Confederate rifle pits on that side of the river, relieved they had been abandoned so quickly.[33] Souvenir hunters such as Gerrish scrounged over an abandoned battery position, where they found a pile of 12 inch sections of railroad iron – the Rebel artillery's answer to resupply problems for solid shot.[34] The less curious and the more pragmatic individuals, like those in the 22nd Massachusetts, started breakfast fires.[35]

Wilson's Cavalry at Wilderness Tavern

(6 miles southeast of Germanna Ford on the Germanna Plank Road.)

As soon as Griffin's infantry crossed into the Confederate works near the ford, Wilson sent his cavalrymen southwest on the Germanna Plank Road to the crossroads near Wilderness Tavern and massed his men in the open fields around it. Colonel George Chapman dismounted and conferred with Wilson in front of the tavern. After studying their maps, Chapman called to an orderly, Private Charles Smith (Company B, 3rd Indiana), and told him

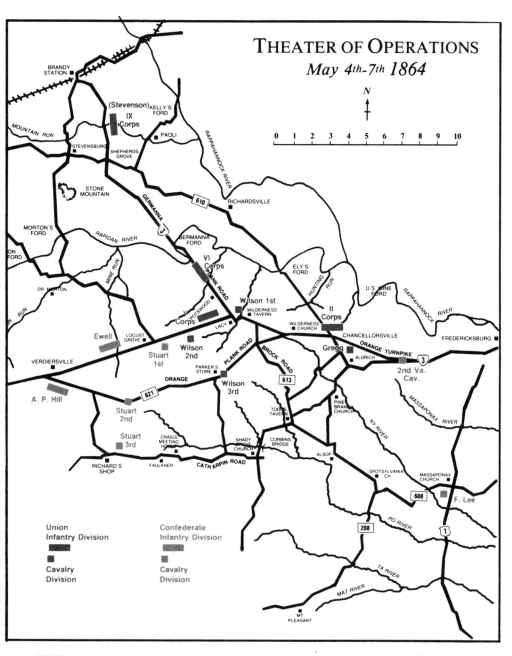

MAP 2: Federal and Confederate troop positions during the afternoon and the evening of May 4, 1864.

to escort one of his aides west on the stone paved Orange Turnpike to find the Confederates.

One thousand yards out on the pike, the two cavalrymen passed over the high open ground north of the Lacy farm. At this point, the road entered the Wilderness, which bordered the northern side of the pike all the way to Mine Run. The woods surrounded the two riders for the next one thousand three hundred yards until the turnpike started a gradual descent into a marshy bottomed, washed out stubble field which the locals called Saunders Field. It measured about four hundred forty yards square. A deep gully cut through the field from northwest to southeast. A plank bridge spanned the washout where the turnpike cut across its path and a wagon track skirted the southern end of the field and crossed the gully at its lowest point. A dense forest of scrub pines and oak lined the top of the swale on the western side of the field.

The two soldiers gently reined to a stop there. Smith spotted videttes from the 12th Virginia Cavalry, who were standing in the road several hundred yards in front of them. With the officer's permission, he dismounted and unsnapped the carbine from his cross belt. He rested the forestock across the saddle of his horse, the reins still in his left hand, carefully sighted in, and squeezed off a single round. The air cracked loudly with the report of the carbine. The weapon recoiled. The horse shuddered. Rather than scatter, the Virginians charged.

"You have played hell!" the aide blurted as Smith swung into the saddle and the two took off for the Tavern at a gallop. A short distance farther east, they pulled up next to a small detachment from the 8th New York Cavalry. Corporal Edward M. Voorhies (Company A), Privates J. Chester Desmond (Company A), Daniel C. Follett (Company B), and Edward Case (Company M) did not pay any attention to the aide who told them to fall back on the division at the crossroads. The corporal ordered a charge instead. The four New Yorkers plowed straight ahead, reaching the bridge over the washout at about the same time that the Confederates did. Smith and the officer watched in horror as the soldiers disappeared from view and the Southerners charged into the swale and met them head on. The sounds of the vicious skirmish subsided quickly. The Confederates, who made short work of Voorhies and his men, clattered over the bridge on the pike after the two cavalrymen.[36]

By the time the Confederates came within shooting distance of the crossroads, Wilson had maneuvered Companies G and L of the 1st Vermont Cavalry across the pike. Private Charles Chapin sneaked a look at his watch. It was 2:00 P.M.[37] The Federals volleyed. Several Confederates toppled into the road. The remaining Virginians wheeled about and high-tailed it back toward where they came from. The two companies of Vermonters, who were under orders to push the Confederates as far as Robertson's Tavern (Locust Grove), five miles to the west, mounted up and drove them to within a mile

Wilderness Tavern looking west toward Lacy's which is in the center of the picture near the horizon.
(MOLLUS, USAMHI)

Saunders Field looking southwest toward Jones' position. The Orange Turnpike is in the foreground.
(MOLLUS, USAMHI)

Confederate works north of the Confederate line looking southeast.
(MOLLUS, USAMHI)

Confederate works south of the Orange Turnpike, looking southeast.
(MOLLUS, USAMHI)

of that place. They halted on the western side of the Wilderness along the edge of a small clearing. The Confederates slowed their pace.

The New Englanders dismounted in the road. Three fourths of them filed into the woods to the north while the horse holders hurriedly pulled the mounts to the rear out of the line of fire. Second Lieutenant Waldo J. Clark (Company G) spied Confederate infantry along the wood line on the far side of the field. He moved his company across the road into the woods on the southern side to take them on the flank. Instead, the infantry swarmed through the woods on three sides of the Union cavalrymen. Rather than be captured, Company G withdrew north to Company L. Together, the two companies slipped back to their horses and raced for the safety of their own lines. The Rebel cavalrymen pursued them as far as Saunders Field before calling off the chase.[38] The two companies dismounted in the woods on the eastern side of the swale and maintained a sporadic picket fire with the Virginians.[39]

Chapman and Wilson mentally brushed the affair aside. They did not realize that Lee's scouts had been keeping him continually informed of the Union route of march. He had already put his army into motion to catch the Northerners on the flank in the Wilderness. The infantry which the Vermonters had stumbled into were the lead elements of Lieutenant General Richard S. Ewell's Second Corps which Lee had ordered to Locust Grove to protect his northern flank. Lee was also mobilizing Lieutenant General Ambrose P. Hill's Third Corps at Orange Court House and Lieutenant General James Longstreet's First Corps, south of Hill. He ordered Ewell not to bring on a general engagement until Hill and Longstreet had time to come up. He had already sent Brigadier General Thomas L. Rosser's Virginia cavalry brigade to picket the Orange Turnpike. Major General Jeb Stuart, whose cavalry corps was scattered from Orange Court House to Guiney's Station to Fredericksburg, took his staff and orderlies on a personal reconnaissance along the Orange Plank Road to explore the Army of Northern Virginia's southern flank.[40]

The V Corps on the Germanna Plank Road

(Near Germanna Ford, 4.75 miles northwest of the Orange Turnpike intersection.)

At 1:15 P.M. the V Corps resumed its march.[41] Every regiment detached flankers in company strength along the western side of the Germanna Plank Road to cover the column.[42] Five miles down the road and about three hours later, Robinson's division, the tail end of the V Corps, bivouacked.[43] Exhausted and dirty after more than twenty miles of hard marching, the sweating soldiers sacked out near Caton's Run, in the vicinity of the Old Wilderness Tavern, on the Germanna Plank Road.[44] Not all of the men reached their camps. First Lieutenant Abner Small (Adjutant, 16th Maine) lamented, "The men unused to marching and heavily loaded straggled far behind, and some of them, together with thousands of blankets and overcoats, were picked up by guerrillas who kept well to our rear."[45] They were on the edge of the foreboding "Wilderness," the scene of a terrible Union defeat exactly one year earlier. Fires were not allowed in that part of the army's line. The men bedded down with their weapons. Not everyone could rest. The veterans in the 83rd New York (Baxter's brigade) did not relish lying in a battle formation so close to where they had been engaged the year before. The thick, tangled underbrush brought back unpleasant memories and reminded them of their tenuous existence.[46] The 12th Massachusetts (Baxter's brigade) ended up on picket in those woods of death.[47] Back at Ely's Ford, the wagon trains finally creaked to a halt. Private John Vautier (Company I, 88th Pennsylvania) wearily glared at the crimson sun above the western horizon and hurled himself to the ground with his weary comrades.[48]

Meanwhile, Griffin's division, at the head of the V Corps, turned southwest along the Orange Turnpike. The 146th New York, after flushing a few of the Confederates from the brush along the road, whom the cavalry had missed, immediately dispatched skirmishers forward to secure the area.[49] Simultaneously, the rest of Ayres' brigade was filing off into the woods north of the pike and onto the large open plateau around the Lacy house.[50] Pickets, under the direction of Lieutenant Colonel Elwell S. Otis (140th New York) pushed to the west and the southwest.[51] As the different brigades spread out in battle lines facing west across the Orange Turnpike, they sent out regiments, rather than companies, into the woods as skirmishers. In Brigadier General Joseph J. Bartlett's brigade, immediately behind Ayres' troops, the 1st Michigan drew the unpleasant assignment.[52] The small regiment of 14 officers and 176 enlisted men left the brigade camp along the dirt track which led from the turnpike to Parker's Store and begrudgingly trudged west. Lieutenant Colonel William A. Throop (1st Michigan) halted his men one and one fourth miles out of camp along the eastern side of Saunders Field, relieving Companies G and L of the 1st Vermont Cavalry.[53] The troopers fell back to the crossroads where they rejoined their division and boiled coffee. Throop placed his right flank on the "Stone Road" (the Turnpike), then spread his men in a tenuous arch, which curved southeast back toward the brigade, until his soldiers connected with the skirmishers from Sweitzer's brigade.[54] Colonel David T. Jenkins (146th New York) and his pickets were posted along Caton Run where it branched southwest across the pike, half of a mile behind him. Neither one maintained contact with the other.[55]

The embers from Ayres' bivouac pulsated red in the night in the woods northwest of the Lacy house. Footsore infantrymen from the 146th New York, who should have been more attentive, wandered to Caton Run, which flowed through the forest from the northeast, and soaked their tired feet in its cool water. The men, surrounded by the ominous jungle of the Wilderness, sensed the silence of the evening more than they ever had before. No one sang. No one joked. Hooting owls and the haunting calls of whippoorwills coupled with the sounds of small game in the woods disrupted the silence and overwhelmed the men with an unshakable dread of the place.[56]

Captain Edwin Bennett (Company C, 22nd Massachusetts) firmly, yet mistakenly, believed that the Army of the Potomac had finally taken the Confederates by surprise.[57] The 62nd Pennsylvania, at the rear of Griffin's division, bivouacked a short distance southwest of the Wilderness Tavern.[58] The division, having been the point of the Army of the Potomac for that day, was going to be rotated to the rear of the column.[59] Jenkins, who commanded the corps' pickets, ordered his men to entrench. He had no idea where the Confederates were.[60] The V Corps' divisions received orders to move south early the next morning in the following order: Crawford's, Wadsworth's, Robinson's, and Griffin's. Sentries were to be posted at every crossroad with flankers well out to the west. The column was to move very slowly with the men staying closely packed together to minimize straggling.[61]

The Sixth Corps at Germanna Ford

Brigadier General Henry L. Eustis' brigade reached the ford at 1:00 P.M. and began crossing the river immediately. After halting for an hour, it continued south, into the Wilderness.[62] Four miles down the road, the brigade stopped for the night. The rest of the corps was strung out as far as the ford.[63] Brigadier General Horatio G. Wright's division camped next in line toward the ford. Around 5:00 P.M., his four brigades flopped down in the fields and woods along Flat Run, north of R. Spotswood's home. In Colonel Henry Brown's New Jersey brigade, six companies of the 15th regiment disappeared into the surrounding forest on picket duty while the remaining four companies settled down for the evening. The 15th New Jersey encamped around a recently abandoned sawmill. The hungry soldiers, upon learning that the owner was a secessionist, quickly turned his stacked planking in the lumberyard into firewood. Before the night was out, they also had ripped down the mill, plank by plank. They split all of the boards and distributed the kindling to every regiment in the division. Some of the more adventurous went so far as to fire up the steam engine which had powered the mill – just to listen to the racket it made and to see it run.

The evening concluded with Chaplain Alanson A. Haines (15th New Jersey) conducting a prayer service. "Some," he sadly recollected, "united in the exercises of prayer and praise for the last time on earth."[64] Other regiments held divine services as well. The chaplain of the 37th Massachusetts conducted church during the evening, which a considerable number of the regiment attended. The night air had turned unexpectedly cool and felt frigid to the sweating soldiers.[65]

Following a refreshing bath in Flat Run, Sergeant Alfred Thompson (49th Pennsylvania) slipped into the woods with Private Samuel Ziegler and one of the Smith brothers in his company. Isolated from the ridicule of their impious comrades, they finished their day with prayer and readings from the religious tracts which the chaplain had distributed during the evening. In his mind, Thompson still saw the sun glinting off thousands of rifle barrels. He could not help but compare the sight with the Vials of Revelation being poured out upon the earth in judgment.[66] The veterans of the 5th Maine (Upton's brigade) preferred eating to praying. Hard crackers, coffee and salt pork weighed more heavily upon them than the conditions of their souls. The bands played familiar tunes into the evening. The men seemed happy and undisturbed by the impending battle.[67]

Surgeon George T. Stevens of the 77th New York (Neill's brigade) reflected upon the beauty he had seen during the day's march. "It was a lovely day," he wrote, " and all nature seemed rejoicing at the advent of spring." In his mind the bluebirds still warbled from the woods which lined the route of march and the wild flowers still bobbed in the dust at the shuffling column's feet.[68]

"Every person.." Private Robert Westbrook (Company B, 49th Pennsylvania) mused in his diary, "left the camp in tears, on account of the smoke..." He had nothing extra to add for the day's events other than a note about the recalcitrant Private John N. Patterson, who, in defiance of the threat of punishment, carried his four shirts with him as he "damned please" despite orders to pack only two.[69]

Brigadier General James B. Ricketts' division camped a short distance south of Germanna Ford. The 151st New York (Morris' brigade) was sent east about 1 mile to guard a stream which fed into Flat Run.[70] The men were hot. Captain Oliver Wendell Holmes, Jr., who was nursing a throbbing headache, complained about how torrid the weather had become by noon that day. He jotted down troop dispositions in his diary. Lee's army was supposed to be at Mine Run, west of the VI Corps. Major General Gouverneur Warren's V Corps was also there. The VI Corps was to proceed another five miles and deploy on the left of the V Corps. Holmes remarked about the division's fine marching and how the many stragglers (apparently from other divisions) had done themselves in by carrying too much excess luggage. "Many of the lame ducks," he sarcastically recalled, "wore boots."[71]

Wilson's Cavalry at Parker's Store

(On the Orange Plank Road, about 3.5 miles southwest of the Germanna Plank − Orange Turnpike intersection.)

The Third Cavalry Division left Wilderness Tavern before dark and headed west on the Orange Turnpike. On the western edge of Lacy's with the woods of the Wilderness to the right flank, the column turned south-

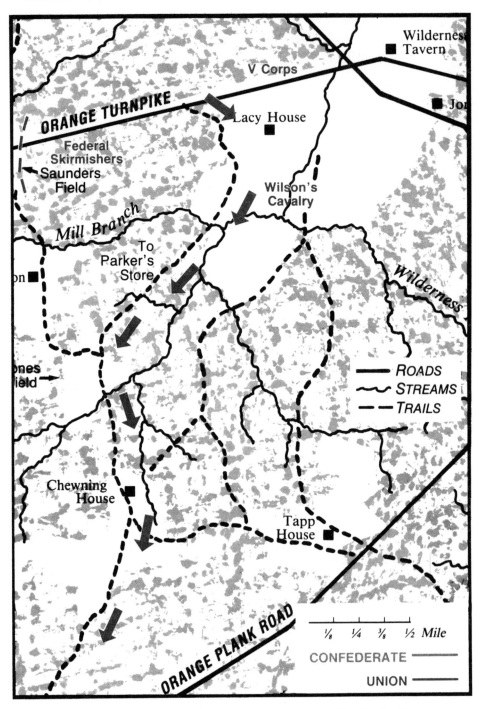

MAP 3: Evening, May 4, 1864 • Wilson's move to Parker's Store.

west on a meandering dirt track which wove through the woods and con-
nected the Higgerson, Jones, and Chewning farms with the Orange Plank
Road at Parker's Store. It was dark when the head of the division reached the
Plank Road, one fourth of a mile east of the store. Wilson sent Lieutenant
Colonel John Hammond with his 5th New York Cavalry west on the road.
The division halted at the intersection, while Hammond dispatched videttes
into the woods west of the store.

At the same time Stuart, commanding the Army of Northern Virginia's
Cavalry Corps, with his staff and entourage of couriers, were scouting the
road from Verdiersville. Colonel Alexander R. Boteler rode near the point of
the command, vainly studying the overgrown woods which surrounded them.
The tree line suddenly exploded along the side of the road. A second volley
illuminated the woods with flashes of orange and blue. Acrid smoke lingered
briefly in the night air before dissipating. The sounds of horses and men
struggling through the brush forewarned the Confederates of a possible
charge. Stuart and his men did not give the Federals a chance to ride them
down. The troopers at the head of the column snapped off several rounds
into the trees and down the road before galloping with the general and his
officers for their own lines.[72]

Hammond initially formed his regiment to receive an attack. When it
never came, he dismounted the 5th New York around the store for the night.
No fires were allowed. The men stood to horse all night.[73]

Brigadier General David M. Gregg's Cavalry Division at Ely's Ford

(3.2 miles northeast of the Germanna Plank – Orange Turnpike intersection.)

The 1st New Jersey Cavalry (Davies' brigade) arrived at Ely's Ford shortly
after 2:00 A.M., at the head of the division column and in advance of Captain
William W. Folwell's pontoon train (Company I, 50th New York Engineers).
Major Hugh H. Janeway quietly led the cavalry's advance guard down into
the hollow along the edge of the Rapidan River to rendezvous with First
Lieutenant Samuel Craig (Company H), who had preceded the regiment upon
a private reconnaissance. The night air was chilly.

At Craig's whispered command, Company H slid from their saddles and
followed him on foot from the ravine to a secluded spot below the line of
sight of the videttes across the river. With their weapons above their heads,
the raiders gritted their teeth and slipped into the freezing water and waded
safely to the Confederate side of the Rapidan. Crawling up the muddy bank,
they slithered into the woods, trying to flank the reserve picket outpost, who
remained huddled about their campfire. The plan went awry because the
pontoniers had advanced too close to the rear of the cavalry column. Gregg,
when he realized that the engineers' creaking wagons and their braying mule

teams were betraying the approach of the II Corps on the ford road, ordered the 1st New Jersey into action immediately. The flurry of activity on the northern bank of the river alerted the lone Confederate vidette on the opposite shore. He fired his warning shot and clattered away into the night. The rest of the outpost rushed to their horses and galloped down the Fredericksburg Road behind him.

Company K of the 1st New Jersey, Captain Joseph Brooks commanding, splashed into the frigid river in pursuit. In the chase which followed, the Union soldiers captured only a dozen horses and men and returned to the regiment tired and somewhat dejected. Craig and the soaked men of Company H, despite their valiant effort, had only wet clothes to show for their efforts.[74] The 1st New Jersey waited upon the southern bank of the river for the rest of the division to come over and join them.

Folwell and his pontoon boats arrived at daylight. By 6:00 A.M. they had laid their canvas pontoons across the one hundred fifty foot wide river. Gregg's cavalrymen churned across the Rapidan to provide security for the engineers and the approaching infantry columns. Major Wesley Brainerd's 1st Battalion of New York Engineers reached the ford shortly after Folwell's men put the finishing touches on their span. Moving to a point on the river where it was about forty feet wider, he set his soldiers to work. It took his three companies (B, F, and G) a little over three hours to string their fourteen wooden boats across the Rapidan. By 9:15 A.M. the pontoon bridge was ready for the II Corps to use.[75]

In the meantime, the cavalry continued toward Chancellorsville which lay three and a quarter miles to the southeast. Small bands of Confederate cavalrymen observed their advance from safe distances along the entire route. Passing through the battlefield of the previous year, the horsemen continued southeast for another one and three fourths of a mile on the same road to Aldrich's. The division halted and camped at the intersection of the Plank and the Catharpin Roads.[76]

Colonel J. Irvin Gregg's brigade (1st Maine, 10th New York, 2nd, 4th, 8th, and 16th Pennsylvania), as was customary, moved to the front of the division to lead the advance on the following day. The 16th Pennsylvania Cavalry drew picket duty at the crossroads.[77] During the evening, Colonel Thomas Munford and his 2nd Virginia Cavalry, which Major General Fitzhugh Lee had sent out from Fredericksburg (eight miles to the east), struck the Pennsylvanians' outposts with about forty to fifty men. It was a short affair. The Yankees captured eight of the Virginians but missed several others who used the confusion to slip behind the Federal lines to reconnoiter the encampments around Chancellorsville.[78] The incident over, the Northern cavalry settled down for a peaceful night, unaware that the Confederates had achieved their objective. Their scouts had infiltrated the Northerners' lines.

The II Corps on the Road Northwest of Ely's Ford

The day greeted the II Corps warm and clear. The early morning march had brought Colonel Samuel Carroll's brigade to Ely's Ford where it patiently huddled along the northern bank while the rest of Brigadier General John Gibbon's division crossed the river. The 14th Connecticut (Carroll's brigade) bunched together in a deep ravine. No fires were allowed which meant no morning coffee. For several hours, the New Englanders sat there, doing what armies throughout history have always done – waiting and more waiting.[79] The brigade finally started to cross on the pontoons at 8:30 A.M. By then, the pleasant morning had turned unbearably hot.[80] Scrambling up the steep, slippery bank on the opposite shore, the veterans gaped at a line of formidable, but abandoned rifle pits across their line of march. The command came down the column to halt and load. With weapons primed, the brigade tramped down the narrow Ely's Ford Road into a dense pine forest.[81] An hour and a half later at 10:00 A.M., the 57th New York (Frank's brigade, Barlow's division) crossed the Rapidan at Ely's Ford. It was half an hour ahead of the rest of the brigade.[82] Brigadier General Alexander Hays' brigade went over, simultaneously, on the parallel pontoon bridge.[83]

Farther ahead in the Wilderness Carroll's men basted in their own sweat. The temperature was hitting the 90 degree mark.[84] Chaplain Charles D. Page (14th Connecticut) watched the soldiers, many of whom had become "soft" from their long winter respite, lighten their packs. When they came across the debris of the brigades which had preceded them, they cast their excess luggage along the roadside as well. Blankets and overcoats sailed through the air along both sides of the column. A number of the soldiers deliberately shredded their blankets to prevent any scavenging Rebels from reclaiming them.[85]

In the early afternoon, Gibbon's division reached the old battlefield of Chancellorsville. Carroll's brigade trudged past a few lines of earthworks. The skeletal remains of unburied Yankees, with pieces of their uniforms still clinging to their sun bleached bones, greeted them before they reached the charred ruins of the Chancellor House in the northwestern corner of the Ely's Ford-Orange Turnpike intersection. A short distance southeast of the once stately mansion, the brigade turned west off of the ford road and marched a considerable distance into the dense woods where it bivouacked. It was 2:00 P.M.[86] Powdery white dust caked the 8th Ohio, which stacked arms and hurled itself to the ground among the remains of the previous year's battle. Before he could sit down, First Lieutenant Thomas Galwey (Company B) received orders to take his company out on picket. Under the direction of Colonel Theodore Ellis (14th Connecticut), he stretched his men over a quarter of a mile front, then advanced them deeper into the Wilderness. While struggling through the dense undergrowth, which laced the trees together, the eighteen year old Galwey peered into the maze of branches over his head and marveled at how effectively they kept the midday sun from reaching the forest floor.[87] Back in the bivouac, First Lieutenant George A. Bowen (Company C, 12th New Jersey) breathed a sigh of relief. In the fading daylight, he scratched in his diary, that they had arrived at Chancellorsville and "had run into no opposition."[88]

Colonel Paul Frank's brigade also arrived at the Chancellorsville battlefield around 2:00 P.M. where it halted to wait for its wagon train, which was strung out for miles behind it.[89] Hays' command, which was still three hours away, halted at the same time for lunch. When it finally arrived at the old XI Corps' earthworks west of Chancellorsville, it found itself among the skeletons and the debris of the previous year's battle.[90] Captain Rudolf Aschmann (Company A, 1st U.S. Sharpshooters) noticed the large number of shell fragments, horse skeletons, and burst shotguns, which littered the area.[91] Not too far away, members of the 141st Pennsylvania (Ward's brigade) stumbled upon some human remains, which still wore kepis bearing the brass insignia of their regiment.[92] Nearly every regiment shared the same macabre experience. The 111th New York, which arrived at Chancellorsville after dark, also discovered the remains of its comrades.[93] Private John Haley (Company I, 17th Maine) recognized the ruins of the Chancellor House as his regiment passed it and he wondered if Grant would repeat Hooker's mistakes from the year before.[94] Many of the soldiers had no idea of where the Confederates were. The men of the 3rd Michigan surmised that the Army of the Potomac was going to wedge itself between Richmond and the Army of Northern Virginia.[95] Hays threw his brigade into the existing earthworks across the Plank Road west of the Chancellor House. Before the men could stack arms, he detached the 17th Maine for picket duty. Haley detested the assignment. The night march and the day's heat had left him too weak, he thought, for such nonsense. The men were quite distressed. They feared another devastating flanking movement similar to the one which had occurred the year before. Haley and his friends tried to reassure themselves that the Army of the Potomac outnumbered Lee's Army of Northern Virginia three to one. Someone started a rumor about water moccasins living in the Wilderness. Haley thought it was bad enough to die from a bullet, but death from snake bite seemed more repulsive.

While trying to quench his thirst from a nearby well, he swallowed a mouthful of the fouled water but was too weak to throw it up. Later in the night, one of the men told him there were Rebels buried in the well from the last year. He did not want to go another forty-eight hours without sleep. Those who could do so, he reasoned, had the constitutions of mules.[96]

The IX Corps Along the Orange and Alexandria Railroad
(15.75 miles northwest of Ely's Ford at Bealton Station.)

While the rest of the Army of the Potomac penetrated the Wilderness around Chancellorsville, the IX Corps, north of the Rappahannock, was just moving out. Brigadier General Thomas G. Stevenson's division got a late start. A train, which derailed during the early hours of the morning, had scattered commissary stores, sugar, and six dead train guards all over the ground behind his camp. It took the willing and hungry volunteers from the 35th Massachusetts several hours to "forage" up the mess. The veterans did not want to leave Bealton Station and the cushy train guard which they shared with the 9th New Hampshire.[97] The 9th New Hampshire had just received its orders to march when a second command arrived in the brigade detailing it and another regiment, the 32nd Maine, to guard the surplus baggage wagons and the excess rations which the division had to leave behind.[98] Stevenson's division stepped out at 7:00 A.M. It crossed the Rappahannock at Rappahannock Station early in the day. Covering the seven miles from Bealton Station, it halted at Brandy Station for about five hours.[99]

In the meantime, thirteen miles northeast of Bealton on the Orange and Alexandria Railroad, Colonel Zenas R. Bliss' brigade passed through Catlett's Station. Continuing a short distance farther, it stopped at noon at Warrenton Junction, where the rest of Brigadier General Robert Potter's division joined its ranks from Bristoe Station, some five miles above Catlett's.[100] In the afternoon, the march continued to Bealton Station, where the division bivouacked.[101]

At 4:45 P.M. Colonel Sumner Carruth's brigade of Stevenson's division set out from Brandy Station for Germanna Ford. The men straggled terribly. Somewhere along the route, the 56th Massachusetts lost half of its men. The misguided battalion strayed six miles off the beaten path before the officers in command admitted their error and countermarched back toward the Germanna Road.[102] Stevenson's division plopped down in the road for an uncomfortable night. It rained on the north side of the Rapidan and the temperature dropped. Fires were not allowed. Captain Z. Boylston Adams (Company F, 56th Massachusetts), who like his men had left his blanket back at Bealton Station, shivered as he slept in the dirt.[103]

At Bealton Station along the Orange and Alexandria Railroad, the 11th New Hampshire and the rest of Colonel Simon Griffin's brigade gratefully threw its blankets on the ground in a field of tall, soft grass and spent a rather pleasant, easy night under the stars.[104] First Lieutenant Lyman Jackman (Company B, 6th New Hampshire) stretched out on his back, his eyes fixed upon the twinkling stars, and his mind hundreds of miles away – at home. He intuitively knew he and his men were walking into a battle. He felt uneasy.[105] The thoroughly tired 9th New Hampshire and the 32nd Maine, having been relieved from train duty late in the day, marched two miles before night enveloped them. Separated from the rest of their brigade, they bedded down in an abandoned campsite, determined to catch up the next day.[106]

May 4, 1864
The Army of Northern Virginia

Brigadier General John Pegram's Brigade Near Somerville Ford
(9.75 miles southwest of Germanna Ford, on the Rapidan River.)

The Yankee pickets around Somerville Ford waxed bold as night settled along the river by doing something they had not done before. They stole down to the river bank and shot at Company A of the 13th Virginia on the southern side of the Rapidan. The Confederates did not betray their positions by returning fire. They quietly waited for their relief, a small party of cavalry videttes, to replace them at 11:00 P.M. Company A marched to a nearby farm called "The Hall" to spend the night. Private George Peyton's cold made him feel very ill, to the point that he felt completely disoriented. His exhaustion soon put him to sleep.[107]

Major General Fitzhugh Lee's Cavalry Division at Fredericksburg
(9 miles east of Chancellorsville.)

Word of the Federal crossing at Ely's and Germanna's Ford's reached Lee's headquarters at Fredericksburg that morning at a most inopportune time. The invasion shattered his plans to conduct a division review at Hamilton's Crossing, south of the city. Major J. D. Ferguson, his assistant adjutant general, posted himself at the crossing during the entire day to intercept the general's special guests from Richmond to explain why the expected review could not take place. Despite the conspicuous lack of cavalry to admire, the dignitaries arrived and a fete of sorts did occur. Captain Robert E. Lee, Jr., his mother and sister, and several other young ladies spent the day with Fitzhugh Lee and his staff. Governor "Extra Billy" Smith, a former brigade commander in the Army of Northern Virginia, being the consummate politician, delivered a brief oration during the day. Two brigades from the division (Lomax's and Wickham's) departed that afternoon toward Massaponax Church, eight miles southwest of Fredericksburg.[108]

Brigadier General Lunsford L. Lomax with the 5th, 6th, and 15th Virginia Cavalry regiments reached the church about dark and went into bivouac. Private Luther W. Hopkins (Company A, 6th Virginia Cavalry) camped with his men in the nearby woods and soon had a low burning fire going. Once the fire had enough embers in it to broil his dinner, the young man reached into his haversack and pulled out several fresh fish. "I don't think I ever ate anything so sweet," he wrote 43 years later.[109]

A. P. Hill's Corps Near Orange Court House

(On the Orange Turnpike, 20.5 miles southwest of the Germanna Ford-Orange Turnpike intersection.)

Orders to prepare to march arrived in Hill's winter camps around 11:00 A.M. Almost immediately, the cooks in Brigadier General Samuel McGowan's South Carolina brigade set to work baking bread. Simultaneously, the enlisted men, according to previous instructions, pulled down their officers' tents and cut them apart to distribute to the rank and file for shelters. Throwing their excess personal belongings into the company streets, the men strapped on their accoutrements and fell into column. The brigade traveled with the corps east on the Orange Turnpike at a quick step. About eleven miles further on, near Verdiersville, the South Carolinians left the corps behind and branched southeast on the Orange Plank Road and did not stop until it came within several miles of Parker's Store.[110]

Chapter Two

"Oh, Captain, I killed one of 'em."

May 5, 1864

The Battle Opens at Parker's Store

(2.75 miles south of Saunders Field)

The sun came up at 4:53 A.M. and bathed the woods around Parker's Store in a haunting gray mist. A light fog nestled in the hollows along the streams.[1] Colonel John Hammond's orderly (5th New York Cavalry) gently nudged Captain William B. Cary (Company I) awake. Hammond wanted Cary to take his squadron (Companies H and I) southwest along the Orange Plank Road to probe the Confederate lines. Determine the Rebs' strength but do not engage them, the orderly instructed him. Cary and his two companies mounted and trotted down the road as ordered.[2] The remainder of the regiment stayed at Parker's Store with instructions to hold there until relieved by the infantry, at which time it was to proceed south for about four miles and rendezvous with the division at Craig's Meeting House on the Catharpin Road.

Brigadier General James H. Wilson led the division out at 5:00 A.M., seven minutes after sunrise.[3] He was well on the way toward developing a wide cavalry screen to protect the southwestern flank of the Army of the Potomac. Confederate cavalry, however, and Major General Henry Heth's infantry division from A. P. Hill's corps quickly thwarted those plans.

Unknown to either Wilson or Hammond, Major General Fitzhugh Lee's scouts, having infiltrated the Northern camps at Chancellorsville, had reported back to Lee at Massaponax Church, eleven miles southeast of the old battlefield. When Lee realized that the Yankees were moving west and had no intention of striking Fredericksburg, he sent a messenger to the army's headquarters near Orange Court House to Generals Robert E. Lee and Jeb Stuart.[4] From the earliest moments of the campaign the Confederate leadership had anticipated what Grant's huge army was attempting to do. Consequently, Stuart ordered Brigadier General Thomas Rosser's Virginia brigade to join Major General Wade Hampton's newly reorganized division in the Wilderness. (Hampton had not arrived at Orange Court House. His "division" consisted of about 300 effectives from Brigadier General Pierce M. B. Young's brigade.) Young was expected to cover the army's front along the Orange Plank Road.[5] Heth's infantry division backed up the scattered cavalry videttes along the pike, while Rosser's command, which had arrived at Richard's Shop from Locust Grove during the previous day, marched east toward the Catharpin Road.

The inevitable collision occurred within minutes after Companies H and I of the 5th New York Cavalry left Parker's Store. One half mile west of Parker's Store, the squadron, still in column of fours, carefully descended a swale where a sluggish stream crossed its line of march. Cary, at the head of the column, quietly studied the muddy water beneath him and the wide morass on the eastern side of the creek, while the column clopped over the plank bridge which spanned the stream. The woods surrounding his men became more foreboding. It was not a good place to fight with cavalry.

Half of a mile beyond the bridge, the Yankees ascended the forested hill which crossed the road and spooked a Confederate cavalry outpost. The Rebels bolted into the woods, disappearing like specters in the ground fog which steamed upward from the creek bottom. Cary halted his column to see what would develop. The sounds emanating from the forest – canteens clanging against other accoutrements, officers shouting commands, tree branches crunching in a rhythmic pattern – told him that an infantry skirmish line was advancing toward his front.[6] The squadron had stumbled into the 47th North Carolina, the skirmishers of Brigadier General William Kirkland's North Carolina brigade.[7]

In compliance with his directive not to start a fight, Cary turned his men about and retired very slowly toward the bridge. The Confederate horsemen slipped into the road a safe distance behind them. Cary wheeled his men

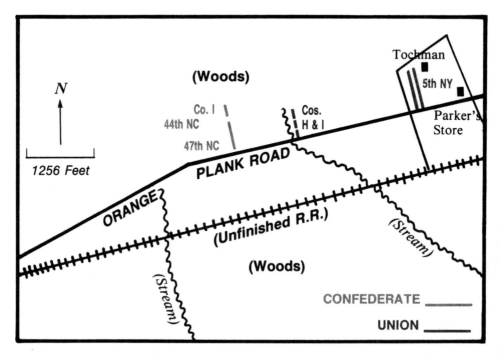

MAP 4: **Early morning, May 5, 1864 • Kirkland's North Carolina brigade forces Companies H and I, 5th New York Cavalry, to deploy west of Parker's Store.**

around again and the Confederates withdrew into the woods. When his men faced east and continued pulling back, the Rebels trickled into sight again. Cary was losing his patience with their cat and mouse tactics. For the final time, the cavalry turned about and once again the Confederates disappeared into the woods. This time, however, Kirkland's infantry brigade fell into line across the road.

From his position Cary could only see the handful of North Carolinians who filled the road and he decided to force them to do something. To determine their strength he had to risk starting an engagement. While the Northern troopers remained mounted in the road, squinting at the infantry which blocked their path, Cary turned to Privates Nick Darsy and Job Coddington (both Company I) and ordered them to fire at the Carolinians. The two enlisted men snapped their seven shot Spencers to their shoulders and took careful aim. He heard the two carbine shots ring down the road. Seconds later, the 47th North Carolina returned fire by files. The volley rolled across the Federals' front from north to south. Cary quickly decided that there were too many Confederate infantry present for him. He frantically turned his two companies around in the road and quickly retreated toward Parker's Store. The skirmishers of the 47th North Carolina struggled through the thick underbrush and the closely set trees in pursuit.[8]

The horsemen retreated as far as the bridge and halted again. Hammond sent a message to Cary from Parker's Store ordering him to dismount and hold his position as long as possible. Cary anchored his left flank on the road and wheeled Company I with considerable difficulty into line to the north. First Lieutenant Elmer J. Barker, commanding Company H, extended the line farther to the right.[9] For a while the mounted troopers fought the interlaced tree branches more than the Confederates, but they managed to form an extended line parallel with the stream.

The Yankees counted off by fours. The horse holders took the mounts to safer positions in the rear of the line. The dismounted cavalrymen advanced into the skirmish line and tore down the fence rails along the edge of the creek to make breastworks. Unsnapping their carbines

First Lieutenant Elmer J. Barker (Company H, 5th New York Cavalry) served as second in command under Captain William Cary (Company I) when the New Yorkers opened the battle along the Orange Plank Road.

(Roger Hunt Collection, USAMHI)

from their cross belts, they hunkered down behind their makeshift cover to await the Rebel infantry attack.[10]

It was not long before the 47th North Carolina attacked the Yankee position. The veteran regiment, however, did not make the anticipated frontal assault. The Carolinians deployed in open order, with the men taking cover behind whatever was available.[11] The New York cavalrymen saw them coming and cut loose with a tremendous volley. Many of their carbine shots went wild, but the sheer volume of fire slowed the Confederates down and convinced Kirkland that he was facing a large force. He pulled Company I, 44th North Carolina, from his main line and sent it into the woods to reinforce the 47th.[12] The Southerners were returning a more accurate fire. They cut down several of Cary's troopers within a few minutes.

Cary, who had remained mounted, continually worked his way through the trees from one end of his company to the other, all the while warning his men, some of whom were quite rattled, to take cover, to conserve their ammunition and to aim at specific targets. He knew that at the rate that they were shooting it would not take long for them to use all of their ammunition. Soon after the initial shots echoed across the creek bottom, he discovered one of his recruits wasting his rounds and recklessly standing in the open. Cary told the man to take cover and to pick his targets. With Cary watching him, the soldier dodged behind a tree, sighted in on a Rebel and squeezed off a round. "Oh, Captain," he exclaimed, while stepping away from his cover, "I killed one of 'em." A second later, a minie ball slammed into the side of his skull and hurled him to the ground. He died without a twitch. Cary rode away to tend to the living under his command.[13]

Daylight to 12:30 P.M.
Saunders Field

While the skirmishing continued west of Parker's Store, the lead elements of the V Corps probed the Confederate defenses along Saunders Field. Around 6:00 A.M., a little over an hour after daylight, an orderly from corps headquarters rode into the skirmish line of the 1st Michigan with orders for Lieutenant Colonel William Throop to retire his regiment to the brigade bivouac near the Lacy house and join the brigade in the line of march. Throop began recalling his outposts from the middle of Saunders Field. About fifteen minutes into the withdrawal, however, one of his skirmishers rushed to him with a report of Confederate activity to the west, on the Orange Turnpike.[14]

Simultaneously, one half of a mile to the east, Colonel David T. Jenkins of the 146th New York, who directed the division's skirmishers, stepped into the road from the woods and faced west. In the distance, about three fourths of a mile off, he believed he saw a large formation on the double-quick moving toward his position. A billowing cloud of limestone dust rose in the sky

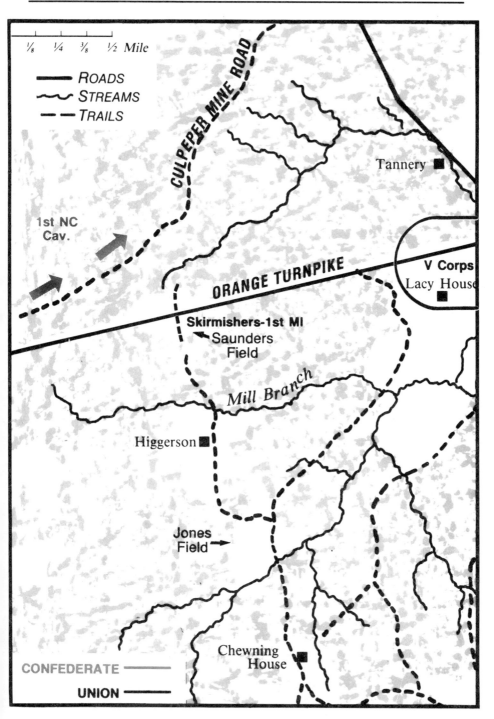

MAP 5: Situation at daylight, May 5, 1864 • Along the Orange Turnpike.

behind several squadrons of the 1st North Carolina Cavalry, which were trotting toward the V Corps' picket line.[15] The horsemen suddenly disappeared
into the woods north of the pike. The seemingly perpetual whitish haze which
rose up behind the horsemen indicated the presence of a much larger force
farther to the west. Jenkins correctly surmised it was an infantry column
and sent more skirmishers into the woods along his front to find the intrud-
ers and to support the 1st Michigan.[16]

Half of a mile beyond Jenkins, Throop knew the Confederates had infantry backing up their cavalry. He stretched his men north across the Orange
Turnpike then sent another company northward behind them as reinforcements. He needed to protect his northern flank from the North Carolinians,
who had taken the Culpeper Mine Road which skirted the wood line along
the northwestern side of Saunders Field. The opposing pickets spotted each
other at the same time. The Yankee infantry melted back into the security on
their side of the field while the 1st North Carolina Cavalry continued its
leisurely walk toward the Germanna Plank Road, two and one half miles to
the northeast. Contented with having made contact, the Northerners nestled
down in their part of the woods to wait and see what would happen. The
northern end of Saunders Field was quiet.[17]

On the Western Edge of Lacy's Farm

A staff officer from V Corps headquarters, who was galloping to Jenkins'
outpost with a directive from Major General Gouverneur Warren (V Corps,
commanding), found him standing in the Orange Turnpike near the center
of his picket line. Jenkins scanned the written instructions. He was to keep
his men well out to the west until the corps had executed the planned march
to the south and had cleared the Germanna Plank Road-Orange Turnpike
intersection.

Scattered rifle shots were echoing from the picket line while Jenkins impatiently scribbled his observations in pencil on the back of the paper.[18] Shov-
ing the instructions back into the sweating aide's hand, the colonel told him
to rein in at the camp of the 146th New York near Lacy's and tell Lieutenant
Colonel Henry H. Curran (146th New York) to send out two companies to
the skirmish line.[19] The aide sped away. Jenkins sent an orderly with the
same information to his brigade commander, Brigadier General Romeyn
Ayres, who, in turn, forwarded the colonel's report to Brigadier General
Charles Griffin, the division commander. Jenkins feared that if Brigadier
General Samuel Crawford's division moved too far to the left (south), he
would create a gap between the skirmishers and the division which could
endanger the entire corps' position. (Griffin, likewise, rushed a message to
Warren.)[20]

Near the Lacy House

The 146th New York had barely sat down to breakfast when the staff officer jerked his foam flecked horse to an abrupt stop in the bivouac. Rebels had appeared on the turnpike, he gasped. Where was Curran? The alarm passed among the men before Curran reached him. The New Yorkers solemnly braced themselves for the inevitable. Curran quietly received his orders. While the staff officer disappeared down the pike to the east, he told First Lieutenants Alonzo J. King (Company C) and William H. S. Sweet (Company F) to get their people to their feet. The hungry soldiers abandoned their unfinished breakfasts. Taking up their weapons at trail arms, they were off at a dog trot toward the picket outposts along Saunders Field.

At the Orange Turnpike, Company F veered to the left and kept well to the side of the road. Company C dashed across the road to the northern side and hugged the wood line while it advanced. Running at a crouch, with the rising sun to their backs, the two companies rendezvoused with Jenkins, who was still in the road. He placed the companies well forward in line on both flanks to cover his skirmishers.[21] Some of the New Yorkers craned their necks to stare between the trees, trying to get a glimpse of the Confederate position. They could barely see the wooded crest on the opposite side of the corn stubbled swale. The occasional crack of a startled Yankee's rifle punctuated the morning's silence.[22]

Showing little concern over normal picket activity, Major General George G. Meade (Army of the Potomac, commanding) refused to delay the V Corps' movement. According to the established scenario, at about 6:00 A.M., Crawford's division took to the winding farm road west of Lacy's which led to Parker's Store, about two and one half miles to the southwest. Nearly an hour later Wadsworth's division followed.[23] Robinson's division had reached the Lacy house, which Sergeant "Jim" Stearns (Company K, 13th Massachusetts) described as a large mansion. The division went prone behind the house to await further instructions.[24] Army headquarters was not going to let an outpost action interfere with its grand scheme to outmaneuver the Army of Northern Virginia.

In the meantime, Griffin directed Brigadier General Joseph Bartlett to take his brigade on a reconnaissance in force along the Orange Turnpike. Around 8:00 A.M., Bartlett detailed the 18th Massachusetts and the 83rd Pennsylvania, under Colonel Joseph Hayes (18th Massachusetts), to reinforce Jenkins. Bartlett, who did not know who was opposing him, told Hayes to find out if he was facing infantry or cavalry. The two regiments left their log and earthen breastworks on the Lacy farm and marched in column down the pike toward Saunders Field.

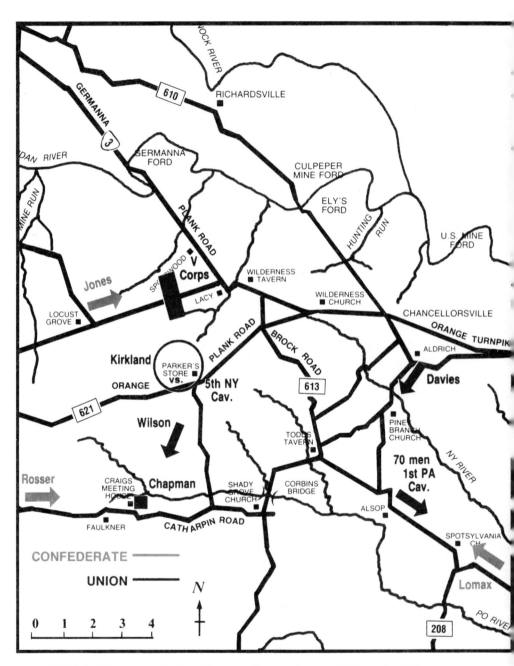

MAP 6: The overall situation on the morning of May 5, 1864.

Brigadier General John M. Jones' Brigade on the Orange Turnpike

Having been on the march since daylight from a point near Locust Grove, Jones' brigade heard the Yankees long before engaging them. The wind, which blew west that day, carried a solitary drum roll from the V Corps' camps into the ranks of the 21st Virginia. Seconds later, the melodious strains of a well practiced band drifted mysteriously overhead. Sergeant John Worsham (Company F) watched his friends, to a man, instinctively clench their weapons tighter. The officers became more intense. "Close up," echoed frequently through the ranks. The Virginians no longer harbored any doubts about the Army of the Potomac's whereabouts.[25]

7:00 – 8:00 A.M.

The Cavalry Situation[26]

While the 5th New York Cavalry engaged Heth's infantry, the cavalry corps of both armies were converging on the southern and western approaches into the Wilderness. Wilson's division moved south of Parker's Store with instructions to reconnoiter west on the Catharpin Road. Rosser's Virginia cavalry was also on the Catharpin Road, slowly approaching the Wilderness from Richard's Shop.

Simultaneously, Brigadier General Henry E. Davies Jr.'s Federal cavalry brigade, which had spent the night near Aldrich's, about five miles northeast of Todd's Tavern, started a leisurely reconnaissance toward the tavern.[27] Seventy troopers from the 1st Pennsylvania Cavalry wandered southwest from Piney Branch Church onto the Brock Road near Alsop's Gate (three miles from Todd's Tavern) and continued on about two more miles to within a mile of Spotsylvania Court House. There they halted to see what would develop. Unknown to the Federals, the 15th Virginia and the 6th Virginia cavalry regiments (Lomax's brigade, Lee's division) were riding toward the court house.[28]

8:00 A.M.[29]

Near Craig's Meeting House

The 1st Vermont Cavalry led Wilson's cavalry division to Craig's Meeting House, seven miles southwest of Parker's Store on the Catharpin Road. Colonel George H. Chapman, commanding the lead brigade, held one battalion (one half) of the 1st Vermont Cavalry, the 8th New York Cavalry and the 3rd Indiana Cavalry back at the meeting house and sent the other half of the Vermont regiment about one mile west to Mrs. Faulkner's place.[30] During the New Englanders' reconnaissance, Wilson placed Colonel Timothy Bryan's three remaining regiments – the 1st Connecticut, the 2nd New York, and the 18th Pennsylvania – in reserve on the north side of Robertson's Run, one mile above the Catharpin Road-Parker Store Road intersection. Three miles separated the two brigades.

Shortly after 8:00 A.M., the advance battalion of the 1st Vermont stumbled into the videttes of the 12th Virginia Cavalry west of Mrs. Faulkner's.[31] The sudden appearance of the Virginians sent the Vermonters scattering back toward the meeting house, firing wildly as they ran.[32] The 1st Squadron (Companies B and I) of the 12th Virginia, led by Captain Lewis Harman (Company I), gave chase. Sergeant William H. Arehart (Company H) watched his friend Private Nathaniel Phillips (Company C) topple from the saddle, dead. Private Sam Slusser (Company H) went down with a leg wound. The companies lost four horses in the running melee.[33] The Virginians raced to within eyesight of the field which surrounded the meeting house, where Chapman's brigade, drawn up in lines of battle around the church, brought the assault to a clattering halt. While his men fought their horses to a stand-still, Harman's frenzied mount carried him helplessly into the waiting Yankees who took him prisoner.[34]

Chapman dismounted the entire 1st Vermont and sent the troopers into the pine forest which bordered both sides of the Catharpin Road. The 12th Virginia also counted off by fours and, with the lead horses going to the rear, melted into the woods to confront the Northerners.[35] The Vermonters, who were armed with Spencer repeating carbines, forced the Virginians to doggedly yield ground and retreat west.[36] The Confederates were buying time and making their rounds count. Private Charles Chapin (Company L, 1st Vermont) tersely noted in his diary that the regiment skirmished "very hard."[37]

Saunders Field

(2.75 miles north of Parker's Store)

At the northern end of the battlefield, Bartlett sent two of his regiments west along the Orange Turnpike to feel out Jones' Confederate brigade. Immediately upon reaching the eastern side of Saunders Field, the 18th Massachusetts deployed to the north and the 83rd Pennsylvania to the south of the Turnpike. Hayes pushed out two companies from each of his regiments as skirmishers to scout the Rebel position in the woods across from them.

Captain Luther S. Bent (Company K, 18th Massachusetts) with Companies I and K cautiously walked west, with their left flank against the pike. Their advance pushed the two Pennsylvania companies off of their course into the swampy lower end of the field. The New Englanders veered across the pike into the woods toward a knoll in their front. To their surprise they did not find any Rebels where they suspected them. The Virginians found them instead.

At approximately 10:30 A.M. the men of the 25th Virginia, leading Jones' brigade, spotted Bent's two companies. Lieutenant General Richard Ewell (Second Corps, Army of Northern Virginia, commanding) ordered Major General Edward Johnson to halt his division and prepare for battle. Jones'

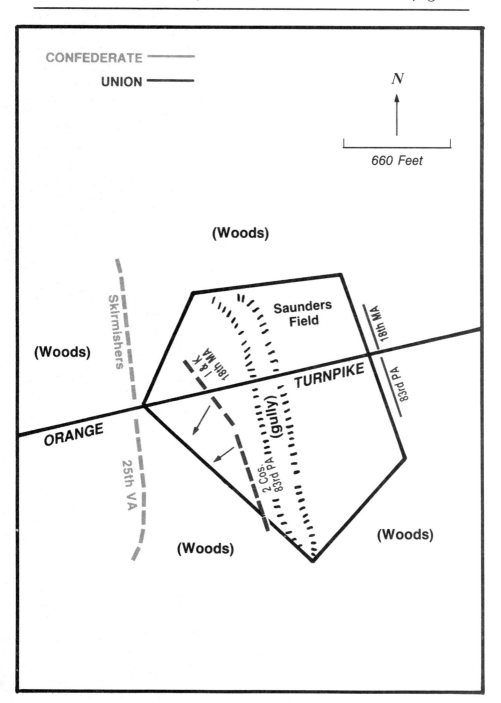

MAP 7: 10:30 A.M., May 5, 1864 • The 25th Virginia encounters Federal skirmishers in Saunders Field.

brigade led the advance, followed by Brigadier Generals George H. Steuart's, James A. Walker's and Leroy A. Stafford's brigades. Reverend Father James B. Sheeran caught up with the 14th Louisiana of Stafford's brigade as the regiment went into line on the south side of the pike. He had never seen the men seem so happy and he could not fathom why. He wrote in his journal, "The poor fellows had little idea of the terrible contest in which they were about to engage."[38]

Between 10:30 A.M. and 11:00 A.M., Colonel John C. Higginbotham (25th Virginia) deployed his regiment forward in extended order. The Virginians fanned out into the woods on the southern side of the Orange Turnpike, while the rest of Jones' brigade tramped to a halt west of the Culpeper Mine Road.[39] "Halt! Load your guns! Shoulder Arms! March!" The commands spattered the column in rapid order. The veteran soldiers mindlessly performed the prescribed military evolutions of each step in seconds.[40]

Meanwhile, the two companies from the 18th Massachusetts, having just crested the hill on the western side of Saunders Field, walked into the approaching skirmishers from the 25th Virginia. Higginbotham, during the sweep up the western side of the hill, discovered that Captain Jehu H. Johnson's 2nd Company E, on the right of the line, had strayed off course and had lost its alignment with the rest of the regiment. He commanded the captain to bring his people back into the formation.[41] Company E's crashing about in the woods below the 18th Massachusetts attracted the attention of Private Charles Wilson (Company I). He sighted in on the Virginians as they moved by the flank and sent a bullet whistling past Private Josiah H. Siple (2nd Company E). The shot signalled a retreat to the equally startled Massachusetts soldiers. Before the New Englanders had time to break over the hilltop into the open, Siple killed Wilson. (He became the Union's first infantry fatality in the battle.)[42] It did not take the Yankees long to return to the 18th Massachusetts and the 83rd Pennsylvania with the disconcerting news.[43]

The opposing infantry laid down on their respective sides of the battlefield to wait out whatever would follow. Jones' brigade advanced into line around the 25th Virginia. A short distance inside the woods, the 21st Virginia placed its right flank on the road, facing east, which forced the 25th Virginia to close ranks and move south of the pike.[44] The 42nd and the 44th Virginia went into line on the right of the 25th Virginia. Then, the 50th and the 48th Virginia completed the brigade's deployment to the south.[45] The division began entrenching.[46] The sounds of their digging echoed some five hundred yards east to the New Yorkers and the New Englanders on the far side of Saunders Field. They listened intently to the Confederate officers yell at their men to fell trees and to dig in.[47] Hayes quickly reported the enemy's activities to Bartlett, who recalled both of his regiments to the works near Lacy's house.[48] Thirty year old Theodore Lyman, a volunteer aide to his

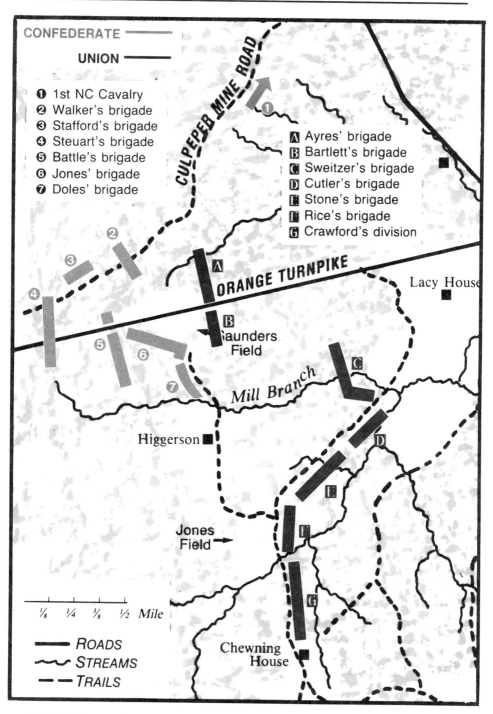

MAP 8: Troop dispositions before noon, May 5, 1864 along the Orange Turnpike.

good friend, Major General George G. Meade, marveled at the Confederates' fortification skills. He wrote his wife, "It is a rule that, when the Rebels halt, the first day gives them a good rifle pit; the second, a regular infantry parapet with artillery in position; and the third, a parapet with an abatis in front and entrenched batteries behind. Sometimes they put this three days' work into the first twenty-four hours."[49]

Captain McHenry Howard, assistant inspector general on Steuart's staff, while standing in the Culpeper Mine Road with the brigade (1st and 3rd North Carolina, 10th and 23rd Virginia), carefully scrutinized the unyielding terrain which swallowed up the Rebel brigade forming around him. The close set scrub oak and low spreading pines made it nearly impossible for any mounted person to negotiate the wasteland. "A more difficult and disagreeable field of battle could not be well imagined," the Marylander recollected.[50] Steuart's brigade fell in on a northeast to southwest line in the sandy track of the Culpeper Mine Road with its right flank across the Orange Turnpike, about six hundred sixty yards west of Saunders Field. The 10th and the 23rd Virginia regiments were on the left of the brigade line. The 1st North Carolina came next with its right on the pike. The 3rd North Carolina was on the opposite side of the "Stone Road" (the Orange Turnpike). To the east, Jones' Virginians, who had disappeared in the Wilderness, snapped rounds at the Federals across the swale.

While Steuart's men struggled through the brush to align the brigade properly, Walker's battle hardened Stonewall Brigade marched by the left flank northeast along the Culpeper Mine Road beyond Steuart's left flank. The 33rd Virginia led the brigade, followed by the 2nd, the 4th, the 27th and the 5th Virginia.[51] The column continued to a point one half mile beyond the Orange Turnpike intersection, where it went into position in the dense woods and faced northeast. The 33rd Virginia fanned out as skirmishers on both sides of the Culpeper Mine Road and advanced toward the Germanna Plank Road.[52]

In the meantime, Stafford's brigade, having lost sight of Walker's men, went into position on the left of Steuart's line, in the woods along the Culpeper Mine Road where it passed the northwest corner of Saunders Field.[53] The command halted beyond the line of sight of Steuart's brigade and failed to contact Walker's Virginians. Stafford, believing that his men had spent an inordinate amount of time in the woods road without instructions, left them on their own while he rode to the right of the line for orders from his division commander, Major General Edward Johnson.

Stafford's assistant adjutant general, Major Henry E. Handerson, uneasily watched the men flop down along the roadside to relax. Some dozed off. Others opened their haversacks to fix lunch. He trooped the line the entire time, all the while savoring the pungent odor of tobacco smoke which lingered in the spring air. He remembered looking down the pike when the brigade came onto the field. The glimpse of sunlight bouncing off the barrel of a Yankee brass field piece in the distance still bothered him. Stafford seemed to be gone forever. Handerson could not understand how his superiors could march men into battle without any directions to govern their movements.[54]

With Johnson's division clear of the Orange Turnpike, Major General Robert E. Rodes' division started maneuvering into position. Brigadier General Cullen A. Battle's brigade forced its way forward into the woods south of the pike to provide close support about one hundred yards behind Jones' brigade.[55] Brigadier General George Doles' Georgia brigade, behind Battle's men, formed a line and right obliqued into the woods south of Battle's brigade, where it eventually aligned itself with and maintained visual but not physical contact with the 48th Virginia on the right of Jones' command.[56]

As Doles' Georgians disappeared into the Wilderness, Brigadier General Junius Daniel's North Carolina brigade went into a battle line west of Jones' brigade astride the turnpike to wait out the situation. Scattered rifle shots reverberated in the forest to the east of the 45th North Carolina, but Sergeant Cyrus B. Watson (Company K) could not see any troops in the brigade's immediate front. Word rippled through the ranks about it coming from some of their own men somewhere in the woods.[57] Brigadier General John B. Gordon's Georgia brigade, at the rear of Ewell's division, slowed its pace to see what was developing.

Saunders Field

The V Corps' forward elements – Jenkins' skirmishers and Companies F and C of the 146th New York – lay in the woods north of the pike listening to the foreboding echoes in the tree line across from them. Finally, the company officers of the 146th New York stepped into the road to better observe the Confederate troop movements to the west. With their field glasses raised to their faces, they peered at the cloud of dust billowing above the horizon. Warren, Griffin, and Ayres trotted up to the group. First Lieutenant William A. Walker (Company C, 146th New York) nervously handed his glasses to Warren.

The corps commander fixed his eyes upon the dark stream of men which poured continuously to both sides of the turnpike. The sun glistened off their bayonets which bobbed in the brown haze enveloping them. Turning to Griffin and Ayres, Warren gasped, "They have discovered our movements. Send for some of the most available troops at once."[58] Orders were issued immediately to suspend the Army of the Potomac's advance.[59]

Private James College (Company C, 146th New York), who was lying in the brush along the forward edge of the woods, did not need field glasses to see the Virginians. Their skirmishers were shooting at him and his comrades from the security of a rail fence on the wooded ridge across from him.[60]

Ayres rushed back to Lacy's to bring up the rest of his brigade. The 140th New York, in their dark blue Zouave uniforms, led the advance, followed by the eight remaining companies of the 146th New York, who were equally resplendent in their Zouave uniforms. The five regiments of United States Regulars came next with the brigade's two Pennsylvania regiments finishing the column. The 140th New York placed its left on the turnpike and four companies of the 11th U.S. fell in on its right.[61] The woods forced Company D, the colors, and the company to their left to position themselves on the right rear of their regiment. The 12th U.S. covered the 11th with the 14th U.S. to its left. The 2nd U.S. with the 17th U.S. on its right continued the line north into the woods for another three hundred ninety-three feet.[62] In the third line, the eight companies of the 146th New York extended from the pike. The 155th Pennsylvania and the 91st Pennsylvania fell into front on the New Yorkers' right.[63]

The regiments had barely settled down on the forest floor when the 18th Massachusetts and the 83rd Pennsylvania noisily marched into the northern end of Saunders Field and part way up the western slope to support their four probing companies. In the woods behind them, the Regulars listened to their incredulous bravado. From their position, a considerable distance to the rear, the Regulars insisted that they clearly understood the commands of the volunteers' line officers when they halted the two regiments. Presently, two distinct, well ordered volleys smashed harmlessly into the trees on the Confederate side of the swale, followed by three vigorous Yankee "huzzahs" and a rousing "tiger."[64] The 25th Virginia, with five feet between each man and with reinforcements from Battle's Alabama brigade, in extended order on its right flank, opened fire. They killed at least two of the bold Federals before the Pennsylvanians and the New Englanders left the field.[65]

Ayres then told Jenkins to let Lieutenant Colonel Henry Curran lead the regiment into action. He wanted Jenkins to take his skirmishers and the two companies from the 146th New York, which were still on the picket line, and reform them to the rear of the brigade. The colonel politely insisted that he lead his regiment. Ayres consented and Jenkins returned Companies C and F to their respective positions in the regimental line.[66]

Once again the V Corps delayed. For about three hours the brigade lounged in the woods. The men were bored. The regimental lines disintegrated into small clusters of men. They were playing mumble-the-peg and craps, joking and telling stories as if they had nothing to worry about. A few men turned over mementoes to their comrades for safekeeping.[67] The officers of the 146th New York inched their way over to Chaplain Edward P. Payson and handed him their valuables which he stuffed into his blouse while he anxiously waited to see his first engagement.[68] Every now and then an officer deliberately crawled up to an enlisted man and jabbed him in the buttocks or the thigh with his sword to watch him jump or to hear him swear.[69]

While Ayres' men wasted time in the woods north of the Orange Turnpike, Bartlett's seven regiments fortified their position. The enlisted men felled trees along the front of the projected line of earthworks, and cut slashings one hundred eighty feet deep. They finished their fortifications by noon. Colonel Jacob B. Sweitzer's brigade connected its right flank with Bartlett's and faced southwest with its left regiment flush against the farm lane that ran from the Orange Turnpike to Parker's Store.[70] The brigade entrenched. The twenty man pioneer detail of the 32nd Massachusetts, being equipped with shovels, axes, and hatchets, were felling trees. The recently promoted Orderly Sergeant Andrew Wilson (Company C, 22nd Massachusetts) refused to shovel dirt on the logs in the fortification. He told his captain, Edwin Bennett, that he did not care much for fighting from behind cover. The regiment had not entrenched at Gettysburg and it did not have to do so now. The "boys" would win the fight from sheer stand up fire power. Captain Bennett did not have the time to argue with the 5'4" sergeant. He stared down into the non-commissioned officer's glaring, dark eyes and very quickly put him in his place. Wilson swallowed his pride and began to dig.[71]

Private Theodore Gerrish (Company H, 20th Maine) fell out with his comrades to enjoy some hot coffee and hard crackers. A commotion rolled along the regiment. The soldiers were cheering Warren as he trooped the line to inspect it. The New Englanders no longer joked about Reb hunting in the woods or about marching into Richmond. Nor were they writing letters home. Things were getting too serious to warrant such frivolous enjoyments.[72]

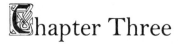hapter Three

"Orr, I am not coming out of that hole alive."

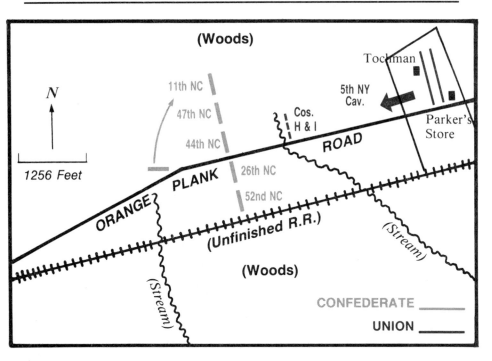

MAP 9: 10:00 A.M.-11:00 A.M., May 5, 1864 • The 5th New York Cavalry holds off Kirkland's North Carolina brigade along the Plank Road.

Around 10:00 A.M.

The 5th New York Cavalry Near Parker's Store

For two hours, Companies H and I of the 5th New York Cavalry held back Kirkland's five regiments in the woods west of Parker's Store. The 47th North Carolina, with the 44th North Carolina on its right, held its original line north of the Plank Road. When the fighting intensified, Kirkland fed his other regiments into the line south of the pike to overlap the New Yorkers' front. The 26th and the 52nd North Carolina connected with the right of the 44th North Carolina at the Plank Road. The 11th North Carolina moved in on the left of the 47th North Carolina and extended the line beyond the 5th New York's right flank.[1] From his position on that end of the line, Private David H. Robbins (Company H, 5th New York Cavalry) could see the Confederate skirmishers steadily advancing through the low ground to envelop the dismounted troopers.[2]

Captain William Cary (Company I) sent an urgent message back to Lieutenant Colonel John Hammond at Parker's Store stating that he could not hold any longer because he was facing a heavy skirmishing force. With that he passed the word along the line for his men to mount up and retreat to Parker's. Those cavalrymen who heard the order slipped back to their horses and evaded capture. They dismounted in the yard west of the store, then melted into the woods along a fence row to stave the attack. Cary had lost all sense of actual time during the severe fighting. It seemed to him that he had only a handful of men left when Colonel John B. McIntosh (3rd Pennsylvania Cavalry), who had just been given the command of the brigade, galloped into the woods. "For God's sake, Captain," the colonel screamed, "hold this line!" Cary shot back that he had been trying to do that but could not withstand repeated infantry assaults. He insisted he did not have enough men to maintain his position.

McIntosh retorted that Cary had to stay where he was until the last minute because the Rebels would raise hell back at the Brock Road if they broke through. The colonel spurred off to the right without giving the weary captain a chance to respond.[3] McIntosh rode back to the rest of the 5th New York, which was still mounted in the yard around the store and told Hammond to put the entire regiment into the line. The troopers dismounted by threes and advanced into the woods. The effective firing strength of the regiment increased to over 290 officers and men, all of whom were armed with Spencers. The woods soon rang with the rapid fire of the Yankees' repeating carbines. The Confederates did not yield their ground. For over an hour they forced the cavalrymen to expend their brass jacketed ammunition. Shortly before 11:00 A.M., the Yankee rate of fire suddenly dropped off and the Confederate skirmishers closed in for the kill.

McIntosh ordered the 5th New York to retreat northeast along the Plank Road.[4] Captain Luke McGuinn (Company A) pushed his horse through the woods on the left of the line, intent upon conveying the command to that flank of the regiment. Riding up to Cary he told him to get to his horse if he expected to get out of those woods alive. The words had barely left McGuinn's mouth when he toppled backward out of the saddle. Cary examined the unconscious McGuinn to determine the extent of his injuries. The large caliber hole in his back and the one in his chest told Cary everything he needed to know. The Rebel Yell echoed through the trees and Cary retreated with his men into the open ground surrounding Parker's Store.[5]

The Confederate infantrymen fired haphazardly into the New Yorkers' backs as they broke from the tree line. A bullet struck down Private Anson Jones (Company A), fracturing his left arm between the elbow and the shoulder. Another round found its mark in Company L when it snapped Sergeant Anthony Cross' arm. Private Charles Westerfield (Company B) rode off the field with a shattered thigh. A bullet slammed Private John W. Slyter (Company K) in the face. Striking him near the hinge of his jaw, it tore out most of his teeth and ripped his tongue away near its base. He rode away, refusing to succumb to his terrible wound.[6] Private David H. Robbins (Company H) swore the Rebels shot down almost fifty men in the few minutes it took for the regiment to escape to the eastern side of Parker's Store. His friend, Private Addison G. White (Company G), went down in the fire and was left upon the field for dead. The regiment also lost Assistant Surgeon Orlando W. Armstrong who was captured while tending to the wounded.[7] The Confederate infantry swarmed toward the cavalrymen who continued to retreat in leap frog fashion, by squads, back toward the infantry on the Brock Road, about three miles away.[8] Since the fighting began at daylight, the New Yorkers had suffered fifty casualties: sixteen killed; twenty-one wounded; and thirteen missing.[9]

Chewning's Farm

Colonel Charles S. Wainwright, chief of the V Corps' artillery, with Warren's permission, caught up with the head of Brigadier General Samuel Crawford's division just as the column crested the clearing around the Chewning house. From the open high ground both officers saw what Crawford had earlier suspected – Northern cavalry was indeed engaging Confederate infantry near Parker's Store. (An hour earlier, before he arrived on Chewning's hill, Crawford had reported the suspected action along the Plank Road in the vicinity of the store to V Corps headquarters.) The point of the division had not quite reached the house when the 5th New York broke and stampeded toward the Brock Road. Crawford immediately sent Wainwright back to Lacy's with a communique to Warren apprising him of the situation.[10]

Crawford haphazardly deployed his Pennsylvania Reserves in a formation which would later cost him one of his regiments. He split Colonel William McCandless' brigade. He placed the 6th Reserves on the extreme right of his line facing southwest. The 10th and the 12th Reserves, from Colonel Joseph W. Fisher's brigade, fell into line on the left. The 13th Reserves straddled the dirt road to Parker's Store and the 1st Reserves went into line facing southeast and east, in conformity with the contour of Chewning's field. He kept the 2nd, 5th, 7th, 8th, and 11th Reserves behind the main line within supporting distance.[11] Then he waited to see what the Confederates were going to do next.

Parker's Store

Kirkland's North Carolinians halted in the wood line west of Parker's Store to give themselves some respite. Colonel William MacRae's North Carolina brigade pushed forward toward the Widow Tapp's, which was almost two miles farther down the road. Kirkland's line melted to the rear. As MacRae's brigade advanced, skirmishers fanned out along his flanks.

Generals Robert E. Lee, Ambrose P. Hill, William N. Pendleton, and a number of couriers and staff officers leisurely trailed behind the main line of infantry. The generals remained in Tapp's broom straw field. Hill and a few of the officers dismounted. Lee and Pendleton stayed on their horses. Presently Jeb Stuart and his staff appeared. They found the generals gathered around the only big tree in the field. While Stuart spurred over to Lee, Lieutenant Colonel Alexander R. Boteler, his volunteer aide de camp, dismounted beside a scrub pine and lay down to sleep. The heat had exhausted him. He passed out under the pine.[12]

Within a few minutes, Companies C and K from the 1st Pennsylvania Reserves broke into the clearing about two hundred yards from Lee and his officers. Lieutenant Theodore Garnett, another of Stuart's aides, stared in disbelief as the Yankees halted and stared back. Without saying a word, the Confederate orderlies, who had suddenly become aware of the Pennsylvanians' presence, turned their heads toward Lee, who at the moment was astride Traveler discussing a map with his generals. The dismounted officers leaped into their saddles and spurred toward Lee.[13]

The sudden pounding of horse hooves nearby shook Boteler awake. He sat bolt upright. The generals, with Lee in front, and their officers were racing toward the Plank Road. Lee, clasping a crumpled map in his hand, galloped past the startled aide, followed by the dismounted Hill, who was not losing any time in clearing the field. Boteler snapped his head to the northwest. A line of Yankee infantry, with fixed bayonets, stood on the edge of the clearing across the trail which led to Chewning's farm. Their bayonets glistened ominously in the morning light. Boteler quickly turned to his horse, only to find it had wandered off a short distance. Slipping alongside the grazing animal, being careful the entire time to keep it between him and the Pennsylvanians, he threw himself into the saddle, and raced away. Any second he expected to receive a volley in the back.[14]

The equally startled Federals melted back into the trees. Just as quickly, the Confederate officers rounded up a squad of infantry and sent them into the woods. A few minutes later, the sounds of scattered rifle fire resounded emptily across Tapp's Field.[15] Crawford would not press the matter with Kirkland's Carolinians without the authorization to do so.

The 46th North Carolina with the 15th North Carolina on its right, placed Company B on the left of the regimental line with its left flank in the Plank Road and maneuvered into battle line on the south side. The 27th North Carolina with the 48th on its left continued the line on the opposite side of the road.[16] Richards' Mississippi Battery from Colonel William T. Poague's Battalion kept abreast of the maneuvering infantry regiments. Heth, much to Poague's disgust, had deployed the four guns in column in the road. "This is one of the many examples of [the] infantry officers' manner of handling artillery," Poague bitterly complained.

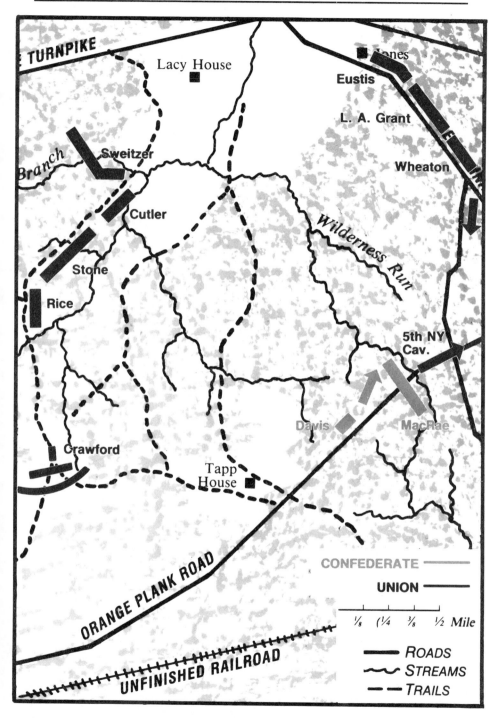

MAP 10: Shortly before noon, May 5, 1864 • MacRae's brigade drives the 5th New York Cavalry from the field.

During the lull created by the relief of Kirkland's brigade, Poague wrangled three of his guns and their caissons from Heth's control. Leaving First Lieutenant W. Frank George and his 12 Pound Napoleon in the road well in advance of MacRae's main line, he retired the three remaining pieces to the rest of the battalion which had rolled into battery on the open plateau on the eastern side of the Widow Tapp farm, three hundred yards west of the Tapp house.[17]

Stuart did not remain idle. Rather than tend to Rosser's cavalry brigade on the Catharpin Road, he ordered his staff to position themselves behind MacRae's skirmishers with orders to push the infantry through the thickets. Boteler resented the duty. "...it was as much as we ourselves could do with the help of our horses to force a passage," he complained in his diary. "When we came out of it, our faces were bleeding with scratches from the bushes and our clothes [were] badly torn."[18]

Colonel William MacRae, commanding Cooke's North Carolina Brigade, pushed the 5th New York Cavalry back to the Brock Road and precipitated a full fledged battle with George W. Getty's veteran infantry division from the VI Corps.

(Clark, I)

While the North Carolinians pushed the 5th New York Cavalry along the Plank Road, Colonel John M. Stone's mixed command of Mississippians and North Carolinians (Davis' Brigade) left the road behind Kirkland's brigade and filed toward the left of the division. They caught up with MacRae's brigade along a wooded ridge which paralleled Wilderness and Poplar Runs, about nine tenths of a mile east of the Widow Tapp's home.[19] Wilderness Run trickled south toward the Plank Road through the marshy swale along their front. The hill rose to another wooded crest about one hundred yards to the east. The Confederate infantry bellied down along the top of the narrow valley rather than venture across the open ground against an enemy with whom they had lost sight.

The VI Corps Along the Germanna Plank Road at J. R. Spotswood's

(2 miles northwest of Wilderness Tavern.)

Shortly after 7:00 A.M., while the V Corps was posturing itself for combat and the 5th New York Cavalry was probing Heth's division, Major General John Sedgwick advanced Brigadier General George W. Getty's three brigades down the Germanna Plank Road and massed them in the fields around the Wilderness Tavern.[20] About one and three fourths mile behind Getty's men, Brigadier General Horatio G. Wright halted his division at the intersection of the Germanna Plank Road and the Culpeper Mine Road. He sent Colonel Emory Upton's four veteran regiments down the dirt track as skirmishers to cover his right flank.[21] Shortly before 10:00 A.M., when it became apparent that the V Corps was going to give battle, Wright received orders to march west and connect with Warren's right flank.[22]

As soon as Upton received the command to advance, he filed his regiments south into the lower end of Mrs. J. R. Spotswood's farm.[23] In the distance the 5th Maine listened to the low, rumbling boom of scattered rifle shots. Fronting his regiments to face west, Upton sent skirmishers forward into the woods.[24] The regiments had barely gotten into formation when shots cracked and popped in the woods. The skirmishers had found Major William H. H. Cowles' dismounted 1st North Carolina Cavalry.[25] Private Maurus Oesterich (Company B) and Private Henry Keiser (Company G) of the 96th Pennsylvania both glanced at their watches and mentally recorded the time – 10:00 A.M. [26]

Behind them, Colonel Henry W. Brown's New Jersey brigade marched into position. From his place behind the regimental line, Sergeant John P. Beech (Company B, 4th New Jersey) could see no other Federal troops in the vicinity of his brigade.[27] To the right, Brigadier General David A. Russell flanked his brigade north into the woods. The regimental officers bullied their way through the briars and the pines to guide the commands into some semblances of battle lines, facing southwest, with their left flanks on the Culpeper Mine Road. The 49th Pennsylvania, being the first regiment in the column, formed the front of the brigade formation. The 119th Pennsylvania fell in behind, completely unobserved by the men to the front. The forest swallowed up the regiment. The 6th Maine was next in the column of regiments. The 5th Wisconsin was moving into line behind the 6th Maine when Russell told Major Enoch Totten to take the five right companies forward and to the right to protect the brigade's northern flank. The Westerners disappeared into the woods while the rest of the brigade waited for something to happen.[28]

Having left Brigadier General Alexander Shaler's brigade north of the Rapidan with the division's wagon train, Wright asked for reinforcements from Getty's division. Around 10:30 A.M., after Upton's men heard the first sounds of skirmishing, and while Wright's division was still maneuvering onto the field, a courier galloped into Getty's headquarters at Wilderness Tavern. Getty, who was not engaged, sent Brigadier General Thomas H. Neill's five regiments north to assist him.[29] Despite the addition of more manpower, Wright did not send his men into the Wilderness until shortly after noon.[30]

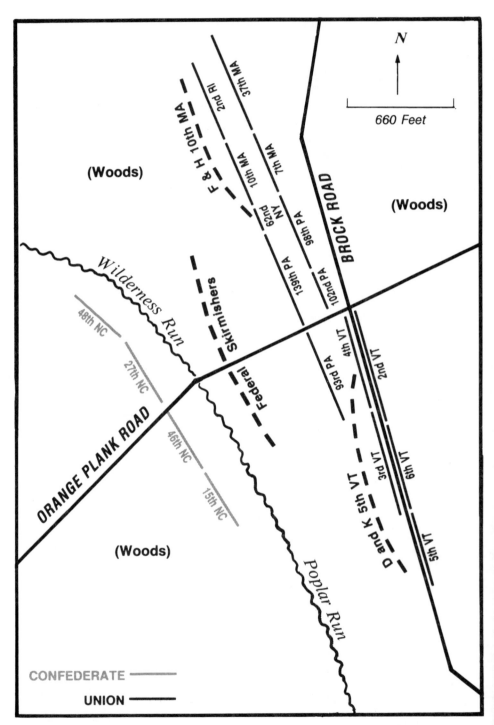

MAP 11: Around 1:00 p.m., May 5, 1864 • MacRae's North Carolinians force Getty's division of the VI Corps to deploy along the Brock Road.

12:30 P.M. – 1:00 P.M.

The Germanna Plank Road–Brock Road Intersection

(1 mile southeast of the Germanna Plank Road-Orange Turnpike intersection.)

By 12:30 P.M., Getty's three remaining brigades, under orders from General Meade, were marching south toward the Germanna Plank Road and the Plank Road intersection. Getty, rather than continue on the Germanna Road, diverted his column southwest along the Brock Road, hoping to intercept the Federal cavalry one mile west of his original destination. The general, his staff and orderlies, acting as scouts, spurred far ahead of the infantry and by pure chance stumbled across the 5th New York Cavalry as it raced for the safety of the rear lines. Getty and his escort came under fire from MacRae's North Carolina skirmishers the moment they rode into the crossroads. Getty sent an orderly back nine tenths of a mile to the Germanna Plank Road to hurry Brigadier General Frank Wheaton's brigade forward. For no immediately understandable reason the Confederates did not close upon the mounted Yankees. They disappeared into the woods and undergrowth on both sides of the road and fired wildly at the officers. (Getty later suggested that the Confederates mistook him and his staff as Federal cavalry.) The officers stalled the Southerners for several minutes without sustaining any casualties.[31]

The rifle fire, however, slammed into the right flank of the 93rd Pennsylvania, then approaching the officers from the north on the Brock Road. Private George H. Uhler (Company A) heard Lieutenant Colonel John S. Long call out, "Forward, double-quick."[32] The 573 man regiment hurried past the Plank Road, their new Springfield rifles at the shoulder shift. It took several minutes for the large column to move clear of the southern side of the intersection.

Halting, the Pennsylvanians mechanically faced right. By command, they leveled their weapons toward the dense woods in front of them, then fired. Not waiting to reload, they charged, trying to flush the Confederates out from their cover.[33] At the same time, Wheaton sent the 139th Pennsylvania into the woods north of the Plank Road.[34] The two regiments pushed the Confederates west some two hundred yards before Getty halted them. Skirmishers fanned into the underbrush as the line pulled back about one hundred twenty-five yards and went prone. The firing ceased as quickly as it began. Within fifteen minutes, the skirmishers reported back. The Confederates had disappeared.[35]

In the meantime, Colonel Lewis A. Grant's Vermont Brigade was double-quick marching south on the Brock Road and taking up position along its western side. Captain Charles J. Ormsbee (Company H, 5th Vermont) with Companies D and K skittered forward into the woods to secure the brigade's front.[36] The 4th Vermont fell in on the right of Grant's formation with its right flank resting at the intersection. The 3rd Vermont went into line on its left.[37] The New Englanders immediately began entrenching. The 2nd, 6th, and the balance of the 5th Vermont (north to south) went prone in the woods on the opposite side of the road behind Grant's first line.[38]

Getty, under orders from Meade, shifted his division to prepare for his own general assault. The 93rd Pennsylvania remained in the brush south of the road. Across from it, the 139th Pennsylvania placed its left flank on the Plank Road about two hundred twenty-five feet beyond the Brock Road.[39] The 62nd New York extended the line to the right. The 102nd Pennsylvania fell in behind the 139th while the 98th Pennsylvania (329 officers and men) covered the New Yorkers.[40]

Brigadier General Henry L. Eustis' four regiments painstakingly worked their way through the labyrinthine jungle toward Wheaton's right flank. Regimental adjutant, First Lieutenant Elisha Hunt Rhodes of the 2nd Rhode Island, grumbled in his diary about the "thick and almost impenetrable underbrush and small trees" through and around which he and his company struggled into formation.

Colonel Lewis A. Grant, commanding the Vermont Brigade, lost most of his men in the two days of fighting along the Plank Road.
(Gil Barrett Collection, USAMHI)

The 2nd Rhode Island with the 10th Massachusetts on its left went into line on the right of the 62nd New York. The 37th Massachusetts and the 7th Massachusetts covered them from north to south.[41] Lieutenant Colonel Joseph Parsons (10th Massachusetts), by Eustis' command, dispatched First Lieutenant L. Oscar Eaton with his Company F and Company H across the brigade's front as skirmishers. They crashed about forty-eight feet into the brush, then bellied down to wait and see what was going to happen.[42]

The Cavalry Fight Along the Catharpin Road
(7.5 miles southwest of the Brock Crossing.)

It took the 1st Vermont Cavalry the better part of three hours to push the dismounted 12th Virginia Cavalry back two miles to the deep ravine which cut across the Catharpin Road about one fourth mile east of Payte's Corner. The Confederates' fierce resistance forced Chapman to dismount most of his brigade into the woods on both sides of the road.[43] He sent word back

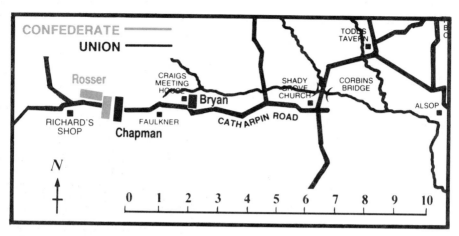

MAP 12: The situation on the Catharpin Road before noon on May 5, 1864.

to Wilson, who was at Craig's Meeting House, that he was desperately low on ammunition. Wilson, therefore, ordered Chapman to halt at the ravine and to go no farther.[44]

While Chapman deployed the 3rd Indiana Cavalry along the eastern lip of the ravine, Wilson prepared a defensive position around the church. Bringing Colonel Timothy Bryan's 1st Connecticut, 2nd New York, and 18th Pennsylvania regiments forward, he placed them in the open field behind the church. First Lieutenant Alexander C. M. Pennington (Company M, 2nd U.S. Artillery) and First Lieutenant Charles L. Fitzhugh (Companies C and E, 4th U.S. Artillery) wheeled their twelve horse artillery guns into battery side by side in the field in front of the cavalry.[45] Wilson rode west with his 50 man escort from the 8th Illinois Cavalry to Mrs. Faulkner's to establish his headquarters.[46]

Near Payte's Crossroads, the fighting became more intense along the skirmish line when the remainder of Rosser's Virginia cavalry brigade arrived upon the field to support the 12th Virginia Cavalry.[47] He kept Colonel Elijah "Lige" White's small 35th Battalion of about 170 officers and men to his rear. They had no ammunition. Rather than deploy them on the firing line where they would be useless, he kept the Virginians trotting from one end of the brigade to the other on the pretense of protecting the flanks from any attempted Federal breakthrough. White repeatedly sent couriers to the rear to find the brigade's ammunition wagons and each time they returned empty handed. The train had not yet arrived from the Shenandoah Valley.[48]

The pickets from the 3rd Indiana Cavalry, having penetrated deep into the pine thickets on both sides of the road, saw the Virginians and reported

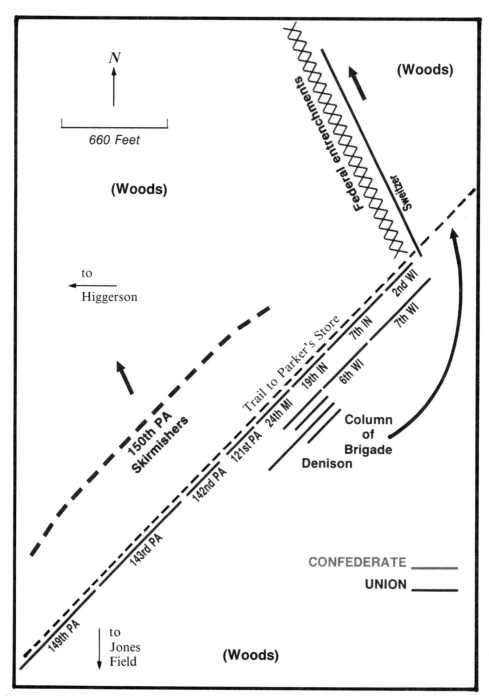

MAP 13: Noon, May 5, 1864 • The positions of Cutler's, Denison's, and Stone's brigades along the trail to Parker's Store.

that information to Chapman at the ravine. By then, Wilson had ridden forward to evaluate the situation for himself. He quickly told Chapman to remount his men and be prepared to retreat toward Craig's Meeting House if the Rebels attacked him in force.[49]

Situation With the V Corps by 12:00 P.M.[50]
Wilderness Tavern
(2 miles northwest of the Brock Crossing.)

Before noon, Brigadier General Charles Griffin's brigade commanders had reported to Warren that their men were in place and ready to advance. Crawford's division, under orders from corps headquarters, was finally evacuating Chewning's farm and marching north on the road toward Wadsworth's left flank. At about the same time that Griffin's division was maneuvering into position along Saunders Field, Wadsworth's three brigades (Rice, Stone, and Cutler) were going into line along the dirt road to Parker's Store. The division deployed, facing northwest, with its left brigade near Jones' Field and its right east of Higgerson's farm.

Brigadier General Lysander Cutler's Iron Brigade held the right in two lines. The 1st New York Sharpshooters disappeared into the woods west of the brigade as skirmishers.[51] The 24th Michigan was on the left of the first line, followed on the right by the 19th Indiana, the 7th Indiana, and the 2nd Wisconsin. The 6th Wisconsin and the 7th Wisconsin covered the 7th Indiana and the 2nd Wisconsin. Colonel Andrew W. Denison's Maryland Brigade fell into column of regiment behind the 24th Michigan and the 19th Indiana.[52] Colonel Roy Stone's brigade continued the division line to the left. The 121st Pennsylvania held the right of Stone's line. The 142nd, the 143rd, and the 149th Pennsylvania completed the formation to the left with the 150th Pennsylvania out in front as skirmishers.[53] Brigadier General James Rice's brigade held down the left of the division. Colonel Jacob Sweitzer's brigade (Griffin's division) linked Wadsworth's division with Bartlett's brigade. Bartlett's men extended to the Orange Turnpike and Ayres' men completed the corps' deployment from the pike to the woods.[54] The original plan called for Griffin's division to march in unison with Wadsworth's. Shortly after Wadsworth's men stepped off, Sweitzer's brigade left the earthworks southwest of Lacy's and pushed north into the woods without their brigadier, who preferred to stay at headquarters.[55] The move left Cutler's right flank unsupported. Colonel Andrew W. Denison's brigade peeled north as well, leaving Cutler and his men without any fire support.[56] The Marylanders moved into the portion of the line formerly occupied by Sweitzer's men.[57]

In the meantime, Stone was deploying his five Pennsylvania regiments for combat on Cutler's left and front. The men of the veteran 143rd Pennsylvania ruefully looked northwest into the foreboding wooded valley between them and the Higgerson farm. "That's a hell of a rough hole to send white men into," Sergeant Avery "Orr" Harris (Company B) heard one man blow through his teeth. "Boys, label yourselves, if we must go down in there," another warned, "as you will never come out." Private Arvin G. Colvin, the youngest member of Company B, looking more dead than alive, approached Harris. "Orr, I am not coming out of that hole alive," he said. Knowing that he probably could not change the boy's mind, Harris tried to convince him to leave the ranks. "Why go in?" Harris asked. "Go back down in the woods, and when the line advances, get out and find the hospital. You look like a corpse now, my lad." "No, Orr, I'll never do that," Colvin insisted. "If I do that the boys will call me a slink and I am going in." Harris told Colvin that the men knew him better than that but the boy refused to listen. The sergeant solemnly recollected that Private Owen Phillips, a member of the color guard and one of the biggest bullies in the regiment, had approached him just before the campaign began and told him, "I am not coming out of the next fight alive."[58]

Stone spread out the 150th Pennsylvania on a wide north-south line which inadvertently overlapped Cutler's front. Very shortly thereafter, the Pennsylvanians drove scattered detachments of Rebels from the brush. A minor firefight erupted with skirmishers popping off rounds at muzzle flashes and noises in the foliage. Captain Roland Stoughton (Company D) went down with a bullet in his right leg below the knee. First Lieutenant John Harter, who had been promoted from sergeant two days earlier, assumed command. Still wearing an enlisted man's blouse and armed with a discarded cavalry scabbard, he led his company forward with genuine determination. Somewhere in the tangle foot, he literally fell over an impromptu "rifle pit" which was defended by three armed Confederate privates and their captain. Brandishing his scabbard like a bludgeon, the spitfire lieutenant cursed the four into surrendering. The demoralized Rebel captain handed his own pistol and sword belt over to Harter, who wore them throughout the campaign.[59]

The rest of the brigade followed the skirmishers by wheeling the regiments to the right. The thick brush in the ravine on the southeastern side of the Higgerson farm slowed their advance. The sharp branches tore the soldiers' clothing and gouged their bodies. The limited space of Higgerson's hill forced the Federals to adjust their front and broke the formation into at least two lines. The 143rd Pennsylvania tried flanking to the left but could not because the 149th Pennsylvania, on its left front, would not yield ground. The pressure for room, however, forced that regiment to move to the left and give way to the 143rd. Once the brigade passed by its right flank, the 149th staggered back to its original position until it overlapped the 143rd from the rear. The 149th apparently mistook their own brigade for Confederates and volleyed at the line of troops which ascended the wooded hillside. Their rounds

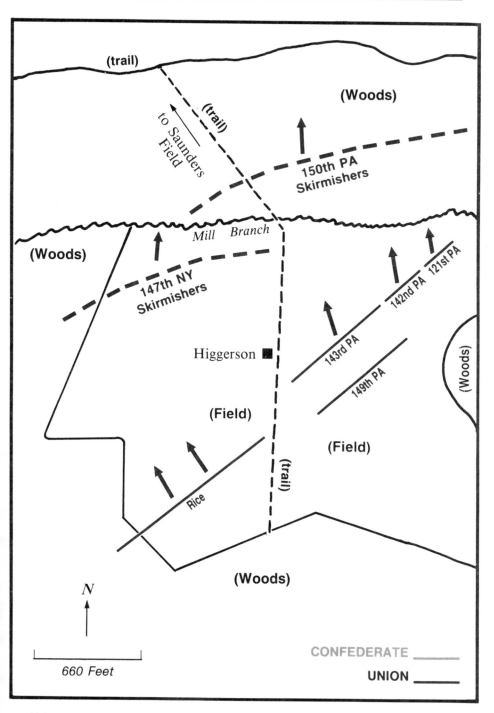

MAP 14: Shortly after noon on May 5, 1864 • Wadsworth's advance against Ewell's right flank at the Higgerson farm.

picked up the dirt at the heels of the 143rd, which continued to struggle to the top of Higgerson's hill.[60]

Around noon, Rice's brigade, supporting the left of Wadsworth's division, deployed for battle and began its advance from the southwesterly trail. The 56th Pennsylvania held the left of the line, with Captain Robert B. Barger's Company H on the left of the regiment.[61] Lieutenant Colonel John E. Cook (76th New York) sent Major John W. Young with Companies B, F, and K to the left to protect the regiment's flank from envelopment.[62] Simultaneously, Major Robert Bard (95th New York) hastened Companies A, E, and I to the front as skirmishers.[63]

To the north the 150th Pennsylvania neared the southern end of Saunders Field. The shooting intensified. Finally, Major George W. Jones, commanding the Pennsylvanians, herded his skirmishers farther to the right to make room for the 147th New York, whose misguided brigade (Rice's) had gotten too close to his command. The New Yorkers, armed with breech loading rifles, increased the din along the skirmish line with rapid fire.[64]

Colonel Edward S. Bragg (6th Wisconsin) and his officers spent a leisurely forenoon gathered around a gigantic oak tree exchanging jokes and quips. Lieutenant Colonel Rufus Dawes strained his eyes as he peered into the tree tops, trying to find the birds which twittered so cheerfully. The sun pierced the forest west of them with lances of blinding light.

The first indication of an advance came with the order to send a company out as skirmishers in preparation for a "reconnaissance," which unknown to the men, meant with considerable force. (Grant brought a new interpretation of skirmishing with him when he took command of the Northern army. Prior to his arrival, a company or a regiment could find itself deployed to the front to find the enemy. Grant skirmished with brigades and divisions, indicative of his perception of how the scope of the war had changed.) Edward Bragg, without thinking, told Captain John Kellogg to take out his Company I. "What word shall I send your wife?" Major Philip W. Plummer fatalistically asked the veteran captain as he got to his feet. "Never mind my wife," Kellogg shot back. "Look after Converse's girl!" Captain Rollin P. Converse (Company B), who was standing nearby, more out of prophesy than in jest, quipped, "Plummer will be shot before either of us, leave your messages with Dawes. He is the only man they can't kill."

The officers walked to their positions in the line and prepared to advance.[65] Private Abram Buckles (Company E, 19th Indiana), the regimental color bearer, gingerly pulled his blouse back over his right shoulder. He was hurting from an old wound, received at Gettysburg. While he was working on the breastworks along the road to Parker's Store, several bone fragments from that injury poked through the surface of his skin. Prior to the advance he was deftly plucking the splinters from his muscle with a pair of tweezers

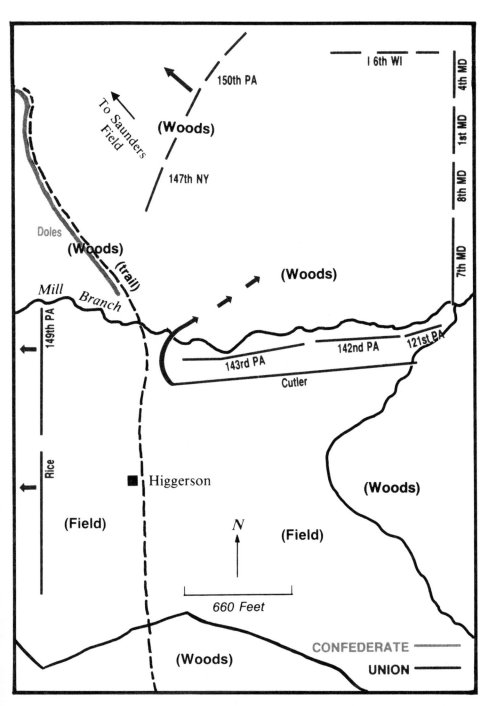

MAP 15: Before 1:00 P.M., May 5, 1864 • Wadsworth's deployment at the Higgerson farm, south of Saunders Field.

which he carried for that purpose. When the order came to move, he kept the colors cased, lest he tear them in the low hanging branches.[66]

The 149th Pennsylvania wheeled west. In passing around the Higgerson cabin, the Yankees destroyed the picket fence which enclosed the yard and the family's garden. Mrs. Pernellia Higgerson defiantly stood in her doorway and verbally harassed the Pennsylvanians as they tramped past her. Calling them "cowardly Yankees," she warned them they would not go very far before they would come back in a hurry.[67] The regiment continued west and formed in a north-south line perpendicular to but not connected with the rest of the brigade.

The remainder of Stone's Pennsylvanians crested the top of Higgerson's knoll, facing north. The 143rd Pennsylvania now held the left of the brigade line. First Sergeant "Orr" Harris did not like what he saw. Stone and his brigade staff rode up on the left of the line not too far from the sergeant and began systematically pulling long draughts from the willow encased whiskey flasks which hung from their necks. It made the sergeant uneasy to see the officers, including one of the 143rd's, getting drunk on the eve of a big battle. The brigade passed over the northern brow of Higgerson's hill and descended into the overgrown swamp created by Mill Branch. It executed a difficult one quarter right wheel through the saplings and elders which dominated the swamp and reformed its line along the wood line on its northeastern side.[68]

Colonel Roy Stone was seen drinking whiskey shortly before John B. Gordon's Georgians smashed his position on the Higgerson Farm.

(Mrs. Rex Album, USAMHI)

The Iron Brigade, moving west in column, passed behind the Pennsylvanians while they were forming their line. The Keystone troops lustily cheered the Westerners. Once Cutler's men cleared the left of the 143rd Pennsylvania, they moved from column into line and disappeared into the woods north of Stone's brigade. Five hundred yards into the woods north of Mill Branch, the Maryland Brigade stumbled into the Kellogg's prone Company I from the 6th Wisconsin. The skirmishers, having forged too far ahead of the brigade line which was then maneuvering through the woods, were trying to find out what was causing the racket up ahead.[69] Cutler's second line had a terrible time trying to keep its interval with the first line, which was 100 paces to the front. The dense forest and underbrush between Lacy's farm and the lower end of Saunders Field made it impossible for the officers of the 6th Wisconsin to see anything but the bobbing flag of the 7th Indiana which was surging deeper into the Wilderness. Before long the entire brigade had become totally disoriented.[70] Along Mill Branch, the nervous recruits in the 143rd Pennsylvania stared into the intimidating woods in front of them, completely unaware that they had actually flanked their own troops.[71]

Brigadier General Horatio Wright's Division (VI Corps) Moves Out Culpeper Mine Road-Germanna Plank Road Intersection.

(1.75 miles northwest of the Germanna Plank Road-Orange Turnpike intersection. 3.75 miles northwest of the Brock Crossing.)

A few minutes past noon, Wright advanced his men into the Wilderness. On the extreme right, Major Enoch Totten and his five companies from the 5th Wisconsin ran too far to the north before turning west. After losing complete contact with the other regiments, they turned in the general direction of the Confederates. The brigade advanced along the Culpeper Mine Road without them. Within short order, on the north side of the road, the 49th Pennsylvania chased a number of the 1st North Carolina Cavalry's dismounted troopers from their cover and sent them bounding back toward their own lines. The Pennsylvanians, excited by the prospect of a good run, threw all discipline aside and crashed through the woods after them. The four veteran companies of the regiment and the color guard swept ahead of the five newly recruited companies intent upon carrying the field on their own.[72]

On the southern side of the Culpeper Mine Road, Colonel Emory Upton decided not to lose his formations to the tangle foot and briars of the Wilderness. He realized it would be foolish to advance in line of battle, therefore, he deployed his regiments by "right of wings" before advancing. Facing the battle lines to the right, each regiment broke into two halves of five companies each. The two men on the right end of each "wing," as the five companies were designated, faced left. Then the men behind them (now on their left), by twos stepped forward and to the right to cover them. By the time the maneuver was completed, each regiment was in two parallel columns of two lines each, all of which faced west. Instead of the individual regiments taking up a front of several hundred feet and four feet in depth, each one occupied a front about eight feet wide (in two columns) and about half the distance of the original battle line.[73]

The junglelike undergrowth snatched at the men's arms and legs. The intertwining briars snagged their clothing and slowed the columns' paces to slower than a walk, and forced the regiments to halt. Nearly a mile into the

Wilderness, Upton's command encountered its first Rebel for that day. During the brigade's last rest, a picket, off to the right of the 5th Maine, shouted, "There is one of the rascals!" and snapped off a round which missed its target. Without warning, several unseen cannons opened fire from beyond the regiment's view. The men heard their roar, then saw their solid shot crashing through the tree tops overhead.[74] The "ball," as the veterans called a big fight, had started.

Chapter Four

"Soldiers, we have always driven
the enemy before us."

❶ The 12th Virginia Cavalry smashes the 3rd Indiana, 8th New York, and 1st Vermont.

❷ 50 men of the 8th Illinois stall the 12th Virginia until Chapman's brigade escapes. Federal artillery stops the 12th Virginia and turns it back.

❸ Thomson's 2 rifled guns duel with the 2nd U.S. Horse Artillery.

❹ The Federal cavalry escapes north.

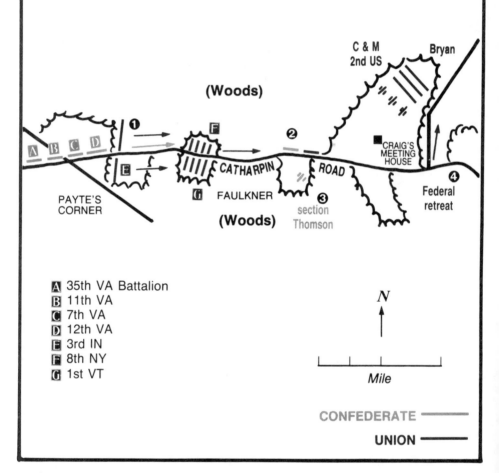

Ⓐ 35th VA Battalion
Ⓑ 11th VA
Ⓒ 7th VA
Ⓓ 12th VA
Ⓔ 3rd IN
Ⓕ 8th NY
Ⓖ 1st VT

N

Mile

CONFEDERATE ———

UNION ———

MAP 16: 1:00 P.M., May 5, 1864 • **The cavalry fight along the Catharpin Road.**

Around 1:00 P.M.

The Cavalry Fighting Along the Catharpin Road

After about an hour of heavy skirmishing along the ravine near Payte's Crossroads, it became evident to Colonel George Chapman that his troopers could not hold the line much longer. While the 3rd Indiana was keeping Brigadier General Thomas Rosser's Virginians at bay, he was massing the 1st Vermont and the 8th New York in an open field which bordered both sides of the Catharpin Road about a half mile from the firing line.[1] Private Charles Chapin (Company L, 1st Vermont Cavalry), having been in the fighting with his company for three hours, was glad to be reunited with his horse. He was looking forward to a much needed rest.[2]

Rosser did not give the Yankees any respite. Captain John W. Emmett, his assistant adjutant general, and his favorite courier, Private Jim Robinson (Company I, 12th Virginia), both of whom were badly injured in the scrape, rode back through the skirmishers along the road, moaning that the Federals had reinforced their line and that the brigade would not have to wait long for a charge to the front.[3] According to Captain William N. McDonald, Rosser's brigade ordnance officer, it never dawned upon the general that he was facing more than a cavalry regiment. He called his dismounted brigade "to horse" in the road and formed the regiments in column of fours to punch a hole through the Yankee position.

Colonel Thomas Massie placed the 12th Virginia Cavalry at the head of the column. The 7th and the 11th Virginia fell in behind and "Lige" White's "Comanches" (35th Battalion) completed the formation.[4] With sabres bared and pistols drawn, the 12th Virginia cut loose with the nerve shattering Rebel yell and boldly charged headlong toward the crude abatis which the Hoosiers had thrown across the road.[5] The suddenness of the attack panicked the 3rd Indiana.[6] Men were scrambling madly for their held horses as the lead riders of the 12th Virginia leaped their mounts over the roadblock and slammed into the Westerners with their pistols cracking.[7]

The Confederates wounded three of the Northerners and captured four more. Chapman tried to salvage what he could

Wounded in the early cavalry fighting along the Catharpin Road, Captain John W. Emmett warned Brigadier General Thomas Rosser that the Confederates would have to charge the Northerners to break through their position.

(History of the Laurel Brigade)

of his formation, but it was useless. While the 3rd Indiana stampeded east down the narrow road, he ordered the 1st Vermont into the fray to stay the rout, which merely added to the confusion. Chapin shot a disgusted glare at his pocket watch before swinging into the saddle. He had only been out of the line for fifteen minutes.[8] The dust kicked up by the 3rd Indiana obscured the 1st Vermont's vision.[9] The Confederates raced head first into the front of the New Englanders. To add to the chaos, Brigadier General James H. Wilson galloped into the disorganized brigade and told Chapman to retreat with all haste to Craig's Meeting House and to fall in behind Bryan's brigade.[10] In minutes, the Virginians killed or wounded several Yankees and captured eleven more before Chapman could execute the withdrawal. Chapin found himself the prisoner of a Virginian who was wearing a Union uniform.[11]

The 8th New York Cavalry did not wait for orders to retire. With the 3rd Indiana leading the way, it galloped for the safety of the meeting house. The 1st Vermont fought as well as the circumstances allowed but was also driven back in quick order. When the lead riders in the 12th Virginia neared Mrs. Faulkner's, threatening to overrun Wilson and his staff, First Lieutenant William W. Long (Company B, 3rd Indiana Cavalry) and his fifty man detachment from the 8th Illinois Cavalry charged pell mell into their path, allowing the general and his staff to escape to the church.

The 8th Illinois sabered and shot its way past Mrs. Faulkner's, leaving one trooper dead, three wounded, and three missing along the Catharpin Road.[12] As the Westerners cleared the killing zone of the two U. S. batteries near the church, eight of the rifled pieces opened fire upon Rosser's men, catching them upon the left flank. The artillerymen emptied a handful of saddles and sent the 12th Virginia scurrying back down the road out of their line of sight.[13] They were going to wait out the artillery pounding which shredded the pines along the road into pulp.

The Northerners had severely mauled the 12th Virginia since they made first contact with the 1st Vermont that morning – five dead, twenty-nine wounded, and one missing. (The Federals lost six killed, thirty-three wounded, and eighteen missing.) With the exception of the Battle of Brandy Station, the regiment had never lost so many men in a single engagement.[14]

Rosser sent a section of guns from Captain J. W. Thomson's horse artillery battery forward into Mrs. Faulkner's yard to return fire against the Federal guns. The two rifled pieces opened fire with shells soon after unlimbering. The Regulars responded immediately. Private George Neese (Thomson's Battery) had not seen such accurate shooting since his crew had run afoul of Yankee gunners during the Maryland Campaign of 1862. The bursting shells showered the sweating Confederate artillerymen with searing hot chunks of iron and cut down so many of the enlisted men that the section's officers were serving the guns.[15] Case shot sent musket balls thudding into the dry earth around them. The Regulars soon killed two battery horses and disabled several others.

With each passing minute, Neese thought he was going to die. He was scared and not afraid to admit it. The Yankees had their range and were plowing up the ground at Mrs. Faulkner's with disconcerting accuracy. Later that day, in an attempt to quell his fear, he sardonically wrote in his diary, "I am afraid that they [the Federals] will harvest me before I will be ripe." To add to the terror, he looked up in the smoke obscured sky to see what appeared to be fearsome new projectiles hurtling through the air into their position. The slow traveling shells emitted thick black smoke and glowed bright red, "like a little bunch of hell," Neese recollected. The incendiary rounds were actually case shot. Having been filled with a pine pitch matrix, they were producing black smoke instead of the standard yellow or white of burning sulphur. The shells fired the tall grass all around the Virginians who refused to yield their ground.[16] The Yankees seemed equally intent upon staying where they were.

About 1:00 P.M.[17]
Saunders Field, Near the Orange Turnpike
(2.75 miles north of Parker's Store.)

For several hours Private Phil Crites (Second Company B) of the 25th Virginia kept his eyes fastened upon the two dead Yankees in the open ground north of the pike and their seemingly over-stuffed knapsacks. Despite warnings from his officers not to venture into the open, he scurried over to the corpses to rifle their possessions. A bullet severely wounded him the second he dropped to his knee next to one of the dead men.

Private Sam Lynch (Second Company B) and three comrades, not waiting for the ambulance corps to come to the front, instantly volunteered to bring in Crites rather than leave him out there to die. "Sam, don't go," his best friend Private John King (Second Company B) pleaded with him. With a quick glance, Lynch propped his rifle against a tree and dashed into the corn stubble. For a moment, King believed the Yankees would allow them to retrieve his grievously wounded friend. But the sharpshooters waited until the four men had Crites in their grasp before opening fire. Lynch collapsed, too wounded to move. The cruelty and the suddenness of the shooting shocked King so badly that he could not remember whether the other three men brought off Crites or not. He desperately wanted to rescue Lynch but could not. Losing his life to save a friend who would probably die did not make sense. "...his death hurt me worse than any other in the war," King lamented. The sight of his friend helplessly writhing between the lines stayed with him until the day he died.[18]

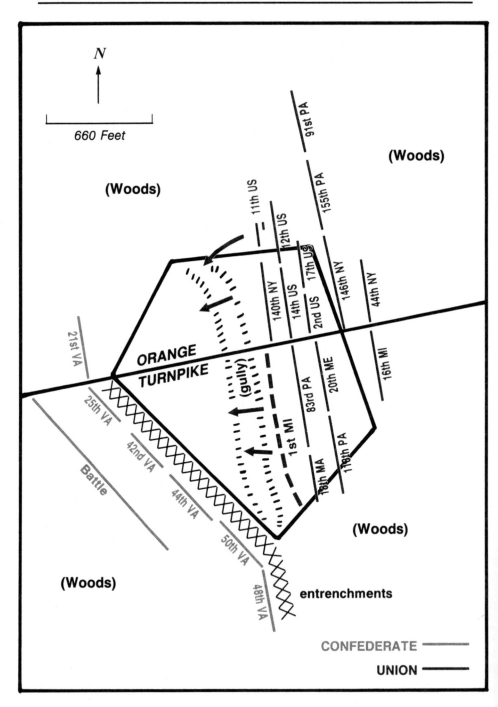

MAP 17: 1:00 P.M., May 5, 1864 • Griffin's V Corps division assaults Ewell's line at Saunders Field.

The 140th New York and the four companies of the 11th U.S. Regulars advanced, without the rest of Ayres' brigade, to the eastern edge of Saunders Field and aligned themselves for an attack. Captain James W. Long, commanding the 11th Regulars, followed behind with the two companies he had kept in reserve.[19] The command rippled along the line to fix bayonets. Minutes later a staff orderly told Colonel George Ryan (140th New York) to move his men across the open ground. As they emerged from the woods, the Federals got their first clear view of the Confederate position.

The wood line across from them puffed white. Bullets thunked into the startled Yankees. Second Lieutenant John Hume (Company F) fell to the ground with a shattered knee. Ryan's horse danced about, severely wounded. He dismounted, his sword still in the saddle scabbard, and sent his horse to the rear. Private William Hurle (Company B) collapsed with a wound. The entire brigade spontaneously went to the ground. Private Mathias Brown, Company B's cook, under the colonel's orders rolled Hurle over and stripped the wounded man of his accoutrements before replacing him in the line. Private Caspar Fromm (Company B), the regimental butcher, also took a disabled soldier's place.[20]

The 140th New York remained prone for several minutes until a staff officer passed the word to advance. Ryan placed himself behind the regiment's center company. "Stand up!" he bellowed. "Right shoulder arms." The regiment responded with precision. "Forward, double quick. Charge!"

With a resounding, deep throated cheer, the 140th New York and the 11th U.S. bolted into the swale well ahead of the rest of their brigade. Ryan, waving his soft felt slouch hat, urged the men forward. The line disappeared momentarily into the gully. The men were not screaming as they surged into view again. A bullet slammed into First Lieutenant Joseph H. Pool's arm as he stumbled after his Company C, the impact hurling him, unconscious, to the ground. The regiment obliqued to the left with the contour of the road until the center company straddled the pike.[21]

Meanwhile, the line of Regulars behind the first wave silently marched forward as if on parade, at the "common time" – ninety steps per minute – toward a waiting enemy. When the regiments reached the bottom land, the right end of the 12th U.S., the 2nd U.S. and the 17th U.S. disappeared into the woods on the northern end of the field and accidentally chased some of Brigadier General Leroy Stafford's Louisianans back toward the Culpeper Mine Road.[22]

The startled Confederates, having stepped into the brush during their respite probably to relieve themselves, had no intention of doing picket duty. They raced back to the brigade yelling about Yankee skirmishers being no more than one hundred yards beyond the woods road. Major Henry Handerson, having been left with the command of Stafford's brigade, hurriedly moved the regiments into line and was going to throw skirmishers forward when the general raced up to the brigade in a fury. He barked at the regiments to retire one hundred yards west. The Confederates did not lose any time executing the order. As they formed another line of battle, the command to load echoed among the trees.[23]

Over one third of a mile away, Ayres' third line crawled into the underbrush along the eastern side of the woods to wait for its turn to go in. The soldiers of the colorfully dressed 146th New York stripped off their knapsacks and pressed themselves as low to the ground as they could to make themselves inconspicuous. They watched in dismay as the first two waves of the brigade stepped into a maelstrom of rifle fire.[24] The Confederates fired by files from the right (south to north). Methodically, like a finely tooled stamping machine, their shots punched across the field with well drilled precision. Gaps appeared in the Federal regiments but the veterans professionally closed ranks and continued forward.[25]

On the left, the 140th New York surged ahead through the corn stubble right into the guns of Brigadier General John M. Jones' Virginians. The right end of the 12th U.S. Regulars became entangled in the briar choked northern end of the field. The undergrowth and the rabbit briars completely disrupted its formation. In an attempt to maintain their own lines, the Regulars slowed their pace and enlarged the distance between them and the 140th New York and the 11th U.S. The New Yorkers veered to the southwest, following the contour of the road, widening the gap between themselves and the Regulars on their right.[26] The 17th Regulars, having observed the rifle flashes in the woods far to their right, suspected the presence of a much larger Confederate force on the right flank, and filed to the left with the 2nd U.S. into Saunders Field behind the 12th and the 14th Regulars.[27]

The Woods North of Saunders Field

By then, Stafford had pushed his Louisianans through the dense brush and woods almost two hundred yards beyond the brigade's original position. Occasional bullets thunked into the trees along the regiments' front. The intensity of the volleying off to the right startled Major Henry Handerson. The trees vibrated with the violent repercussions of the intense volleying on that flank.[28]

Bartlett Goes into the Fray – South of the Pike

While Ayres charged across the upper end of Saunders Field, the rest of the division joined in the assault. The 1st Michigan initiated the attack by advancing in a wide arc which covered the brigade front across the southern half of Saunders Field. The same volley which slammed into the 140th New York with a thunderous roar, enveloped the Michiganders. The Yankees walked into it on the western slope of the field. The Rebels' muzzle blasts, at point-blank range, were literally knocking large numbers of men in the small regiment off their feet. A bullet snatched Captain David Stanway (Company G, 1st Michigan) from the ground and sent his fragmented arm sailing in several directions. His clothing smoldered from the burning powder. The inside of his wound was sizzling from the sulphur as it penetrated his arm in the track of the ball.[29] The men passed around their severely wounded captain into the edge of the forest and engaged the Rebel skirmishers in hand-to-hand combat. A minie ball thudded into Private George W. Sawyer (Company E, 1st Michigan). The bullet bored through his chest immediately below his right nipple, perforated his lung, and exited through his back very close to his spine. He hobbled from the field with an entry wound which would never heal.[30] The musketry proved too overwhelming. The 1st Michigan retired, leaving behind 64 officers and men dead, wounded, or missing.[31]

Bartlett then attacked, with his brigade in two lines. The 44th New York held down the right of the line north of the turnpike, with its left on the road. The 16th Michigan went into position on its left.[32] The 83rd Pennsylvania and the 18th Massachusetts fell in to the south, respectively. The 118th Pennsylvania covered the 18th Massachusetts and the 20th Maine formed behind the 83rd Pennsylvania.[33] When the division buglers blew "the Advance" the brigade, with the exception of the 16th Michigan and the 44th New York, rose in unison and bolted toward the open ground in front of the woods.[34] The Confederate skirmishers in the open ground between the lines retreated, snapping off random shots as they went.[35] Their bullets splattered into the 20th Maine which was approaching the eastern edge of Saunders Field. Private Theodore Gerrish (Company H, 20th Maine) carefully noticed every detail of the action. The stunted pines which clawed him as he ran through them were dying from the bottom up.[36]

One of the rounds smashed Colonel O. S. Woodward (83rd Pennsylvania) in the left leg, just below the knee. The regiment continued on past its colonel, while one of the men helped him to the rear. The command devolved to Lieutenant Colonel DeWitt McCoy.[37] On the western edge of Saunders Field, the Confederates temporarily regrouped. Turning, they unleashed a volley into the 83rd Pennsylvania and the 18th Massachusetts which, to the approaching 20th Maine, on the far side of the stubble field, seemed to gouge impressive holes in the front line.[38] The two regiments split apart in the momentum of the charge and independently struck the woods and the Confederates retreated again.[39] The 83rd Pennsylvania, which caught up with the Rebel skirmishers, did not bother to take prisoners. They left a handful of dead Rebels in their wake.

The Pennsylvanians outflanked Generals Richard S. Ewell, Jubal Early, Robert E. Rodes, and John M. Jones with their headquarters staffs and couriers, who had assembled in the first swale in the turnpike west of Saunders

Field. Jones, his aide-de-camp, Major Samuel J. G. Moore, Captain Robert D. Early, and Lieutenant Randolph Ridgely immediately mounted up and spurred toward their scattering troops. Jones was frantically trying to rally his panicked Virginians. Despite his threats and pleas, his men streamed past him in a total rout. Their sudden exodus swept Captain Robert D. Early from the front. Wheeling his frightened horse about, he galloped to Jones' assistance. The Federals cut the captain down in a flurry of small arms fire before he could reach his friend. Moore went down in the same volley with a bullet in the thigh. Ridgely hurriedly dismounted and, with the help of two enlisted men, shoved Moore onto his horse. At the same instant, Captain Reuben Cleary, assistant adjutant general to Robert E. Lee, helplessly watched two of the Pennsylvanians corner Jones on the picket line and demand he give his arms to them. When he refused to surrender to someone of inferior rank, they shot him down then stole his sword.[40]

Brigadier General John M. Jones, C.S.A., died at the hands of two Union soldiers rather than surrender. They stole his sword.
(Battles and Leaders, Grant-Lee Edition)

Crashing through the briar entangled woods, the screaming Yankees dodged and darted around trees and bounded over logs. They lost track of the distance, of the time, and of each other.[41] The 18th Massachusetts strayed too far to the left and dragged most of the 83rd Pennsylvania with it.[42] The regiments tramped over the Confederate wounded and swarmed around 40 dejected Confederates, who were walking east without an escort.[43] The 118th Pennsylvania and the 20th Maine (south to north) charged toward the gap created by the fragmented front line. The 118th Pennsylvania, in the wake of the first line's attack, picked up the 18th Massachusetts' 40 demoralized Confederates in Saunders Field. The Northerners hurriedly stripped the Rebels of their weapons and accoutrements and sent them to the rear without a guard. Since they did not have the time to walk them personally to their lines, they turned them loose on their honor to get there on their own.[44]

The bullets pocked up the stubbled ground like rain pelting a dried field, Gerrish fearfully remembered. Out in front, Brigadier General Joseph J. Bartlett, in his best uniform, spurred his horse across the open ground ahead of the two regiments.[45] A little under one hundred yards into the junglelike forest, the Federals ran into Battle's Alabamians.[46] The confused Yankees tried to reorganize their brigade line, which allowed Jones' Confederates enough time to rally. The Federal officers lost too much time bullying and shouting their soldiers back into formation.[47]

One of Early's couriers had unfurled the division's new colors in the breeze on the western side of the first swale west of Saunders Field. The Saint Andrews Cross filled the field in the upper left hand corner. Three parallel bars, alternating red, white, and red, tied into a flaming red, vertical bar on the right end of the banner. A large, inverted "L" spanned the center of the three bars and another inverted "L" was centered in the red band below the saltier.[48] Colonel John Higginbotham (25th Virginia), now commanding Jones' very scattered brigade, regrouped about 50 men from the 25th Virginia and reported to Early and Ewell. Early shoved his headquarters flag into the colonel's hands with orders to plant it on the hillside and rally whom he could. Higginbotham complied but no one stood by him. None of his men were returning to the fray. His regiment left 6 killed, 2 wounded and 86 captured upon the field – a loss for which the men unfairly blamed the rest of their brigade.[49]

Early did not have time to waste. Turning to Major John W. Daniel he blurted, "Major, you will find Gordon a short distance up the pike; ride to him as fast as you can, and tell him to bring up his brigade as quick as possible. Tell him too not to get his men out of breath, for they will have to charge as soon as they get here."[50]

Demoralized Virginians from Jones' command broke into the open ground west of the Wilderness into the face of Brigadier General Junius Daniel's halted brigade. They frantically blurted the news of their general's death on the skirmish line because he refused to surrender. They also brought word of how they had shattered at the Yankees' first fire. Daniel did not need any special instructions to attack. He responded to the situation as soon as his front cleared of stragglers.

"Attention, Battalions!" he yelled loud enough for everyone to hear. "Battalions forward, the center the battalion of direction, march!" Advancing at the quick step, the North Carolinians trampled down the fresh budding brush on the edge of the Wilderness and disappeared into the woods, guiding in the direction in which they assumed Battle and his brigade had gone. A very short distance into the forest they walked into the rifles of the 18th Massachusetts and the 83rd Pennsylvania. The briar entangled scrub brush along the brigade's front burst into white smoke followed instantly by what Sergeant Cyrus Watson (Company K, 45th North Carolina) recalled was the near deafening roar of musketry. Bullets whacked the bark off the trees above the Confederates' heads. For the most part, the Federals had fired too high. A few men in the 45th North Carolina plummeted to the forest floor.[51]

The Southerners responded without orders. They leveled their weapons and randomly fired at the smoke which still enshrouded the trees along their front.[52] The badly rattled Lieutenant Colonel DeWitt McCoy (83rd Pennsylvania) hailed over Colonel Joseph Hayes of the 18th Massachusetts and suggested that both units quit the field.[53] For the most part, the encircled enlisted men did not stand on orders from their officers. They ran, Captain Amos M. Judson (Company E, 83rd Pennsylvania) reminisced.[54]

The North Carolinians cheered and dashed forward into a briar thicket which they quickly clubbed to the ground. Hastily glancing at the casualties who were lying in a contorted string in the woods, Watson mistakenly assumed that their volley had swept about half of the Northerners' line away.[55] Daniel's rifle fire slashed and thunked into the trees through Bartlett's first line into his second. The 20th Maine, having just reached the western side of Saunders Field, recoiled briefly under its impact. The bullets, which seemingly materialized from the shadows of the trees, startled the daylights out of Gerrish.[56] The Pennsylvanians and the New Englanders plowed into the woods, through the swarm of refugees from the front line of the brigade, who disrupted their formations.[57]

The 118th Pennsylvania regrouped inside the woods and braced itself for the worst. Rather than run, Colonel James Gwyn halted the regiment and bellowed the command to "about face." The veterans valiantly attempted to retire with some dignity but the Confederates seemed too close behind.[58] Whooping and hollering as they charged, Daniel's North Carolinians slammed minies into the Federals' backs.[59] Honor quickly surrendered to common sense. In short order, the Pennsylvanians scattered into clusters of frightened soldiers, with each group fending for itself.[60] The dense undergrowth swallowed them up and broke them away from the left of the 20th Maine as they ran for their lives.[61]

Before Bartlett's left wing cleared the woods, a bullet smacked into Hayes' head. He rode off the field desperately but not mortally injured. Another bullet wounded First Lieutenant Timothy McCarty (Company H, 18th Massachusetts) in the arm.[62] By the time the 20th Maine, with its right on the Orange Turnpike, reached

Rather than face annihilation, Colonel James Gwyn (118th Pennsylvania) ordered his men to retreat during Joseph Bartlett's assault across the southern end of Saunders Field.

(MOLLUS, USAMHI)

the small clearing in the woods opposite Battle's Alabamians, most of the 83rd Pennsylvania had abandoned the field, as had the 18th Massachusetts and the 118th Pennsylvania.[63] The woods resounded with the continuous crackling of musketry much like a bursting, interminable string of fire crackers. Intermittent brush fires crackled and snapped throughout the area. The pungent smoke mingled with the low hanging veil of burned powder, reducing visibility to a few rods. The men's eyes were stinging and watering. Their sweat and tears were tracing little rivulets down their powder blackened cheeks. Unable to see their targets, they were sniping at the shadows and the puffs of smoke which dotted the jungle in front of them.

Major Ellis Spear of the 20th Maine, who could not determine whose troops were in front of him, advanced the regimental colors into the clearing ahead of the right wing of the regiment. The right half of the regiment filed into the field, leaving the left half in the trees on its southern flank. Minie balls whistled into the regiment from the right flank and the rear. Steuart's Virginians and North Carolinians were beginning to roll up Ayres' brigade in the woods and in the field north of the pike and were wheeling toward the New Englanders on their southern flank. Stragglers from other regiments were wandering into their formation. Captain Walter G. Morrill (Company B, 20th Maine), on the right, shouted at his company and the men from the other commands to form a line at a right angle to the rest of the regiment, facing north. They executed the maneuver and temporarily stymied the Rebel drive. A bullet hammered Morrill in the face, knocking him down. Jarred but not dead, he painfully worked himself to his feet, bandaged his face with his handkerchief, and tried to continue the fight.[64]

The 20th Maine could not withstand the onslaught. Casualties were rapidly increasing. Enlisted men assisted Morrill, who was choking on his own blood, to the rear. Other injured men staggered from the firing line. Spear told the regiment to retreat. Gerrish heard the command and turned about to run. He took one step. His left leg went numb and he fell flat on his face. He felt nothing from his hip to his foot. He sheepishly glanced down at his foot, believing he would find it gone. The minie ball had bored through his left ankle, leaving the foot attached to his leg. The leaves on the forest floor and surrounding the pine trees burned dangerously close to him. The adrenalin was pumping through his system. His heart thumped violently. He did not want to burn alive nor did he care to waste away in a Confederate prison pen. Rising to his feet, he attempted another step. But, when he bent his knee, he collapsed. Again, he attempted to support his weight. He flexed his knee and crashed to the ground. The next time he struggled upright, he kept his leg straight, and for some unexplainable reason, found he could limp at a rather fast clip.[65]

Ayres' Brigade – North of the Pike

While Bartlett and his men became engulfed in the maelstrom on Ayres' left front, the left wing of the 140th New York slammed into the woods south of the pike. The entire regiment volleyed blindly into the trees while the right wing stopped on the eastern face of the woods. Steuart's Confederates slammed headlong into the 140th New York and exploited their success.[66] The 21st Virginia clambered wildly through the overgrown woods in an attempt to force the skirmishers from the 140th New York from the field. They loaded and fired on the run, all the while making as much racket as possible to frighten the Northerners. Sergeant John Worsham (Company F) found himself staring down the barrel of a rifle. A quick glimpse absorbed the detail of the stump it rested upon and the Union Zouave who was leveling it at him. A handful of Confederates, Worsham included, instantly brought their weapons to bear upon the equally startled Yankee and called at him to surrender. The fellow made a start to run when the short teenager to the sergeant's left dropped him with a single shot. The boy, who had straggled several weeks before because his wooden bottomed shoes had torn his feet up, redeemed his honor among his comrades. In short order, they smashed through the right of the 140th New York and destroyed its line.[67]

Many of the New Yorkers took cover behind trees and stumps. Wounded men continued to fall to the ground. A musket ball struck twenty-one year old Private Eugene H. Dunning (Company I, 140th New York) a glancing blow in the head and sent him staggering dizzily toward the rear.[68] A minie ball struck a private in Company C in the face just below his right eye. It exited through his palate and upper jaw on the opposite side, taking his left eye tooth and three more teeth with it. At the same time another ball ripped into his foot. Dropping his weapon, he limped away from the fighting.[69] Colonel George Ryan (140th New York), still clenching his hat in his hand, dashed from the center of his regiment south across the pike toward the left end of his line, which had disappeared into the woods. All the while he was yelling at his men to stay firm.

Colonel George Ryan (140th New York), during the entire attack across Saunders Field, while waving his hat above his head, cheered his men onward by running from one end of the regimental line to the other. He came out of the action unscathed.

(Under the Maltese Cross)

Captain Porter Farley (Company B) who stood behind his men just north of the pike, had lost sight of the left half of his company. As the colonel darted out of sight, Farley glanced about, trying to see what was left of the regimental line and its officers. "My God, they've knocked my leg to pieces!" The captain wheeled around to see Captain William S. Grantsyn (Company H) writhing on the ground in terrible pain. Nearby lay Captain Henry G. Hamilton (Company K). Two of his men were stooping over him, futilely attempting to shake him into consciousness. When they failed to rouse him, Farley mistakenly assumed his fellow officer had died. To the left rear, First Lieutenant Joseph H. Pool (Company C), who had regained consciousness and had followed the regiment into action, blacked out against a tree stump on the southern side of the road. Seconds later, Ryan, still screaming for the men to hold their ground, and still waving his hat, bounded across the road, heading north. "He had hardly gone," Farley later wrote, "and I felt my heart sinking in the realization that my men were reduced to a handful."[70]

Worsham and his men rounded up over one hundred prisoners and sent them rearward while the rest of the regiment surged ahead. When the Virginians hit the pine forest bordering Saunders Field, they instinctively went prone. Meanwhile, Steuart's North Carolinians and Virginians, who were moving up behind the 21st Virginia, also dove to the ground. Unable to see more than twenty yards in any direction because of the interlaced pine branches, Worsham decided to go forward alone. Darting south, across the road, he whipped east to the top of the ridge overlooking the swale. The rumbling and clatter of charging caissons made him snap his eyes to the front. The sight which greeted him in the open ground to the northeast stopped him cold.[71]

Two 24-pounder howitzers from Company D, 1st New York Artillery, under the personal direction of Captain George B. Winslow, trotted down the pike and across the bridge over the gully in an attempt to support the 140th New York.[72] Winslow and the section commander, Second Lieutenant William H. Shelton, hurriedly dismounted and helped the artillerymen, who had run alongside the limbers, manhandle the trails of the large guns around into position south of the pike. The veteran gunners rolled their two pieces by hand almost to the top of the eastern slope of the hollow. Minie balls whistled and hummed about them like swarming bees, Shelton recalled. He staggered momentarily under the impact of a spent ball which glanced off the knee flap of his heavy leather boot.[73]

Before Worsham could respond he realized the two artillery pieces were pointed at him. The sergeant hurled himself behind a large tree alongside the road. At the same time Private W. E. Cumbie (Company F) bolted into the open to see what was happening.[74] The Federal guns opened with solid shot and the infantry accompanied their fire with an unexpected burst of musketry.[75] Cumbie toppled into the road, mortally wounded, and Worsham ran back to his company.[76]

To the west, one of those cannon balls caught Chaplain James Sheeran (14th Louisiana) and a number of Confederate surgeons by surprise. They heard the whizzing of the incoming round about one second before it thudded into the pike not fifty yards off to their right. The doctors were too close to the front to guarantee their patients' safety and their own. They retreated about a quarter of a mile to set up their field hospital. At the same time Major John W. Daniel, on Early's staff was putting the spurs to his "Old Whitey" and disappearing down the Orange Turnpike in search of Brigadier General John B. Gordon's Georgia brigade.[77]

The incoming Yankee rifle shots peppered the main Confederate line which had impatiently lain in support several hundred yards to the rear of the wood line. Twigs, pine needles, and splintered bark rained down upon the heads of the prone Virginians and North Carolinians of Steuart's brigade. Captain McHenry Howard posted himself near the right of the brigade while Steuart assumed his place near the center of the line. Major General Edward Johnson galloped past the captain, shouting that he was not to bring on a general engagement.

A minute or so later Johnson again singled out the assistant inspector general. "Remember, Captain Howard," he anxiously cautioned him, "it is not meant to have a general engagement." "But, General," Howard protested, "it is evident that the two lines will come together in a few moments, and whether it is intended to have general engagement or not, will it not be better for our men to have the impetus of a forward movement in the collision?" "Very well," Johnson sighed, "let them go ahead a little."[78]

Worsham staggered into his company and found Colonel Hamilton Brown (1st North Carolina) standing among the Virginians. The sergeant reported the situation in Saunders Field to the colonel. Brown, a firebrand of an officer, unhesitatingly called, "Forward, men!" at anyone within earshot.[79] Howard, who was nearby, having glanced to his left in an unsuccessful attempt to find Steuart, unsheathed his sword and cried out, "Forward!" The Rebel yell resounded through the forest above the tremendous crash of musketry.[80] Winslow saw that the troops backing up the 140th New York and the U.S. Regulars to its right had not kept up with the guns. He immediately told his men to wheel their pieces into the hollow to the western edge of the gully.[81] Confederate sharpshooters, in the tree tops on the opposite side of the clearing, methodically picked off the section's horses. Several of them plunged wounded or dead into the stubble near the edge of the wash out, while a couple, with their slain riders, remained upright in their traces.[82] The remaining artillerymen manhandled the two pieces into position.[83]

The Eastern Side of Saunders Field

The bugler of the 146th New York blared "The Attention." "Attention! – Take Arms! – Fix bayonets!" Colonel David Jenkins called out. "Forward march!" Ayres' fourth line calmly stepped out at the "common time" with its weapons at the shoulder. The left wing of the 146th New York, being at the narrowest part of the woods, emerged from cover first. As the three left companies came into the open, Jenkins continued, "Forward, double-quick!" The order traveled through the regiment from the center to both wings as the company officers repeated it in succession. With their line intact, the New Yorkers marched across the stubble field, heading for the wash out in the center of the hollow.[84]

The Confederate volley which sent the artillery skittering down hill, hammered into the Regulars of Ayres' first three lines when they reached the western edge of Saunders Field, and as the 146th New York reached the eastern lip of the ditch. A second rapidly executed volley punched huge holes through the Regulars' two lines.[85] Part of the 2nd U.S. hit the dirt. The rest of the regiment and the entire 17th U.S. broke ranks and streamed rearward, while the 12th U.S. and 14th U.S. plowed ahead in a very ragged formation into the woods. First Sergeant Louis Dugal (Company F, 146th New York) watched in disbelief as his company ran over the top of the prone 2nd U.S.[86]

The blast destroyed the unit integrity of the two Regular regiments on the right of the formation. The 12th and the 14th U.S., with the center companies and the colors of the 11th U.S. cast aside all semblance of their original formations. Quickly, Lieutenant Sartell Prentice (Company F, 2nd Battalion, 12th U.S.) later recalled, it seemed as if the two regiments overran two light lines of breastworks before crashing into a third line to which the Confederates stubbornly clung.[87]

All around Dugal soldiers were taking hits. Men suddenly threw their arms into the air, reeled and fell. Others were hurled flat upon their backs. The unnerving death rattle in the throats of the dying resounded ominously among the cries of the wounded. While a stream of injured trailed rearward in the wake of the charge, he suddenly became aware of his own quick breathing.[88] Without warning, the air exploded to the left of the line, followed by a suffocating sulfuric cloud and the scorching heat of a blast furnace. Winslow's gunners had each emptied a single round of canister at the right oblique across the left front of the 146th New York.[89]

Infuriated by the snipers, who were killing their fellow Yankees, the gunners feverishly loaded and discharged two more rounds of canister into the mass of troops which they saw in the smoke to their front. The cast iron canister balls ripped gory holes into the backs of the frightened 140th New York.[90]

Captain Porter Farley (Company B, 140th New York) heard the first rounds clatter into the woods around him. Unable to tell where the noise originated from, he stepped into the road, where, to his horror, he saw the "Number One" gunners reloading their field pieces. He panicked. Hurling himself into the drainage ditch on the northern side of the road, he hugged the ground until the next two bursts whistled overhead. He then dashed across the road with no intention of stopping until he reached the woods on the Federal side of the field. As far as he knew, there was no longer any regiment left to hold any ground.[91]

Meanwhile, the left of the 146th New York was scrambling out of the gully and rushing the woods to the front. The men were firing as they advanced. Many were not stopping to reload. The Confederates were falling back, fighting from tree to tree. They retreated to their breastworks and poured a deadly fire into the Yankees.[92] The 146th New York's left companies threw themselves to the ground on the edge of the woods. Firing prone was no easy matter. Following each round, the individual soldier had to roll onto his back to reload. It slowed a man's rate of fire to about one round a minute.[93]

A dense, asphyxiating pall of burned powder hung low in the pines and the blooming dogwoods, making it very difficult to tell friend from foe. Individuals, carried away by the lust of battle, were darting back and forth through that eery mantle, bayoneting and clubbing isolated Rebels who had not retreated. Within a minute or two, the left wing of the 146th New York was in the woods. The regiment reformed and both sides ceased fire. The New Yorkers believed they had won the field.[94]

The 155th and the 91st Pennsylvania regiments, on the right of the brigade, having struggled through the same underbrush and woods which ensnared the Regulars several minutes before, had gotten separated from each other.[95] On the far right, the 91st Pennsylvania found the woods relatively open but the trees were too thick to see any appreciable distance. After advancing about one furlong, the regiment passed over the swampy depression which drained into Saunders Field. First Lieutenant Thomas F. Walter (Company A), who was standing on the extreme right of the regiment, did not like his situation at all. The sounds of the raging battle to the left echoed ominously overhead. He envisioned a longer Confederate battle line sweeping down upon the regiment's exposed northern flank. In the dense forest, it was impossible to detect any friendly line to his front.

Pot shots suddenly zipped overhead. Skirmishers were skittering through the woods to the front. A few steps farther brought the Pennsylvanians under fire from an unseen Confederate regiment. Walter thought the Confederate force was smaller than his regiment, but he was not sure. An exploding bullet burst in front of his face, cutting his cheek and temporarily blinding

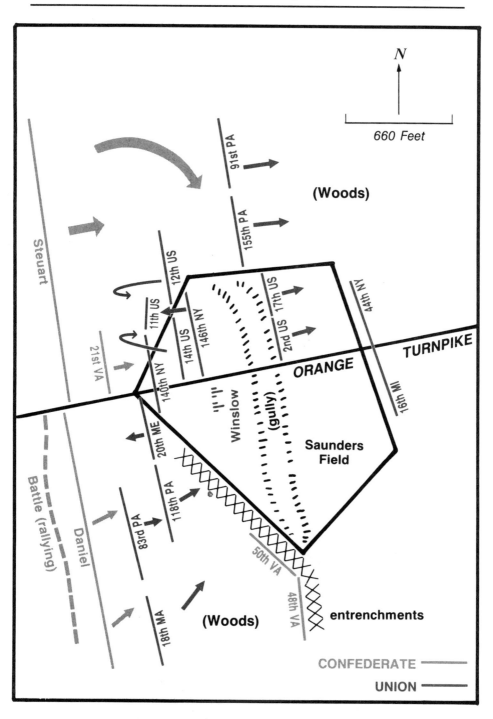

MAP 18: 1:00 P.M.-1:30 P.M., May 5, 1864 • Ayres' and Bartlett's brigades are stopped by Steuart's and Daniel's Confederates.

him. Before he fully recovered, the regiment flanked south and east, leaving the stunned lieutenant among others isolated in the swamp. Rather than run, they formed a tiny rear guard and skirmished while they retreated. Company A came off the field with one man slightly wounded and rejoined the regiment back at the jump off point in the woods on the eastern side of Saunders Field. (The 91st suffered 11 casualties.)[96]

Announcing their advance with their terrifying Rebel yell, the 10th and the 23rd Virginia turned south rather than pursue the timid 91st Pennsylvania. A volley raked the stranded 155th Pennsylvania.[97] The Pennsylvanians valiantly attempted to hold their ground. An enlisted man, without orders, cut down a Confederate captain with a well aimed shot. Several Confederates tossed their officer onto a blanket and carried him away. The two Confederate regiments sprang upon the brightly dressed Zouaves with a fury until the two lines became entangled. "Throw down your guns! Drop your colors! Surrender!" the Rebels demanded in between shouts and curses. Color Corporal Thomas J. Marlin, who had not unfurled the 155th's colors, turned about and pushed his way through the briar entangled woods to the rear. Within seconds, the Rebels had taken out 45 men. The regiment turned and streamed for cover. The Virginians chased them into the woods north of the pike and suddenly halted on its border. The Pennsylvanians ran back through the trees to a point several hundred yards into the woods where they went prone and sporadically began to return fire against the Southerners, whom they could not see. The fighting cost the 10th Virginia dearly. Major Isaac Coffman went down in the melee, mortally wounded. His superior Colonel E. T. H. Warren, of Harrisonburg, Virginia, died instantly when a bullet ripped through his throat.[98]

The center of the 146th New York had just crossed to the western side of the gully when the Confederates struck. Their musketry instantly swept away six of the color guard. The color bearer, Private George F. Williams (Company B), jerked violently when three rounds thudded into him in rapid succession. As he collapsed, another of the guard grabbed the standard from his grasp and carried the flag a few yards before he was killed. Corporal Conrad Neuschler (Company I) snatched the flag staff before the colors hit the ground and bolted toward the rear.[99] The

While trying to escape across Saunders Field with the colors of the 146th New York, Corporal Conrad Neuschler (Company I) was wounded when he fell into the gully which ran through the field.

(Richard K. Tibballs Collection, USAMHI)

right wing of the regiment fled to the east like jumped game. Hurling their rifles to the ground, the men were snatching their canteens and pressing them to the backs of their heads as they ran – vain attempts to shield themselves from ugly wounds. Officers, finding themselves suddenly alone, madly dashed about trying to find their men.[100]

Twenty-three year old Lieutenant Colonel Henry H. Curran (146th New York), resplendent in his gold laced dress uniform, and sporting his college pin on his chest, stumbled into the underbrush in front of the Rebel earthworks. Unable to determine exactly where he was, he placed his hand upon the shoulder of a fellow officer who was standing nearby. "This is awful!" he shouted. The frightened junior officer cried back, "Where are all our men?" "Dead," Curran spat, at which a bullet crashed into the back of his head and hurled him forward onto his face – dead.[101]

Lieutenant Colonel Henry H. Curran (146th New York) died in Saunders Field when a round struck him in the back of his head.

(NYSAG, USAMHI)

Squads of New Yorkers stumbled over the battered corn stalks and dropped face first to the ground. A large number dove into the gully to escape capture and others, like the distracted Neuschler, who were not watching where they were going, fell headlong into it.[102] Sergeant J. Albert Jennison (Company C), who saw the colors disappear with the unfortunate Neuschler, leaped in beside the wounded corporal. Pulling the flag from the dazed color-bearer's hands, Jennison clambered out of the ditch and took off at a zigzagging run for the woods to the east. Bullets were zinging about his ears and picking up the dirt around his feet, but he got away unharmed.[103]

First Lieutenant William A. Walker (Company C, 146th New York) could barely make his way on his stomach. A bullet had passed horizontally through his neck di-

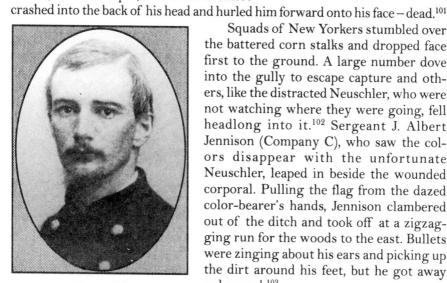

Twenty-eight year old Colonel David T. Jenkins died in the slaughter at Saunders Field. His body was never recovered by his men.

(Under the Maltese Cross)

rectly below his ears. A second one had shattered his forearm, and a third had bored through his leg at the thigh. When another wounded officer tried to assist him from the field, he refused his help. Telling his own comrade to escape while he could, Walker remained behind and was captured.[104] Thirty-six year old Private Franklin L. Palmer (Company C) escaped despite a head injury from a minie ball which cut his scalp and drove a needle sized bone sliver from his skull onto the dura mater. (The injury permanently damaged his hearing and sight, and impaired his memory, but did not prove fatal.)[105]

Confederates were pouring freely through the gaps in the Yankee lines. The 12th and the 14th Regulars became isolated from the rest of the brigade and tried to retreat into Saunders Field to regroup. They collided with the prone 11th Regulars. Meanwhile, the left companies of the 146th New York, which remained prone on the edge of the pine thicket, had no idea what was going on to the north. Twenty-six year old First Lieutenant William H. S. Sweet (Company F), who was standing twenty paces behind his company, glanced through the trees to the north only to find the field swarming with Rebels. A second contingent was advancing down the pike toward the two artillery pieces, enveloping the Yankees from the south. "We were in a bag and the string was tied," Sweet thought.[106] Soldiers who were trapped in the woods vainly attempted to club and bayonet their way out. A round struck Sergeant Louis Dugal's left knee and dropped him to the ground. Dugal (Company F), nevertheless, attempted to reload. Two more minie balls – one in the right arm and the other in the right shoulder – pounded into him as tried to charge the cartridge. His rifle clattered on the forest floor and he fell close to the base of the Confederate earthworks, too stunned to move.[107] Chaplain Edward Payson (146th New York), who had not stayed behind during the assault, as the men had suspected he would, grabbed a weapon and defended himself. His blouse stuffed with the officers' treasures, he fought side by side with Captain Joseph H. Durkee (Company A) until they both escaped.[108] Colonel David Jenkins leaned on his sword and wiped the sweat and blood from his face with his handkerchief. His men never saw their twenty-eight year old colonel again. Cut down in the musketry, he fell to the ground and was not picked up during the retreat.[109]

With soldiers swarming everywhere it became difficult to tell one side from the other. Captain Isaac P. Pail (Company G), who was lying next to Private Carrol S. Waldron (Company G), pulled the private's rifle down while he attempted to draw a bead upon the Confederates who had surrounded them. "Don't fire," the captain shouted. Waldron complied and with 14 of his own company and 130 more from the rest of the regiment, gave up the fight.[110] Colonel Stephen D. Thurston (3rd North Carolina) marveled at the speed with which the Yankees surrendered. Caught in the kneeling position, they simply grounded their arms and walked west through Steuart's Confederate brigade without any guards.[111] An adrenalin crazed Virginian struck Private William A. Palmer (Company A) in the head with a rifle butt and kept going without stopping to check on the dazed New Yorker. Palmer crawled off when the field seemed clear.[112] The 21st Virginia, 1st North Carolina, and the 3rd North Carolina swept southeasterly across the 146th New York, heading directly for Winslow's two guns.[113]

Wadsworth's Assault Near the Higgerson Farm

(About .5 miles south of the Orange Turnpike.)

Brigadier General Lydsander Cutler's brigade occasionally advanced in line to the front, and at other times it moved by the flank in a futile attempt to maintain contact with Bartlett's brigade, which it never saw.[114] The 6th Wisconsin became entangled in a thicket while the 7th Wisconsin (on its right) kept on going. Above the noise of breaking branches and trampled brush, Lieutenant Colonel Rufus Dawes (6th Wisconsin) heard Colonel Ira Glover (7th Indiana) move his regiment into the "double-quick." Colonel Edward Bragg (6th Wisconsin) snapped at Dawes to rush the regiment forward as fast as he could while he bolted ahead to keep the Hoosiers in sight.[115] The Westerners pushed through Denison's Maryland brigade which had accidentally gotten between Cutler's two lines. The Marylanders opened ranks to let them pass.[116]

The front line of the brigade suddenly tripped into the overgrown, swampy southern end of Saunders Field at about the same instant that Bartlett's men struck Jones' left wing. Private Abram Buckles (Company E, 19th Indiana) unsheathed the National flag and shook the folds out of it. The 48th and the 50th Virginia, which were hiding in the trees and bushes on the western side of the clearing, opened fire immediately. Federal soldiers were dropping at a frightening rate along the line.[117] A battle cry exploded along the front of the Iron Brigade as its lead regiments bolted into the clearing.[118] The 24th Michigan, on the far left of the line, ran over the top of the prone 147th New York (Rice's brigade) and the 150th Pennsylvania (Stone's brigade), which had strayed too far north of their brigades. They had thrown themselves down to the ground upon hearing the heavy infantry line crashing through the woods behind them. The impetus of the assault carried away half of the Pennsylvanians and dragged the rest of the Iron Brigade into the mess.[119] In the attack Colonel Roy Stone's brigade remained behind. Cutler's men were on their own.

Waving the flag from one side to the other, Buckles screamed for his men to follow him. A short way into the partially open ground a bullet knocked him down. Buckles kept the flag aloft until another member of the color guard, Private Daniel Divelbess (Company G), pulled them from his hands. A short distance beyond, Divelbess went down, never to get up again.[120] Mean-

Major Albert M. Edwards (24th Michigan) captured the colors of the 48th Virginia in the hand-to-hand fighting south of Saunders Field.
(Roger Hunt Collection, USAMHI)

while the 24th Michigan and the 7th Indiana took on the 48th and the 50th Virginia in hand-to-hand combat.[121] The rifle fire, which cut down saplings as well as men, thrashed the 48th Virginia. A bullet snatched the regimental colors from Color Sergeant Winfield Carter's hands. At the same time, a second round struck him in the leg four inches above the knee. He hobbled rearward without his flag. Another man picked them up.[122] Major Albert M. Edwards (24th Michigan) knocked down the second color bearer and wrenched the colors from him.[123] Private John Opel (Company G, 7th Indiana) grabbed the flag of the 50th Virginia.[124] The regiment took about two hundred prisoners.[125]

The 24th Michigan, rather than reform, chased the demoralized Confederates deeper into the woods ahead of the rest of the brigade.[126] In their haste, the Michiganders brushed past the prone 4th Georgia, the left regiment of Brigadier General George Doles' small brigade. The 4th quickly formed a hinge on the 12th Georgia, to its right, and pulled back its left to form an "L" with the rest of the brigade. Having not yet fired a round, the Georgians remained on their stomachs, patiently waiting for the 150th Pennsylvania to walk into their line.[127] The 12th and the 44th Georgia volleyed into the Pennsylvanians at point-blank range.[128] The Yankees responded with equal ferocity. They gave the 44th a terrible beating. Captain Ashbury Hull Jackson's old Company C lost more men than any com-

During the height of John Gordon's counterattack at the Higgerson farm, Surgeon Abraham Harshberger (149th Pennsylvania) cooly directed the evacuation of the Federal wounded to their own lines.
(Mrs. Rex Album, USAMHI)

pany in the regiment. A bullet shattered both of Sergeant William J. Whitehead's arms. Two rounds slammed into Private William P. Bearden – one in the shoulder, the other in his leg. Private John J. Griffith left the field with a broken right arm. A minie clipped off part of Private Needham F. Hunt's ear. Privates Levi C. Cooper and Joe B. Langford went to the rear with flesh wounds. Private Gilmer Tiller disappeared in the fighting and was never heard from again.[129] Behind Cutler's first line, the stranded 6th Wisconsin helplessly listened to the volley as it stumbled through the jungle to assist its comrades.

Gordon's Assault – Western Side of the Wilderness

(.5 miles west of the Culpeper Mine Road-Orange Turnpike intersection.)

Major John W. Daniel, at Early's request, intercepted the head of Gordon's column about one half of a mile from Saunders Field. He anxiously rattled off his message to the general. Gordon twisted about in the saddle and with characteristic self-composure replied, "Major, do me a favor – give the instructions yourself to each of your regimental commanders while I ride to the front and see the situation."

"Certainly, General," Daniel gasped.

The staff officer relayed the orders and the column quickened its pace. The brigade alternately trotted, then quickstepped, to pace the men's gait and to keep them from overexerting. Private I. Gordon Bradwell (Company I, 31st Georgia) suddenly became aware of their situation. Unlike the other battles in which he had taken part, no artillery bombardment and no skirmish fire echoed through the woods to forewarn him of the approaching conflict. First, he saw the column up ahead branch to the left and to the right, like peeling a leaf of grass in half down its center seam. Presently, the wounded from Doles' brigade groped through the woods to the right front and trailed west along both sides of the brigade.[130] Fourth Sergeant Francis L. Hudgins (Company K, 38th Georgia) paid particular attention to the ordnance wagons and the ambulances which forged through the infantry formation in their hurry to get west. Instead of the sporadic cracking of skirmishers, he distinctly heard the steady rattle of musketry. He did not have to listen more intently to realize they were marching into a full blown battle.[131]

In the meantime, Gordon had reached the rear of the forward line. Ewell leaped his horse over the tangle foot and brush at a full tilt and reined to a clattering stop next to Gordon. Early was not too far behind him. Gordon winced as Ewell's wooden left leg came dangerously close to his knee cap. "General Gordon," Ewell emphatically spat, "the fate of the day depends on you, sir." "I think I can change the situation here," Gordon sonorously replied, while not possessing any idea of how he and his men were going to do it. "Try your hand," Ewell told him.[132]

Daniel reached the three generals in time to see Gordon, sword in hand, twist about in the saddle to shout his orders to his fast approaching brigade. "Forward into line, on the right," he called out, "right oblique, and load as you march."[133] The 61st Georgia filed off at the right oblique, the men loading their weapons as they went.[134] The 26th Georgia, being the next in line, moved to the left of the Orange Turnpike to mark the end of the line. The 60th Georgia went to the right; the 31st Georgia peeled left with the 13th Georgia going in the opposite direction. The 38th Georgia, bringing up the rear of the brigade, marched into the center position.[135] A Federal shell burst in front of the regiment. Daniel watched in horror as an enlisted man in the front rank collapsed into the arms of the man behind him. He could hear the Yankees crashing through the woods to their front and judged them to be about two hundred yards distant.[136]

Ewell rode away. Gordon pranced his horse along the brigade front, as was his custom while winding up for a "brave up" talk. The general's face seemed to glow as he trooped the line, hat in hand. "Soldiers, we have always driven the enemy before us, but this day we are going to scatter them like the leaves of the forest....," Bradwell recalled before the general passed out of earshot. The general wheeled his horse around the right end of the brigade and rode behind the men, this time cautioning them not to raise the Rebel yell nor to discharge their weapons, which they had become accustomed to doing while advancing. The brigade was to reserve its fire until it was on top of the enemy. With a rush they were to drive the Yankees from the ground and win the day for Lee.

Gordon gave the order to advance. The regimental commanders repeated it as did the line officers.[137] At the far left of the line Private John E. "Ervin" Spivey (Company E, 26th Georgia) lived up to his nickname, "Gordon's Bull." When the order reached his regiment, he sucked in his breath and let out his terrible, deep throated bull snort which reverberated above the noise on the field.[138] The six regiments walked into the dense underbrush and forced their way toward the Federal lines.[139] At about a distance of one hundred yards Gordon's six regiments heard Wadsworth's division crashing through the woods to their front.[140] Nearing the right rear of Battle's Alabamians, Gordon happened upon his old regiment, the 6th Alabama. "Steady, 6th Alabama," he cautioned while his regiments pushed passed the right flank. "We will," echoed at his back as he followed his soldiers farther south into the Wilderness.[141] Once the brigade cleared the right rear of Doles' Georgia brigade, it flanked east in line of battle.[142]

The Situation Near Mill Branch

The day was going badly for Stone's stagnant brigade. Lieutenant Colonel John Musser (143rd Pennsylvania) rode into the woods well ahead of his

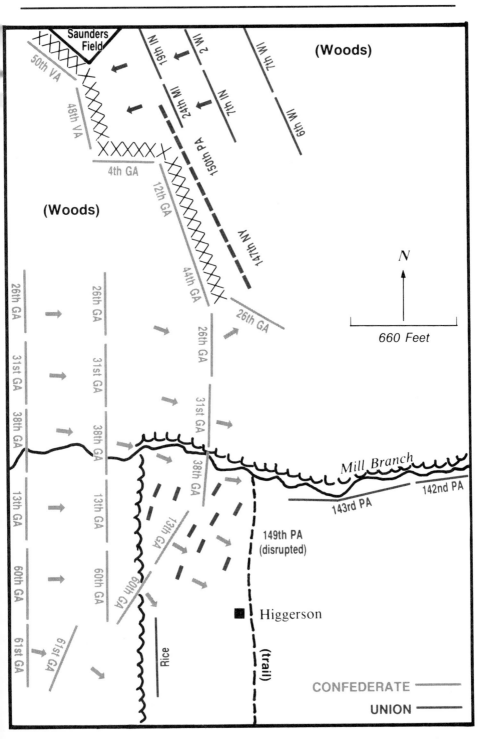

Saunders Field

50th VA

48th VA

4th GA

12th GA

44th GA

26th GA

31st GA

38th GA

13th GA

60th GA

61st GA

(Woods)

19th IN

2 WI

7th IN

24th WI

7th IN

4th WI

6th WI

150th PA

147th NY

26th GA

26th GA

31st GA

38th GA

13th GA

60th GA

61st GA

(Woods)

Mill Branch

142nd PA

143rd PA

149th PA
(disrupted)

Higgerson

Rice

(trail)

N

660 Feet

CONFEDERATE ———
UNION ———

MAP 19: After 1:30 P.M., May 5, 1864 • Gordon's Georgia brigade shatters Wadsworth's division and flanks the Iron Brigade.

line to reconnoiter the regiment's front. He had barely disappeared when a recruit on the right of the regiment fired blindly into the woods. Two or three rounds followed, then a volley roared out. First Sergeant "Orr" Harris (Company B) instinctively brought his weapon to the ready but did not fire. The right wing of his company, comprised mostly of recruits, broke and ran toward Higgerson's. Musser suddenly galloped into Company B. "What in thunder did you shoot at?" he bellowed, "I have been out in there a quarter of a mile, and didn't see a Reb." The veterans who remained in the ranks shouted that the fellows who had done the shooting had deserted the line.[143] Unknown to any of them, Gordon's brigade was moving in on the 149th Pennsylvania from the west. The Confederates merely angled their line toward the sounds of the firing. Pursuant to Gordon's instructions, the men did not fire until they were on top of the Northern position.[144] Their volley caught the stunned 149th Pennsylvania on the front. The Yankees counterfired then ran.[145]

Harris heard the severe rifle fire and stepped back from the line to see what was going on beyond the regiment's left flank. The swarms of blue uniforms crashing down through the swamp from the west told him that the 149th Pennsylvania had broken. He returned to his company and told the men around him they had better fall back to Higgerson's hill. The orderly retreat lasted seconds. The bulk of the regiment broke ranks and streamed east along Mill Branch. They, in turn, disrupted the 142nd and the 121st Pennsylvania.

"My God, look there!" one of Harris' men screamed. The sergeant watched the man snap off a round and run. He momentarily stepped into the man's place, totally unprepared for what he saw. Confederate infantry were running through the marsh. Their unearthly Rebel yell rent the air punctuated by shouts for the "damned Yankee" to surrender. Harris bolted south as fast as he could.[146] The air echoed with yelps, howls, and screams amidst incessant, rolling crashes of small arms fire. "We could scarcely hear a gun fire," Private George W. Nichols (Company D, 61st Georgia) remembered, "and could hardly tell when our own guns fired, only by the jar it gave us."

Bradwell watched the Pennsylvanians' front crumble. Scores of them threw their hands in the air to surrender. The victorious Georgians halted momentarily to round up their prisoners, one of whom was Colonel Edmund Dana (143rd Pennsylvania).[147] Once they had regrouped, the Southerners headed pell mell toward Stone's survivors, who had regrouped in his second line on Higgerson's hill a short distance beyond their first position.[148]

The attack caught Surgeon Abraham Harshberger (149th Pennsylvania) and his stretcher bearers too close to the firing line. With bullets zipping closely about him, he turned toward brigade surgeon F. C. Reamer (143rd Pennsylvania), who was standing close behind him, and asked the doctor to retreat farther to the rear and establish a brigade medical depot. Harshberger gathered in his litter bearers and ran back about six hundred forty feet across the open field to the abandoned barn on the hill east of Higgerson's house. He found Doctor William F. Humphrey (149th Pennsylvania), and assistant surgeons Uriah Q. Davis (148th Pennsylvania) and John L. Morris (150th Pennsylvania) there. Humphrey sent a man after the brigade ambulances.[149]

Not too far to the north, the hard pressed remnants of the 143rd Pennsylvania were tenuously hanging on to their position. Musser rode into his line with the Confederates on his heels. His wounded horse splashed blood with every labored step. The Federals did not maintain their position long.[150] But the attack had isolated Gordon's brigade from the rest of the Rebels.[151] The quick thinking Gordon, ever one to exploit a military advantage, realized he had penetrated the Union lines and knew his men would be "swallowed up" once the separated Union regiments realized where he was. He quickly split his brigade three ways.

The 26th Georgia wheeled north and with Doles' Georgians took Cutler's Iron Brigade from the left flank and the rear. The 31st and the 38th Georgia pressed east, driving Stone's brigade back toward Lacy's. The 13th, 60th, and 61st Georgia swung south and took Rice's brigade on the right flank.[152] The dense pine thickets and the undergrowth fragmented the Confederate troops into disorganized squads which, in the seemingly impenetrable thickets, ballooned into "brigades" to the frightened Federal regiments. The 31st Georgia floundered about in the woods in "detachments" of one or more men.[153]

Back in the middle of Higgerson's farm, the surgeons of Stone's brigade saw their infantrymen streaming from the woods west of their position. The doctors and their orderlies frantically jostled most of their casualties into the ambulances which had just arrived from Lacy's. Unable to bring in all of the wounded, the doctors resigned themselves to rescue those whom they had in hand, then hurried northeast toward a ravine near the Lacy house.[154]

At the same time, Major John W. Young of the 76th New York (Rice's brigade) came back to the regiment from the skirmishers with word of a large Confederate force, which extended well to the south of Rice's brigade, moving in on the command.[155] Captain Robert B. Barger (Company H) on the left of the 56th Pennsylvania saw them as well and had just reported their approach to his colonel when the right of the line – Stone's and Cutler's brigades – collapsed.[156] (The 61st Georgia, which remained more intact than the 13th Georgia and the 60th Georgia, on its left, strayed too far south.) The still invisible 13th and 60th Georgia regiments, to the front of the brigade, continued to pound the confused Yankee soldiers. The colors of the 76th New York went down twice in quick order. Private Albert Hilton (Company A) picked them up only to get killed a second later. Captain Samuel M.

Bryam (Company D) pried them from under his body and bore them from the field.[157] The 56th Pennsylvania left many fine men in the woods, among them the newly promoted First Lieutenant Henry C. Titman (Company G), who fell with his presentation sword in his grasp.[158]

The retreat happened so quickly that Major John W. Young (76th New York) and Private James Cinnamon (Company D) found themselves stranded between the two armies. A Rebel soldier rushed upon them demanding, "Halt! you are my prisoner." Rather than answer, the major turned on his heel to run. "Halt!" the soldier insisted, "or I'll blow your damned brains out!" The lock clicked ominously behind Young, who turned around to find the weapon leveled at his head. Cinnamon took off running. "Halt!" the Reb screamed. The rifle cracked and a ball lifted the private's cap off his head, sending it ahead of him into the woods. Cinnamon did not look back but kept on running.[159]

Half a mile back in the woods, a handful of officers rallied about 350 men from the 56th Pennsylvania and the rest of the brigade. Seconds later, an aide from Wadsworth arrived and ordered them back to Lacy's.[160] Much farther to the west, Companies B, F, and K of the 76th New York and A, E, and I of the 95th New York, having accidentally passed beyond the Confederate right flank, did not know where the Rebels had gone. They did not have long to wait.

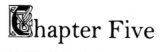

Chapter Five

"I can't go no farther."

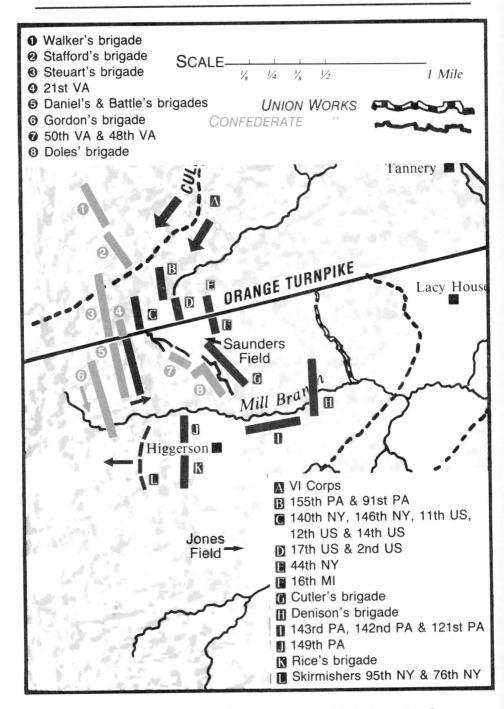

① Walker's brigade
② Stafford's brigade
③ Steuart's brigade
④ 21st VA
⑤ Daniel's & Battle's brigades
⑥ Gordon's brigade
⑦ 50th VA & 48th VA
⑧ Doles' brigade

SCALE ———————————————————————
⅛   ¼   ⅜   ½   1 Mile

UNION WORKS
CONFEDERATE   "

Tannery ■

ORANGE TURNPIKE

Lacy House ■

Saunders Field

Mill Branch

Higgerson ■

Jones Field →

A VI Corps
B 155th PA & 91st PA
C 140th NY, 146th NY, 11th US, 12th US & 14th US
D 17th US & 2nd US
E 44th NY
F 16th MI
G Cutler's brigade
H Denison's brigade
I 143rd PA, 142nd PA & 121st PA
J 149th PA
K Rice's brigade
L Skirmishers 95th NY & 76th NY

MAP 20: The situation after 1:30 P.M., May 5, 1864 along the Orange Turnpike.

1:00 P.M. — 1:30 P.M.

Steuart's Counterattack in Saunders Field

Overcome with their exhilarating victory, Steuart's North Carolinians and the 23rd Virginia raced southeast across Saunders Field. Daniel's five North Carolina regiments burst into the open ground on the southwestern side of the swale at the same time that Winslow's guns fired into the backs of the 140th New York. The blast startled Sergeant Cyrus Watson (Company K, 45th North Carolina) as his regiment bolted into the open ground and swept past the Federal guns, leaving them for Steuart's command.[1]

Second Lieutenant Obediah R. Scott (Company C, 1st North Carolina) with a mixed party of stalwarts from his regiment and the 3rd North Carolina lunged toward the field pieces.[2] A handful of frightened survivors from the 146th New York hurled themselves behind the dead artillery horses in the road to keep from getting cut down in the fire which swept the area. Wounded men crawled and limped pitifully back toward the eastern side of the field.[3]

Sergeant Cyrus B. Watson (Company K, 45th North Carolina) and his regiment reached the southern end of Saunders Field at the same time Steuart's brigade slammed into Ayres' brigade and flanked it.

(Clark, III)

A fragment of Company K (118th Pennsylvania) hit the dirt around the pair of 24 pounders.[4] The artillerymen, upon seeing a few more of their horses go down — killed or disabled — quit the field.[5] Sergeants Theodore B. Fryer and Samuel Nugent with Private George W. Stotsenburg and a handful of exhausted infantrymen turned their weapons upon the gunners and attempted to shove them back to the pieces. They failed. The artillerymen abandoned the guns to the exasperated infantry, who also turned and ran.[6]

Many men of the 146th New York flopped into the southern end of the gully. By then Scott and his veterans of the 1st North Carolina had captured the guns. Rifle butts cracked skulls. A few of the slower running gunners turned and parried against bayonet thrusts until the blunt steel struck home. For several desperate moments it became impossible for anyone outside of the melee to distinguish between Yankee or Rebel. Winslow hobbled off the field toward his own lines, bleeding from a bullet wound beneath his shoulder blades.[7] He left his horse and his section commander, Second Lieutenant William H. Shelton, behind.

Shelton, who managed to get back to his guns, found them abandoned. He slipped off his wounded Morgan to unhitch the dying lead horse of the team nearest to him, turned his back to the mob which was surrounding him, and unsnapped the near–side traces at the horse's collar. But, when he reached around to release the other trace, he heard, "Surrender." The lieutenant slowly faced about and found himself staring down the barrels of Colonel Hamilton Brown's two cocked revolvers. "Give me that sword," the colonel of the 1st North Carolina demanded. Shelton defiantly unhooked the clasp and let the sidearm fall to the ground. Brown assured the young officer he would be escorted to the rear by a commissioned officer and not a rank and file soldier if he would give up. The disgusted artilleryman started with his guard to the rear. Shelton took but a few steps when Brown snatched up the dangling reins and swung into the saddle of his newly acquired Morgan.[8]

Colonel Hamilton A. Brown (1st North Carolina) captured Second Lieutenant William H. Shelton (Company D, 1st New York Artillery) and the lieutenant's fine Morgan.

(Clark, I)

The fighting around the lower half of the gully devolved into a shooting and a shouting match. Stubborn New Yorkers, trapped in the wash out, vainly screamed at the swarm of Virginians and North Carolinians on their flanks and front to quit the fight while the Rebels demanded the same from them. Captain John L. Cantwell (Company F), Second Lieutenant Robert H. Lyon (Company H) and their adjutant, First Lieutenant Theodore C. James of the 3rd North Carolina and some enlisted men wheeled the cumbersome guns around to use them against the fleeing Yankees only to discover they had no ammunition. The frustrated Carolinians attempted to shoulder the two 24 pounder howitzers up the road to their lines while the rest of their brigade pushed the Yankees toward the far side of the field.[9]

Without warning, panting soldiers from the 20th Maine burst into the clearing west of the Confederates, running like frightened cattle in every direction as fast as they could possibly go. Brigadier General Joseph Bartlett, who was still mounted, charged into Saunders Field with his horse stretched out at a full gallop. He came abreast of Private Theodore Gerrish (Company H, 20th Maine), who was struggling past the far end of the ditch. Bartlett, a superb rider, calculated the gait of his plunging horse. At the correct moment, he expertly leaned forward in the

❶ Daniel's North Carolina brigade gets involved in a fire fight with the 44th New York, then retires.
❷ Battle's and Steuart's men charge through Daniel as he retires from the fight.
❸ The 44th New York withdraws.
❹ The 21st Virginia finds itself isolated behind the Federal lines and retires.

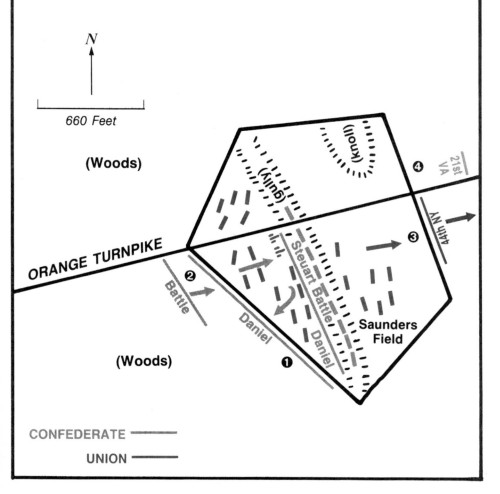

MAP 21: 1:30 P.M., May 5, 1864 • The Confederates take Saunders Field.

saddle. The well trained animal vaulted itself up and forward near the lip of the six foot deep gulch above the Confederates who cowered in the bottom and gracefully launched itself across the twelve foot expanse. In an instant, the startled Gerrish mentally captured every detail of the jump. The horse's eyes came to life. Its nostrils flared and its ears leaned forward. When the horse was half way over the gully, a stray rifle ball whacked into its taut flank. The horse dropped its head under the slug's impact, jerked its hind quarters high into the air, and landed with a terrible crash onto its back, with the general still on it. Gerrish stared in disbelief at Bartlett, who wriggled from beneath the animal's corpse, and staggered off toward the Union lines. The private followed him to safety.[10]

The 44th New York moved to the front to relieve the survivors of the first two lines of Bartlett's brigade and formed a line of battle in the pines on the eastern face of the field, determined to give battle. Daniel's North Carolinians, who were approaching from the southwest, dropped to their knees to slug it out volley for volley with the stubborn New Yorkers. In the terrifying excitement Watson of the 45th North Carolina lost any sense of time.[11] The blood lust consumed the men. They behaved more like mindless machines than humans as they repeatedly loaded and fired at the Federals in the pines across from them.

Several minutes later, Battle's Alabamians, having shattered the 20th Maine, broke into the open ground, behind the North Carolinians.[12] The newly arrived Alabamians crashed through Daniel's brigade from the rear and dove for cover in the ravine. They delivered a well aimed volley into the New Yorkers, forcing them to go prone.[13] Captain Seth F. Johnson (Company I, 44th New York), who had joined the regiment as a private, perished in the fighting.[14] A large caliber musket ball, whizzing into Company C from a higher elevation, slammed into Corporal Elnathan Meade's left temple and knocked him out.[15] Using the momentary lull, the North Carolina Brigade, without orders, retired to the woods on the western side of the swale.[16] A large portion of the Alabamians, when they realized they were in a dangerous position, scrambled out of the gulch after them.[17]

During the fracas, Lieutenant Colonel James N. Lightfoot (6th Alabama), with the regimental banner in his hand, sprang onto one of the deserted field pieces and proclaimed its capture. Brown and a considerable number of his veterans popped up from the gully, almost beneath Lightfoot's feet and vigorously reasserted their claim upon the guns. Embarrassed and outnumbered, the Alabamian graciously acknowledged his error in judgement and fell back to the western side of the field, where the rest of the brigade was reforming.[18] The North Carolinians from Steuart's brigade did not get past the eastern side of the swale. A scathing fusillade from the 44th New York forced them back. The Confederates attempted another charge, which quickly weakened when the Yankees rose up and volleyed into their broken ranks.[19]

Meanwhile, the hounded Northerners who survived the onslaught slid into the forest on their side of Saunders Field and lay on their backs panting.[20] The 18th Massachusetts did not stop running until it reached the breastworks in the edge of the woods on the western side of Lacy's farm. Major Thomas Weston (18th Massachusetts), the sweat profusely running from his hairline, his face flushed, and heart palpitating out of control, lost his senses. He became "temporarily insane" before collapsing from sunstroke.[21] In their hurry to escape, the soldiers of the 83rd Pennsylvania lost their colors and Color Sergeant Alexander Rogers (Company F) to the Rebels.[22] Captain Bradford R. Wood (Company C, 44th New York), in all of the noise, misunderstood the command for the regiment to retire and, instead, shouted for his company to advance. With the Rebels on the retreat, Company C and a handful of soldiers to either flank dashed into the open ground, firing as they advanced. When he glanced over his shoulder and saw the regiment retreating from the right toward the Lacy house, Wood realized he was alone upon the field. He yelled for his men to pull back and tapped First Sergeant Samuel McBlain (Company E) on the arm to get him to pull out.[23]

The Woods on the Eastern Side of Saunders Field

The 21st Virginia, just north of the pike, plowed east parallel to the road as the Federals fled east and south. A large detachment of the Confederates, including Sergeant John Worsham of Company F, penetrated at least two hundred yards into the woods without contacting any of the enemy. They found themselves alone, the only Confederates to break into the Union lines. The regiment halted and hastily decided to withdraw as a body.[24]

Without warning, Colonel Emory Upton's brigade from the VI Corps stumbled into the 21st Virginia's left flank when the Confederates crested the wooded ridge on the northern side of Saunders Field. The Virginians left wheeled, delivered an effective volley, then started running toward the woods south of their original jump off point.[25]

Lieutenant Colonel Edward Carroll, at the front of the 95th Pennsylvania, fell from his horse with a bullet in his forehead. Several men collapsed – dead or wounded.[26] Captain Alexander Boyd and First Lieutenant David Gordon (both from Company A) with Captain William Byrnes (Company F) charged with their companies into the rear of the 21st Virginia. In the hand–to–hand encounter which followed, the Pennsylvanians captured thirty Confederates while losing three men themselves.[27] During the retreat, one of the Southerners disappeared into the secure looking gully.[28] Having found it impossible to escape to their own lines many of the men in the 1st and the 3rd North Carolina piled into the ditch from the opposite direction.[29] While the Rebels were withdrawing across the bloodied stubble field, the rest of Upton's brigade arrived. The 96th Pennsylvania moved forward and established a line with its skirmishers on the knoll in the open ground beyond the woods. The 95th Pennsylvania, 121st New York and the 5th Maine went prone in line inside the woods below the brow of the hill.[30]

In the Wilderness – West of Saunders Field

During the Confederate counterattack First Lieutenant Holman Melcher (Company F, 20th Maine) and his mixed force of 17 men from Companies F and H had forged ahead of the regiment and the fighting. After tramping west then northwest, Melcher suddenly realized that he had not seen any Rebels and that the rest of the regiment had disappeared. He immediately called First Sergeant Ammi M. Smith (Company F) to his side to discuss the situation and the options they had open to them. Presently one of his men calmly walked up to him. "Lieutenant," the fellow said with a rather perturbed air, "come this way and let me show you something." The two loped over to the Orange Turnpike, where the soldier anxiously pointed east and exclaimed, "See that!" The lieutenant's blood literally turned cold. A chill quaked his body. A large column of Confederate infantry (21st Virginia, 1st North Carolina and 3rd North Carolina) was running across the pike, half a mile east of his men and heading south into the Wilderness. He was cut off.[31]

The Woods North of Saunders Field Along the Culpeper Mine Road

To the right of Upton's hastily forming brigade, Brigadier General David Russell's lead regiment, the 49th Pennsylvania, was trying to reorganize itself. Colonel Thomas H. Hulings halted his five untried companies of draftees on the south side of the Culpeper Mine Road just before it turned south toward Upton's right flank. He had completely lost track of his four veteran companies when they disappeared into the woods in front of him. The rest of the brigade was crossing the road behind him and moving forward through his rookies. Bullets whacked into the trees and men were getting hit.[32]

The 119th Pennsylvania shifted south and connected with the right of the 96th Pennsylvania (Upton's brigade). The undetached battalion of the 5th Wisconsin fell in on its right. Brigadier General Thomas Neill's brigade was marching due west to fill the gap created by Russell's shift to the southern side of the trail. Companies D and G of the 49th New York, acting as Neill's skirmishers, fanned out into the woods to provide cover fire while the five regiments were maneuvering into three lines. The 49th New York, with the 7th Maine on the right formed the first line. The 61st Pennsylvania covered the rear of the 49th New York. The 43rd New York, with the 77th New York to its left, fell in behind the Pennsylvanians.[33] The two lead regiments advanced cautiously up to the wooded ridge which ran south into the swale between the V Corps and Steuart's brigade.[34]

Brigadier General Leroy Stafford's Louisianans struck the top of the opposite ridge about a minute or two after the Neill's Mainers and New Yorkers had gone into position. The Yankees poured a hot fire into the front of his brigade. Unable to see either Walker's Virginia Brigade on his left or Steuart's on his right, Stafford immediately ordered his men to halt and return the volley. A musket ball disabled Major John W. Crosby of the 61st Pennsylvania. Striking him in the right side of his head, it ripped away a part of his scalp and bruised his skull. Captain William M. Dawson (Company G) also went down with a wound.[35] Major Henry Handerson concurred with Stafford's decision. It would have been foolish and suicidal to cross that open ground.[36]

While the Louisianans slugged it out with Neill's command, Walker's "Stonewall Brigade" maneuvered into line in the woods below the crest of the ridge on Stafford's left. His right flank rested nearly at a right angle to the Culpeper Mine Road. The 33rd Virginia and the left wing of the 2nd Virginia melted into the woods to the northeast and north as skirmishers. Within seconds after the shooting erupted to Walker's right rear Major Enoch Totten's five companies from the 5th Wisconsin cut loose into Walker's right flank. Delivered from a distance of forty yards, the unexpected burst of riflery shattered the 5th Virginia, Walker's right regiment. Frightened soldiers stampeded into the 4th Virginia which broke and collided with part of the 27th Virginia.[37] Walker rose in the stirrups yelling, "Remember your name!"[38] Colonel William Terry (4th Virginia) threatened and taunted his regiment into line and restored order. The colonel swung his rattled command back until it stood facing southeast at a ninety degree angle to the rest of the brigade. Their counter volley exploded in the faces of the Wisconsin men.[39]

The Lacy House

While Company C of the 44th New York bounded back through the woods toward the earthworks it had thrown up near Lacy's, Captain Bradford R. Wood mentally tabulated their losses. Private Sydney Burroughs (Company E), who had applied for a lieutenancy with a black regiment, lay among the slain. (Burrough's commission, awarded posthumously, was forwarded to his father.)[40] The regiment lost 62 killed and wounded in that half hour.[41] Privates Orrin Watkins and Stephen P. Dye (both from Company C) pulled their horribly wounded comrade, Corporal Elnathan Meade (Company C) to his feet. With blood streaming from a huge ghastly wound in his left temple, he awakened to find himself being supported between them. His friends slung his arms across their shoulders and dragged the semiconscious corporal into the crowded Orange Turnpike. From there, they continued east toward the Lacy house. On the way, they hauled aside a hospital party and placed him upon their stretcher. A harried surgeon deftly fingered Meade's bloodied, swollen head for the exit wound. He quickly found a knot below and slightly to the front of the corporal's right ear. Without anesthesia, the doctor excised the ball. Because he did not need to waste any more of his time upon a dying man, he directed the stretcher bearers to take him to the hospital tent, which was a short distance away. They left Meade upon a makeshift bed of pine boughs in a vacant corner of the huge tent.[42] Not too far away, the two men from the 83rd Pennsylvania who killed General John M. Jones, approached Dr. William Stewart, their regimental surgeon, and offered him the general's sword. The doctor, who was nursing a slight wound in the palm of his right hand, "declined the loot," as he recorded, and went about his business.[43]

The Woods North of Saunders Field Near the Culpeper Mine Road

Handerson, Stafford's assistant adjutant general, could not believe the wheezing infantryman who had run up to him blurting something about a large force of Yankees sweeping through the woods on the brigade's left (northern) flank and the rear. He dug the spurs into his horse and pushed the animal through the maze of low hanging branches in that direction. Several rods from his original position, he spied the flank of Totten's Wisconsin line crashing through the woods against Walker's Virginians. Wheeling his horse about, he hurried to the center of the brigade to Stafford's side. As soon as Handerson informed him of the situation, the general ordered him to maneuver the 1st Louisiana, the brigade's left regiment, at a right angle to the line to meet the assault. Lieutenant Colonel James Nelligan, commanding the fifty man regiment, panicked while attempting to execute the command. Wildly swinging his sword above his head, he cried for his men to rally around him. The scared soldiers milled around him in a confused huddle rather than square off against the Westerners. Handerson, who did not have time to argue with the befuddled officer, watched the Yankees pass by the regiment's front without disturbing it before he turned his horse around and returned to the general's side. Stafford took the bad news for what it was and directed Handerson to ride quickly to the right and make contact with Steuart's brigade. The major worked his horse into the thick woods and disappeared from sight.[44]

Behind Neill's Brigade

Shells screamed over Neill's brigade from the two Confederate 12 pounders under the command of Lieutenant Michael Garber, which had just rolled into battery in the Pike on the western side of the swale.[45] One burst in the woods under the mounts of two newspapermen who had been following the VI Corps for a good story. Major General John Sedgwick's staff officers advised the reporters, one of whom was Jerome D. Stillson of the *World*, to leave for safer ground, which they did. Lieutenant Colonel Thomas Hyde of the 7th Maine (Sedgwick's staff), who had dismounted to adjust the bit in his horse's mouth, saw them riding east.[46]

The New Jersey Brigade was trotting toward the major to reinforce Neill's brigade. Incoming rounds from the west spattered the line. One bored through the heart of Color Sergeant Theodore F. Phillips (Company G, 1st New Jersey) killing him instantly. Color Sergeant Peter Brobson (Company A) jerked the National colors from Phillips' hands and carried the standard forward.[47]

Hyde's sixth sense picked up the whoosh of a solid shot coming in and he instinctively turned his face, mouth agape, to follow its course through the trees. The round decapitated one of the Jerseymen as he ran by the colonel. The head struck Hyde full in the face, splattering his uniform with brains and blood. The impact threw him onto his back and momentarily stunned him. Staring numbly up at his fellow staff officers who had gathered around

him, Hyde vaguely remembered seeing Sedgwick gaze down at him with genuine sorrow. Someone said something about him being dead. Then two of the officers dismounted to help him to his feet. Hyde, however, gained his feet by himself and spent the next fifteen minutes spewing the brains from his mouth and cleaning himself up.[48]

The sudden deluge of shells and shot smashed into the New Jersey Brigade. An explosive round burst over the 1st New Jersey, killing First Lieutenant Benjamin Moffett (Company F) and wounding Captain William H. Tantem and Second Lieutenant John N. Hulfish (both from Company B). Captain H. C. Warner (Company A) staggered rearward with a wounded arm. With bullets striking the front as well, it was not safe to remain upright. The brigade

Three officers from Maine. Left: Colonel Edwin Mason (7th Maine). Center: Major Thomas Hyde (7th Maine), who nearly lost his head to a cannon ball. Right: Lieutenant Colonel Selden Connor (7th Maine) later colonel of the 19th Maine. All three saw action in the Wilderness.

(MOLLUS, USAMHI)

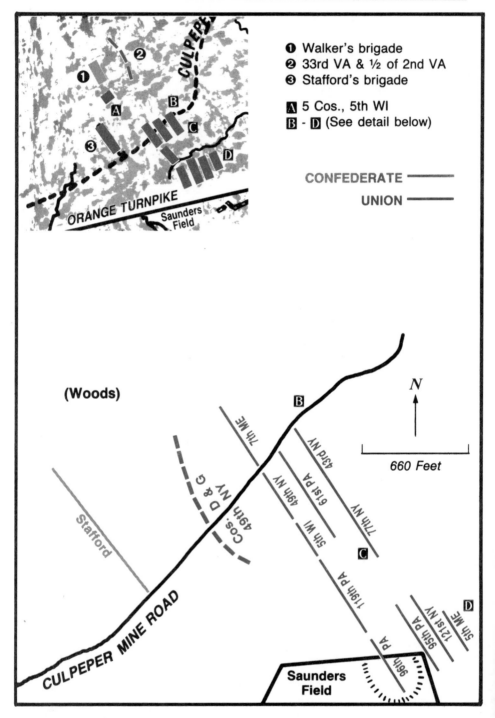

MAP 22: 1:30 P.M.-2:00 P.M., May 5, 1864 • Stafford's brigade encounters the VI Corps.

halted less than one hundred yards beyond the dazed Hyde to reform its line. A bullet in the chest killed Color Sergeant Brobson (Company A). Color Sergeant C. A. Pettie (Company G) caught the colors as they fell. With their line restored, the Jerseymen went prone.[49]

Artillery rounds pounded Neill's front line as well. A solid shot whooshed into the 61st Pennsylvania. Sergeant Joseph Seville (Company G) who was standing behind his men did not see the cannon ball. It struck him full in the face with such force that it ripped his head off without knocking his body down. The headless corpse tottered for what seemed like an interminable amount of time before it toppled over.[50]

Stafford's Brigade

Realizing that he could not sustain his position much longer, Stafford began breaking his men to the rear by the right. Moving by files, the regiments quickly slipped back through the trees toward the rear. The general remained on the line, carefully shepherding his men to safety. When the rattled 1st Louisiana sidled by him, he turned his back upon the Yankees. A minie ball struck him in the armpit. The bullet bored through his body, severed his spine and shattered his shoulder blade. Stafford dropped to the forest floor. His men quickly carried him off the field.[51]

In the meantime, Handerson continued toward the right of the line. Sword drawn, he pushed his horse briskly through the brush behind the line. His horse nearly trampled Captain Alexander O. Boarman (Company A, 1st Louisiana), who was prone in the undergrowth and weaponless. What was he doing there? Handerson queried. Hiding from the Yankees, Boarman quietly answered. Handerson raised his right arm to shield his face from the low hanging tree branches and pressed south. He did not believe the captain.[52]

Less than one hundred yards to the east, Lieutenant Colonel Thomas Hulings (49th Pennsylvania) had caught up with his overly ambitious veteran companies and the color guard. He found Privates Robert S. Westbrook, William Blatt, Billy White, and John Ginethan (all of Company B) in the woods a short distance north of the southwest turn in the Culpeper Mine Road and told them to return to the regiment, which he was reforming in the Wilderness southeast of them.

The enlisted men, who were running west at the time, darted to the left, and broke into the dirt track of the road before turning east. Fifty yards from where they started, a Confederate horseman, with an unsheathed sword, suddenly appeared in front of them.[53] They automatically brought their weapons up, charged, and yelled for the man to surrender. Handerson saw their bayonets bearing down upon him and heard rifle hammers double click to full cock. As he threw his sword to the ground and raised his left hand, the major looked up to see more of Company B about fifty feet away.[54] With their bayonets not more than a foot from the major's face, the badly startled Westbrook wondered why no one had blown the Rebel's head off.[55] The Yankees did not stand on formality. They grabbed Handerson by his tunic and jerked him from the saddle. One of them yanked his pistol out of its holster before turning him over to Privates Peter McGonigal and Ed Miller (both Company B). McGonigal, who was bleeding from a head wound, and Miller, who was also wounded, hustled the major east as fast as they could. Along the way to the Wilderness Tavern, where the Army of the Potomac had a prisoner depot, they picked up Stafford's courier. Handerson was glad to have the company.[56]

The four remaining Pennsylvanians about faced and ran back to the point where Colonel Hulings had first confronted them, and reformed with a larger number of their company who had retreated that far. A volley flamed and roared at close range from behind the line. The men hit the ground in unison. Crawling around to face east, the Pennsylvanians vehemently cursed and snapped off several rounds at the line of infantry behind them. When Westbrook and his men recognized the troops as the 119th Pennsylvania of their own brigade, they shouted at them to cease fire. With all of the smoke hanging in the trees and the limited visibility, accidents like that were bound to happen. Company B regrouped itself and retired to the main body of the regiment, which left the 119th Pennsylvania on the front line. On the way back, Westbrook came across Private James McCord of his company. A minie ball had gutted him. He was standing upright, futilely trying to press his entrails back into his body with his hands.[57]

Saunders Field

The northern part of Saunders Field quieted down and the panting Union soldiers started bringing in the wounded whom they could reach within the fringes of the woods on the eastern side. The brush on the northern end of the field and the dry leaves along the Confederate front caught fire from the muzzle flashes. A strong wind fanned the flames into the stubble field as well. The dense, suffocating smoke drove would be rescuers away. Wounded men, unable to crawl into the ditch between the lines or to reach the turnpike, screamed horribly as the flames ignited their clothing or touched off their cartridge boxes. The "pop", "pop" of the live rounds reminded one of the New Yorkers of a local celebration. The small explosions seemed almost delightful. From where he sat he could not see the metal tins, which held the cartridges in the boxes, tear and gouge ghastly holes in the sides of the men who still wore them around their waists. The sickening, tangible smell of frying human flesh hung over the woods.[58]

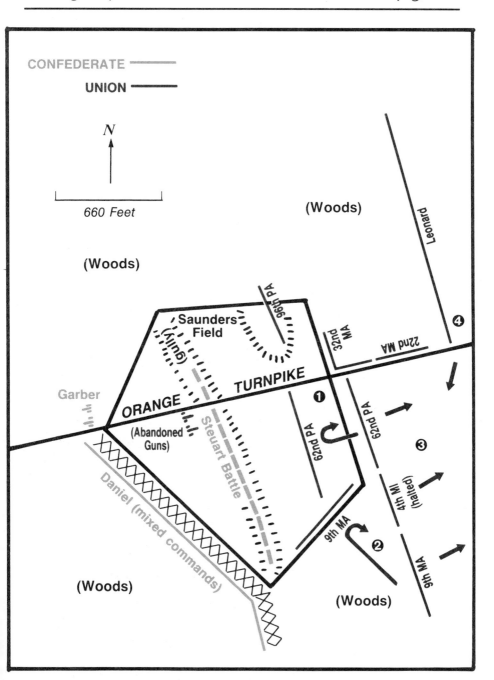

MAP 23: Afternoon, May 5, 1864 • Sweitzer's brigade attempts to recapture Captain Winslow's abandoned guns in Saunders Field.

1:30 P.M. – 4:00 P.M.

Sweitzer's Brigade

Colonel Jacob Sweitzer's brigade left the earthworks southwest of Lacy's and pushed north into the woods without their brigadier, who preferred to stay at headquarters.[59] Skirmishers from the 32nd Massachusetts fanned out to the front to cover the brigade's advance.[60] In the first line, the 9th Massachusetts, 4th Michigan, and 62nd Pennsylvania (south to north, respectively) veered west into the woods south of the Orange Turnpike, headed for the position formerly held by Bartlett's brigade.[61] From the second line, Private Robert G. Carter (Company H, 22nd Massachusetts) incredulously watched a fellow who had deserted once before about face and take off for the rear. He was never seen again.

The 22nd and 32nd Massachusetts wheezed north across the Turnpike. To their left front, the 62nd Pennsylvania kept on going. The two regiments halted momentarily to allow Company C, 22nd Massachusetts, to return to the line. They lost two men. Private Elbridge Perry died near Saunders Field. The other casualty, Private Charles Lamos, limped into the regiment inside the woods. His best friend, Private Hugh Gilligan, very tenderly asked Lamos if he had any money. "No," Lamos replied weakly. He had sent it all home to his widowed mother. Gilligan told him money would be useful in a hospital, whereupon he jerked out a thick roll of bills from his inside blouse pocket. Without blinking, he counted off thirty dollars and stuffed them into his friend's hand. He shoved the remaining bankroll of over two hundred dollars into his shirt again and watched Lamos wander back toward the field hospital. (Gilligan could always rely on his poker buddies in the 118th Pennsylvania for future funding.)[62]

The 22nd and the 32nd Massachusetts reached the eastern edge of the field. The 22nd went prone in the brush along the pike facing south. The 32nd continued the line to the right then refused its right companies to face west.[63] The regiment boldly planted its colors in the turnpike.[64] A canister charge swept the Orange Turnpike, wounding thirteen more soldiers.[65] (The 32nd Massachusetts lost 19 men that day.)[66] The detached 62nd Pennsylvania, which lost contact with the 4th Michigan somewhere in the woods, emerged from cover and advanced into the middle of the field, where it was flanked and forced back to the woods.[67]

At the same time, the 9th Massachusetts plowed through the pine forest to the south and flushed a party of skirmishers from the edge of the forest who broke north toward the pike. Confederates in the gully emptied an unexpected, rapid volley into the regiment as it stepped into the open. A minie ball, whistling in from the right, gouged out Colonel Patrick Guiney's left eye. The round, which completely destroyed the eye socket, lodged in the left side of his face, near his ear.[68] He stumbled from the field, blinded. The regiment veered to the right, heading for the two silent artillery pieces which were bedecked with Confederate flags. A devastating fire knocked down too many men before they gained any appreciable amount of ground.[69] Lieutenant Colonel Patrick T. Hanley (9th Massachusetts) called out for the regiment to retreat to the earthworks at the southwestern corner of the Lacy farm.[70] The 62nd Pennsylvania and the 4th Michigan left the field with Hanley's regiment. To the north, the 22nd Massachusetts, and the 32nd Massachusetts engaged the Confederates for at least half an hour.[71]

Near Mill Branch
Denison's Maryland Brigade

In the woods at the southern end of Saunders Field, Colonel Andrew Denison's four Maryland regiments, having lost sight of Cutler's brigade, stayed back a considerable distance within the forest to await the results of the fighting to their front. The 7th Maryland stood in line on the left with its southern flank in the northern end of Higgerson's field. Mill Branch ran through that end of the regiment at right angles. The 8th Maryland continued the brigade formation to the right, followed respectively by the 1st and the 4th regiments.[72] Scores of prisoners and their escorts and the two stands of colors taken by Cutler's men flowed rearward around the Marylanders. Presently the large amount of wounded and their inordinate numbers of "helpers" indicated that the Federal assault had gone sour. An aide came in from the front wildly demanding to know who commanded the brigade. The officer he spoke to told him to hunt out Denison. "No time," the aide blurted, "tell him the Rebels are driving our right, and there is no support on that flank." The line officer hurriedly reported the message to the colonel who nervously answered that he had just heard the same news about the left flank.

Up ahead, the Confederates virtually encircled Cutler's first line. The regiments shattered and fled toward the rear. The stranded 6th Wisconsin, in the disconnected second line, while rushing after the 7th Indiana, charged into an ambush. "Look to the right," Major Philip W. Plummer yelled. Lieutenant Colonel Rufus Dawes, commanding the right wing of the regiment, shot a frightened glance in that direction. He saw a very large line bearing down upon his tiny regiment from the right front. Yelling at Plummer to form the left wing at right angles to the right battalion, Dawes turned his attention to that end of the line. A round snuffed out the major before he received the command. Bullets materialized from the smoke obscured trees around the 6th Wisconsin. The volley knocked down about forty Westerners, killing Captain Rollin P. Converse (Company B) and wounding First Lieutenant James L. Converse (Company G).

Dawes ordered his battered regiment to retreat. The Confederates pressed the advantage, firing and hollering their dreadful yell the entire time. The 6th Wisconsin leapfrogged through the brush before halting to return fire. When the Rebels recoiled, the Northern soldiers ran back a few more paces, loading as they did so, then turned and fired again.[73]

To the south, the 31st and the 38th Georgia rolled up Stone's brigade, catching it on the flank. Stone's Pennsylvanians gave way first, which exposed Rice's right flank and Cutler's left and rear. Denison's Marylanders caught the Iron Brigade's wild retreat full force. In the open ground behind the left wing of the 7th Maryland, Brigadier General James Wadsworth frantically rode into the mass of wounded men. Colonel Charles E. Phelps (7th Maryland) noted how the general's white hair flared out behind him as he excitedly shouted, "Where is my second line? Bring up my second line!"

The words had barely escaped his lips when Cutler's refugees swarmed and crashed through the forest. The Rebs were too uncomfortably close. The Marylanders gaped in awe as men in the 26th Georgia snatched fleeing Yankees by the collars and jerked them onto their backs.[74] Hundreds of unescorted Northerners wended their own way to the Confederate rear lines. Snatched up in their overwhelming drive, many of the Georgians would not leave the firing line to take care of the prisoners.[75]

Private I. Gordon Bradwell (Company I, 31st Georgia), whose regiment had accidentally strayed too far to the left, found himself part of a scattered formation. He recognized a comrade or two pushing his way through the scrub pines around him but found nothing resembling a regimental strength line.[76] The Marylanders withheld their volley until the bulk of their own men were clear of the line of fire. The sudden explosion of the Yankees' rifles at close range halted the Rebel drive.[77] The terrific volley burst from the pines in front of Bradwell. Bullets clipped the needles off the trees above his head.[78] The 26th Georgia, to his left, quickly broke into groups of sharpshooters before the smoke cleared. For several minutes, the opposing sides fought, shooting at the billowing smoke among the trees. A round killed Colonel Charles Phelps' horse.[79]

Bradwell shot a harried glance to the left but saw no one. To the right he noticed a Confederate squad, but could not see anyone he recognized. The anxious private stepped up behind a small tree. He felt totally alone and had no desire to die without anyone being present to mark his place or to verify the fact to his kin.[80] Without warning, a gray clad soldier emerged from the ground to his right. The ghostlike person dashed to within a few feet of the Yankees and abruptly disappeared from sight. Two more men followed the first one very quickly. Two more did the same seconds later, then more, until at least thirty soldiers had crossed the bullet swept forest to that forward position. Wherever they had dropped out of sight, Bradwell reckoned it had

❶ The 4th Maryland exposes the brigade's right flank.
❷ The 1st Maryland and part of the 8th Maryland retreat, firing as they go.
❸ The rest of the 8th Maryland and the 7th Maryland fight a delaying action, then retreat.

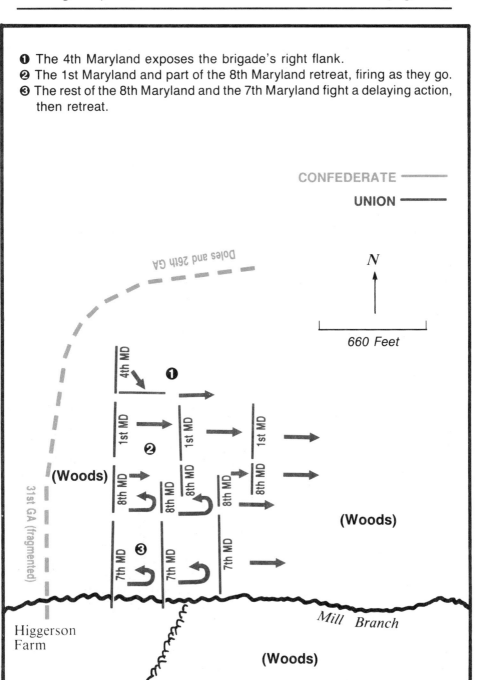

MAP 24: Afternoon, May 5, 1864 • Doles' and Gordon's Confederates herd Denison's Maryland brigade from the woods north of Higgerson's farm.

to be relatively safe. Ducking low, he darted after them. Diving to the ground, he tumbled into a gully which was filled with friends from his regiment. He immediately opened fire across the level ground, under the low branching pines into the Yankees.[81]

The field became relatively silent, the two sides apparently ceasing fire from mutual exhaustion. As the smoke settled, Phelps trooped his regimental line only to discover that the lull was allowing the Rebels time to envelope the brigade's right flank.[82] Colonel Richard N. Bowerman (4th Maryland), under orders from Denison, wheeled the regiment back at right angles to meet the assault. The Confederate muzzle blasts betrayed the length of their formation, which overlapped the 4th Maryland's right wing. Bowerman retired his regiment twenty paces by files to the right, where it halted and volleyed again. The movement exposed the rest of the brigade to a raking fire. The 1st Maryland and the right wing of the 8th Maryland fell back to protect themselves without telling the southern end of their formation. As they retreated, Bowerman side shuffled his 4th Maryland back another thirty yards. He reported his problem to Denison before pulling out of the action entirely.[83] Unable to bear the crunch and with the brigade broken into echelons, the 1st Maryland and the right wing of the 8th Maryland quit the field also in a hurry.[84]

It did not take too long for Lieutenant Colonel Rodolphus T. Pride (31st Georgia) to tumble into the ditch with his men. He immediately told the Georgians to charge. The veterans, who knew the Yankees outnumbered them about twenty to one, ignored him.[85] The 7th Maryland and the part of the 8th Maryland which had stayed put, found themselves between two fires – from the Southerners to the front and from their own men to their rear. The enlisted men were wavering. Sergeant Noble H. Creager (Company E, 7th Maryland) quit the firing line with two bullet wounds.[86] The regiment seemed ready to collapse. The color guard and the line officers did everything in their power to urge the men to maintain their posts. In a fit of bravado, Captain David T. Bennett (Company E, 7th Maryland), with revolver drawn, stepped in front of the line to duel with a Confeder-

Captain David T. Bennett (Company E, 7th Maryland) decided to fight a duel with a Confederate officer and received a pistol ball in the face as a result of his bravado.

(Roger Hunt Collection, USAMHI)

ate officer. They exchanged shots simultaneously. Bennett missed. The Confederate did not. A pistol ball tore into Bennett's face, temporarily disabling him.[87]

Nearby, Pride demanded that his small company leave its secure ditch and attack the Marylanders. One foolhardy individual stood up. A bullet cut him down instantly. Bradwell stood up beside the colonel to load his rifle. He felt a ball whip by his side and heard it thunk into Pride's stomach. The bullet in exiting between the upper coat buttons of the colonel's swallow tailed coat whirled the officer around. His face paled, lost all of its ruddy tone, and he collapsed to the bottom of the ditch. A couple of the men snatched up the colonel's body and took off with it at a dog trot through the woods. Bradwell did not have the time to grieve over a man whom he mistakenly thought was dying.[88]

Finally Denison rode up and personally told Phelps to retire the 7th Maryland. The veterans broke to the east by the rear rank, according to the book, loading as they moved. The line turned and volleyed a couple of times before reaching the southwestern corner of Lacy's field.[89]

When the firing ceased, the Georgians leaped over the edge of the gully and ran into the Yankee position. Bradwell never forgot what he saw. A few dead Yankee soldiers lay in a relatively neat line among the pines. Blood trails, which seemed brownish in the increasing darkness, meandered over the mottled brown carpet of pine needles as if someone had taken a paint brush and walked away with it dangling by his side. Nearby, he found a few silver cornets, and several drums, the heads of which had all been shot out.[90] Colonel Clement A. Evans (31st Georgia) found his lost men there and started the long trek back to the brigade. To the southwest and the northwest, musketry still echoed in the encroaching night.[91]

Crawford's Division at the Chewning Farm

Crawford's Pennsylvania Reserve Division had lingered upon the Chewning farm too long to be of any use to Wadsworth's shattered division. His front line regiments had pushed Kirkland's North Carolina skirmishers back upon the eastern fringe of the Chewning farm. While flanking the Confederate drive along the Plank Road, he overextended his command. It was not very long after Gordon's Georgians split and stove in the Federal line at Higgerson's that Crawford realized that he had been left out on a hook. Colonel William McCandless took Company K from the 11th Reserves in his second line and stuck them far out on the brigade's right rear. Private Elijah Bish (Company K) looked to the north and saw what appeared to be a small body of Confederate infantry coming in from the rear of the division. Bish instinctively knew that something had gone awry with Wadsworth's division. Company K turned about to face what appeared to be the Confederate skirmish-

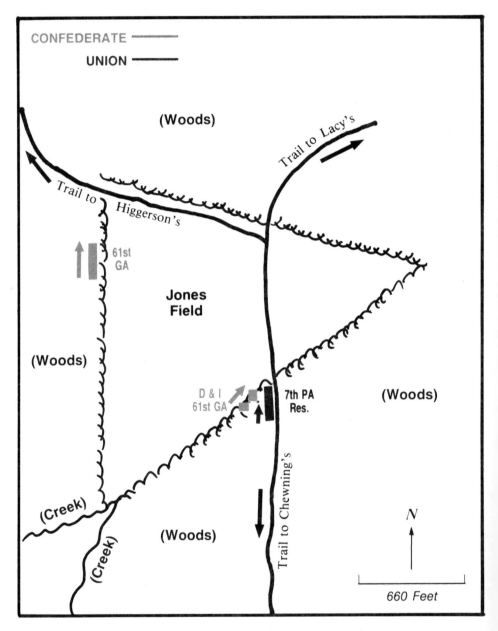

MAP 25: Afternoon, May 5, 1864 • Companies D and I, 61st Georgia snare the 7th Pennsylvania Reserves near Jones Field.

ers from the 61st Georgia along an old fence row when Captain Edward
Scofield ordered his men not to open fire. Look at their blue uniforms. They
were Federals, the captain insisted.

The Pennsylvanians, who soon realized they were in a bad fix, fired wildly
into the Georgians. The Confederates overlapped the company and struck
Crawford's division from the flank and the rear. Colonel Samuel M. Jackson
of the 11th Reserves pulled his regiment and the 2nd Reserves from the
division's second line to meet the attack and give the rest of the division time
to withdraw. The two regiments charged the fence row, drove the Georgians
back into the woods and opened the road to Lacy's. With the 7th Reserves
posted as the rear guard, the entire division escaped northward.[92]

Jones' Field

The overextended 61st Georgia, following its brief encounter with
Crawford's V Corps division temporarily lost track of the Federals. The regiment stumbled north until it reached the southern side of Jones' Field. Major James D. Van Valkenburg (61st Georgia) suspected that the Federals had
split left and right to go around the field, but he was not sure. (Actually, the
Pennsylvanians had stayed on the road from Parker's Store to Lacy's.) While
one part of the regiment slipped north through the woods on the upper part
of the field, Van Valkenburg covered the southern flank with Company D
and a portion of Company I. As his men lay down to watch the clearing, First
Lieutenant Eugene Jeffers (Company I, 61st Georgia) arrived with orders
from General Gordon to retire. The two companies had just begun to move
northwest when they spotted a Yankee regiment tramping north through
the pines in front of them. "I felt bad," Private George W. Nichols (Company
D) wrote with considerable understatement, "for we did not have over forty
men and there were about five hundred Yankees."

The Georgians suddenly halted. Van Valkenburg unsheathed his sword
and quick stepped toward the Yankee colonel, whom he saw clearly. He bra-
zenly demanded the Federals' surrender, whereupon, Major LeGrand B.
Speece (7th Pennsylvania Reserves) hollered back for the Confederates to lay
down their arms.[93] At that the Pennsylvania Reserves tried flanking to the
left and to the right simultaneously. The Confederates were shooting into
them from all sides. Private Frank B. Ellis (Company H) crumbled to the
ground – dead – beside his captain, Jacob Heffelfinger.[94] Van Valkenburg did
not yield. Instead, he called over his shoulder for General Gordon to bring
forward a brigade to take care of the obstinate regiment which he had cut off
from its own supports. Captain Stephen H. Kennedy, Sr. (Company D, 61st
Georgia) loudly gave the command to forward. The enlisted men picked up
the order and relayed it along their imaginary regimental lines in equally
authoritative voices.

At that, Speece told his men to ground their arms.[95] When the small Confederate party started to encircle them, forty men bolted into the woods, escaping capture.[96] "Officers to the front," Van Valkenburg demanded. Kennedy snatched the colors from the shamed Federal color guard. After the twenty captains, and lieutenants, and their major fell in at the head of the column, the Rebels walked their captives northwest toward the Orange Turnpike. The Pennsylvanians said nothing.[97] They had no reason to brag or to cheer. Forty shabby looking Rebels had tricked three hundred three veteran Yankee soldiers into surrendering without a struggle.[98]

When the Confederates shot down Private Frank B. Ellis by his side, Captain Jacob Heffelfinger (Company H, 7th Pennsylvania Reserves) realized that the 61st Georgia had "bagged" his regiment. (MOLLUS, USAMHI)

Cutler's Brigade

Somewhere in the woods behind the Maryland Brigade, Lieutenant Colonel Rufus Dawes (6th Wisconsin) lay with his men, trying to catch his breath. Presently, Colonel Edward Bragg (6th Wisconsin) staggered into the regiment. Shortly thereafter, an enlisted man from Company I came into the line as well with sad news. "Captain Kellogg is killed, I am certain of it," he gasped.[99] (He was mistaken. Kellogg returned to the regiment later.) In an effort to save the men he had left under his command, Colonel Bragg carefully pulled his regiment farther to the east and to the safety of Lacy's field.[100]

Leonard's Brigade

Colonel Samuel Leonard's brigade, which was moving in column on the north side of the Orange Turnpike, filed to the right and swung into line in the pines some distance behind the 22nd Massachusetts and the 32nd Massachusetts.[101] Company D, 13th Massachusetts, First Lieutenant Edward F. Rollins commanding, penetrated deeper into the woods ahead of the other regiments as skirmishers. The brigade deployed into line of battle and trudged into the overgrown jungle. Occasional bullets from Saunders Field zipped through the trees around the 13th. Private Nat Seaver, who stood directly in front of his file closer, Sergeant "Jim" Stearns (Company K), tumbled forward onto his hands and knees. Stearns, who believed Seaver had "caught one," leaned over him to check his condition. The 25 year old soldier clutched his chest and painfully rasped out something about heart disease. The ex-

citement of battle was aggravating his condition. The extremely compas-
sionate Stearns gently laid his pale and trembling friend under a shrub. He
then draped his overcoat over the bush to provide Seaver with more shade.
With that, he moved after the regiment. The sergeant hated the cursed one
inch long horse briars which gouged his arms and legs and scratched his face
as he forced his way through the tangled forest.[102]

One of Private Robert G. Carter's officers (Company H) of the 22nd
Massachusetts nestled down behind a log, keeping as low as he could from
the incoming fire from across Saunders Field. As he lay there he blew through
his teeth that he wished he would get a "thirty days' scratch." A second later,
a musket ball, which ricochetted off a nearby tree, bored through his shoulder and exited through the shoulder blade. Standing upright, he wobbled
rearward.[103]

Leonard's overly anxious regiments were standing too close behind the
22nd Massachusetts. Private Channing Whittaker (Company B, 39th Massachusetts) never forgot that afternoon. The regiment took position in a grove
of small oaks, the largest of which measured, perhaps, eight inches in diam-
eter. First Lieutenant William T. Spear (Company B) stood in his usual position as file closer – three paces behind the second rank and a few paces to the
left rear of Whittaker. He was calmly enjoying the relative quiet of that sector of the field. Captain William W. Graham (Company B) lounged in front
of his men, leisurely leaning against one of the oaks, facing his company.
Every now and then a stray ball splattered into a nearby tree trunk or sang
above a fellow's head but never anything to cause any real concern.

Spear, for no accountable reason, suddenly turned about on his heel and
stepped away from the line. At the same time, a shell burst overhead and a
hot fragment imbedded itself in the forest floor where he had been standing.
Simultaneously, a minie ball, fired from close range from the east, slammed
into Graham's tree right above his head. In an instant, the captain dove for
cover. Orderly Sergeant Joseph J. Allison (Company B) shot along the company looking for the fool who had discharged his weapon.[104] At the same
time more nervous infantrymen along the line leveled their weapons and
opened fire.

The wounded officer from the 22nd Massachusetts, who happened along
the front of the regiment on his way to the rear, hit the ground while the
bullets sailed over his head. Shouting loudly not to kill him, he pulled himself
along on the forest floor until he was well clear of those trigger happy "fresh
fish."[105] The Rebels had taken out over three hundred men from his brigade
in less than an hour and he did not care to be a fatality.[106]

Quite a few of the rounds struck the ranks of the 96th Pennsylvania
which was lying down in the woods a short distance away. Private Henry
Keiser (Company G) had just rolled onto his side to see who was making all

the racket by crashing through the woods behind him when the rattled men from the 39th Massachusetts opened fire. The rounds pattered the ground all around him and two passed right across his chest. By the time the New Englanders ceased fire, two men in Company G had been hit.[107]

Allison tracked down the culprit. Grabbing the recruit by the collar, he brutally jerked the fellow from the rear rank, and rattled his body from head to foot. All the while he threatened personal bodily harm and worse should the man ever again discharge his weapon without orders.[108]

The Lacy Farm

Very shortly after the 9th Massachusetts hunkered down behind the headlogs on the western side of the Lacy farm, Sweitzer spurred up to Lieutenant Colonel Patrick T. Hanley and bellowed, "Why don't you take your regiment in?" "We have been in, and just come out!" Hanley shot back. "Well," the flustered Sweitzer blurted, "take 'em in again." The powder stained soldiers, who were lying nearby talking about their recent skirmish, could not believe their commander when Hanley shouted, "Fall in, Ninth." The regiment obeyed and was about to step off when a frantic staff officer reined in next to Hanley and yelled, "General Griffin's orders are not to take the Ninth in again." The embarrassed Sweitzer wheeled his horse about and spurred toward the corps' headquarters at the Lacy house, where the men later learned he had spent the entire day.[109]

The Germanna Plank Road–Orange Turnpike Intersection

By 4:00 P.M. Privates Ed Miller and Pete McGonigal (both Company B) of the 49th Pennsylvania had reached the Germanna Plank Road with their prisoners – Major Henry Handerson and one of Stafford's couriers. The two Yankees left their charges at the prisoners' depot near the intersection where they were lined up with other captured Confederates in single file. The soldiers in charge of the depot asked their prisoners to give them their names, rank, and regiments. All the while, malingerers and rear guard personnel harangued the Confederates about their uniforms and their personal cleanliness. It did not take long to get Handerson angry. "Boys!" he warned them, "Do you think it brave and manly to insult unarmed prisoners? Before long you yourselves may occupy a similar position." The rebuke did not change their behavior but it made the major feel better.[110]

Leonard's Brigade on the Eastern Side of Saunders Field

Not too long after the "friendly fire" incident, Leonard filed his five regiments south across the turnpike toward the position formerly held by the 4th Michigan, 62nd Pennsylvania, and 9th Massachusetts.[111] In so doing, he forgot to recall First Lieutenant Edward F. Rollins (Company D, 13th Massachusetts) and his skirmishers.[112] Confederate shells pelted the road with searing fragments. The veterans instinctively halted to survey the situation. They decided to run the gauntlet between shell bursts. A battalion, ducking low, bolted to the safety of the woods on the other side of the road when a shell exploded in the valley to the west. Sometimes an intrepid squad of a dozen men deliberately left cover to draw the gunners' fire, and then about one hundred men would skip across the pike while the projectile's burst of smoke obscured the artillerymen's sight.[113] Stearns, his mind fixated upon the peculiar "swi—s-s-s-h" of the shells, darted into the pines south of the pike right after he saw the muzzle flashes of the Rebel guns. He swore the brigade took heavy casualties changing position.[114] The men were too tense to check their losses accurately.

Once his men were safely on the southern side of the pike, Leonard reformed his brigade facing south, with the right flank presented toward the firing. At the command to march, the four regiments wheeled right and tramped west, completely lost. They eventually found themselves on the eastern side of Saunders Field. Shortly after the brigade went prone in the pine thickets along the edge of the swamp, Stearns heard an invisible line of men crashing through the seemingly impenetrable brush along the regiment's front. "Halt, front," an invisible officer cried out, "right dress, order arms." "What regiment?" one of the New Englanders' officers hailed. "South Carolina," came the response in a syrupy Southern drawl, "the Flower of the South."[115] There was no response from Leonard's hidden brigade. Shooting one another at point-blank range did not seem advisable. The Yankees lay quiet, hoping the Rebels would probe no further into their position, which they did not.

To the right, the 39th Massachusetts went prone on the reverse side of the slight grassy ridge which overlooked Saunders Field. Stunted pine trees, with their browning lower branches nearly touching the ground shielded the prone New Englanders from the prying eyes of the skirmishers on the opposite side of the swale. Colonel Phineas S. Davis lowered himself to the ground but his second in command, Lieutenant Colonel Charles L. Pierson, refused to lie down with his men or his fellow officers. Despite the minies which clipped the trees and showered the soldiers with pine needles and sappy bark, Pierson steadily paced from one end of the regiment to the other calmly and collectedly admonishing fidgety individuals to "lie down" and take it easy. His cool courage inspired Private Channing Whittaker (Company B) who adored him. Even later in the day, when the regiment inched closer to the crest of the ridge, Pierson retained his self composure. His men would follow him anywhere.[116]

The Woods North of Saunders Field

As the firing waxed hotter Major General Jubal A. Early committed the rest of his division into the battle. Brigadier General Harry Hays' five Loui-

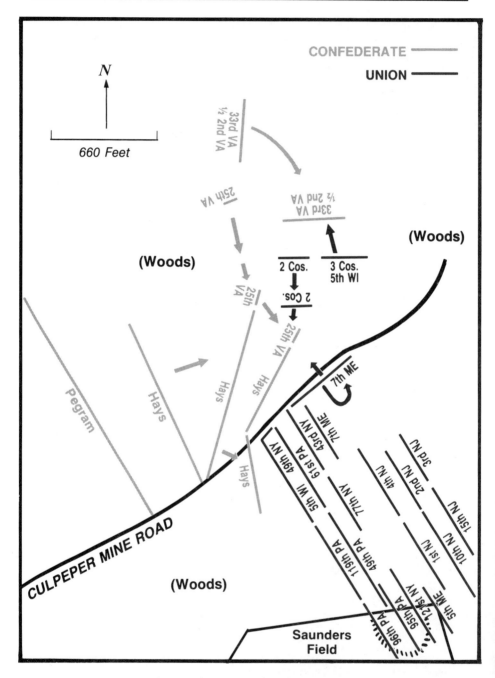

MAP 26: 4:00 P.M., May 5, 1864 • Hays' brigade smashes itself against Neill's VI Corps brigade and the 5th Wisconsin.

siana regiments doublequicked northeast on the Culpeper Mine Road toward the signs of the firing. On the way over to the left of the line General Richard Ewell, at Colonel John C. Higginbotham's insistence, detached the badly mauled 25th Virginia to accompany the Louisianans.[117] The colonel proudly led his fifty men and the regimental colors up the trail behind Hays' brigade.[118]

When Hays arrived upon the field, he found that Stafford's brigade had fallen back into line on the left of Steuart's command. The "Stonewall Brigade," with the exception of the 33rd Virginia and the left wing of the 2nd Virginia, having squared off with the five companies of the 5th Wisconsin, yielded the ground to the Yankees who decided not to press their advantage. The brigade retired fifty to seventy–five yards farther east of its original position.[119] Sergeant Mord Lewis (Company C) of the 2nd Virginia rushed up to Lieutenant Colonel William W. Randolph blurting something about Lieutenant Samuel Grubbs (Company C) having gone down with a bullet in his head out on the skirmish line. After rechecking his regiment's position, the colonel rushed into the undergrowth with the sergeant to retrieve Grubbs' body. Several feet away from the line a rifle ball slammed into Randolph's head. He died two hours later.[120]

As the Louisianans rushed into position they passed alongside the mortally wounded Stafford. Stretched out under a shade tree and in unspeakable pain, he said repeatedly in response to every word of encouragement that he was prepared to die. It was the men's duty to give their lives as the last full measure of devotion, he insisted.[121] The Louisianans disappeared into the woods to the east before Brigadier General Pegram's Virginia Brigade (behind them) could come to their support.

Pegram's brigade followed Hays' brigade to a point in front of and to the left of Stafford's rallied brigade.[122] Orders sounded along the line to construct breastworks. The soldiers of the 49th Virginia, Private William Waugh Smith (Company C, 49th Virginia) recollected, did not "cotton" to fighting from behind a wall of any kind. Rather than seriously attempt to obey the order, they rolled a few dead trees together, piled on a couple of fence rails and lazily tossed loose dirt or stones into the shoddy earthwork. Having never fought behind breastworks before, they preferred to meet the Yankees in the open.[123] The 52nd Virginia, to the left of the 13th Virginia, did not feel like working either. They had never fired a hostile round at the Federals from behind an earthwork before and did not intend to do so now. As Captain James Bumgardner, Jr. (Company F) put it, "...they had always whipped the Yankees on open ground and...the Yankees were not such damned fools, as to attempt to drive them out of breastworks."[124]

They did not have long to wait. Hays' Louisianans crashed into the woods between Stafford's brigade and the remnant of the Stonewall Brigade. The

Louisianans walked into a brisk fire from Totten's battalion of the 5th Wisconsin, which discharged its weapons and fell back through the woods toward the skirmishers of the 7th Maine on the north end of Neill's line. Fighting from tree to tree, the Confederates steadily wove their way through the woods, pushing the skirmishers of the 7th Maine less than two hundred yards until they came to the edge of the small clearing upon which Stafford's earlier assault had stalled.[125]

The forest along the Federal line became relatively quiet. The 7th Maine, having shot away all of its ammunition on Stafford, had retired to Neill's second line to the right rear of the 49th New York. It was sitting at right angles to and detached from the New Yorkers who had to pull back their right wing to cover the vacated position.[126] The New Englanders, feeling relatively safe, faced by the rear rank and refilled their cartridge boxes.[127] To the south, the 43rd New York, and the New Jersey Brigade (in two lines) rested in formation, facing west.[128]

At the same time that Hays' men reached the clearing, Lieutenant Colonel George Huston with his 33rd Virginia, the 2nd Virginia, and the 25th Virginia, which had attached itself to his right flank, came crashing through the woods into the gap created by the battalion of the 5th Wisconsin when it pulled away from the front and left of the Louisianans.[129] The two Virginia regiments from the "Stonewall Brigade" swung east, striking the Wisconsin skirmishers. The 25th Virginia pivoted south and connected with the 6th Louisiana, Hays' left regiment.[130]

The steady spattering of the skirmish line, sounding much like the patter of rain on leaves in a forest, suddenly increased in intensity to the rear of the 7th Maine.[131] Their skirmishers skittered toward the main Federal battle line, alerting the troops to the new Confederate drive. The 4th New Jersey, which stood in the woods south of Neill's brigade fixed bayonets and brought their weapons to "charge bayonets."[132] Colonel Edwin Mason (7th Maine) brought the regiment to its feet at the same time that the 25th Virginia wheeled right with part of the 6th Louisiana to take the New Englanders from the rear.[133]

Mason immediately pivoted the 7th Maine to face west, which exposed the right flank of the New Jersey Brigade to an enfilade. The Confederates unleashed a terrific volley into the Jerseymen. The brigade responded with an angry and deliberate fire by the right oblique into the backs of the Mainers who were to their right front.[134] Rather than get slaughtered by the riflery from the front and Federal bullets from the rear, Edwin Mason screamed, "Change front to rear on tenth company!" The veteran soldiers about faced and by companies from the right began to swivel back into their former position.[135] The Confederate infantry punched holes in the regimental line. The man next to Captain Albert A. Nickerson (Company E) pitched forward across his feet. The captain quickly stooped over to see if the man was dead. He was not. Nickerson straightened himself up and twisted about to yell for a stretcher when he felt something sting him sharply. For a second or two he thought he was walking on air, then he suddenly realized he had been shot through both legs just above the knees. Numbed and bleeding profusely, he turned to Lieutenant Eli H. Webber (Company B) and told him to take over the company. With the assistance of Corporal Charles Lowell (Company C), the captain left the field for the rear.[136]

The New Jersey regiments could not advance because of the narrow front. With incoming rounds whistling overhead, they could do nothing but wait it out.[137] The 119th Pennsylvania, the left battalion of the 5th Wisconsin, the 49th New York and the 7th Maine (south to north) held their ground and hammered the Confederates on their front and flank.[138] Their rifle balls slapped into the trees around Pegram's men who were behind Hays' line. The tremendous roar of the volleying frightened Private George Peyton (Company A, 13th Virginia) so badly that his hair raised up under his hat. The 13th Virginia, 52nd Virginia, 58th Virginia, and 31st Virginia flopped down behind trees, stumps and their miserable low breastworks to let the shooting pass over them.[139] Captain Samuel D. Buck (Company H, 13th Virginia) peered into the brush and woods along his front but he could not see anything clearly within fifty yards.[140]

The 49th Virginia, on the right of the brigade, blazed away into the fluttering shadows among the trees to its front. In the smoke and the confusion, the Virginians mistook Hays' men for Yankees massed on regimental front.[141] Their bullets took out quite a few of the Louisianans and probably did strike some of the Federals as well. Sergeant Edward W. Stephens (Company E, 8th Louisiana) dropped to one knee to fire. A minie ball, coming in from behind, gouged through both sides of his buttocks and dragged some of his intestines through the track as well. He died upon the field where he was hit.[142]

All along the Union line, ambulance corpsmen from the different regiments struggled through the woods and the underbrush to drag the wounded away from the battle. The strain of pulling semi-ambulatory or totally disabled men through the briars killed Sergeant Louis A. Bronz (Company C, 96th Pennsylvania). After carrying a wounded man across his shoulders for over a mile, he collapsed. Rasping in German, "I can't go no farther," he died in the arms of his friend, Private Maurus Oesterich (Company B).[143]

With rounds coming in from both directions, Harry Hays' men doggedly tried to slug it out with the VI Corps troops. It was no use. The 7th Maine peppered the 6th Louisiana and the 25th Virginia from the front. To the north, behind the 25th Virginia, Totten and his battalion of the 5th Wisconsin struggled against Colonel George Huston's 33rd Virginia and the left wing of the 2nd Virginia, which were pressing the Westerners from the west and the northwest. Rather than retreat from the action, Totten saw an opportunity to pull a maneuver more typical of Robert E. Lee than of a Federal officer.

While three of his five companies slugged it out with Huston and his men, he detached Captains Samuel White (Company D) and George E. Hilton (Company G) with their two companies to the south. The two Federal companies raced through the woods, screaming and firing as they went. Sweeping down upon Hays' Louisianans and the 25th Virginia from the rear, they tore into them with a vengeance.[144] Simultaneously, the 7th Maine, with the 4th New Jersey, charged into the Southerners from the opposite side.[145] In the resulting hand-to-hand melee, Colonel John C. Higginbotham, Private John R. King, and possibly a few others of his fifty men from the 25th Virginia, escaped through the milling Yankees to their own lines.[146] Buckshot plastered First Lieutenant Joseph S. Heston (Company D, 4th New Jersey) in the face beneath his ear, stunning him.[147] The Jerseymen obliqued southwest to cut off Confederates who were trying to escape. About one hundred of the Rebels threw their arms to the ground to escape annihilation. One of them, however, darted behind a tree and snapped off a round into the milling ranks of Company B. The minie ball whistled close by Captain Robert S. Johnston's head and scared him into a frenzy. With drawn sabre, he charged the Confederate screaming for his men to show no quarter. A number of enlisted men quickly leaped onto their frenzied captain and physically restrained him. Sergeant John P. Beech (Company B) breathed a sigh of relief. Had Johnston been allowed to kill the Rebel he could have triggered a senseless massacre of the other disarmed prisoners.[148]

Twenty minutes had elapsed since Hays came onto the field. Unwilling to sustain more losses, he ordered a retreat. He left over 250 men and the bulk of the 25th Virginia's detachment in the woods as casualties or prisoners. His brigade numbered under 500 effectives.[149] The Confederates cut down their share of Union soldiers as well. The 7th Maine alone lost 81 of its men, including Webber of Company B, whom the Rebels dropped seconds after his friend, Captain Albert Nickerson (Company E), limped off the field.[150] The 49th New York, to its left, lost under one third of that number.[151]

Chapter Six

"Death was in every shot."

4:00 P.M. Until Dark

The Gully in Saunders Field, North of the Pike

By late afternoon, only detached squads from Steuart's Confederate brigade remained in the gully between the lines. The Rebels, having trapped a handful of Yankees in it when they overran the field, robbed them of their canteens. Captain Emmett E. DePriest (Company H, 23rd Virginia) and his thirsty stalwarts soon discovered that the Northerners had carried whiskey instead of water into the fray. While the battle was waning around them, the captain, his men, a fellow or two from the 21st Virginia, and their prisoners squatted down in the bottom of the ditch and became thoroughly drunk.[1] The more they imbibed, the louder they became. Presently an argument broke out between one of the 21st Virginia and his prisoner which the two decided to settle in a "manly way." Defying the steady skirmishing across the field, they clawed their way out of the ditch into the road. Staggering to their feet, they stripped off their tunics to their shirt sleeves and drunkenly squared off with one another. For a few moments, the pickets on both sides stopped shooting to excitedly watch the match. From the security of the woods on the western side of the field, Sergeant John Worsham (Company F, 21st Virginia) and his comrades cheered on the two combatants. A smattering of Yankee skirmishers also joined in the hullabaloo. The Reb quickly knocked the Yankee down and they both rolled into the gully. The shooting commenced again.[2]

5:00 P.M.

Earthworks on the Lacy Farm

The 118th Pennsylvania left its bivouac at Lacy's at 5:00 P.M. and spent the next two hours on picket.[3] Time seemed to stand still. The veterans, drained from the day's events, mentally blocked out the stench of the roasting human flesh in the woods across from them. They heard the fires crackling and that peculiar "popping" of the exploding cartridge boxes but they could not – they would not – hear the screams of the wounded until years later when they were no longer in the Wilderness. Throughout the evening rifles flared in sporadic fits of anger, triggered by helpless men who could do nothing to relieve the suffering of the men dying between the lines except to blindly retaliate. A genuine madness existed in the Wilderness which fostered more bitterness and more hatred.

When a comrade fell, the historian of the 118th Pennsylvania truthfully recorded, the veteran trained himself to think, "What of it? The next turn may be mine." He bluntly continued, "Manifestations of grief rarely follow the fatal casualties of war. It is better that it should be so. The business of war is to kill and maim, and the quicker this is accepted as a hard and bitter necessity the better are the soldiers."[4] The veterans of Bartlett's brigade became "better soldiers" but at a fearful price – both emotionally and physically. The charge across Saunders bloodied field cost them 511 officers and men. At 7:00 P.M., the 118th Pennsylvania returned to the earthworks, which had been constructed earlier in the day, and bedded down for the night.[5]

6:00 P.M. – Sunset
The Woods North of Saunders Field
Confederate Position Along the Culpeper Mine Road

It did not take the Confederates long to reinforce their weak trench line. Pegram's regiments were shuffling north to allow room for what was left of Hays' brigade to shift into the line between them and Steuart's exhausted veterans. Battle's Alabamians straddled the Orange Turnpike with Daniel's North Carolinians and Gordon's Georgians to the right in the woods.

Walker's Virginians and Stafford's Louisianans were in the forest in reserve behind Pegram and Hays. Despite their tremendous casualties they were not too exhausted to go hunting. During the brief lull, Colonel Zebulon York (14th Louisiana) raced after a frightened fox which he accidentally spooked from cover. A wild turkey, fluttering out of the brush near the brigade line, brought down upon itself Rebel yells and a disorderly flurry of musketry. A handful of Louisianans were scrambling after a rabbit, which bounded over the low works into the woods between the lines. Catching it bare-handed, they trotted victoriously back to their own lines to their howling friends.[6]

The ferocity of Hays' battle had convinced Pegram's men that they had to construct better breastworks. No sooner had the shooting ended along their front than they feverishly pitched into building something more substantial than what they had. Officers and enlisted men were working together. Captain Samuel Buck (Company H, 13th Virginia) grabbed a tin plate and scooped up dirt to tightly pack the chinking between the stacked logs.[7] First Lieutenant Robert D. Funkhouser (Company D, 49th Virginia) pried up clods of earth with the point of his sword.[8] Private William W. Smith (Company C, 49th Virginia) later wrote, "Seeing that Grant would charge us in breastworks, the men set to work to show him something worth charging and with axes and other implements [we] soon had a stout log wall in front [of us]."[9] By 6:00 P.M., as the sun began to throw dark shadows over the backs of the Confederates into the trees along their front, they had put together a sturdy line of works measuring some three to four feet in height.[10]

They finished none too soon. On the left of Pegram's brigade, the skirmishers under First Lieutenant Cyrus B. Coiner (Company G, 52nd Virginia) suddenly cracked off rounds into the Wilderness before scampering rearward through the undergrowth to the safety of the earthworks.[11] On the extreme right, Captain Buckner M. Randolph (Company H, 49th Virginia), commanding the brigade skirmishers, was keeping up a prolonged fire to delay what appeared to be a strong Federal advance on brigade front.[12]

The Federals in the Woods North of Saunders Field

Brigadier Generals Thomas Neill's, David Russell's, and Truman Seymour's brigades of the VI Corps made a combined attack shortly after sunset (7:00 P.M.) in conjunction with several V Corps brigades to retake Saunders Field and the wooded ground to the north. The 119th Pennsylvania, a battalion of the 5th Wisconsin, the 49th New York, 4th New Jersey, 6th Maryland and 110th Ohio formed the first line from south to north, respectively. The 49th Pennsylvania, 61st Pennsylvania, 77th New York, and 43rd New York completed the second line. (The 7th Maine, having been relieved by Seymour's two regiments, had moved to the rear.) The rest of the New Jersey Brigade, in three lines, backed them up.[13] As the infantry moved out, the 15th New Jersey peeled away from the column to the south at Major General John Sedgwick's request to fill a gap in his line.[14]

The regiment moved to the smoldering wooded hill which the 96th Pennsylvania had secured earlier in the day. As the scattered musketry pelted their masked line, the Union infantry started scraping up dirt to protect themselves from an enemy whom they could not see. The 121st New York went to ground at the eastern base of the hill behind them with orders not to fire for fear of shooting their own men. One of the New Yorkers, in throwing himself down, accidentally jabbed a bugler, Private Thomas J. Hassett (Company F), in the right side of the neck with his bayonet, inflicting a "slight" wound.[15]

Every now and then, the Jerseymen responded to the Confederates with a shower of minie balls but, generally, they dug for their lives. When Lieutenant Michael Garber's section of Confederate artillery opened up on the men on both sides of the pike, some of the shells dropped short. The bursts rattled the tree tops and showered the men with wood chips and bark. A bullet zinged through Companies A and E of the 15th New Jersey and bored a hole through Captain John H. Vanderveer's throat seconds after a shell fragment shattered his hand. By then, Assistant Surgeon Charles E. Hall had appeared on the field. He dressed the officer's wounds and sent him back toward the Germanna Road with two drummers. (The captain never returned to active duty again.) Shortly thereafter, stray rounds wounded two more men.[16]

On the right of the line Seymour dispatched Captains Luther Brown (Company I, 110th Ohio) and Clifton H. Prentiss (Company F, 6th Maryland) with their companies forward to find the Rebel skirmishers. They immediately walked into Pegram's brigade sharpshooters. At the first sounds of musketry the 4th New Jersey, 6th Maryland, and 110th Ohio fixed bayo-

❶ Pegram smashes the 4th New Jersey, 6th Maryland and 110th Ohio.
❷ Hays drives back the 49th New York, 5th Wisconsin and 119th Pennsylvania.
❸ The 43rd New York, 77th New York, 61st Pennsylvania, and 49th Pennsylvania try to smash the Confederate lines with a third assault.
❹ - ❺ Four of Penrose's regiments meet a similar fate.

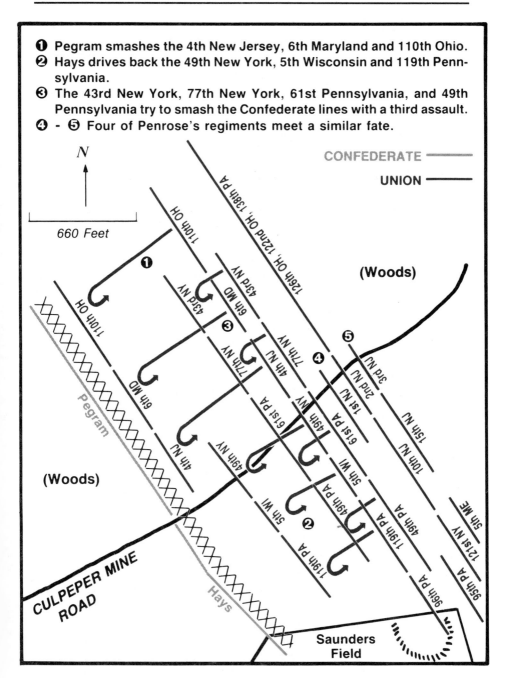

MAP 27: 6:00 P.M., May 5, 1864 • The VI Corps' debacle north of Saunders Field.

nets, then stepped off.[17] Pegram's brigade remained silent while their skirmishers skittered through the woods and bounded over the works. Buck,
who was standing on higher ground behind his company of the 13th Virginia, stared down the slight ridge into the hollow at the solid line of Federals
which halted not one hundred yards away and mechanically volleyed. Their
rounds went high. The three Northern regiments charged. The 4th New
Jersey obliqued left. The 6th Maryland veered off to the northwest for a
short distance, dragging two enlisted men from Company B, 4th New Jersey,
with them. Sergeant John P. Beech and Private John Duncan maintained contact with the left of the Maryland line, thinking that the rest of their regiment would incline in the direction of the charge.[18]

The Virginians stayed down behind their earthworks – silent, waiting.
At forty yards, the command to return fire rang down the line. Rising en
masse, the Confederates volleyed point-blank. The 6th Maryland recoiled
under the blast but rallied, closed ranks, loaded and returned the volley. The
three Federal regiments aimed at the muzzle flashes which rapidly sputtered
from the dark woods to their front. A bullet wounded Colonel John W. Horn
(6th Maryland). Captain Adam B. Martin (Company H) went down with a
fatal wound.[19] The slaughter continued for several minutes.

The Virginians and Hays' Louisianans raked the Federals repeatedly with
methodical, alternating volleys by files from the right and the left oblique,
cutting them down like a scythe going through high grass.[20] Rounds slammed
into Company D of the 6th Maryland, wounding First Lieutenant Charles
A. Damuth and his brother, Color Sergeant Jason Damuth. Corporal James
E. Heffner and First Sergeant Grayson M. Eichelberger (both from Company D) dragged the dying color bearer to the rear.[21] The 4th New Jersey,
6th Maryland, and the 110th Ohio broke ranks and streamed rearward.[22] A
few of the men stopped to snap rounds into the smoke. One of the bullets
struck Pegram in the knee as he sat astride his horse behind the Confederate
works.[23]

The 119th Pennsylvania, 5th Wisconsin, and 49th New York crunched
through the woods from the 6th Maryland's left rear, and melted under more
intense firing. Corporal Ira B. Newkirk (Company E, 5th Wisconsin) reeled
under the impact of a minie ball which bashed in his forehead between his
eyes and pushed fragmented bone down onto his brain casing.[24] Neill's support troops, the 61st Pennsylvania, 77th New York, and 43rd New York,
quickly replaced them. The tremendous Confederate musketry knocked down
large numbers of men. Corporal Thomas Beisty (Company A, 43rd New
York) caught a bullet in the upper side of his head.[25] Colonel George F. Smith
(61st Pennsylvania) dismounted and sent his horse to the rear. He wanted
his men to see him that day to refute camp gossip about his ability to discharge his duties under fire. Unable to withstand the extreme pressure, Neill's

three regiments stubbornly withdrew from the action but not before the 61st Pennsylvania had expended 100 rounds of ammunition per man without gaining any advantage upon the field. The smoldering forestocks on their Springfield rifled muskets scalded their fingers on the rifle barrels.[26] The New Jersey Brigade, in two lines, advanced into the vacated position.[27] The fighting took a heavy toll among the Jerseymen.[28]

"Death was in every shot," Captain Samuel Buck (Company H, 13th Virginia) recollected, "and we held fast to our works."[29] The attack went awry from the start. Incoming small arms fire from the invisible Rebels in conjunction with the seemingly impenetrable woods stymied the Federal attack on the left of the line. The 49th Pennsylvania, while marching by the right oblique to assist the 119th Pennsylvania and the Jerseymen, took several casualties, a large portion of them from the Confederate artillery section in the pike on the opposite side of Saunders Field. The regiment did not go very far before turning back. A rifle ball stung Sergeant Alfred Thompson (Company A) in the body. His captain and lieutenant ordered him to the rear, but he refused to go. He felt his wound was too slight to leave the line.[30] Thirty-five year old Private Jonathan Wiser (Company E) was not so fortunate. He went to the rear with a bullet lodged in his skull which the doctors did not attempt to extract.[31]

The 6th Maryland and 110th Ohio had walked into a death trap. Their half an hour in combat cost them 262 officers and men out of 986 engaged – a loss of 27 percent.[32] Stray balls pelted Seymour's second line, wounding about eight of the prone soldiers in the 138th Pennsylvania. Private James W. Davis (Company A) listened apprehensively to the steady crack and patter of riflery to the west of his regiment. Unable to see the Rebels, he hugged the ground to wait out the mess.[33] Not too far away, Sergeant Grayson Eichelberger (Company D, 6th Maryland) was tenderly cradling Sergeant Jason Damuth's head in his lap. Corporal James Heffner sat across from them. Their dear friend was bleeding to death with each passing minute and they could do nothing to prevent it. In the darkness Eichelberger distinctly heard the whippoorwills, which had serenaded the regiment to sleep the night before, singing plaintively all around them. Their calls had not forecast good fortune for the 6th Maryland as Horn had predicted.[34]

Sergeant Barclay Cooper (Company B, 126th Ohio) went down when two musket balls struck him simultaneously – one in the right side of his face, just below his earlobe, and the other in the scrotum. The bullet in his face gouged a pea sized hole through the back of his palate and imbedded itself in his left cheek bone behind his eye. The one through his scrotum, luckily, missed his testicles but left one of them completely exposed to the elements. His friends evacuated him to the field hospital a short distance to the rear, where he lay unattended until the next day.[35]

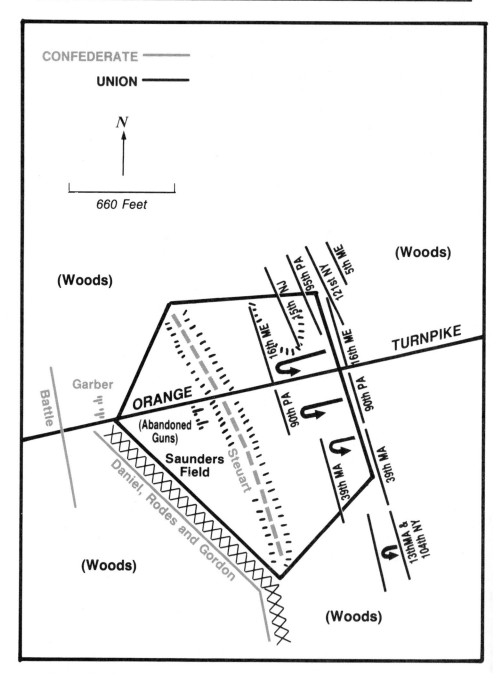

MAP 28: Dusk, May 5, 1864 • Leonard's brigade makes a final attempt to reclaim Captain Winslow's two abandoned guns.

Saunders Field

At sunset Colonel Samuel Leonard sent his brigade into the swale between the lines to capture the two abandoned guns south of the turnpike.[36] The men stood up in full view along the lip of the swale. Private Channing Whittaker (Company B, 39th Massachusetts) stared ruefully at the blinding sun which silhouetted the regimental line in a supernatural light as it started to slip below the western horizon.[37] The brigade charged down the slope. The right of the 16th Maine passed over the prone 95th Pennsylvania as it headed for the guns in the pike. The woods thundered and roared under the tremendous blasts of musketry.[38] Battle's and Steuart's reformed Confederate brigades, with an artillery section from Garber's Virginia Battery in the turnpike, hammered the Yankees as they came into the open ground.[39] The 90th Pennsylvania was caught in the field and nearly destroyed. In a few minutes, the Confederates struck down 94 out of 340 men.[40] Muzzle flashes slashed through the dark woods on the western side of the swale striking the Yankees who stumbled about trying to find a hidden enemy.[41] Several men in the 13th Massachusetts took hits. Private Lyman Haskell (Company K) staggered away from the skirmish with a bullet hole in his chest. Three other men in Company K became lost in the dark and turned up a few days later.

First Sergeant William Rawson (Company K) turned about and ran. Shedding his hat, cartridge box, waist belt and rifle, he took off at a fast clip back through the woods toward the Orange Turnpike.[42] Half way into Saunders Field Leonard ordered his men to quit the fight. They retreated to their side of the field and bedded down. After dark, ammunition bearers found the prone line and distributed cartridges to the exhausted soldiers.[43]

Lieutenant Holman Melcher (20th Maine) and His Detachment

Cut off during his regiment's attack against Saunders Field, Melcher decided that he and his seventeen enlisted men from Companies F and H would take the Rebels between them and their own lines from the rear. Sergeant Ammi M. Smith (Company F) posted himself on the left of the line while the lieutenant took his position on the right. The small detachment stole through the woods until within fifteen feet of the Confederate skirmishers, who were busily shooting at the Federals across Saunders Field. Each Yankee sighted in on his own target. At the command, the woods rang with the unexpected volley. Before the smoke cleared, the Mainers lunged through the brush, screaming, "Surrender or die!"

A surprised Confederate turned and leveled his rifle in the face of one of Melcher's soldiers. The hammer snapped coldly on the nipple. The weapon misfired. Angered beyond reason, the Yankee teenager rammed his bayonet into the Confederate's chest. Tears streaming down his face, the boy pushed the struggling gray coat to the ground and pinned him there. "I'll teach you, old Reb," he screamed, "how to snap your gun in my face!"

Another Southerner, his back to Melcher, lowered his weapon at a Yankee private at point-blank range. Melcher stepped forward and swung his sword at the Reb's back. The tip of the dull weapon clipped the soldier's scalp and slit his tunic all the way down the middle. The stunned Rebel threw down his rifle surrendering, while the remaining Confederates scattered, leaving their casualties and 32 prisoners on Melcher's hands. (He counted two dead and five wounded.) The Rebel line quickly reformed and snapped a few rounds into the brush at the Yankees' backs.

The lieutenant did not waste any time in leaving. His prisoners, however, when they realized they outnumbered the New Englanders and were so close to their own lines, slowed their pace and showed signs of turning on their captors. Melcher drew his seven shot revolver, halted all of them, and threatened his prisoners, "The first man who does not keep up in his place will be instantly shot." When he ordered the doublequick, the Confederates listened. The lieutenant brought all of his party into the Federal lines.[44]

Chapter Seven

"Show the enemy you have won laurels..."

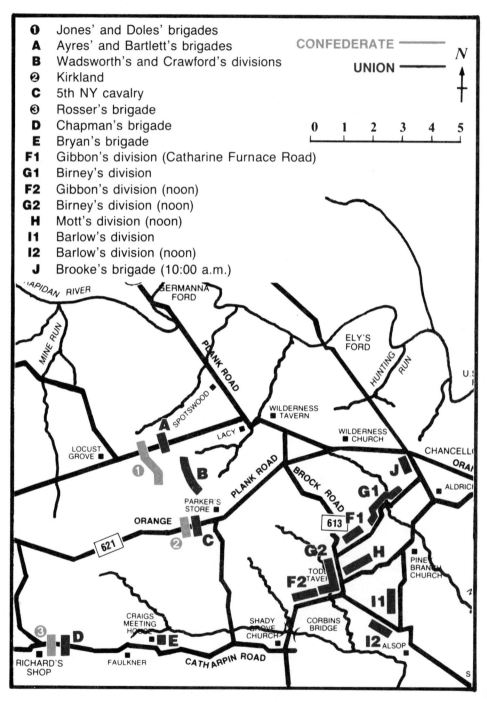

① Jones' and Doles' brigades
A Ayres' and Bartlett's brigades
B Wadsworth's and Crawford's divisions
② Kirkland
C 5th NY cavalry
③ Rosser's brigade
D Chapman's brigade
E Bryan's brigade
F1 Gibbon's division (Catharine Furnace Road)
G1 Birney's division
F2 Gibbon's division (noon)
G2 Birney's division (noon)
H Mott's division (noon)
I1 Barlow's division
I2 Barlow's division (noon)
J Brooke's brigade (10:00 a.m.)

CONFEDERATE ———
UNION ———

0 1 2 3 4 5

MAP 29: Situation by noon, May 5, 1864.

May 5, 1864: Dawn to Noon
II Corps Bivouac Near Chancellorsville

(2.5 miles east of Wilderness Tavern)

Private William Kent (Company F, 1st U. S. Sharpshooters) did not want to wake up that hot morning, but his stiff body, dust clogged throat, and the annoying Virginia flies goaded him into consciousness. The smell of a greasy breakfast lured him to a sitting position. When his chum, Second Sergeant Cassius Peck, invited him to the spring along the Orange Turnpike, he went along. Rather than contend with the long breakfast queue, the two strolled west on the Pike. Peck pointed out where the company had fought the year before and farther along the road he showed Kent where "Stonewall" Jackson was fired upon by his own men. Kneeling down, Kent plucked several flowers from the spot and secreted them away in his prayer book for Miss Lizzie Ellery, back home - a friend who admired the great Confederate general. The two sharpshooters returned to the spring, which gushed into the road from beneath the roots of a large tree. All about them lay the debris of battle - empty ammunition crates, scarred trees, bleaching bones draped in tattered and faded shrouds of unrecognizable uniforms. They were back in the company bivouac by 4:30 A.M. in time to join the advance into the Wilderness.[1]

At 5:00 A.M., the 8th Ohio (Carroll's brigade) called in Company B from the skirmish line and prepared to march with the rest of the II Corps. The sun bathed the regiment in insufferable heat, which seemed to radiate from the boards in the plank road. By 6:30 A.M. Brigadier General John Gibbon's division advanced toward Todd's Tavern, which was four and one half miles south of the Plank-Brock Road intersections.[2] Major General David Birney's division followed Gibbon shortly thereafter. The 17th Maine (Hays' brigade), having been called in from picket at daylight, was not in a joyful mood because the regiment had received orders to fall in before the men had had time to heat up their beef ration. The column wound its way a short distance past the ruins of Catharine Furnace on the Furnace Road en route to the Brock Road.[3] The march was brutal in the intense heat. By 8:00 A.M. the soldiers of the 124th New York (Ward's brigade) were staggering.[4] While Gibbon's men stumbled forward, Brigadier General Francis C. Barlow's division halted and countermarched back to the road which ran southeast from Chancellorsville to Aldrich's. At the Aldrich farm, Barlow's column turned southwest onto the Catharpin Road and, around 7:00 A.M., resumed the march to Todd's Tavern.[5] Brigadier General Gershom Mott's division followed behind.[6] Colonel John R. Brooke's brigade (Barlow's division), rather than proceed south to the Catharpin Road as the rest of the division had, did not leave its bivouac near Chancellorsville until 10:00 A.M.[7] Pursuant to orders, the 2,300 man brigade turned southwest on the Catharine Furnace Road with orders to stay with the division trains.[8]

The head of the Gibbon's division reached Todd's Tavern around 8:30 A.M. Pushing beyond the Tavern, southwest on the Catharpin Road, for another mile and a half, he halted to await further orders.[9] Birney's division marched into Todd's Tavern about an hour behind Gibbon.[10] He had thrown out the 1st U.S. Sharpshooters as flankers long before reaching the Tavern. Captain Rudolf Aschmann (Company A) expected some kind of confrontation at any moment. Not finding any enemy at all surprised and alarmed him and he wondered how long they would have to go before making contact with the Rebels.[11] Mott's division lurched to a stop on the Catharpin Road behind Birney's command. Meanwhile, Barlow's division, after shuffling about two miles southwest on the Catharpin, forked south on the Piney Branch Road.[12] His brigades turned north on the Brock Road and arrived within shooting distance of Todd's Tavern about 9:30 A.M. He could not march onto the Catharpin Road because Birney's division was turning west on the road at the Tavern, blocking his line of march.[13] The intense heat drained both the column's men and animals of their energy. Captain Josiah Favill (Company A, 57th New York), a recently appointed member of Barlow's staff, felt quite relieved when the column stopped in the small clearing along the roadside. They did not get much respite. All too quickly, the division moved out.[14] By splitting Hancock's II Corps three ways, Grant had provided flanking cover for his supply trains and the rest of the army while his cavalry reconnoitered toward Shady Grove Church.

In Hays' brigade, Private John Haley (Company I, 17th Maine) did not like what he saw when Birney's command reached Todd's Tavern. Aides were rushing frantically one way then another.[15] A staff officer, horse foaming at the mouth, raced north along the Brock Road, past the 124th New York (Ward's brigade) alarming the men that trouble was afoot.[16] Birney then massed his two brigades in the southern end of the large field which surrounded the Tavern. As soon as the pickets went out, Ward's regiments stacked arms. Many of the newer men threw themselves beside their weapons and slept. The veterans boiled coffee. They believed the hot drinks would insulate their bodies from the heat.[17] Hays formed his brigade in line of battle before allowing the men to break ranks for hard crackers and coffee.[18]

One and a half miles southwest of the Tavern on the Catharpin Road, the lead regiments of Gibbon's division listened apprehensively to the loud, rumbling thunder of artillery fire which was rolling intermittently through the woods on their right flank, and indicated action north of their position.[19] Second Lieutenant Thomas Galwey (Company B, 8th Ohio) correctly surmised that the Confederates were pressing Warren's V Corps and Sedgwick's VI Corps. The inevitable reversal of direction came within the half hour.

Shortly before 10:00 A.M., Gibbon's division turned about and doublequicked a short distance toward Todd's Tavern, only to stop again.[20]

Major General Winfield Scott Hancock, II Corps commander, with Lieutenant Colonel C. H. Morgan, chief of staff, galloped through the men who crowded the roads around the Tavern and started north on the Brock Road. He issued orders to advance while he struggled through the tangle of men who blocked his route.[21] Intercepting the head of Mott's division as it filed north alongside Birney's stalled command, Hancock ordered Colonel Robert McAllister to rush his seven regiments toward the Brock-Catharine Furnace Roads intersection.[22] He then disappeared in a burst of dirt clods and dust up the Brock Road.

A short distance into the advance, Mott ordered McAllister to detach only two regiments to the crossroads. He immediately sent the 5th and 8th New Jersey, under the direction of Colonel William J. Sewell (5th New Jersey), to the intersection. He then halted his remaining five regiments in the road to await further orders.[23] His stop set off a chain reaction, halting Colonel William Brewster's brigade which was marching in the road behind him. The "short halt" which McAllister described in his official account escalated into a couple of hours. At the same time Gibbon's division was marching into Todd's Tavern from the southwest.

Noon to 2:00 P.M.[24]

Finally, a courier sent Gibbon's command quick marching farther north along the Brock Road, where it stopped again to await the movement of Birney's two brigades (Hays' and Ward's), which had bottled up the Brock Road in front of his division.[25] Barlow's division was choked to a stop at the junction of the Catharpin Road and the Brock Road, south of the Tavern.[26] They did not hear the artillery fire from the woods to the north until shortly before noon. Within the half hour, the brigades were in column and dog trotting toward the sounds of the guns. At first the veterans of the 124th New York (Ward's brigade) believed they were going to rescue a besieged cavalry probe, but the intensity of the small arms fire indicated something much bigger.[27]

Hays' brigade, leading Birney's column, ran into Mott's traffic jam south of the Plank-Brock Roads intersection. Rather than order the men to clear the way, they impatiently plowed into the center of the column. Hays was in there with them. When he noticed the white diamonds on the soldiers' kepis, he shoved into the confused mob "tearing and swearing" as Private John Haley (Company I, 17th Maine) recorded in his diary. "Get out of the way, you damned white patches," he swore at Mott's soldiers.[28] A cavalryman accidentally brushed the general with his spur. "God damn your old heels!" Hays cursed.[29] Spurring and slapping their way through the mass of troops,

Hays and his staff galloped away from the head of the column, yelling for the men to catch up.[30] At the rear of the brigade, the 1st U.S. Sharpshooters tried to keep up, despite the blockage. Private William Kent (Company F) distinctly remembered his fat captain rasping out, "Come - on, boys," while he struggled heroically to maintain the lead himself. His sweating riflemen, who were gagging on the dust kicked up by the troops in front, did not have the energy to swear at him for his valiant effort.[31]

In the meantime, Hancock, having reached the crossroads, contacted Brigadier General George W. Getty, whose VI Corps division was holding the Confederates at bay. Hancock immediately hurried Colonel C. H. Morgan north to inform Meade of his arrival.[32] Hays reached the Plank Road shortly thereafter.

2:00 P.M.

The Cavalry Fight Along the Catharpin Road

(7.5 miles southwest of the Brock Crossing)

With the Confederates' line of sight obscured by the tremendous clouds of billowing smoke in Mrs. Faulkner's grass yard, Brigadier General James Wilson began pulling his Federal cavalry division from Craig's Meeting House, north along the road toward Parker's Store. Colonel Timothy Bryan, whose videttes from the 18th Pennsylvania Cavalry had patrolled the road since the Yankees arrived at the church, told him that Confederate infantry had cut off their retreat at Parker's Store. The news stunned Wilson. He could not go back to the Catharpin Road without risking interception by Rosser's cavalry and he could not get through to Parker's Store. Instead he diverted his column east on a back trail which intercepted his line of march a little over fifteen hundred feet north of Robertson's Run. Colonel George Chapman's rattled and bloodied First Brigade led the withdrawal followed by Bryan's Second Brigade, less the 18th Pennsylvania which was assigned the rear guard with the division's two batteries. First Lieutenants Charles L. Fitzhugh's and Alexander Pennington's artillery retired by sections down the road, covering the Pennsylvanians.[33] While Pennington rolled four of his six guns behind the main body of cavalry, First Lieutenant Carle A. Woodruff, with a section (two guns) from Pennington, loosed a couple of warning shots, then followed slowly down the crowded road. A section of Fitzhugh's guns silently rolled after him.[34]

The Confederates' two rifled guns at Mrs. Faulkner's sent a couple of shells whirling after the Yankees, before limbering up and cautiously moving north into the open ground around the meeting house. Private George Neese, one of the gunners, swore that the two pieces forced the Federals to retreat by flanking them. Their objective gained, the Confederates rested by their guns and Rosser's tired horsemen waited in the Catharpin Road for the order to advance.[35] The delay gave the escaping Yankees just about enough time to get to Corbin's Bridge on the Po River, five miles from Craig's Meeting House.[36]

2:00 – 3:00 P.M.[37]

Plank-Brock Road Intersection

(1.75 miles southeast of Wilderness Tavern)

As soon as his brigade caught up, Hays deployed the men across the crossroads in two lines of battle. The 4th Maine fell in with its right flank on the southern side of the Plank Road in the Brock Road. The 57th Pennsylvania and the 63rd Pennsylvania quickstepped into formation on the north side of the pike.[38] The 105th Pennsylvania halted immediately east of the 63rd Pennsylvania, on the eastern side of the Brock Road.[39] The 93rd New York fell in to its right. The 5th Michigan and the 3rd Michigan, covered the 4th Maine on the south side of the pike.[40] At the rear of the column, the 1st U. S. Sharpshooters and the 17th Maine lumbered forward on the troop cluttered road, trying to work their way to the front. The soldiers were stacking arms along both sides of the Brock Road. The 5th Michigan threw itself down on a small knoll on the eastern side of the dirt track and kindled fires for a late lunch.[41]

Ward's brigade, having failed to close with Hays' column, halted within half a mile of the Plank-Brock Roads intersection.[42] Rather than go into action to support Hays, he also allowed the men to stack arms in the woods on the road's eastern side. Within minutes, the worn out soldiers of the 124th New York were sleeping near their weapons. While they slept, the engineers moved into the brush along the road's western berm and started constructing breastworks.[43] Mott's division moved into the gap between Ward's and Hays' men and began entrenching.[44]

Early Afternoon: Time Uncertain
The Lost Skirmishers of the 76th and 95th New York Regiments

(An abandoned farm, 1 mile west of Higgerson's.)

Company B (76th New York) got caught in an open field behind the Confederate right flank and was shot up from the hidden Rebels.[45] An officer told the remaining five companies to retreat to a small body of dwarf pines behind them. The Confederates were pursuing them too closely. The New Yorkers turned around and forced the Confederates to pull back. The Southerners regrouped and, with their fearful yell ringing in the air, charged again. The hail of Yankee bullets staggered them but did not stop them this time. Taking cover behind a rail fence which bisected the field north to south, the Rebels returned the musketry round for round.

The Northerners, while firing down a sparsely wooded hillside, retreated to a thicker section of woods behind them. But the right of their line collapsed without warning under another charge. Part of Company B, 76th New York, responded to the situation. A brief hand-to-hand struggle settled the matter in the New Yorkers' favor. A staff officer, whose name no one remembered, having gone forward with the skirmishers, decided the situation was well in hand. Wheeling his horse about, he rode about eight hundred feet east into a Confederate skirmish line. Shots rang out. He was wounded and captured. The officers of Company B whispered instructions to retire to the right to Companies F and K and the three companies from the 95th New York. The fifteen line officers conferred to decide upon their next course of action. A black servant to one of the officers walked into the group with a report of sighting Rebel cavalry nearby.

At that, the officer in charge of the skirmishers ordered the men to fall in and march toward the sounds of the battle, which appeared to be behind them. Not too far away, a private was attempting to escort a prisoner into the Federal lines when a Southern colonel reined in across his path. "Halt!" the colonel loudly demanded, "Where are you going?" "To the Union Army," the disconcerted private growled while staring down the muzzle of the revolver which was aimed at his skull. "Give up that gun to the prisoner," the officer shot back. Turning his attention upon the Rebel private, he snapped, "March him back to our camp!" The colonel rode away, congratulating himself upon having reversed an undesirable situation. The Confederate enlisted man waited until the colonel disappeared among the pines. Turning to the startled Yankee, he shoved the weapon back into his hands. "Take it and march me to your camp. I've done with this confederacy!" The two joined the skirmishers, while they were stepping off toward the supposed direction of the Yankee lines.[46]

3:30 P.M. to 4:15 P.M.[47]

The Higgerson Farm

(.63 mile south of Saunders Field and the Orange Turnpike)

Companies B, F, and K of the 76th New York, with Companies A, E, and I of the 95th New York, finding themselves in the yard of the Higgerson home, had no idea where they were. The captain in charge of the skirmishers walked up to the house and inquired if the owner knew where their bivouacs of the previous night - the "Gold Mills" - were. "Sartinly," Benjamin Higgerson drawled. "How far is it?" the captain queried. "Wall, I reckon it is about two miles." "Can you take us to it?" "Couldn't think of it, " the Southerner insisted, "When I'm gone, who knows who might tote off my wife and young uns. Couldn't think of it, sir." "No excuses will do, sir," the captain sternly

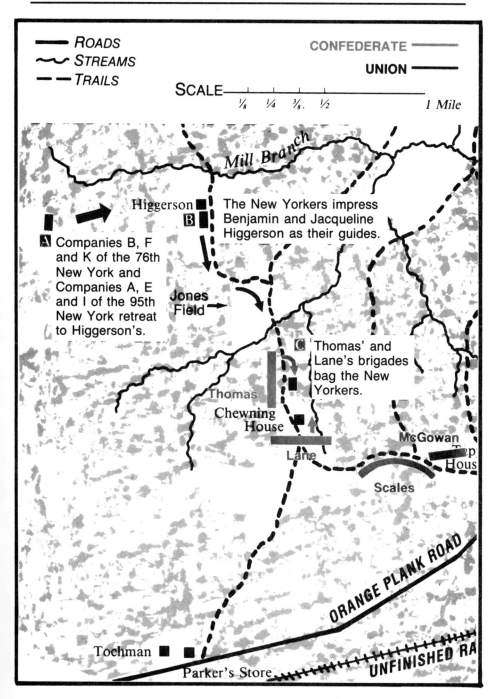

ROADS
STREAMS
TRAILS

CONFEDERATE
UNION

SCALE

⅛   ¼   ⅜ .   ½   1 Mile

Mill Branch

Higgerson

B

The New Yorkers impress Benjamin and Jacqueline Higgerson as their guides.

A Companies B, F and K of the 76th New York and Companies A, E and I of the 95th New York retreat to Higgerson's.

Jones Field →

C 'Thomas' and Lane's brigades bag the New Yorkers.

Thomas

Chewning House

Lane

McGowan

T'p Hous

Scales

ORANGE PLANK ROAD

Tochman

Parker's Store

UNFINISHED RA

MAP 30: 3:30 P.M.-4:15 P.M., May 5, 1864 • The lost skirmishers of the 76th New York and the 95th New York walk into Wilcox's Confederate division.

persisted, "You must act as our guide." Higgerson's nine year old daughter, Jacqueline, overheard the conversation and pushed in between her father and the Yankee officer. "Oh, sir! you would not think of taking my father? What should we do were some accident to befall him?" The captain tried to brush her aside with the hollow reassurance, "No accident will befall him, madam. We'll send him back safely when he puts us upon the right track."

She asked to go along. The officer consented, probably thinking the Rebels would not fire upon civilians. Very shortly thereafter, the skirmishers reached a back road which Higgerson reassured them went directly to their old bivouac. It ran to the Chewning place, then to the Tapp farm, about two miles to the southeast. The captain allowed Higgerson and his daughter to melt into the forest at the southwestern corner of the field.[48]

Near the Chewning Farm

(1.07 miles southeast of Higgerson's)

Unknown to the lost Federals, Major General Cadmus Wilcox's Confederate division was finally arriving upon the field from Mine Run. Brigadier General Edward L. Thomas' four Georgia regiments led the division, followed in turn by Brigadier Generals James H. Lane's North Carolinians (five regiments), Alfred M. Scales five North Carolina regiments, and Samuel McGowan's five regiment South Carolina Brigade. That large division of just over six thousand officers and men were moving northwest on the very back road which the V Corps had intended to take to the Plank Road that morning.

The division's skirmishers, under Captain John G. Knox, while slipping through the woods northwest of the Chewning place, ran into the six companies from the 76th New York and the 95th New York as they stumbled south in the darkened woods along the back road which intersected Wilcox's division.[49] Flames stabbed through the trees surrounding the Northerners. New Yorkers pitched to the ground. First Lieutenant William Cahill (Company B, 76th New York) was hit in the shoulder. At the same time a couple of rounds shattered his other arm. He dropped to the ground, helpless.[50] One of the bullets nicked Private Wilber F. Swaringen (Company K, 28th North Carolina) in the leg, badly bruising him but not knocking him down.[51]

The Yankees took to their heels, only to be rounded up by the sharpshooters who struck them from the front and Thomas' brigade who had encircled them.[52] None of the 76th New York escaped capture. The Confederates also seized Company E (95th New York) as a unit along with parts of the other two companies from the lost skirmish detachment. The unfortunate New Yorkers were going to come closer to Lee's headquarters than most of the Army of the Potomac that day.[53] Lane's North Carolinians captured one hundred thirty-nine enlisted men and eight officers, many of whom were wounded. Private George W. Hall (Company G, 14th Georgia), the cook for his "mess" of four men, went into the action with his faith in Christ as his shield. He came away unscathed and boasted that Thomas' brigade captured several hundred Federals.[54]

The Widow Tapp Farm
(1.0 mile southeast of Chewning's)

While Lane and Thomas cleared Chewning's farm of Yankees, Wilcox maneuvered the two remaining brigades of his division (Scales' and McGowan's) to face north in the 40 acre field around the Widow Tapp's house. Lieutenant Colonel William T. Poague's artillery battalion was in battery west of the house. Lee and Stuart stood near the guns watching the fighting in the woods which raged in the lower land east of their position.

The South Carolinians took a breather and laid down in the grassy field to rest. Second Lieutenant James F. J. Caldwell (Company B, 1st South Carolina Volunteers) sincerely believed that the regiment would not become engaged because it was so late in the day. General combat took time to develop, particularly in such hostile terrain. Theoretically armies needed cleared fields and plenty of daylight to fight and the natural condition of the Wilderness plus the late hour

During the afternoon action at the Chewning farm, Brigadier General James H. Lane, C.S.A., and his men captured 147 men from the 76th and the 95th New York regiments.

(Clark, Vol. I)

in the day ruled out any possibility of a normal, prolonged fight.

Far to the left, Ewell's division thundered away at the V Corps troops in Saunders Field. To the right front, small arms fire cracked along Poplar Run. Amidst the disturbing racket in which men were dying, the Reverend Mullaly, chaplain of Orr's Rifles, called the religious soldiers in the regiment into a tight covey about him. Caldwell anxiously shifted his attention from the fighting to the north, to that which was occurring to the east, then to the cluster of Christians huddling near their chaplain while he led them in prayer. The bright green leaves of the trees surrounding the field reminded him of more placid times. Finally he locked his eyes upon the hardened veterans and their preacher. Tanned, ragged, and hairy, they knelt with bowed heads

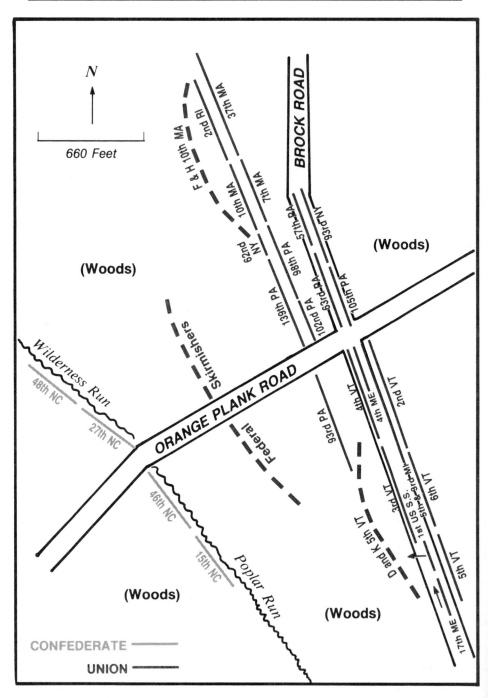

MAP 31: 2:00 P.M.-3:00 P.M., May 5, 1864 • II and VI Corps troops mass along the Brock Road.

and, with apparent genuine contrition, asked God to shrive them of their sins. Caldwell studied the blue sky, trying to suppress the sudden rush of emotion which he found swelling within him. "It was one of the most impressive scenes I ever witnessed," he recalled.[55]

On the Brock Road, South of the Plank Road

While Wilcox shifted his division south toward the Widow Tapp's farm, the Federal troops along the Brock Road continued deploying for battle. The lead regiments in Alexander Hays' brigade parted to both sides of the Brock Road to allow the 1st U.S. Sharpshooters (Berdan's Sharpshooters) to pass to the front of the column.[56] Major Charles P. Mattox, commanding the sharpshooters, brought the regiment to a halt on the left flank of the 3rd Vermont, with the 17th Maine falling into line immediately to the south.[57] The major called the regiment to attention.

Moving by the left flank, the sharpshooters stepped over the western bank of the Brock Road and entered the Wilderness. The 17th Maine shifted north to the left of the 3rd Vermont. The Berdans disappeared into the woods, then fanned out to the north in open order - one man every six feet -until the right flank (Company A) anchored itself on the Plank Road.[58] Private William Kent (Company F, 1st U.S. Sharpshooters) disliked the closely set trees because they blocked his field of fire. Yet, they were too skinny to protect his hind quarters. He became so preoccupied with the intense shooting to the north that he failed to hear the occasional rounds being fired at him and the men who walked near him. Despite the distant roar which echoed through the woods off to his right flank, in his sector, he became acutely aware of the snapping twigs under his feet and how silent and surreal the forest seemed. Every crunching step he took resonated too loudly for his liking.[59]

He was not the only soldier concerned about the relative quiet of the woods. Private Locke (Company F, 1st U.S. Sharpshooters), a recruit, worked his way to Kent's side. "Where are the Rebs?" he lowly asked. "I don't know," Kent whispered back. "How far do we go?" the rookie persisted. "I don't know," the veteran responded. "When should we run back?" "I don't know," Kent patiently replied. He let the scared boy talk all he wanted to. It comforted both of them somewhat. If they were still talking, they were still alive.[60]

Several hundred yards and less than fifteen minutes after it left the Brock Road, the regiment broke free of the saplings and stepped into a gently sloping field. The brush was lower. Large trees dotted the ground here and there. While the regiment descended into the swale, Kent locked his eyes upon a very thick belt of willows along the low, marshy northern end of Poplar Run. Mattox pranced his horse from one end of the line to the other, trying to realign his regiment in proper formation.[61]

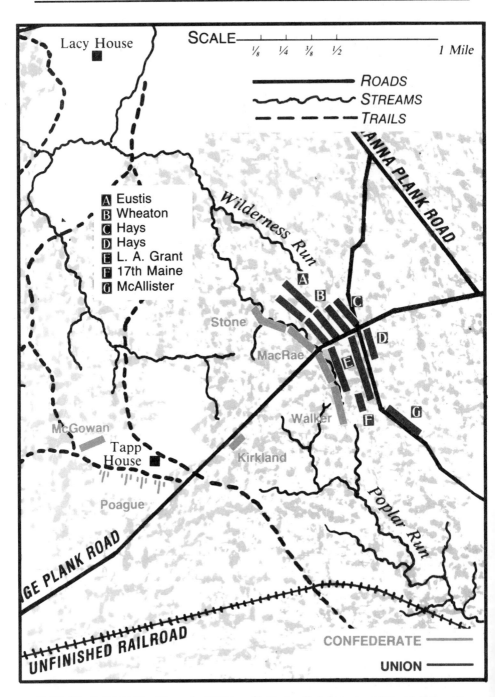

MAP 32: 3:30 P.M., May 5, 1864 • Getty's division and Hays' brigade push west on the Orange Plank Road against Heth's Confederate division.

North of the Plank Road

Meanwhile, Getty's division of the VI Corps, under orders from Meade, advanced as ordered before the rest of Birney's II Corps' troops had properly aligned themselves. At 3:30 P.M., about the same time that the 1st U.S. Sharpshooters were advancing into the Wilderness, Getty forwarded the brigades on the right of his division. Brigadier General Henry L. Eustis' brigade, on the northern end of his line, found it impossible to march on regimental front through the densely wooded and overgrown terrain. The 10th Massachusetts and the 2nd Rhode Island moved forward "by right of companies to the front." Instead of marching on a wide line, each regiment broke into ten separate columns, each company presenting a two man front, and pushed west through the tangle foot and horse briars.[62] In the seemingly impenetrable forest it appeared impossible to maintain a linear brigade formation. To help guide his command, Colonel Oliver Edwards, whose 37th Massachusetts marched behind the 2nd Rhode Island, called for volunteers to walk abreast of the brigade's first line to observe the fighting when it did break out and to keep him informed of conditions at the front. Corporal Theodore A. Church (Company G) stepped out with the volunteer squad and disappeared into the woods.[63]

The four veteran regiments of Brigadier General Frank Wheaton's brigade maintained their alignments on Eustis' left as well as the circumstances allowed.[64] A little over six hundred twenty-five feet away, along the western crest of the swale through which Wilderness Run flowed south toward Poplar Run, Major General Henry Heth's Confederates impatiently waited for the Federals to walk into the muzzles of their weapons. Colonel John M. Stone's Mississippian, Floridian, and North Carolinian Brigade covered about a five hundred foot front on the left of the division line, about nine hundred feet north of the Plank Road along the ridge bordering Wilderness Run. The 26th Mississippi, newly arrived from the West, was on the left end of the brigade, with the 42nd Mississippi to its right.[65] The 55th North Carolina was to the right center of the brigade. The 2nd Mississippi, 11th Mississippi, and 1st Confederate Battalion (Florida) filled in the area to the left and the right of the North Carolinians.[66]

Stone told Captain O'Neil, in charge of the brigade skirmishers, to send his men onto the opposite bank of Wilderness Run. The sharpshooters smartly stepped to the front right of their respective regiments and fell into double ranks. "One! Two! One! Two!" echoed along the files as the men formally counted off by two's, preparing to descend into the creek bottom.[67]

Colonel William MacRae's eighteen hundred man brigade straddled the Plank Road. The 48th North Carolina and the 27th North Carolina connected with Stone's right regiment. The 46th North Carolina and the 15th North Carolina continued the formation on the south side of the road.[68] Brigadier General Henry N. Walker's Virginia, Alabama, and Tennessee Brigade was still south of the Plank Road behind Brigadier General William Kirkland's brigade.[69] MacRae's skirmishers, led by First Lieutenant Francis Marion Wishart (Company A, 46th North Carolina), rushed into the undergrowth along both sides of the road. Wishart's good friend, Quartermaster Sergeant John M. Waddill, apprehensively listened to the party crash through the tangle of small, closely set trees.[70] A few minutes later, they inadvertently walked into the approaching skirmishers from Getty's division.

Companies F and H of the 10th Massachusetts, who covered the front of the 10th Massachusetts and the 2nd Rhode Island, opened fire upon MacRae's and Stone's skirmishers before O'Neil had time to deploy his battalion of sharpshooters forward. Colonel William A. Feeney (42nd Mississippi) shouted at Lieutenant Robert F. Ward (Company B) to extend his men in open order as they descended into the swale along the creek. Ward never saw his colonel alive again. A Yankee bullet cut Feeney down before his men returned to the regiment.[71]

O'Neil's skirmishers opened the fight on the eastern side of Poplar Run against Eustis' brigade.[72] Dashing halfway up the eastern bank of Wilderness Run swale, no more than sixty yards away from their main line, the Confederates halted and went prone. Bullets cut through the dense brush and whacked into the close set trees. Ward, depending upon which way he looked, could not see anything beyond thirty to eighty yards away. O'Neil darted over to Ward and told him, "Lieutenant Ward, take charge of the right wing of the battalion, and don't retire until you can see the enemy's colors."[73] In other words, the captain expected the lieutenant's five companies to drive the Federal skirmishers back upon their regiments and bring on a major engagement, which is exactly what they did.

Seconds later, a Confederate bullet struck First Lieutenant L. Oscar Eaton (Company F, 10th Massachusetts) in the leg and sent him staggering back through his regiment, which was maneuvering into line of battle.[74] Some of those rounds splattered into the observation detail from Company G of the 37th Massachusetts in Eustis' second line. One of them hammered into Corporal Theodore Church's forehead, killing him instantly.[75] Companies F and H of the 10th Massachusetts, now under Second Lieutenant Alfred E. Midgeley (Company H) clambered eastward through the trees attempting to get back to their lines before the brigade opened fire in their faces.[76]

A short distance away, Ward wanted to see the Yankees' colors so he would know how close their battle line was to him and his men. Poking his head above the lip of the ridge he spied the colors of the 2nd Rhode Island not more than seventy yards off. The color bearer was clutching the bunting close to the staff, evidently unwilling to unfurl them in the slight breeze which rustled through the woods. "...it was not necessary that it should be unfurled so that I could count the stars and stripes," Ward later recounted. He promptly had his company of sharpshooters retreat, unaware that the rest of battalion had already withdrawn to the brigade line. Stone, having impatiently waited until most of his skirmishers had gone prone in their positions on the left of their respective regiments, gave the order to fire. The filed leaders of the 2nd Rhode Island and the 10th Massachusetts shot back. Rifle and musket rounds suddenly whistled and zinged over the heads of Ward's Mississippians from both directions. While both sides reloaded, the twenty-four frightened Confederates were running up the ridge into their assigned space on the left of the regiment.[77]

On the opposite ridge, Company F (10th Massachusetts) and only part of Company H escaped to safety before the 10th Massachusetts and the 2nd Rhode Island began firing at the Confederates. Midgeley and his section of Company H threw themselves to the ground as the minie balls clipped off the branches over their heads. Pinned between the lines, they hugged the leaf covered ground, hoping not to get killed.[78]

Farther to the south, the skirmishers from the 48th North Carolina peppered Wheaton's brigade. The 139th Pennsylvania and the 62nd New York, his two front regiments, unable to see where the incoming shots originated from, halted inside the wood line along the eastern lip of Wilderness Run swale and pointed their rifles toward the thick ribbon of willows and brush along the creek bottom. They fired on command. Wishart and his North Carolinian skirmishers paid heavily for their temerity. Quartermaster Sergeant John M. Waddill (Company B) of the 46th North Carolina who was lying inside the tree line on the opposite ridge, just south of the Plank Road, said the Northern regiments literally cut the skirmishers down in their tracks.[79]

South of the Plank Road

Simultaneously, on the south side of the road the Vermont Brigade was catching up with the rear of Wheaton's left regiments. Companies D and K of the 5th Vermont passed through the 93rd Pennsylvania, which was filing north across the road to join the left end of Wheaton's second line.[80] The two companies of skirmishers from the 5th Vermont, who were almost opposite those of Wheaton's brigade, apparently spotted the Berdans bobbing about in the woods ahead of them, and halted, rather than collide with their formation. The 4th Vermont passed through them and formed a line along the top of the creek valley.[81] The 3rd Vermont, moving by the oblique, went into line on the left.[82]

A terrific volley burst from the woods along Wheaton's front.[83] Unobserved by the Federals across from them, Stone's and MacRae's brigades stood up and fired at ranges varying from fifty to one hundred yards. The

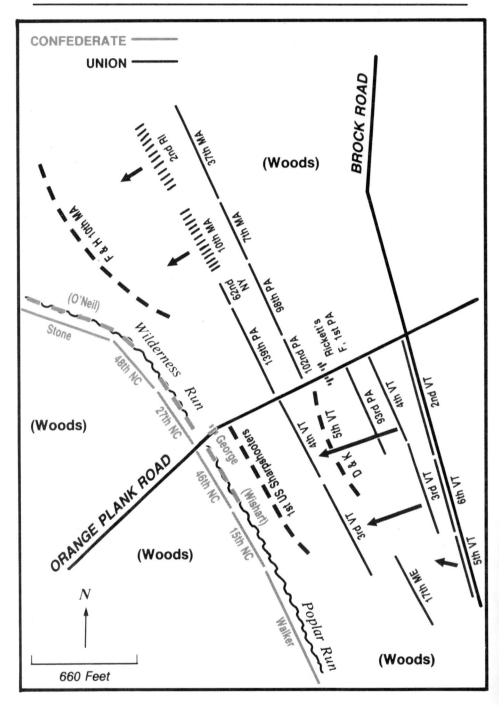

MAP 33: 3:30 P.M., May 5, 1864 • Detail of the opening battle along the Plank Road between Getty's division and Heth's Confederate division.

thunderous roar of some three thousand rifles firing almost in unison momentarily stunned the Federals. Soldiers pitched from the line, struck down by bullets which seemed to materialize in the air around them. Squads of wounded men crawled or limped rearward.[84]

The Widow Tapp's Farm
(1.73 miles southwest of the Brock Road)

The ferocity of the assault abruptly terminated Chaplain Mullaly's prayer service with the contrite South Carolinians of Orr's Rifles. The officers shouted their men into formation, faced the brigade south and attempted to quickstep the regiments toward the already congested Plank Road. The 1st South Carolina Volunteers led the column of regiments, followed by Orr's Rifles, the 12th, 13th, and the 14th South Carolina. Striking the trail which meandered into the road, the regiments filed southeast in files of two by the left flank toward the sound of the shooting. Word rippled through the ranks that the brigade was moving to support Heth's division.[85]

South of the Plank Road

Unable to determine what was happening in the thick woods to his front or to see through the smoke across the Plank Road, Major Charles Mattox (1st U.S. Sharpshooters) rode over to Captain Rudolf Aschmann (Company A), whose company anchored the right flank on the Plank Road, and asked whether the entire line had fallen back or not. Aschmann, who could see no more than fifty feet from where he stood, told the major that it was quiet on the left flank and that they probably were not being hard pressed over there.[86]

The words had hardly left Aschmann's mouth when the sharp cracks of breech loading rifles resounded from the left. Sixty-eight feet from the creek bed and the willows, Private William Kent (Company F) heard the solid volley roll in from the north. Without orders, he loosed a round into the willows. The recruit, Locke, who was still to his left, gasped, "What is it? What are you firing at?" "Fire and you'll see," Kent yelled as he shot another round. The frightened private fired wildly into the trees. Simultaneously, the entire left wing of the Sharpshooters opened fire at will. In an instant, the 46th North Carolina in full battle line emerged from cover firing point-blank into the startled Berdans.

Just as he fired his third shot, Private Dick Cross (Company F) jerked forward into the brush on Kent's right side, dead before he thudded to the ground. Instinctively, Kent glanced to his left. No one was there. Private Locke, and Kent's brother-in-law, Private Spafford A. Wright (Company F) were running back toward the top of the hill. As he turned to escape, Kent helplessly watched a handful of Rebels break from the willows and jerk the surprised Major Charles Mattox from his horse - the price he paid for being foolishly brave.

Major Charles P. Mattox (17th Maine) rode into William MacRae's North Carolinians along Poplar Run and was captured.

(Roger Hunt Collection, USAMHI)

The scattered Berdans formed a tenuous line three hundred twenty feet east of the slope to return a ragged volley. The Rebs were on them in too many numbers. The regiment broke and ran. "I'm hit. Don't leave me, boys." Locke and Kent quickly jerked the badly wounded Wright to his feet and tried carrying him by pulling his arms over their shoulders. A few yards farther on, they decided to support him, which must have increased the injury to his shattered upper arm. He slowed their pace too much. By mutual assent, they let Wright go and dashed for the earthworks along the Brock Road. Within a second, Kent heard the distinctive spat of a minie ball impacting his knapsack and he absorbed the full blow of something striking him between the shoulder blades. He did not drop but tottered unsteadily toward the works.[87]

While Wheaton's two front line regiments exchanged fire with the North Carolinians and the Mississippians north of the pike, the 4th Vermont came on line across from them and gave the Confederates a good stand up fight.[88] Private Henry A. Amidon (Company K, 4th Vermont) went to the rear breathing through a bullet wound in his chest. Like many who were wounded in the lungs, he was dead before the day ended.[89] The 3rd Vermont, having obliqued to the left over the top of the prone skirmishers from the 5th Vermont, also joined in the fighting.[90]

A pair of artillery shells whirled overhead from the east, fired by Captain R. Bruce Ricketts' section of Company F, 1st Pennsylvania Artillery, which had gone into position in the Plank Road, about two hundred twenty yards west of the Brock Road intersection.[91] They burst over McGowan's South Carolina Brigade as the 1st South Carolina Volunteers started across the Plank Road while moving south. The searing hot fragments pelted the ground around the shuffling Confederates and miraculously injured nobody.[92]

The sudden report of the guns disturbed Lieutenant Colonel William T. Poague and the gunners of his artillery battalion which had gone in position on the eastern edge of the open plateau surrounding the Widow Tapp farm. With his sixteen guns in position on defensible ground, almost one mile behind Heth's most advanced brigade, he had no need to worry about being overrun. The infantry, however, needed fire support, which he could not provide. He could not risk hitting his own men by rounds which fell short.

Heth had ordered First Lieutenant W. Frank George's single 12 Pounder Napoleon from Richard's Battery A, Mississippi Artillery, into the Plank Road to help the infantry out while the rest of the battery retired to the slightly higher ground around the Widow Tapp's.[93] The artillerymen carefully wove their limber and gun through the infantry which thronged the road and went into battery in the road, twenty yards in front of MacRae's prone infantry. The Federal infantry concentrated their fire upon the crew. George and several of his men were wounded as were the horses at the limber. The Federals drove them away from the field piece. From that moment on until the end of the day, the Confederates along the Plank Road had no artillery cover whatsoever.[94]

South of the Plank Road

Presently, the 17th Maine, behind the 3rd Vermont, came into the line on its left rear. Private John Haley (Company I, 17th Maine) could see only trees and undergrowth.[95] The breast high tangle foot, which laced together the saplings along their route of march, destroyed whatever order the two regiments were trying to maintain. During the 17th Maine's approach to the front, it walked into some resistance from skirmishers who harassed its left front. Unable to see through the foliage, the soldiers fired at the Confederates' muzzle flashes. As his regiment herded the Rebs west, Haley increasingly worried about an ambush. The persistent roar of the musketry in the distance and on both flanks reminded him of a raging surf striking the shores of Maine.[96] Private Daniel Brown (Company I, 17th Maine), who had harbored a death premonition, tumbled to the forest floor mortally wounded. His shrieks reverberated above the incessant firing, disconcerting those who recalled the prediction. As Brown died, Haley anxiously recalled the last thing Brown had said that morning, "If I go into any fight, I hope to Jesus Christ that I shall be shot before five minutes." Some things were better left unsaid, Haley wrote as an afterthought. Daniel Brown had not had time to fire his second shot. The fighting continued and Haley became increasingly weaker. He nearly passed out. His nose bled profusely. Unable to staunch the flow, he, nevertheless, stayed with his regiment.[97]

Rather than have his regiment stand and be slaughtered, Colonel Thomas O. Seaver (3rd Vermont) charged his men through the open swale to take the Confederates out head on.[98] His New Englanders ran into Walker's eight regiment brigade.[99] They sent a flaming wall of lead from the western crest of the creek swale, costing Seaver more men than he cared to lose. Frantically looking behind him for support from the 17th Maine and coming under fire from his unprotected left flank, he quickly moved his line back into

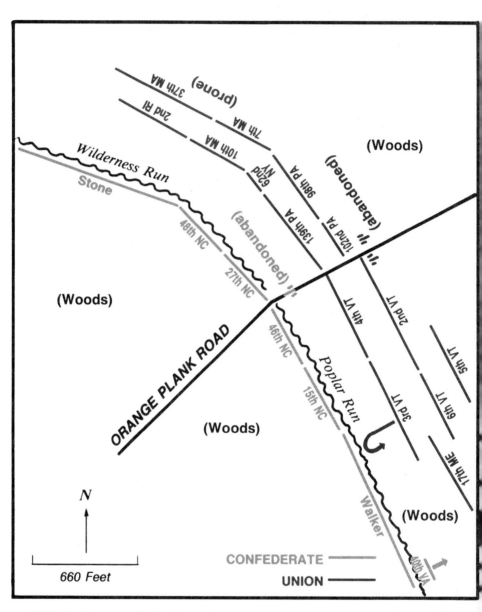

MAP 34: By 4:00 P.M., May 5, 1864 • A stalemate develops along the Plank Road.

position on the left of the 4th Vermont.[100] Walker's men stayed back in the woods with the exception of the skirmishers of the 40th Virginia. They slipped around the left flank of the 17th Maine, supporting the 3rd Vermont from the left rear, and edged their way toward the Brock Road.[101]

North of the Plank Road

Initially, the 139th Pennsylvania and the 62nd New York, rather than lie down, decided to fire standing up. The regimental officers soon realized the folly of trying to wage war upright, and ordered their men all along the line to go prone. To the far right of the line, the 10th Massachusetts and the 2nd Rhode Island crawled into the regulation regimental lines. Bullets, zipping and whistling through the trees, from the front as well as the flank, knocked down men in the rear regiments as well. The 37th Massachusetts, supporting the 2nd Rhode Island, quickly lost several men to rounds which passed through the Rhode Islanders' ranks. One of those bullets hit Captain Joseph L. Hayden (Company H) in the thigh, permanently disabling him. Both the 37th and the 7th Massachusetts, on its left, laid down rather than be slaughtered by an enemy to whom they could not respond.[102]

The Confederates fared no better than the Federals in the maelstrom which swept the woods on both sides of the creek. "...one of the severest engagements of the war ensued," Captain Kenneth Raynor Jones (Company I, 27th North Carolina) entered in his diary.[103] A fellow officer in his regiment, First Lieutenant James A. Graham (Company G) wrote his mother with considerable understatement, "Our company suffered severely." A bullet gouged out Sergeant Thomas Byrd Whitted's left eye. Sergeant Olin F. Hatch went down with a wounded left leg. Private George M. Dorothy got hit in the face. A bullet shattered Private Martin Delany's right arm. Another minie grazed Private Egbert H. Strayhorn's neck.[104] The Yankees were reducing the regiment by the handfuls.

Lieutenant Robert Ward (Company B, 42nd Mississippi) quickly lost track of the number of men he sacrificed during the first sixty minutes of shooting. The Yankees had killed or wounded nineteen of his twenty-four prone sharpshooters. The lieutenant, having squatted down behind a white oak sapling a few feet behind his men, got as low to the ground as he could without lying down.[105] He could theoretically boast that he had remained upon his feet throughout the action.

South of the Plank Road

The Vermonters, firing from the ground, devastated the 46th North Carolina. Company K alone lost fifty-three of sixty-five engaged. Many of them were chest, thigh, and facial wounds.[106] The volleying waxed into an incessant roar which drowned out all other sounds. Time blurred. The Federal lines merged as the men in the front line ran out of ammunition and retired from the fighting. The 3rd Vermont withdrew behind the 6th Vermont, which inched forward to take its place. A bullet cracked Private Alfred F. Douglas (Company I, 6th Vermont) on the right side of the head, cutting his scalp to the bone. The frightened nineteen year old tried to get away from the fighting only to discover that he could not move his legs very well. The blow to his skull partially paralyzed him from the thighs down.[107]

On the right, the 2nd Vermont crept into formation nearly on line to the left of the 4th Vermont.[108] The 5th Vermont remained to the right rear of the 6th Vermont in support.[109] The 2nd Vermont, initially, attempted to maintain the regulation firing line, but the Confederate fire quickly negated that option. In short order, the regiment lost Colonel Newton Stone and its acting major, who were killed outright, and Lieutenant Colonel John S. Tyler, who was mortally wounded.[110] A bullet struck Private George A. Arnold (Company G, 2nd Vermont) on the right side of the head, leaving him with a severe headache and nothing more. Another member of his company, Private Norman J. Nichols, was also shot in the head. That minie ball destroyed his right eye and exited through his upper jaw on the opposite side.[111] Moments after entering the fight, while kneeling to cap his rifle, Private Wilbur Fisk (Company E, 2nd Vermont) narrowly escaped with his life. A bullet split his kepi in half and knocked it off his head, leaving him with a slightly grazed skull. "We all had narrow escapes," he noted shortly thereafter with considerable New England understatement.[112]

2:30 P.M. – 4:00 P.M.

Corbin's Bridge on the Po River

(5.5 miles south of the Brock Road intersection)

Once he was sure he would not come under Federal artillery fire, Brigadier General Thomas Rosser sent his four cavalry regiments charging east on the Catharpin Road in an effort to cut off the retreating Federal column. The 12th Virginia Cavalry again led the madcap race. They were trying to make up for lost time by galloping in column of fours along the dirt road after an enemy which they hoped would be at their objective.[113] The 7th and the 11th Virginia, with the 35th Virginia Battalion in the rear, followed after the lead regiment with equal speed. With each minute the column became more engulfed in its own dust and the regiments became more scattered. In particular, the unfortunate 35th Battalion could see nothing through the insufferable cloud of dirt which blanketed the woods and the road to its front.[114]

Sometime between 3:00 P.M. and 4:00 P.M. Brigadier General James H. Wilson and his staff, riding between the 18th Pennsylvania Cavalry and the rest of Colonel Timothy M. Bryan's cavalry brigade, reached the Catharpin

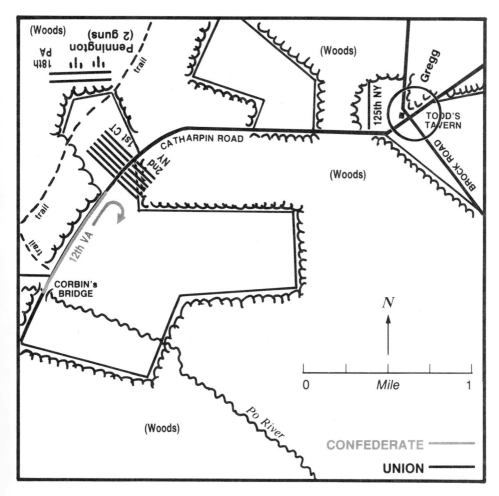

MAP 35: 3:00 P.M.-4:00 P.M., May 5, 1864 • The 1st Connecticut Cavalry and the 2nd New York Cavalry temporarily repel the 12th Virginia Cavalry on the Catharpin Road.

Road about one fourth of a mile east of Corbin's Bridge only to discover that the point of Rosser's Virginia Brigade had just reached the hill a quarter of a mile west of the bridge. Wilson and his escort spurred into the road behind the 1st Connecticut and the 2nd New York Cavalry leaving his rear guard and a section of Pennington's guns in the woods behind him.[115] The two regiments wheeled about and deployed on squadron front in mounted lines in the clearing on both sides of the Catharpin Road, prepared to fight.

The 12th Virginia clattered across the wooden bridge over the Po and stormed headlong into the Yankees' waiting carbines. The small arms fire thundered across the open ground. The Virginians recoiled under the blast, retreated a short distance and charged, only to be shattered again.[116]

The rest of Rosser's brigade slowed its pace to catch its breath while the 1st Connecticut and the 2nd New York withdrew into the woods behind them. In the meantime, the 18th Pennsylvania rode about a mile farther north along a parallel country road and went into position in the woods northwest of a square, overgrown field which bordered the Catharpin Road.[117] The 1st Connecticut faced about in front of the 2nd New York in the woods on the northeastern border of the same field to let the Confederates catch up. They did not have to wait long. Lieutenant Colonel Thomas Marshall (7th Virginia) raised himself in the stirrups and, turning to his command which was strung out in column behind him, called out, "This is the Laurel Brigade. Show the enemy you have won laurels and can win them again. Come on." The Rebel yell echoed ominously overhead.[118] The 7th Virginia Cavalry burst over the wooded ridge opposite the Yankees and rushed down on them with pistols blazing. Rosser positioned himself on the hill to the Virginians' left as they spurred into the pine and sumac studded field. At the same time, Captains Preston P. Johnston's and James W. Thomson's batteries rolled into position on the ridge to his left to provide close support.[119] Scattered rifle shots, not an organized volley, pelted the Southerners, which convinced Second Lieutenant Charles H. Y. Vandiver (Company F, 7th Virginia) that the Federals were weakening. The lieutenant waved his shotgun over his head like a sword yelling, "Come on, my boys! Come on, Company F! Follow me!" The bone chilling yelps of the Confederate cavalrymen resounded over the thunder of the horses' hooves as they surged forward.[120] In vain, the Yankee officers tried to keep their men in formation.

The 11th Virginia, with Major E. H. McDonald at the front, galloped toward the rear of the 7th Virginia. The 7th, which continued to lose its unit integrity during the charge, opened ranks, allowing the 11th to slip into the formation as the charge continued. The Confederates literally slammed into the two Yankee regiments. The very brief hand-to-hand fight unhorsed men on both sides. Pistol shots snapped in the air. First Sergeant John F. Johnson (Company F, 7th Virginia) reeled in the saddle, struck in the neck by a pistol

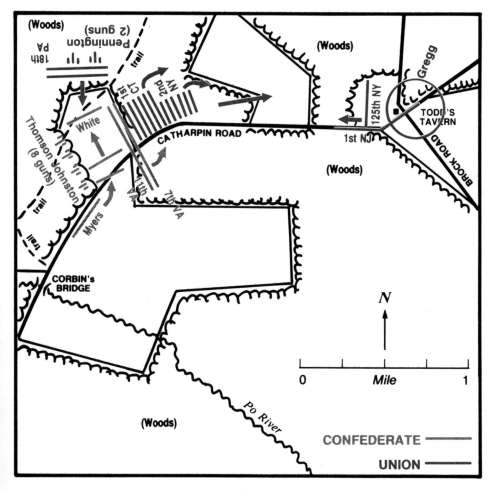

MAP 36: 3:00 P.M.-4:00 P.M., May 5, 1864 • Rosser's Virginians break Bryan's Federal cavalry brigade on the Catharpin Road.

ball. Private John W. Smith, Rosser's clerk, died in the melee. The Federal rounds seemed to go wild. They wounded no less than five horses.[121] The 1st Connecticut quit the field with seven wounded, leaving the 2nd New York to bear the brunt of the assault. The two Virginia regiments bolted into the trees. Shots were exchanged. Private James F. Wood (Company F), who was riding next to Vandiver, had just rounded up three Yankees when a bullet killed Vandiver's horse, sending him to the forest floor in a heap. The jarred lieutenant recovered quickly, telling Wood to take their three prisoners to the rear and find him a horse while he continued the fighting on foot. The Confederates took prisoners by the dozens as they chased the Yankees east toward Todd's Tavern.[122]

The three front companies of Colonel Elijah White's 35th Virginia Battalion ("Comanches") added to the confusion when they crashed into the woods on the left rear of the 11th and the 7th regiments and ran head-first into the waiting mounted soldiers of Lieutenant Colonel William P. Brinton's 18th Pennsylvania. Major William B. Darlington ordered the 1st Battalion (6 companies) forward. The "Comanches" charged into the Yankees despite their rifle fire. The Pennsylvanians fought there briefly, then retreated a short distance. Then, Major John W. Phillips' 2nd Battalion joined the 1st Battalion in a counterattack. But White's Virginians sent them reeling. Darlington went down with a severely injured leg. Again the two sides reformed and charged at each other, the Federals with carbines and White's men with bared sabres.

Meanwhile, Captain Frank Myers' 1st Squadron (two companies) of White's Battalion, had finally caught up with his own brigade. The charge along the Catharpin Road had left Myers with about twelve men from the two companies in his squadron. Myers halted to allow the others to catch up. Rosser, who had ridden nearer to the road to better observe the fighting, listened intently to the staccato rapping of carbine and pistol shots which reverberated from the pine forest to his front. The general twisted around in the saddle and saw Myers attempting to reorganize his troopers.

"Let 'em out, Myers," Rosser yelled, "let 'em out! Old White's in there, knocking them right and left."

Myers darted out in front with his small Company A screaming like banshees after him. Using the shouts, the firing, and the clanging steel in the woods as his guide, he struck the Catharpin Road and wheeled left, heading directly for what he assumed was the Federal right flank. He envisioned himself saving the day by enveloping the Yankees from the west. Instead of overriding the Yankee flank, his men galloped directly into one of Pennington's waiting field pieces. They were located a short distance inside the forest, on the north side of the back road which the 18th Pennsylvania had taken to escape to Todd's Tavern. The artillerymen sent a case shot with a short fuse whining toward the front of the Virginians' formation. The shell burst overhead and a sulfuric cloud of acrid smoke engulfed the cavalrymen. Searing hot shell fragments hurtled past the men's ears and musket balls pattered the ground around the foam flecked horses, which made them buck.

While the startled Confederates regrouped, the wily Federals limbered up and trotted north after the 18th Pennsylvania, which by then, having broken off its engagement with the rest of White's "Comanches," was also heading for safer ground. Instead of following the dirt track east, because the "Comanches" had blocked the way between them and the gunners, the Pennsylvanians broke to the rear through the swampy pine woods. The horses slung mud in every conceivable direction. Pine branches slapped and gouged the troopers as they ran for their lives.[123] When Myers realized that the Yankees had gotten away, he sent his men trotting into the forest on the eastern side of the field where they united with the rest of the battalion. The vicious fighting had provided White's Virginians with about thirty prisoners and more importantly, with their sidearms.

Having spent the entire day without ammunition, they equipped themselves with the Yankees' loaded pistols and carbines. Then, White led his partially armed battalion down the Catharpin Road to support the 7th and the 11th Virginia regiments in their pursuit of the 2nd New York toward Todd's Tavern.[124] Along the route, the "Comanches" picked up more weapons from Connecticut and New York cavalrymen who were being escorted to the Po as prisoners.[125]

Captain Frank M. Myers (Company A) of White's "Comanches," under direct orders from Rosser, led a saber charge against the 18th Pennsylvania Cavalry.
(History of the Laurel Brigade)

Todd's Tavern and the Brock Road

(On the Brock Road, 4.2 miles south of the Plank Road)

Wilson, having ridden ahead of his brigade, arrived at Todd's Tavern sometime before 3:00 P.M. and found Brigadier General David Gregg, who commanded the Second Cavalry Division, and the 125th New York Infantry from Brigadier General Francis Barlow's II Corps brigade massed there. Brigadier General Henry Davies' cavalry brigade had just arrived from the

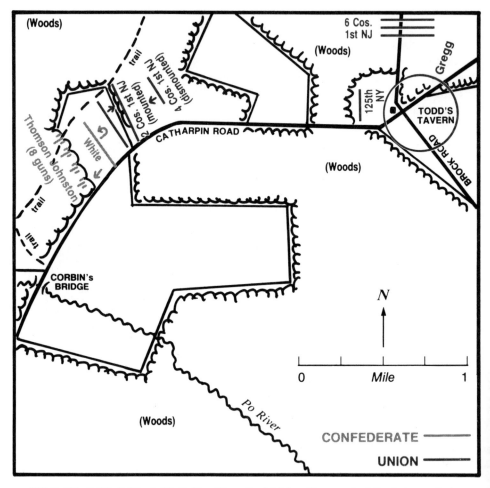

MAP 37: 3:00 P.M.-4:00 P.M., May 5, 1864 • Rosser's Virginians fight
the 1st New Jersey Cavalry to a standstill west of Todd's Tavern.

vicinity of Piney Branch Church with part of the 6th Battery, New York Light Artillery. Davies had already detached Lieutenant Colonel David A. Gardner with five companies of the 1st Pennsylvania Cavalry, the other half of the 1st Massachusetts Cavalry, and a section from the 6th New York Light Artillery south on the Brock Road toward Alsop's Gate to cover his flank.[126] Gregg, upon seeing Wilson's beaten troopers stream from the woods west of the tavern, immediately told Lieutenant Colonel John W. Kester (1st New Jersey Cavalry) to send a squadron down the Catharpin Road and to back it up with the rest of the regiment. Kester ordered Captain James H. Hart with Company A and the other company of the 1st Squadron forward.[127]

Hart and his two companies trotted past the rattled 2nd New York which burst into the clearing north of the road. A few seconds later, he sighted the 7th and the 11th Virginia regiments fast approaching in the road. The quick thinking officer charged without waiting for the rest of the regiment. The Confederates at the head of their column got off several rounds which hit Second Lieutenant Theodore Michenor and two men from Company A.[128] Private Jacob Baker (Company F, 7th Virginia Cavalry) cornered a frightened German and forced the man to surrender his sidearm to him. The German, who knew the weapon was unloaded, turned his horse about and started for the Federal lines. "If you don't come, I'll shoot you!" Baker warned the Yankee as he leveled the man's service revolver at him. "Dere ish no load in it," the German yelled back. "I beliefsh I will go pack." The flustered Confederate noticed the 1st New Jersey getting by him on the flank, wheeled about, and dashed for the ridge east of the Po River.[129]

The New Jersey cavalrymen galloped around their casualties, bent upon smashing into the Virginians, who rather than engage in hand-to-hand combat, turned on their heels and broke for the security of their brigade. The chase continued for another quarter mile to the next clearing in the pine woods. The sight of White's 140 "Comanches" clattering in column down the road with sabers drawn abruptly checked the Yankee charge. The 7th and the 11th Virginia escaped to the left and the right, sweeping around the 35th Battalion as if it were a boulder in a raging flood. White's men plowed east with the men screaming the dreaded Rebel yell at the startled Federals.

Hart quickly deployed to the north in an extended mounted formation. Their carbines cracked and flamed before the men melted into the pine forest behind them. A short distance into the woods, the Jerseymen ran into two more dismounted squadrons from their regiment. Hart's men rallied on its skirmishers while Kester, with the regiment's mounted twelve man color guard, trotted down the road abreast of them. The increased volume of small arms fire from the Yankees' repeating carbines and their own fierce yelling turned back White's battalion which was attempting to take the woods in a battle line.

While the Confederates were breaking to the rear and his own skirmishers were pushing ahead of him, Kester turned around in the saddle to call up the remaining three squadrons of his regiment only to find them gone. (Unknown to him, Davies had ridden forward during the advance and had recalled those six companies to Todd's Tavern to form a buffer between the Rebels and the rest of the brigade which had not formed yet.) The colonel did not have time to locate his missing companies. Forming his twelve men in column of four, he told the color sergeant to conspicuously display the flag and the men to raise as much dust as possible. The suddenness of their charge sent the few dismounted Virginians who had lagged behind scurrying for the protection of their side of the field.[130]

White and his mounted men did not stop running until they reached the wooded hillside behind them.[131] By then Thomson's and Johnston's Virginia Batteries and some dismounted cavalrymen had gone into position behind a makeshift barricade along the western edge of the field where the action had begun that afternoon. The "Comanches" regrouped in the road behind the guns and waited for the Federals who were having trouble managing their 200 man skirmish line in the thick pines across from them.[132] White's Virginians, who had shot away most of their captured Federal ammunition, did not want to rally in the road. The men complained about their predicament. They considered it suicide to stay there against apparently superior odds.[133]

Todd's Tavern

The 125th New York Infantry was sent into the woods northwest of the crossroads to back up the hard pressed cavalry.[134] The New Yorkers took up position on the southern edge of the woods.[135] Chaplain Ezra D. Simons (125th New York) nervously watched the cavalry fall back from Corbin's Bridge to the crossroads. He instinctively suspected a hot action.[136] Gregg reinforced the infantry with the 6th Ohio Cavalry and the remaining battalion (6 companies) of the 1st Massachusetts Cavalry.

The Brock Road, North of Todd's Tavern

At the same time, two miles to the north, fighting broke out in the dense woods to the left front (northwest) of Barlow's slow moving column. Almost immediately a thunderous volley roared through the woods in front of the breastworks along the road.[137] While Colonel Thomas A. Smyth was maneuvering his brigade into position along the Brock Road, about one and one fourth miles south of the Plank Road intersection, the II Corps artillery started rolling into battery on the high open ground east of its position.[138] Barlow had already sent word to Brigadier General John R. Brooke, whose brigade was still guarding the division wagons at Catharine Furnace to come to his support. The order reached Brooke at 4:00 P.M. He set his large brigade in motion along a tortuous back trail which he believed would take him to the Brock Road.[139]

Colonel Nelson A. Miles' brigade was stalled in the Brock Road, behind the artillery and Colonel Paul Frank's brigade remained at Todd's Tavern to cover the left flank near the Catharpin Road intersection.[140] An unfinished railroad bed slashed through the woods, south of Miles' left flank, about seven hundred yards north of the Furnace Road intersection. This left a dangerous gap between Miles and Frank which the Confederates could readily exploit.

Chapter Eight

"Give them Hell, boys."

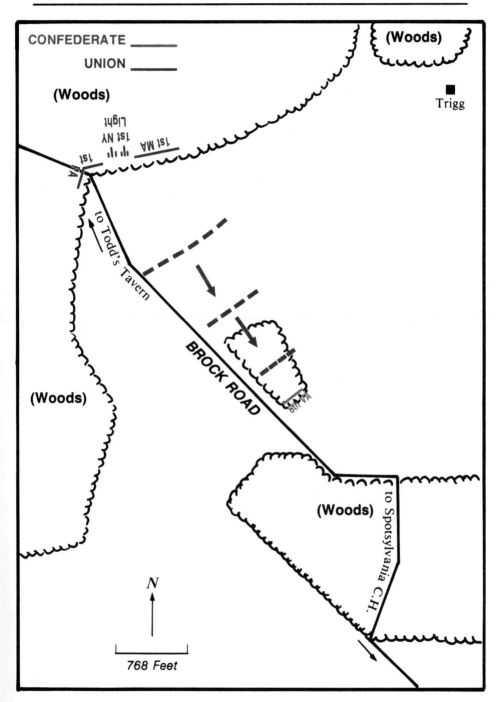

CONFEDERATE _____

UNION _____

(Woods)

(Woods)

Trigg

1st RI Light

1st NY

1st MA

1st PA

to Todd's Tavern

BROCK ROAD

6th VA

(Woods)

(Woods)

to Spotsylvania C.H.

N

768 Feet

MAP 38: 4:00 P.M., May 5, 1864 • Cavalry skirmish on the Brock Road at Alsop's Gate.

4:00 P.M. to Dusk

The Cavalry Engagement at Alsop's on the Brock Road

(3.0 miles southeast of Todd's Tavern)

Late in the afternoon, the 15th Virginia Cavalry (Lomax's brigade) left Spotsylvania Court House in column of twos and headed north ahead of the 6th Virginia Cavalry. The regiment startled the seventy man detachment from the 1st Pennsylvania Cavalry, which had spent the better part of the day picketing the Brock Road above the court house. The Yankees immediately bolted north toward Alsop's Gate.[1] The Virginians charged blindly ahead and chased the Yankees into the clearing around the Alsop house. The Pennsylvanians galloped into the woods north of the field where they intercepted the six companies from their own regiment which had just arrived from Todd's Tavern. The cavalrymen dismounted in the woods on both sides of the Brock Road along the tree line.

The dismounted Pennsylvanians caught the Confederates in the open and volleyed into the moving column at point blank range. The rounds struck about a dozen Virginians, among them Lomax's assistant adjutant general, Captain C. Powell Grady, who left the field with a bullet in his elbow. One of

The 1st Pennsylvania Cavalry stalled Brigadier General Lunsford L. Lomax's Confederate cavalry brigade at Alsop's Gate south of the Wilderness until Federal reinforcements arrived from Todd's Tavern.

(History of the Laurel Brigade)

the other Virginians was not so fortunate. A bullet bored through both sides of his mouth and ripped his tongue nearly off. His friends dragged him to cover, then sent him to the rear with his tongue hanging by a shred from his mouth.[2] The Confederates reeled about and scattered for the cover of the woods on the southeastern side of the property. They returned fire and settled down for some long range skirmishing. The sounds of their riflery echoed ominously south along the Brock Road for about a mile into the advancing column of the 6th Virginia Cavalry. Private Luther W. Hopkins (Company A), near the front of the regiment, had kept his eyes upon the two point men who were riding in the road about two hundred yards ahead of him. Suddenly he heard two distinct shots. The troopers halted. The men counted off by fours and dismounted. The number four men led the horses rearward while the rest of the com-

mand unsnapped their carbines and cautiously advanced in skirmish formation toward Lomax's relief.[3]

The battalion from the 1st Massachusetts Cavalry joined the six companies of the 1st Pennsylvania Cavalry along with two guns from the 6th Battery, New York Independent Light Artillery.[4] By then, the dismounted troopers of the 6th Virginia had relieved the 15th Virginia Cavalry on the skirmish line. From the start the 6th Virginia ran into heavy opposition. As part
of Company F stepped into the open ground in Alsop's field, the New York
artillery hurled two shells into them. One ripped off an enlisted man's leg.
The other burst above Company F, showering the advancing soldiers with
shell splinters. A fragment slapped the heel of a man near Private Samuel
Rucker (Company F). The fellow yelped loud enough to scare the man next
to him who asked if he was hurt bad. No, not hurt bad at all, the wounded
man grinned, but he thought it might hurt worse. His friends laughed at his
stupid response and pressed deeper into the clearing.[5]

The Confederates did not linger long at Alsop's. The dismounted Federals,
who outnumbered them, pushed forward into the field and started to herd
them rearward. Bullets zipped through the Virginians' extended formation,
hitting the men in Company A with slivers of bark and snapped twigs. Hopkins
and his cousin, Private James Dallas Leith, stuck together throughout the
retreat. Fighting from tree to tree, they shot at the Federals who were quickly
closing in on their position. At one point, they hid behind the same tree. A
bullet grazed Leith's lips as he stepped from behind his cover and fired. Turning to Hopkins, he exclaimed, "Wasn't that a close shave." A second later a
round grazed Hopkins' trigger finger just as he took aim.

The Virginians grudgingly retired to the rail fence which bordered the
southern edge of the woods north of the Brock Road where they laid down
to wait out the inevitable assault. Scattered Federal rounds slammed into the
fence rails. A carbine slug hit into the fence rail directly in front of Rucker's
head. He instinctively ducked down, considerably shaken. The impressive
size of the Federal force drove the 6th Virginia back to the crest of a small
hill behind their line.[6] The New Englanders pressed to within fifty yards
when the 6th Virginia opened fire. The shots ripped through the Federals
and forced them to retreat. For a while the field fell silent as both sides gathered themselves for another attack. When it did not occur, the Confederates
crawled over the fence on the crest of the hill and started to rifle two of the
Federal wounded, who had fallen not sixty feet from their position. One of
the Virginians jerked a photograph of a young girl from one of the injured
men. "I guess that's his sweetheart," the Rebel said, while showing it to a
friend. The Yankee, who was bleeding profusely from a bullet hole in his
chest, opened his eyes and painfully rasped, "No, it is my sister." Hopkins'
captain, stood nearby, staring at the two dying men when one of his troopers

observed, "Captain, these men came up to surrender, and were shot down." One of the two Federals loudly denied the charge. The captain ordered his men to carry them behind the Confederate line despite the Yankees' protests. They did not want to die as prisoners of war.[7]

Following the assault against the hill, the Pennsylvanians and New Englanders retired to the northern edge of Alsop's field and the Confederates generally kept themselves inside the wood line on the opposite side. The fighting fizzled into occasional exchanges of small arms fire which resulted in one dead and a dozen or more wounded to the Confederates. Once again Leith and Hopkins took cover behind the same tree. Hopkins saw his cousin kneel down to load his weapon when a carbine ball crashed into Leith's forehead and ripped away the front part of his skull. The boy flopped to the ground, his brain exposed to the elements. Orders came along the line to pull back. The 3rd Virginia Cavalry (Wickham's brigade) was arriving on the field to relieve the 6th Virginia. One of the troopers told Hopkins they should take Leith back to the rear. Hopkins would not hear of it. Why bother with the dead? They had their hands full with their own wounded. Hopkins' comrades refused to leave his grievously wounded cousin. Binding Leith's bloodied head in a handkerchief, the veterans half carried and dragged the dying boy a mile to the rear where they placed him in an ambulance on the Brock Road. (He lived another ten days, long enough for his father to come in from Loudoun County to be with him when he died.)[8] With the threat of a Confederate incursion from the south neutralized, the 1st Pennsylvania went on picket while the 1st Massachusetts slipped north to Todd's Tavern. The 3rd Virginia Cavalry posted an overextended picket line south of Alsop's Gate and the 6th Virginia retired to Spotsylvania Court House with the 15th Virginia.[9]

4:15 P.M. − 5:00 P.M.[10]

South of the Brock-Plank Road Intersection

While the front roared incessantly with musketry, the handful of skirmishers from the 40th Virginia infiltrated the woods immediately west of the Brock Road and took cover in a small gully within fifty feet of the Federal engineers who were feverishly reinforcing the berm of the road. The Virginians saw the southern end of Hays' brigade resting along the higher bank on the eastern side of the road and ambushed Company C of the 5th Michigan as it broke ranks for lunch directly in front of them.

Their disorganized firing startled Orderly Sergeant Harrison Caril (Company C), who swore several volleys were fired at his men. Company C, without orders, snatched up its weapons and bolted into the woods. The Virginians easily repelled the attack, forcing the Yankees to take cover in a ditch alongside the road. Several unexpected explosions crashed among the West-

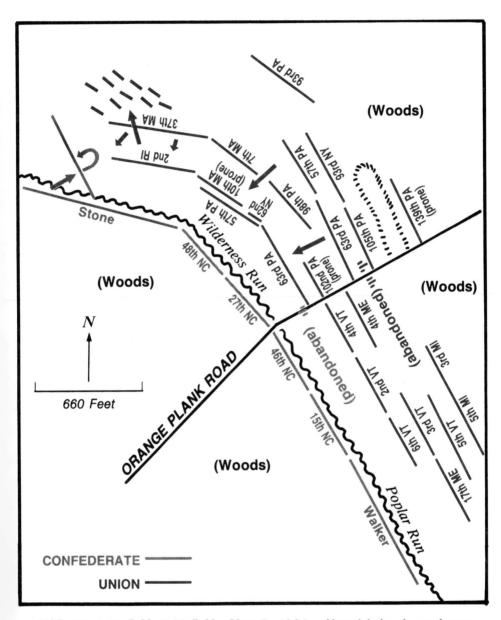

MAP 39: 4:15 P.M.-5:00 P.M., May 5, 1864 • Hays' brigade replaces Wheaton's men on the line and Stone's Mississippians turn the 2nd Rhode Island.

erners. Hot fragments seared flesh and knocked some of the Yankees onto their backs. The Confederates lobbed a few more hand bombs into Company C which stubbornly retaliated with rifle butts and bayonets.

Company C bought enough time for Colonel Lewis A. Grant, whose Vermonters were running out of ammunition, to bring the rest of Hays' brigade to their support.[11] Private Royster S. Marsh (Company G, 40th Virginia) carelessly rose from cover to drop one of the Michiganders when a minie ball crashed into his jaw. The bullet exited through the back of his neck. The impact hurled him onto his back where he lay helplessly upon his knapsack, unable to disengage himself from his harness. Blood rolled into his blanket, saturating it. His comrades retreated toward their regiment, leaving him to drown in his blood.[12]

About four hundred yards west of the Brock Road, the Vermont Brigade wavered. The 3rd Vermont and the 6th Vermont (on the left of the line), having sustained almost three hundred casualties, withdrew from the fighting which allowed the 5th Vermont to move into their position.[13] The 5th Vermont walked into a relentless firestorm of musketry. A bullet shattered Lieutenant Colonel John R. Lewis' left arm. His men carried him away immediately and the command of the regiment devolved upon Major Charles P. Dudley.[14] About the same time that Dudley took over the regiment, three of Hays' regiments came upon the rear of Grant's Vermonters and reinforced his line. The 3rd Michigan and the 5th Michigan closed on the backs of the 5th Vermont.[15] The 4th Maine moved into position behind the 2nd Vermont and the 4th Vermont.[16]

5:00 P.M. – 6:00 P.M.[17]

North of the Plank Road

The North Carolinians and the Mississippians across the ravine from Wheaton's and Eustis' brigades mauled those two commands badly. The 139th Pennsylvania, having used all of its ammunition, inched rearward to the eastern slope of a small hill behind their line while the 102nd Pennsylvania filtered through their formation and replaced them on the firing line.[18] The prone 102nd started absorbing hits. Bullets, whipping in close to the ground, produced a number of ghastly facial wounds.

Twenty-two year old Private Robert Harper (Company M) lost his sight when a minie ball smashed into his forehead above his right eye and literally popped the eye out of its socket. An incoming round struck Private John Keil (Company K) in the face. Destroying his left eye, the projectile passed behind his nose and struck him in the back of his upper jaw on the right side. Keil spat out his molar and crawled away from the regiment, too dazed to realize that the ball was still lodged in his jaw. Seventeen year old Private Caleb R. Foster (Company B) escaped serious injury when a ball cracked the top of his skull. (Back at the field hospital the surgeons quickly removed a couple of bone fragments from the outer layer of his crown and put him aside to recover.)[19]

Farther to the north, some of Stone's Mississippians flanked Eustis' brigade from the right front and ambushed the 2nd Rhode Island. Captain Joseph McIntyre (Company E) died in the first fire. Chaplain John D. Beugless caught a bullet in the wrist as he raced to the captain's side.[20] The regiment broke and ran to the rear. In the dark, ominous woods they could only see the muzzle flashes from the Confederates' weapons stabbing through the wall of trees surrounding them. The adjutant, First Lieutenant Elisha Hunt Rhodes, listened to the birds serenely chirp from the branches overhead as if nothing were occurring beneath them.[21] The 10th Massachusetts, on its left, was snatched up in the fighting. "Men fell like leaves in autumn," Lieutenant Colonel Joseph B. Parsons wrote.[22] Private Michael Moffatt (Company F) went down with a slug in one of his lungs.[23] Rather than retreat, the New Englanders hurled themselves to the forest floor and returned fire.[24] The remainder of Company H, having been pinned between the rifles of their own men and the Rebels, used the confusion to run to the safety of their own lines. Several of them did not make it. Second Lieutenant Alfred E. Midgeley (Company H) crumbled with a smashed right knee, which eventually cost him his leg and his life.[25]

The 37th Massachusetts lurched into the line vacated by the 2nd Rhode Island. The incoming rifle fire tapered off quickly as the Mississippians withdrew from the fight. The parting shots struck down Captain Joseph L. Hayden (Company H) and eleven enlisted men. Hayden was shot in the thigh and Private Clement H. Russell (Company F) came away with a bashed in skull and no memories of the action. (The bullet drove several bone splinters into his brain and left him blind and mentally disabled for the rest of his life.)[26] The regiment did not become further engaged for the rest of the day.[27]

In the meantime, the right wing of Hays' brigade approached the field from the Brock Road. The first line consisted of the 57th Pennsylvania and the 63rd Pennsylvania (from north to south) and the second line of the 93rd New York and the 105th Pennsylvania (north to south). The four regiments, in ascending the small ridge between them and Wheaton's prone line, moved over the top of the prone 139th Pennsylvania. Descending into the valley along the Wilderness Run, they walked into the small arms fire which passed over the 102nd Pennsylvania to their front. The two lines went to ground without orders. The 63rd Pennsylvania incurred several casualties. Shortly thereafter, Hays' first line rose up and advanced over the hard pressed VI Corps troops. Several feet beyond the prone 102nd Pennsylvania, they dropped to the ground and returned fire.[28] Two bullets bored, simultaneously, into twenty-one year old Private William Elder (Company F, 63rd Pennsylvania). One smashed his right foot. The other stove in the side of his face, shattered his forehead, and destroyed his eye. His friends carried him to the rear where the surgeons amputated his foot.[29]

"Give them Hell, boys!" someone from the 63rd Pennsylvania screamed. The oath of defiance rippled from flank to flank along the line. The Rebels responded with increased musketry. A ball whistled into Company B and thudded into Second Lieutenant Andrew G. William's left temple. It severed the muscle which voluntarily controlled the wrinkling of his brow.[30] Casualties hobbled to the rear from the Federal position in greater numbers. Willing volunteers abandoned their posts to drag the disabled over the hill behind them.[31]

One by one, Wheaton's regiments retired toward the Brock Road, leaving the defense of Wilderness Run to Hays' men. The 57th Pennsylvania, on the right front of the brigade, took a fearful beating. It lost 153 of 357 effectives, including its colonel, Peter Sides.[32] Unable to sustain the fight any longer, it withdrew from the firing and allowed the 93rd New York to crawl into its place.[33]

South of the Plank Road

In the meantime, Colonel Robert McAllister, whose brigade had been strengthened by the return of the 5th and the 8th New Jersey regiments, was pushing the 26th Pennsylvania into the woods on the left rear of the 5th Vermont as skirmishers. Leaving Major Samuel G. Moffitt (26th Pennsylvania) in command, McAllister returned to the Brock Road to confer with Mott, his division commander, who advised him to put Colonel William J. Sewell (5th New Jersey) in charge of the skirmish line. Mott said he would advance the rest of the division to McAllister's support.

McAllister's eight regiments climbed over their breastworks along the Brock Road by right of companies to the front only to have the woods destroy their regimental formations.[34] The long, needle sharp "cat thorns," which laced the scrub oaks together, savagely tore at the soldiers' uniforms. The Yankees forced their way into the more open woodland west of the tangle foot.[35] McAllister vainly attempted again to create a battle line.[36] Colonel William Sewell (5th New Jersey) sent the regiment's right wing (5 companies) forward to assist the 26th Pennsylvania. The remaining five companies fell in on the right of the brigade, at which point the 8th New Jersey moved into line on its right flank. The 7th New Jersey, the 11th New Jersey, the 16th Massachusetts, and the 1st Massachusetts completed the formation to the left.[37] The 6th New Jersey and the 115th Pennsylvania formed to the rear in support.[38] While McAllister's men struggled to the west, Colonel William Brewster's Excelsior Brigade sidled into the Wilderness from the southeast and was moving by the oblique northwest toward McAllister. In the dense

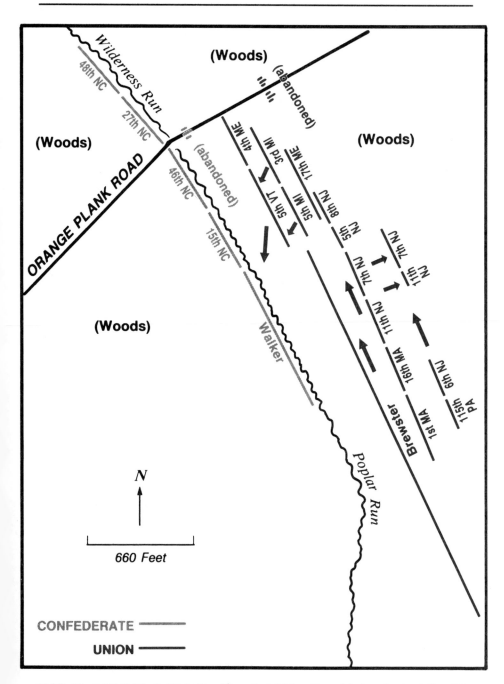

MAP 40: 5:00 P.M.-6:00 P.M., May 5, 1864 • Hays' brigade and the 5th Vermont attempt to turn the Confederate right along Poplar Run.

forest Brewster had no idea that his seven regiments were cutting off McAllister's advance.[39]

At the same time, Colonel Lewis A. Grant rode over to Major Charles Dudley (5th Vermont) and, pointing toward the saplings in the creek bottom, yelled something about the Confederate position being less protected there than it was farther to the right. Grant asked, Could the major and his regiment, if supported by the 3rd Michigan and the 5th Michigan, break through the Rebels' southern flank? "I think we can," Dudley gasped in reply. While the major passed the word along to his regimental officers, Grant trotted to the II Corps regiments behind him. Colonel Bryan R. Pierce (3rd Michigan) and Lieutenant Colonel John Pulford (5th Michigan) agreed to the plan. The officers got their men to their feet. The soldiers all the while cheered, "We will."[40]

Pushing his horse a few hundred feet southeast, Grant came upon Brewster's II Corps brigade which had halted on the eastern side of Poplar Run. Without introducing himself to Captain Abram L. Lockwood (Company A, commanding the 120th New York), he rode along the front of the regiment and told the men they were backing up another regiment, which was not too far to the front and that they should not load their weapons. With that cautionary note, the Excelsior Brigade shoved deeper into the Wilderness without deploying skirmishers.[41]

Simultaneously, the 5th Vermont with the 3rd Michigan and the 5th Michigan behind it, charged southwesterly into the swale along Poplar Run.[42] A chase started. Through the dense smoke First Sergeant Harrison Caril (Company C, 5th Michigan) saw a large number of the Confederates throw down their weapons and run.[43] Those who remained on the line, however, devastated the 5th Michigan, taking out many men and a considerable number of the line officers.[44] The corporals and sergeants moved into command positions and urged the men to press the Confederates back.[45]

Brewster's brigade closed to the right and the two Michigan regiments dove to the ground, leaving the 5th Vermont on its own.[46] The sudden movement of the Vermonters and of the Excelsior Brigade across his line of march constricted McAllister's front, throwing the 11th New Jersey and the 7th New Jersey into some confusion. Unable to maintain their regulation formations, the commanding officers of those two regiments were forced to yield ground.[47] As the 11th New Jersey reached a partially open ridge, Lieutenant Colonel John Schoonover pulled three of his companies to the rear and placed them in reserve, thereby allowing his seven remaining companies to maintain their original alignment.[48] His refusal to yield any more space forced Major Frederick Cooper to step his 7th New Jersey several paces to the rear which reduced McAllister's front by an entire regiment.[49]

The 26th Pennsylvania and the five companies of the 5th New Jersey had slowed down too much for McAllister's liking. He spurred through the woods and commanded the skirmishers to pick up the pace. A few yards deeper into the Wilderness, hostile rounds zinged over the brigade front. The Jerseymen and the Pennsylvanians on the skirmish line melted into the brush as they went to ground and McAllister sent his main line over them into the battle.[50] The 5th Vermont, with its two support regiments and the right of Brewster's brigade, overlapped the front of the 8th New Jersey. McAllister halted his regiments. The 8th New Jersey laid down to keep itself from getting chewed up like the Vermonters and the Westerners across its front.[51]

The Plank Road

Grant, having sent the 5th Vermont into the swale, did not remain upon the field. His two right regiments did not have enough ammunition with which to continue the battle. Their rifle fire had dwindled to almost nothing. The 2nd Vermont and the 4th Vermont opened ranks to allow the 4th Maine to move onto the firing line. After having lost over 450 officers and men in less than an hour, they had seen enough fighting for one day.[52] Private Wilbur Fisk (Company E, 2nd Vermont) felt a ball graze his left side as he stepped rearward. "Two inches farther to the right and that ball would have made an end of me," he wrote. He did not stop retreating until he reached the Brock Road.[53]

Across from Eustis' and Grant's brigades, the Confederates consolidated their men for a counterattack. Kirkland's North Carolina Brigade crawled into position behind MacRae's beleaguered men. The 44th North Carolina placed its right flank on the northern side of the Plank Road. The 26th North Carolina maneuvered into line on its right, with the end of its left company in the road.[54] The 11th North Carolina was next in line with the 47th North Carolina finishing the formation to the right.[55] Within a short while Major General Cadmus Wilcox's four brigades (Lane, Scales, McGowan, and Thomas) marched south from the Widow Tapp's farm to reinforce the Southern position.

The rest of Lewis A. Grant's brigade withdrew toward the Brock Road and the II Corps troops replaced them in the line. Grant dispatched his acting aide-de-camp, Second Lieutenant Horace French, into the valley to order the 5th Vermont from the field. The lieutenant never reached the regiment.[56] He had barely descended into the swale between the lines when Kirkland's and Walker's Confederate brigades struck the Federal line.

North of the Plank Road

On the northern end of Heth's division an orderly from Lieutenant Colonel Alfred H. Belo (55th North Carolina) brought Adjutant Charles M. Cooke away from the firing line with orders to report to Belo. Cooke found Belo sitting against a small poplar behind the regiment. Belo grimly told him that Stone was probably going to order the brigade to charge and he wanted Cooke and his former company, with Company C (the color company) to keep the regimental flag well to the front. Braving a steady fusillade of bullets, the adjutant trooped the two companies and alerted the men to the proposed assault. Realizing that it was suicidal to do so, they quietly protested. They would go if the colonel insisted upon it but they did not like the idea.[57]

When Lieutenant Colonel Alfred H. Belo (55th North Carolina) ordered his men to take part in a "forlorn hope" along the Plank Road, his men protested the order but said they would obey him anyway.

(Clark, III)

Henry Heth pulled the 26th Mississippi (Stone's brigade) from the left of the line and quick marched it south toward the Plank Road. It halted and went prone behind the 27th North Carolina, just north of the Plank Road. The corpses appalled Captain W. M. Graham. Some of the bodies lay on their backs or stomachs. Others had died in the act of firing, their corpses frozen in the kneeling position.[58]

While this was happening, Hays' brigade was moving into Wheaton's former position. The 63rd Pennsylvania held the left of the brigade with its left on the Plank Road. The 93rd New York was on its right. The 105th Pennsylvania and the badly shot up 57th Pennsylvania formed his second line (south to north) a short distance behind the first one.[59] Presently, Hays showed up between them. Passing behind the colors of the 63rd Pennsylvania, he rode another fifty feet or so and reined his horse to a halt. Private Samuel Dunham (Company K, 63rd Pennsylvania), who had rolled onto his side, fastened his eyes upon the old man. Hays seemed to reach for his sword but he pulled his canteen to his mouth instead and was fighting with the twisted strap to get a good swig of whatever he had in it.

The general's head snapped back under the impact of a minie ball which hit him into the forehead through the corps badge on his hat. Hays' hand convulsed upon the reins. His body swayed back in the saddle. The horse responded to the shift in the general's weight, wheeled about on its hind legs and raced toward the east, dumping the general's corpse upon the ground.[60] Twenty men from Company H broke from the line and ran for cover behind the ridge to the rear. The rest of the regiment followed soon after and the 105th Pennsylvania bolted from the second line into the first.[61]

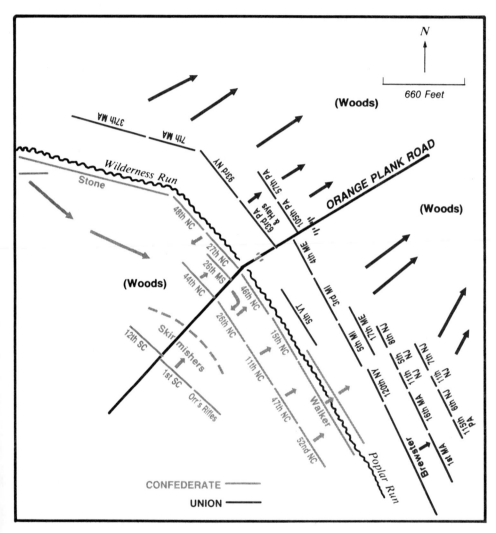

MAP 41: 5:00 P.M.-6:00 P.M., May 5, 1864 • The VI and II Corps troops are driven back to the Brock Road.

Colonel F. Marion Boone (26th Mississippi), across the swale from Hays' brigade, noticed the commotion to his front and to the south. Several minutes after the regiment went prone behind the 27th North Carolina, he tapped Graham on the shoulder. He told the startled officer, "Go tell Captain Gallagher to move forward."

The captain found Gallagher standing behind his company, staring to the front. The moment Graham spoke to the captain, a bullet thunked into Gallagher's forehead. The "old" Mexican War veteran crumbled to the ground without a word. Despite that sudden jolt to his system, Graham delivered the command to advance to Lieutenant Luther, then dashed to the left to rejoin his own company. The 26th Mississippi was up and running south by files before the captain reached his men. At the same time, the 44th North Carolina dashed forward to relieve the 27th North Carolina. First Lieutenant James A. Graham (Company G, 27th North Carolina) heard them coming through the brush when a minie ball whacked into his left leg about three inches above the knee. After making sure that the bone was still intact, he hobbled to the rear unassisted. The thought of landing a good sixty day furlough encouraged him to stagger a little faster.[62]

Lieutenant Colonel William T. Poague sent Sergeant C. R. Dudley, Corporal Samuel Handy, Private Perk Stewart and three other members of his battalion into the front lines to retrieve the abandoned 12 pounder from his Mississippi battery. Dudley stared intently at the prone infantrymen's powder blackened faces as he crawled with his volunteers up to the 44th North Carolina. The sweat rolled down over their cheeks, streaking their faces. Through the smoke, Dudley barely discerned the silhouette of the field piece. With the bullets sweeping the low ground in front of him, he did not want to act too rashly. He did not have to wait long. A long line of Federal infantry (probably the 105th Pennsylvania) materialized out of the smoke, seemingly on top of the guns. What was left of the 44th North Carolina fired a well aimed volley. The Federals "almost instantly disappeared before the unerring aim of that line of infantrymen," Dudley wrote.[63]

Major Charles M. Stedman (44th North Carolina) peered through the smoke from his hurriedly established firing line. He saw Richard's artillery piece, with its wounded and dead mounts still trapped in their harnesses behind the gun. Second Lieutenant Robert W. Stedman (Company A) noticed the gun also and loudly volunteered to drag it away if forty enlisted men would help him. The North Carolinians took off at a run for the gun at about the same time that the 26th Mississippi crossed the pike.[64]

The section of artillery which Captain R. Bruce Ricketts (Company F, 1st Pennsylvania Artillery) had placed in the Plank Road several hundred yards to the east swept the path of the North Carolinians and the Mississippians with canister. The blast of cast iron cut down most of Stedman's men before they reached their objective. Stedman went down with a canister ball in his body.[65]

South of the Plank Road

Hundreds of minie balls stripped the bark from the black jack saplings a few inches above the ground. As Major Charles M. Stedman (44th North Carolina) lay there expecting to die, with bark chips flying close to his ears and body, he suddenly realized how much the saplings reminded him of the apple trees back home and how, in the spring, the rabbits gnawed away at their bases.[66] He felt relieved to hear the order to charge.[67] Kirkland's brigade bolted into the open ground.

Walker's Virginians, Tennesseans and Alabamians, on Kirkland's right flank, fired at the 8th New Jersey, then swarmed into the low ground along Poplar Run.[68] On the northern flank, rifle fire killed Second Lieutenant Horace French's horse. The Vermonter went down with his mount. The Confederates snatched him up and dragged him into their lines.[69] Instead of facing left and

Lieutenant Robert W. Stedman (Company A, 44th North Carolina) and forty volunteers were cut down by canister when they dashed into the Plank Road to rescue an abandoned Confederate field piece.

(Clark, III)

reinforcing the 46th North Carolina south of the Plank Road, the Mississippians halted to let Kirkland's North Carolina Brigade pass through to support Walker's charge on the right. The 26th Mississippi, rather than get hit by more rounds, retired from the fighting. As they did so, a ball plowed into the back of Lieutenant Roberts' skull (Company A), killing him instantly. While Kirkland and Walker pushed the Vermont Brigade from the field, the Mississippians laid down to escape annihilation.[70]

Kirkland's brigade advanced over the prone 46th North Carolina and 15th North Carolina south of the road. Colonel William MacRae, commanding Cooke's brigade, was among the men lying on the ground. Captain Edward R. Outlaw (Company C, 11th North Carolina) heard MacRae sneer, "Go ahead; you will soon come back."

The 26th North Carolina, the 11th North Carolina, the 47th North Carolina, and the 52nd North Carolina (north to south), which had just rejoined the brigade from Parker's Store, drove back the 4th Maine. The Confederates threw themselves to the ground along the brow of the eastern lip of the creek hollow to protect themselves from a possible counterattack.[71] In the

Lieutenant Rowland S. Williams (Company I, 13th North Carolina) went into battle with his friend, Captain Robert H. Ward, singing "Lorena."

(Clark, I)

meantime, Walker's soldiers swept around both sides of the 5th Vermont. Major Charles Dudley (5th Vermont) found his regiment in a very tenuous situation. Surrounded by dense brush and darkening forest, with rifle fire stabbing the deepening shadows around his men, he quickly discovered that he had outdistanced his connecting units. The Confederates struck down his men in large numbers. In a matter of minutes he had lost over seven line officers and one hundred enlisted men. Captain Charles J. Ormsbee (Company H), commanding the skirmishers, did not leave the Wilderness. He died in the fighting near the Plank Road.[72] The scattered shots spattered up and down the entire division, catching Brewster's brigade by surprise. Sergeant James Kron (Company C, 120th New York) pitched forward from the regimental line – dead. The New Yorkers immediately scattered for the cover of the trees and hit the dirt. A minute later a volley crashed into the far left of the regiment, followed quickly by a second well timed delivery. The 120th New York, unable to respond with its empty weapons and too confused to load them, broke and ran toward the Brock Road. The rest of the brigade left the line, regiment by regiment.[73]

The Virginians herded the 5th Vermont and Brewster's Excelsior Brigade back upon McAllister's New Jersey Brigade, the 3rd Michigan, the 5th Michigan, and the 17th Maine.[74] Rounds slapped into the 11th New Jersey.[75] When the last regiment of the Excelsior Brigade scrambled through the woods on the left of the 1st Massachusetts, the New Englanders also quit the line. That regiment, in turn, collapsed the 16th Massachusetts. The 11th New Jersey, with the exception of Captain Edward T. Kennedy (Company C), the color guard, and the color company, abandoned the brigade.[76] Seeing the 11th New Jersey panic and scatter, the men of the 5th New Jersey retreated and dragged all of the 8th New Jersey with it. Only the colors and a few enlisted men, under the command of Captain George M. Stelle (Company F, 8th New Jersey), held their ground.[77]

The sudden assault alarmed Colonel Lewis A. Grant whose brigade had not yet reached the breastworks along the Brock Road. Having lost Second Lieutenant Horace French (Company F, 3rd Vermont) to the Confederates and, with his second aide-de-camp, Second Lieutenant John W. Bain, Jr. (Company G, 2nd Vermont) down with a facial wound, he and his assistant inspector general, Captain Addison Brown, Jr. (Company F, 4th Vermont) could not expect to rally his battered brigade. It sickened Grant to watch the North Carolinians ascend the slope which his men had held for so long and hurl themselves to cover among his casualties.[78] The Yankee dead lay so thick that Captain Edward R. Outlaw (Company C, 11th North Carolina) and his men used them as "unnatural" breastworks.[79]

In the twilight Wilcox's division came into line by brigades. Brigadier General Samuel McGowan's South Carolina Brigade struggled south through the forest to form in a brigade front facing east.[80] The soldiers found themselves stepping into a Dantean nightmare. Sporadic fires crackled and snapped in the woods along both sides of the road and toward the front. The flames flickered and shot upward against the darkening sky. Suffocating clouds of smoke drifted across the road, stinging the men's eyes. Dead horses, Federal corpses wearing the familiar yellow piping of cavalrymen, discarded carbines and the spent carbine shell casings which littered the place told Private Berry Benson (Company H, 1st South Carolina) everything he needed to know about the 5th New York Cavalry's running fight from that morning.[81]

The brigade fanned out to both sides of the Plank Road, several hundred yards west of the front lines. Orr's Rifles and the 1st South Carolina formed south of the road with the 1st's left flank in the pike. The remaining three regiments fell in north of the road with the 12th on the right. The 13th and the 14th continued the formation to the north.[82] The 1st South Carolina sent its sharpshooters east well in advance of the rest of the regiments and on the north side of the road.[83] As soon as the commands aligned themselves, McGowan ordered them forward. The South Carolinians shoved their way around and through the dense saplings and undergrowth, cheering as they went.[84]

Brigadier General Alfred M. Scales' North Carolina Brigade followed McGowan. First Lieutenant George Mills (Company G, 16th North Carolina) and his men struggled around the ambulances and supply wagons which clogged the Plank Road in both directions. To the left (north) he spied Poague's silent artillery battalion. Moments later, the brigade moved by column south into the woods behind Kirkland's stalled line and McGowan's moving brigade.[85] The 16th North Carolina placed its left on the Plank Road and wheeled into line.[86] Skirmishers fanned out to the front.

At the rear of the brigade Captain Robert H. Ward (Company I, 13th North Carolina) softly recited, "Years creep slowly by, Lorena; the snow is on the grass again..." to his close friend, First Lieutenant Rowland S. Williams (Company I). Williams clapped the captain on the shoulder. The captain grinned. Having recently recovered from his Chancellorsville wound, Ward confided in his lieutenant that he wanted a flesh wound so he could go home again to his wife. As an afterthought, the captain blew through his teeth, "Would to God that it may only be a flesh wound."[87]

In the Plank Road – Western Side of Poplar Run

Sergeant C. R. Dudley and his five volunteers from Poague's Battalion waited until McGowan's South Carolinians and Scales' North Carolinians had disappeared into the increasing shadows and the smoke from the east, then dashed into the road to haul in Richard's solitary 12-pounder. The artillerymen found three of Stedman's uninjured men trying to manhandle the gun around in the road. With bullets materializing from the woods to the east, the nine men defiantly shouldered the gun back into their lines. (It stayed in the road south of Tapp's until dawn the next day.)[88]

Chapter Nine

"What are our sabres for?"

5:00 P.M. – 6:00 P.M.

North of the Plank Road

Hays' badly mauled brigade withdrew from the fight, with the men shooting fitfully into the trees at the muzzle flashes from the sharpshooters of the 1st South Carolina. The Confederates came close enough to the Brock Road to spatter the 19th Massachusetts while it led Brigadier General Alexander Webb's huge brigade past the crossroads. The brigade deployed as soon as it came abreast of the Plank Road-Brock Road intersection.[1] The twenty man Company B of the 19th Massachusetts fanned out to the front north of the Plank Road as skirmishers with orders to hold back the Rebs so the troops in front of them could retire to the breastworks along the Brock Road for ammunition.[2]

The seemingly distant musketry on the left flank sounded like a storm to First Lieutenant Thomas J. Hastings (Company D, 15th Massachusetts). He gaped incredulously at the brigade column when it swayed off to the side of the Brock Road, like a sail flapping in a gale, to avoid the incoming rounds, and allowed Colonel Samuel Carroll's men to go into line. The small arms fire sounded like a gigantic waterfall cascading over a precipice and the 15th Massachusetts seemed to be in the midst of it. The regiment dodged back into the road before deploying farther north, and Hastings momentarily glanced over his shoulder. His eyes locked onto a woman. She sat astride a horse on the rise of ground east of the brigade, calm and composed. While the brigade disappeared along the earthworks north of its approach, the vision of his "stoic goddess" lingered indelibly upon his mind.[3]

Carroll's brigade steadily approached the Plank Road intersection and worked its way through Webb's meandering column. The ominous sounds of a severe infantry engagement reverberated through the woods on the left (western) flank.[4] The regiments rushed across the intersection and deployed north of and perpendicular to the Plank Road behind the stranded Company B of the 19th Massachusetts.[5] The two lead regiments, the 10th New York (on the left) and the 12th New Jersey (on the right) doublequicked by the left flank into the woods on a northwesterly course from the Plank Road.[6] The closely packed trees and dense tangle foot slowed their pace. The Yankees pressed forward more cautiously.[7]

South of the Plank Road

In the meantime, the skirmishers from the 16th North Carolina (Scales' brigade) stumbled over the prone 26th North Carolina. They pressed east through the Poplar Run swale and soon became engaged with the rear elements of Grant's Vermonters and Hays' left wing. Their shots echoed west over the rest of the brigade as it trotted into position. Brigadier General Alfred M. Scales' four regiments maneuvered into regimental fronts and

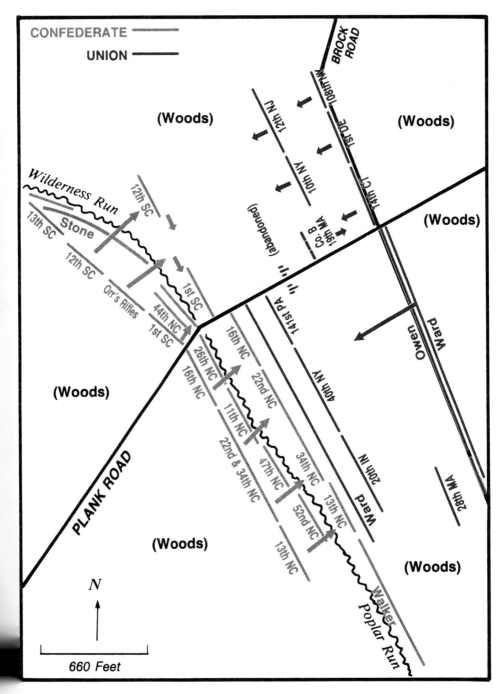

MAP 42: 5:00 P.M.-6:00 P.M., May 5, 1864 • Ward's men hold the Federal line along Poplar Run.

advanced. Colonel John R. Lane (26th North Carolina) could not get his battered regiment to move out with the 16th North Carolina, which was crunching through the woods behind it. He harangued his exhausted men with oaths. Some stood. Others laid down. The confused officers and men could not decide on what course of action to take. Lie down, First Lieutenant George Mills (Company G, 16th North Carolina), heard the livid colonel shriek, and let a fighting regiment step over them. The 26th North Carolina cascaded to the ground and the 16th North Carolina pressed forward.[8] The 11th North Carolina trailed into the fray with them, while Walker's large brigade doggedly surged ahead on the right front.[9]

Southwest of the Brock Road Intersection

The burst of musketry which drove Brewster's and McAllister's regiments from the ground near the Poplar Run, brought Ward's slumbering troops to their feet. Within minutes they were running north on the Plank Road to relieve Mott's division below the crossroads. The 2nd U.S. Sharpshooters (Berdan Sharpshooters) spread out in extended order, with their right flank on the Plank Road and slowly disappeared into the thick underbrush of the Wilderness. Unable to maintain contact with their men, the officers told the regimental musicians to direct the line in its advance with bugle calls. As they neared the swale along Poplar Run, sporadic Confederate rifle fire clipped through the trees over their heads. The buglers sounded "Fire at will." The line halted momentarily, then advanced. The Confederates opened fire upon the Berdans within seconds after they reached the open ground on the ridge east of the creek. The sharpshooters dove to the ground or dodged behind trees and did not sustain many casualties from the hundreds of bullets which cut the branches and leaves off the brush over their heads.[10] Ward deployed his brigade in two lines. The 3rd Maine, 86th New York, 124th New York, 99th Pennsylvania, and the 110th Pennsylvania jumped over the earthworks along the roadside and disappeared into the seemingly impenetrable woods. About forty-four yards farther east, the 141st Pennsylvania placed its right flank in the Plank Road to anchor the second line. The 40th New York and the 20th Indiana went into line on its left.[11]

Up ahead, Lieutenant Colonel Charles Weygant (124th New York) gaped at the scores of Federal casualties who stumbled among the trees in front of them. They mindlessly shoved and jostled their way through the approaching relief forces. A large portion of the non-wounded refugees from Mott's shattered division fell in with Ward's regiments, something peculiarly Confederate for the better disciplined Federals. The line passed over the sharpshooters and relieved Captain George M. Stelle (Company F) and his few stalwarts of the 8th New Jersey. At the same time Lieutenant Colonel John Schoonover (11th New Jersey) personally told Captain Edward T. Kennedy

(Company C) and the color company of the 11th New Jersey to rejoin their regiment.[12] The 124th New York halted with the rest of the line to realign itself.[13]

In the dense growth, Ward's men blazed at the muzzle flashes from Scales' North Carolinians who advanced more like skirmishers than organized infantry. The Confederates doggedly resisted the attack, refusing ground by the inches.[14] The Federals pushed their way through the woods. The 124th New York captured a few Rebels, who were surrendering, two or three men at a time.[15]

North of the Plank Road

In the labyrinthine woods, already obscured in a low sulfuric cloud of small arms smoke, Company B of the 19th Massachusetts found itself coming under fire from the sharpshooters of the 1st South Carolina who ranged across their left flank and the rear. The veterans knew immediately they could not hold their posts. "By the right flank, double quick," Captain John G. B. Adams (Company B) screamed. The startled New Englanders dashed to the rear much quicker than the prescribed 120 steps per minute. The Rebs were so close upon the Yankees' heels that Adams, in glancing over his shoulder, clearly saw them overrun and capture eighteen year old Private James Thompson (Company B). Another man in the command disappeared among the trees – wounded.[16]

Behind the New Englanders, the 108th New York, 1st Delaware, and the 14th Connecticut (Carroll's brigade) rushed into position along the Brock Road.[17] The three regiments flanked into the woods under the same unexpected burst of heavy fire which, coming in from the left and the left front, had also surprised Adams' men.[18] A stray round slammed into Private John Uzelmeyer (Company I, 14th Connecticut). The impact fractured his skull and destroyed his left eye.[19] The 14th Connecticut responded as soon as its last company cleared the Brock Road intersection. The men bolted over the natural earthen berm on the western side of the road and ran directly into a heavy volley along its entire front. The Confederates dropped thirteen enlisted men and two officers.[20] Private James Crinyan (Company H) received his third wound of the war as he limped into action. A minie ball glanced off the forty-eight year old's unbelievably tough skull. Bruising his scalp, it cracked his skull's outer table and gave him a headache which stayed with him for the rest of his life. Dizzied but conscious he turned back toward the Brock Road.[21] The shots which passed through its ranks struck home in the 7th West Virginia which was forming behind it. A minie ball struck Private John Mellott (Company D) in the chest, perforating his lung. He was carried from the field to the nearest hospital.[22]

The 14th Connecticut stumbled forward, groping in the increasing darkness to reform itself.[23] Their unexpected resistance sent the skirmishers from the 1st South Carolina scampering back toward the western side of Poplar Run while the South Carolina Brigade was approaching the field from the west.[24] The 1st South Carolina and Orr's Rifles anchored the line south of the Plank Road with the 12th, 13th, and the 14th regiments continuing the formation to the north of the pike. With more bravado than common sense, the Confederates lustily cheered and yelped long before reaching Heth's decimated brigades. "We should have charged without uttering a word," Second Lieutenant James F. J. Caldwell (Company B, 1st South Carolina) lamented. Bullets which whistled through or over Stone's and MacRae's brigades plopped among the ranks of the approaching South Carolinians before they reached the front. The regiments, fragmented by the terrible underbrush and forest west of Poplar Run, struggled more toward the left front in response to the terrible firing from that direction, pulling all of the regiments to the northern side of the Plank Road. Running over the top of the prone North Carolinians and Stone's bloodied men, they screamed louder than ever.[25] Berry Benson and the rest of the sharpshooters, who were being flushed through Wilderness Run valley at that time, looked up as the brigade crested the rise.

The approaching Federals in Ward's brigade saw them as well. A tremendous wall of flame rolled across the front of McGowan's brigade taking out a frightful number of men. Color Bearer Andrew M. Chapman (Company G, 1st South Carolina) spun around when a bullet slammed into his face. He staggered to the rear to have his wound bound before returning to the fight.[26] In the confusion the 44th North Carolina, which remained prone behind Orr's Rifles and the 1st South Carolina, volleyed into them. Orr's Rifles were huddled upon a knoll on the northern side of the pike making it a conspicuous target for the Yankees on the ridge across from them as well as from their own troops who were behind them. Presently, Lieutenant John H. Tolar (Orr's Rifles), found himself commanding the left wing of his regiment. A bullet bored into his head as he attempted to lead his five companies in a charge through the woods. He died instantly, fulfilling his prophesy to his wife that he would never see her again.[27]

Unable to charge, Orr's Rifles and the 1st South Carolina abruptly halted and loosed two poorly organized volleys into the smoke enshrouded ridge east of them. The Rifles could no longer endure the horrendous beating they were taking and retreated from the fight, leaving the 1st South Carolina on its own. The regiment shifted to the right to fill the gap. With the nearest troops over one hundred fifty yards to the north and no apparent supports upon its right, the 1st Regiment huddled lower in the belt of saplings on the western side of the swale and prayed that the Federals would keep shooting high. They did not. The South Carolinians started taking more hits and went prone upon command.[28]

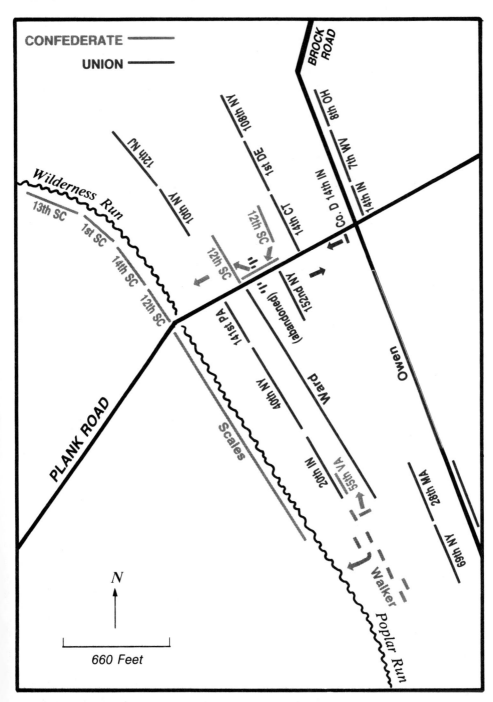

MAP 43: 5:00 P.M.-6:00 P.M., May 5, 1864 • The Federals secure their position on the Plank Road.

Private Berry Benson (Company H, 1st South Carolina) found his battalion on the right flank of the entire brigade with its right flank on the Plank Road. He stole into the road to get a better view of the situation east of the regiment's position. Everywhere he looked, he could only see the shadows of the forest. In the distance he believed he saw the silhouette of an abandoned caisson or a gun. He could not tell for sure which it was. A solitary Yankee suddenly loped into the open and took cover behind the carriage. Seconds later a ball whizzed past Benson who immediately replied in kind. The two exchanged no less than four shots at each other in a little over a minute – a shoot-out in every sense. A stray ball penetrated Benson's blouse behind his left shoulder. It grazed the back of his shoulder, burned a track across his back, glanced into the wooden frame of his knapsack and stopped there. By then, the fighting had worsened south of the road.[29]

South of the Plank Road

Less than a quarter of a mile into the Wilderness, Ward halted his brigade line and ordered the second line to entrench.[30] Lieutenant Colonel Charles Weygant (124th New York) stared at the thickest growth of saplings he had ever seen. Eight to fifteen feet tall with small tufts of leaves at the top, they were no thicker than a man's wrist. Ward's brigade pried its way through the springy stands and wedged its way to the opposite side, where the veterans saw Walker's brigade and Scales' rallied North Carolinians, who were waiting for them on the western crest of the depression.[31] Confederate riflery then hit the Federal lines. The 3rd Maine found itself coming directly into the line of fire. Private Ashbury F. Haynes (Company F, 3rd Maine) heard the distinctive zip of a minie ball pass over his left shoulder, barely missing his neck. It struck the man behind him in the forehead. The fellow's sudden death shocked Haynes. Before long the regiment was taking more casualties.[32]

The 99th Pennsylvania absorbed its share of the fire as well. Eighteen year old Private Robert W. Thompson (Company D) had turned around for a moment when a minie ball hit him in the back of the head several inches below his crown. The bullet impelled a bone fragment measuring one inch by one half an inch into the dura mater and stopped. His friends carried him from the field mistakenly believing that they would never see him in their regiment again. Sergeant J. C. Moore (Company H) reeled under the impact of a ball which gouged a groove across his forehead and scraped his skull but did not knock him down.[33] The 124th New York reformed with customary Yankee precision and unleashed a devastating volley into the Confederates, who threw themselves to the ground like cascading dominoes. A volunteer skirmish line immediately dashed forward to round up prisoners.[34] Ward's men successfully fought the Rebels to a standstill and for about half an hour the field became relatively quiet. Ward moved his second line forward to the relief of his first line.[35] The movement of the troops initiated a Confederate counterattack.

The 55th Virginia, on the northern end of Walker's brigade, flanked Ward's front line and prepared to take the 20th Indiana from the rear. Hobart Ward discovered the Butternuts crashing through the woods behind him and ordered the 20th Indiana from the left of the line to face to the rear to meet them head on. The Westerners withheld their fire until the 55th Virginia finished maneuvering into battle formation and had started their charge. Unable to halt, because of the momentum built up at the double-quick, the Confederates dashed right into the muzzles of the Yankees' roaring weapons. Color Sergeant William Richardson (Company F, 55th Virginia) went down in the fury. A comrade quickly snatched the colors. When the smoke cleared, the surviving Virginians were either breaking to the rear or dropping their guns to the ground. Sergeant William P. Thompson (Company G, 20th Indiana) coolly walked up to the second Rebel color bearer and jerked the flag from his hands. The Hoosiers took twenty prisoners to the rear.[36]

North of the Plank Road

The South Carolinians along the Plank Road first learned of the rout when demoralized North Carolinians inundated the road. "Rally! Rally!" echoed through the frightened men as their officers frantically attempted to rally them. Private Berry Benson (Company H, 1st South Carolina) heard men calling to each other by name, trying desperately not to get swallowed up in the mob. "This is Saturday evening market in Augusta," he heard himself mutter. The horde of fleeing soldiers destroyed the 1st South Carolina's formation. Noticing a couple of his comrades, Benson called them over to himself. Pretty soon he had effectively organized eight riflemen, himself included.[37]

In the meantime, the rest of the brigade attempted to advance east through the dense thickets. To the north, the 14th South Carolina and the 13th South Carolina ground to a halt in the rolling, entangled ground along the Wilderness Run. The 12th South Carolina, on the right, surged ahead, unaware that it had become separated from the rest of the brigade.[38]

South of the Brock Road Intersection

Brigadier General Joshua T. Owen's brigade arrived at the Plank-Brock Roads intersection ten minutes behind Carroll's men.[39] With words of encouragement from the rest of the brigade, who were not advancing with them, the 152nd New York, by column of companies, crawled over the breastworks along the Brock Road, formed and disappeared into the heavily overgrown woods. The underbrush disrupted their regimental line.[40] On the north side of the Plank Road, the 12th South Carolina, having passed the New Yorkers' right flank, engaged the 14th Connecticut in a fire fight. Almost immediately musketry, fired from the concealed 152nd New York, hit the Confederates from behind.[41] Struck from behind by rounds which they presumed came from the southwest, the South Carolinians faced by the rear rank, left wheeled into line parallel with the Plank Road, and blindly opened fire into the Federals whom they could not see.[42]

Back at the Brock Road intersection, the 8th Ohio startled a squad of South Carolinians in the thickets south of the crossroads, who had inadvertently penetrated the Federal lines. A few shots were exchanged and the Federals occupied the narrow, northeasterly running ridge at the Brock Road intersection. Second Lieutenant Thomas F. Galwey (Company B) mistakenly thought it was about 4:30 P.M.[43] The 8th Ohio shifted north, leaving room for the 7th West Virginia and the 14th Indiana to move into the line.[44]

In response to the ambush, Captain Francis Butterfield on Carroll's staff, galloped into the 14th Indiana with instructions to bring them forward. The Westerners struggled free of their knapsacks. Dense smoke from the intense riflery to the front smothered the road in a sulfuric cloud. Colonel Lewis A. Grant whose troops had been engaged in the battle before Carroll's brigade arrived, coolly rode up to Major General Winfield Scott Hancock at the intersection as the regiment unhitched itself. Sergeant Owen T. Wright (Company D, 14th Indiana) momentarily wondered how they stayed alive amidst the intense small arms fire, then brushed it aside as protection from the smoke screen.

Captain Washington W. Hulser (Company E, 152nd New York) from Owen's brigade pitched forward onto the forest floor, mortally wounded by the Confederate fire which swept above and below the Plank Road. The regiment broke and streamed back toward the Brock Road. A few paces to the rear, the frightened soldiers ran into Lieutenant Colonel George W. Thompson (152nd New York), who was standing alone with his drawn sword. Within several minutes, he and his officers had rallied the regiment. Not long afterward, the untried New Yorkers returned fire by the book. They sent several organized volleys into the trees along their front. The noise and the violence of their riflery calmed the men considerably. In all probability, they inflicted severe wounds upon the trees around them while damaging the Confederates little, but they needed the reassurance which the volume of fire gave them more than the actual knowledge they had killed any of the enemy.

With only silence in front of them, the 152nd New York ceased fire and retired to the recently deforested yet brush strewn ground between the Brock Road breastworks and the woods. Deploying a picket line, the bulk of the regiment laid down upon its arms on the right of its brigade. Captain Robert S. Seabury, the brigade assistant adjutant general, went to the exhausted regiment and, presenting it with the brigade guidon, he personally congratulated them upon their outstanding bravery. After he left, the soldiers continued to chatter and reassure themselves of their personal fearlessness.[45]

Meanwhile, Butterfield was leading the 14th Indiana into the crossroads. In the racket and the confusion, only Company D responded. First Lieutenant Charles H. Myerhoff (Company D, 14th Indiana) quickly concentrated on his objective – Captain R. Bruce Ricketts' two abandoned artillery pieces – and the impetuous Confederates who were racing down the Plank Road, between the Federal lines, to recover them. The Confederates beat the Yankees to the guns and were attempting to turn them about when Company D – having run two hundred twenty yards – slammed into them. In the melee which followed, the Southerners yielded the field but not before the Yankees suffered three casualties. Orderly Sergeant George Faucett (Company D) went down on the right of the guns just as the company overran the Rebels. By then the left of the regiment, responding to the sudden movement, had come on the line.[46] The 12th South Carolina beat a disorganized retreat back toward its jumping off point.[47]

McGowan, whose South Carolinians had been totally disorganized by their forlorn charge and by the fleeing troops from Heth's division, regrouped his men. The 12th South Carolina placed its right flank on the Plank Road with its left flank running north west from the road. The 14th South Carolina came next in line followed by the 1st regiment and the 13th regiment. Orr's Rifles, in the confusion, had wandered far off to the left along Wilderness Run, completely separated from the rest of the brigade.[48] As the South Carolinians maneuvered into line on the western bank of Wilderness Run they crowded Stone's position. Stone, who mistakenly believed he was being relieved by Brigadier General Edward L. Thomas' regiments, retired all of his regiments but one to the south side of the Plank Road. The terribly reduced 42nd Mississippi in the increasing darkness did not know that it had been left on its own hook. It remained upon the western bank of Wilderness Run a little under half a mile north of the Plank Road.[49]

North of the Plank Road

About four hundred fifty feet north of the Plank Road, the 10th New York and the 12th New Jersey descended the gradual slope toward Wilderness Run and the narrow swamp created by its drainage. They halted near the stream to wait for the rest of their brigade to come up, without knowing that they had passed north of the 12th South Carolina which had closed upon the Plank Road.[50] It seemed to take forever. The closely interlaced tree tops blocked out what sunlight was left in the day. First Lieutenant George A. Bowen (Company C, 12th New Jersey) noticed that it had already become night and that the regiment had been in position almost an hour.[51]

South of the Brock Road Intersection

For several hours, Barlow's division officers and their staffs busied themselves by riding up and down the Brock Road, acting important and forcing the dusty soldiers, who were working along the troop choked thoroughfare to construct cover.[52] Finally, as the 152nd New York took cover behind the breastworks on the Brock Road, Colonel Thomas Smyth sent the 28th Massachusetts forward into the jungle to the left front of Owen's brigade to support Ward's exposed left flank.

The New Englanders, his only regiment armed with rifles, had persistently drawn skirmish duty because of the accuracy of their weapons and this day proved to be no exception to the rule. They provided cover fire to the front against Walker's right flank, which they could hear but not see while the rest of the brigade entrenched.[53] Skirmishers from the 69th New York joined them shortly thereafter and for a while the fire waxed hot.[54] They started taking hits. A minie ball horribly disfigured Private Michael Murphy (Company G) when it smashed into his face. Tearing the skin away from his cheek it shattered his upper jaw and destroyed part of his palate.

Back at the Brock Road, a private in Company B, 63rd New York, was hit in his mouth by a ball which fractured his upper jaw immediately beneath his nose, split the carotid artery, and lodged in the back of his neck behind his tonsil. (Unlike Murphy, who survived and returned to duty much later, that man hemorrhaged to death on May 31, 1864.) Another man in Company B, Private Owen Fitzpatrick, was shot in the back of the head. The bullet penetrated his kepi, and ricochetted off his crown. The impact, which fractured his skull and left him with a piece of fabric imbedded in the one quarter inch dent in the back of his head, temporarily blinded him in his right eye. (He would survive the war but suffer from epileptic seizures until he died.)[55]

South of the Plank Road

Brigadier General James H. Lane's North Carolina Brigade was marching south by the flank into the woods below the Plank Road when unexpected rounds from a skirmish line struck his column from the northeast, where he assumed McGowan's brigade still occupied the ground. He immediately ordered Colonel William M. Barbour of the 37th North Carolina to wheel his regiment away from the rest of the brigade and go into line, facing north, along the northern side of the Plank Road. Simultaneously, Major Palmer (A. P. Hill's staff) told Lane to halt his command in the woods behind Scales' command, which was still actively engaged several hundred yards to the east. For several minutes, the veteran Confederates stood in formation listening to the battle. The trees reverberated ominously with a seemingly continuous, almost monotonous roar of incessant small arms fire. Around them nasty little brush fires snapped and crackled. In some places, pine trees, enveloped in flames, added to the hellish atmosphere. The eye searing heat of burning pitch and the black coal-like smoke of smoldering pine needles and burning sap combined with the sulphur of the gunpowder to darken the sky prematurely. The brigade was in the bowels of Hell itself.

That is where Lieutenant General A. P. Hill met Lane. Part of Scales' brigade had fallen back, Hill explained and he wanted Lane's North Carolinians to bolster the gap. He ordered Lane to connect with McGowan's right and to re-establish the line.

Lane cautioned Lieutenant Colonel William Lee Davidson of the 7th North Carolina to watch out for McGowan's men on his left and to not fire into them. He then gave the command to advance, which like most of the other movements in the Wilderness, began neatly enough but soon lost all of its cohesion.[56] The encroaching darkness, and the dense woodland disoriented the brigade, which veered much farther south than originally intended. The interval between Lane's left flank and the Plank Road widened from the original one hundred yards to five hundred yards. The 7th North Carolina, instead of connecting with the 1st South Carolina of McGowan's brigade, relieved the 13th North Carolina, which it found in the creek bottom, on the right of Scales' line.

Stray rounds, fired blindly into the darkness by the Yankees across from the two regiments, passed overhead. The 13th North Carolina right about faced to leave the field when a bullet struck Captain Robert H. Ward (Company I). He crumbled to the ground next to his first lieutenant, Rowland S. Williams. A quick probing found the entry wound in the back of the captain's right leg. The swelling around the knee indicated that the ball had not exited. Williams and another man tenderly struggled to their feet with the captain cradled in their arms. Ward had gotten his second wound and another sixty day furlough to his beloved wife.[57]

Lane's brigade filled out the line to the right with the 33rd, the 28th, and the 18th North Carolina.[58] To the north, Scales mistakenly believed that Lane's men were covering his brigade from the rear, instead of extending the formation to the right. He ordered a withdrawal. The command was whispered through the ranks from man to man to retire from the field. But, not everyone received the word to pull out. The 38th North Carolina, having become detached from its brigade before Scales and Walker assaulted Hays' and Grant's Vermonters, found itself wandering on its own behind Lane's right flank. Lieutenant Colonel John Ashford swung his regiment east and aligned it with the right flank of the 28th North Carolina (Lane's brigade) which forced the 18th North Carolina, under the command of Colonel John D. Barry, to shift to the right. It then shifted south with the 18th North Carolina almost to the northern edge of the unfinished railroad bed which ran east to west along the brigade's right flank.[59] Very shortly after it came on line,

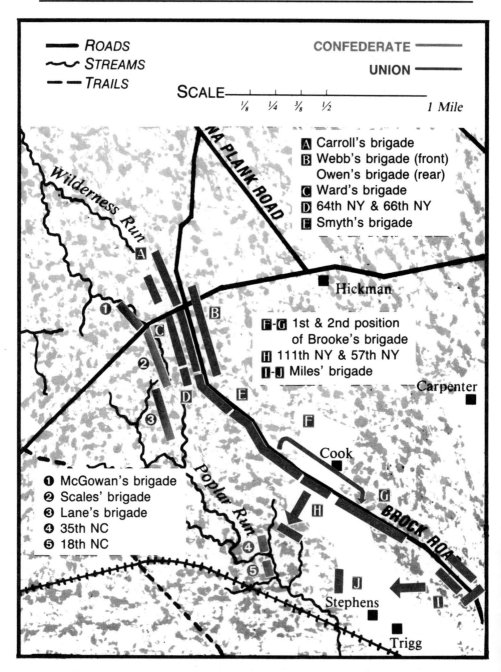

MAP 44: 6:00 P.M.-dark, May 5, 1864 • North of the Plank Road, Carroll's brigade drives back McGowan's South Carolinians. Scales and Lane hold their own against Gibbon's, Birney's, and Barlow's divisions of the II Corps.

Lane's brigade slogged east through the marshy ground around Poplar Run against an unseen enemy.

South of the Brock Road Intersection

Several times Barlow dispatched his staff officers to Smyth's Irish Brigade to assist its skirmishers. Captain Josiah Favill (Company A, 57th New York) and his fellow officers did not enjoy the work at all. The dense undergrowth snatched at his mount and, at times, physically restrained it. The suffocating, blinding smoke from the hundreds of discharged small arms blanketed the forest in a sulfuric mantle which cut visibility to about twenty yards in many places.

Presently, Colonel Nelson A. Miles' five regiments went into position near Smyth's left flank. The 26th Michigan, on the left of the brigade, sent two companies forward to the south as skirmishers while the remainder of the regiment laid down in the woods just west of the Brock Road, facing south. The regiment lost one man – wounded.[60] The 61st New York, and the 183rd Pennsylvania remained back at the Brock Road to entrench while the 140th Pennsylvania (on the left) and the 81st Pennsylvania (on the right) stepped into the woods west of the road and struggled through the thick vegetation to rear of the 26th Michigan. Facing southwest, those two regiments continued the brigade formation.[61] In moving into the woods, they did not contact Smyth's skirmishers who were to the north.[62]

Todd's Tavern to the II Corps on the Brock Road

Instructions had already gone down the Brock Road to Colonel Paul Frank, before 4:00 P.M., for him to bring his men up to Barlow's division. The 57th New York and the 111th New York were on their way north while he attempted to close further to the right and cover the left flank as ordered.[63] The right of his brigade – the 39th, 52nd, and 126th New York regiments – tramped several hundred yards to the right but did not get as far as the railroad bed. The men entrenched along the western side of the Brock Road.[64] The 125th New York stayed at the Catharpin Road to cover the army's flank.[65]

The Cavalry Fight Along the Catharpin Road

(5.5 miles southwest of the Brock Road intersection)

While the bulk of the II Corps maneuvered and fought to maintain its position along the Brock Road, the 1st New Jersey Cavalry doggedly played a cat and mouse probing attack against Rosser's battered cavalry on the hill east of Corbin's Bridge. Lieutenant Colonel John W. Kester, while keeping his color guard in the road, pushed his tiring skirmish line of two hundred fifty dismounted troopers (six companies) west. Thomson's and Johnston's Virginia Batteries announced their presence the minute the thirteen man

Yankee column left the cover of the woods and rounded the southwesterly bend in the road into the open where the fighting had started two hours earlier. Several rounds of canister tore up the ground in front of the Yankees, pelting the cavalrymen with clods of dirt. Undeterred, the Federals continued into the open ground until they suddenly became aware of Colonel Elijah White's mounted column in the road and the dismounted troopers who were massing on both sides of the guns.[66]

The New Jersey men wavered but their officers shoved them forward. From his position next to White at the front of the 35th Virginia Battalion, Captain Frank Myers (Company A), sighted the 1st New Jersey's regimental colors bobbing conspicuously in the dust cloud which the canister had churned up and mistakenly thought that an entire Federal regiment was charging down upon his small battalion. He panicked and turning to White pleaded, "Colonel, how can we fight those fellows with no ammunition? We'd as well have rocks as empty pistols." "What are our sabres for?" White grimaced while unsheathing his blade. The bloodied Virginians followed his example. With swords drawn and at their shoulders they galloped after their impetuous colonel who had already spurred his horse full tilt toward the advancing Northerners.[67] The dismounted Yankee cavalrymen heard the yelping Rebels and shattered rearward into the woods with the Confederates close behind.

Part way through the pines, Captain Moses W. Malsbury ((Company M, 1st New Jersey Cavalry) managed to get his squadron to horse. Hurrying his men into line alongside the road, they turned about and volleyed into the Rebels at close range. Simultaneously, Color Sergeant James Dalziel (Company B) wheeled about and, with a handful of troopers, countercharged the Virginians. White's men gave ground when the Federals blasted them at point blank range. The Yankee carbines cracked louder than usual in the confines of the woods. The pursuit lasted a few hundred yards when White turned his men about and raced into the Federals again. His skirmish line overlapped the disorganized Yankee formation and forced it to yield ground.

5:00 P.M. to Dark[68]

It took Brigadier General John R. Brooke's 2,300 man column an hour and a half to cover the three miles between Catharine Furnace and the Brock Road. Striking the road at 5:30 P.M., one mile below the Plank Road intersection, he was turned left and told to entrench that wing of Barlow's division. Moving south, he threw his regiments into line in the Brock Road and filled the gap between Frank's and Miles' brigades.[69]

Around 6:45 P.M., the brigade took to the road again, this time behind the 57th New York and the 111th New York (both Frank's brigade) and hauled north for half of a mile. The two New York regiments swung into position behind the earthworks on the western side of the Brock Road to the right of

Miles' brigade.[70] Brooke's soldiers tramped past and swung into line on their right.[71]

The Cavalry Fight Along the Catharpin Road

White's Confederates chased the remnants of the 1st New Jersey Cavalry, who by now had remounted, back to the clearing half a mile west of Todd's Tavern, where Captain John Hobensack's two companies from the 1st New Jersey and the 6th Ohio Cavalry, backed by the 1st Massachusetts and Captain Joseph W. Martin's 6th Battery, New York Light Artillery, rode into the open to reinforce their line. The 16th Pennsylvania Cavalry, supported by most of Colonel J. Irvin Gregg's brigade, formed in line behind the battery in support.[72] At the sight of their reserve, Dalziel wheeled again, and waving the colors, led the remaining skirmishers of the 1st New Jersey toward White's startled men in the road.

Some of the cavalry worked its way through the woods on the Confederates' right flank to cut them off. Captain Frank Myers with Sergeant Jack Dove and Corporal Jim Whaley (both from Company A) at the back of the 35th Battalion saw the Yankees cautiously trying to encircle them. Pulling their mounts to the south, the three Rebels rapidly snapped off rounds from their captured service revolvers into the dense pines and screamed commands to non-existent cavalrymen to charge the Northerners. The Yankees reined to a halt and blindly sniped with their repeating carbines at the shadowy horsemen to their front. The three Confederates returned fire for several minutes until the rest of the battalion came galloping back toward the Po. Myers and his two men fell in with the column and did not stop running until they reached the western side of the river.

Artillery shells from Martin's Federal battery whined overhead and burst in the air. Once the Confederate cavalry cleared Thomson's and Johnston's line of fire, back at the first opening in the woods, the Confederate artillery loosed a few parting rounds into the Yankee cavalry, who in the increasing darkness had slowed their pace considerably. One shell wounded a couple of Martin's battery horses. Another injured several men in the 1st Massachusetts.[73]

Dark: 7:00 P.M.

The Cavalry Situation South of Todd's Tavern

(3.0 miles southeast of Todd's Tavern)

Following the action west of Todd's Tavern, the 8th Pennsylvania Cavalry was detached to do picket duty along the Brock Road near Alsop's Gate. The regiment halted a short distance north of Alsop's and bedded down for an uneasy night in the pines which blanketed the area. The six companies of the 1st Pennsylvania Cavalry which had engaged the Rebels earlier in the day slipped behind them to get some much needed sleep.[74] The 15th Virginia used the lull to retreat to the woods about a mile south of the Yankees and rejoined their brigade there. The Yankee carbines accounted for two Confederate fatalities and twenty-one wounded.[75]

The 4th Virginia Cavalry (Wickham's brigade) walked from Spotsylvania Court House to the forward position and went prone along the edge of the pines as skirmishers to support the 3rd Virginia Cavalry which had replaced the 6th and the 15th Virginia regiments on the line. Every now and then a masked artillery piece roared from the Federal side of the field and showered the prone Confederates with branches and needles.[76]

West of the Po Near the Catharpin Road
(5.5 miles southwest of the Brock Road intersection)

Rosser's wearied brigade bivouacked on the western bank of the Po. The Federals had inflicted an estimated 173 casualties upon his small brigade while his men had accounted for over three hundred Federal losses.[77] The equally exhausted Federal cavalry retired to Todd's Tavern. During the night a courier from Major General Fitzhugh Lee arrived at Rosser's headquarters informing him of the inconclusive scrap along the Brock Road with Brigadier General David Gregg's Federal division.[78]

Along the Brock Road North of the Railroad Bed
Colonel Thomas Smyth recalled the skirmishers from the 69th New York and the 28th Massachusetts to allow the 64th New York and the 66th New York (Brooke's brigade) to cover his withdrawal. While those two regiments moved west through the brush, Smyth swung back his left flank toward the Brock Road, forming a right angled line.[79] In the meantime, Brooke countermarched his remaining four regiments – the 2nd Delaware, 53rd, 145th, and 148th Pennsylvania – south on the Brock Road to the support of Miles' brigade, anchoring the Federal left across the Brock Road near the unfinished railroad bed. Captain Josiah Favill (Company A, 57th New York), who was patrolling the forward position in front of Miles urged his horse west, away from the Brock Road. The darkness disoriented him.[80] Suddenly, amidst the racket echoing through the forest, a familiar voice hailed him by name. It was Lieutenant Colonel David L. Stricker of the 2nd Delaware (Brooke's brigade). Stricker warned him to wheel about and return to the brigade, which had halted in the Brock Road, facing west. He responded without question.[81]

Favill resumed his position behind the four regiments of Brooke's brigade while they cautiously moved a very short distance into the woods between Miles' command and Frank's two detached regiments, the 57th New York and the 111th New York.

Colonel Alford B. Chapman (57th New York) joined him and they trooped the line together. Chapman, who had left the regiment for detached staff duty, seemed particularly conspicuous in the colorful sash of the division's picket officer.[82] The normally affable colonel was depressed and somber. He confided to Favill that he feared he was going to die. His friend tried repeatedly to "shake him" of his premonition, but to no avail. Chapman insisted he was going to perish.[83]

To the north, the 64th New York and the 66th New York, under the command of Lieutenant Colonel John S. Hammell (66th New York), unsuspectingly stumbled into what appeared to be another Federal regiment which was moving by the left flank in files across their front. At first, the New Yorkers halted to yield right of way to the thin column as it crashed through the brush within ten feet of their line. At a closer look, the Yankees realized the men in front of them were Confederates. Hammell immediately ordered his veterans to open fire.[84]

Lieutenant Colonel William L. Davidson, believing his 7th North Carolina had driven Smyth's two Irish Brigade regiments from the field, carelessly advanced the left wing of the 7th north to exploit the situation. In so doing, he presented the battalion's right flank to the full front of Hammell's two New York regiments. The disorganized Yankee fire caught over half of the 457 Rebels at close range. Second Lieutenants S. Layne Haymen (Company E) and William H. Haywood (Company K), with three enlisted men, died in the tumult. Sixty enlisted men and Second Lieutenants John W. Ballentine (Company E) and Edward B. Roberts (Company I) hobbled away with powder burn wounds.[85] The New Yorkers charged into the badly shaken and bewildered Rebels and captured 37 severely jarred officers and enlisted personnel, including Captains John G. Knox (Company A) and Walter G. McCrae (Company C).[86] Second Lieutenant Newman Burkhardt (Company K) grabbed Davidson.[87] A sudden, head shaking burst of musketry from the southwest immediately followed the attack on the 7th North Carolina when the rest of Lane's brigade and the 38th North Carolina volleyed wildly in the supposed direction of the Federal lines. According to Lane, the musketry sounded like the violent roar of a fire in a canebrake.[88]

The unexpected shooting broke off the conversation between Favill and Chapman. Barlow spurred up to the two men, asking for a volunteer to investigate the commotion. Chapman responded immediately.[89] Seconds later, after he dashed into the woods, the North Carolinians killed him.[90] Favill, in the rear of the division, heard of his friend's death within minutes, but before he had a chance to absorb the doleful news, Barlow personally sent him forward into Brooke's brigade. In the excitement he temporarily blocked out what he had heard, like words spoken in a dream.[91]

Meanwhile, Miles' skirmishers, having advanced southwest through the woods to within sight of the unfinished railroad bed, collided with the 18th North Carolina and the 38th North Carolina.[92] Barlow, in response to the riflery, sent the 57th New York and the 111th New York from their position on the left of the 64th New York and the 66th New York to relieve the out-numbered skirmishers in the woods near the railroad bed. When they darted into the woods, one of the 57th's officers stumbled across Chapman's corpse. The sight unnerved him. He yelled, "Your Colonel is killed, avenge your Colonel!"

Bullets pinged and thudded into the two regiments from about one hundred yards. Sergeant Minard McDonald (Company H, 111th New York) stared at the sporadic gaps in his line. The thick underbrush and the billowing rifle smoke darkened the woods prematurely. His men could not see whom they were fighting.[93] Three times in half an hour, the New Yorkers charged only to find themselves facing more intense riflery than they had originally anticipated.[94] They took casualties, among whom was twenty-one year old Private Warren Slocum (Company G). He was horribly wounded when a bullet destroyed his left eye, left upper jaw, and his forehead. (Much to everyone's amazement he survived despite constant pain and dizziness.)[95] Outnumbered, the 57th New York fell back, with the men darting from tree to tree to provide cover fire. First Lieutenant Gilbert H. Frederick (Company B) watched his men drop to the forest floor in quick succession as the Confederates returned fire. Private Theodore Taylor (Company C) kneeled down behind a tree and was raising his weapon to get a clean shot when a round hit his chest and killed him. A bullet struck Frederick when he tried to roust several of his men from a cluster of trees. The enlisted men hurriedly picked him up and escaped through the woods to the Brock Road.[96] A rifle ball knocked nineteen year old Private William Seymour (Company G) to the ground. The bullet penetrated his face immediately below his left ear lobe, glanced downward, cut through his pharynx, struck his right collar bone and ricochetted out of his body without hitting his arm. He lay on the ground, unconscious, until a friend dragged him away to a field hospital. (When he regained his senses, he discovered that he could not move his right arm and he had no feeling in his face between his chin and his right eye.)[97]

Private Thomas Alfred Martin (Company B, 38th North Carolina), who was just north of the railroad bed, saw nothing through the interwoven pine and cedars on the southern end of Poplar Run. The sharp, nerve rattling cracks of the Federals' rifles told him his regiment was uncomfortably close to the Yankees, but he could not see the muzzle flashes to indicate their exact position. He watched Third Lieutenant Stephen H. Poplin (Company B) fall down among the trees wounded, but in the darkness Martin lost track of him.[98] Major James A. Weston (33rd North Carolina), whose regiment was farther to the left, stood with his men in the oozing mud of the Poplar Run creek bottom knowing full well that the Yankees were but yards in front of his position. Rifle bullets sang through the woods and randomly struck down men – among them Lieutenant Isaac L. Farrow (Company H). He bled to death in the leaf covered muck.[99]

Lane's regiments put up a determined resistance despite the poor visibility. His men freely used their ammunition in hopes that more was forthcoming from the wagons along the Plank Road. Behind him some of Scales' men had thrown together logs to construct a pitiful excuse for an earthwork. Private Berry Benson and his seven South Carolina riflemen from the 1st South Carolina found a regiment lying down behind the works. Stepping over them, they pushed toward the front until they ran into Lane's brigade. Lane happened to turn around in the saddle as the eight men rushed toward his position. Mistaking the squad for ammunition runners, he called out, "Are you bringing in cartridges?" The plucky South Carolinians pulled their cartridge boxes above their waists and flapped them by the cross belts. One of the men howled, "Yes, in our cartridge boxes." "That's right!" Lane shouted back.

The sharpshooters fell in with the North Carolinians, who were coming under a terrific fire. Benson distinctly noticed the absence of any large trees and the horrendous undergrowth he had seen elsewhere in the woods. The trees were slender and very close set. "Men were falling thick and fast all about," Benson vividly remembered, but "we could only now and then see one or two as they flitted here and there." Smoke hung in the trees and the area reeked of sulphur. Private Duncan Leach (Company G) disappeared in the woods, mortally wounded as did Private Eldred Rhodes (Company G) a few minutes later. Benson estimated the Carolinians fought with the Federals for about an hour, with neither side daring to charge. At one point the Southern line buckled but the officers pushed the men back into the ranks and it held. The shooting ceased around 8:00 P.M.

After obtaining a note from the North Carolina officer nearest to them explaining their absence from their own regiment, Benson and his five remaining sharpshooters picked their way through the woods toward the Plank Road. The note clearly stated that the South Carolinians had remained with the Tar Heels and had not deserted.[100]

Chapter Ten

"Grant will whip! Grant will whip!"

Night
Saunders Field, South of the Orange Turnpike
Colonel Samuel Leonard's Brigade

The brief foray into Saunders Field had been a costly one. The 104th New York took two casualties. The 39th Massachusetts accounted for seventeen more. The 16th Maine, being one of the regiments closest to the pike and the guns, came back without twenty enlisted men and one officer – all of whom were taken prisoner, which raised their casualties to forty for the day.[1] Almost immediately a call went out for volunteers for picket duty. Private Channing Whittaker, (Company B, 39th Massachusetts) stepped forward. He found himself nearly halfway down the eastern side of the swale. He was scared. The dying sun savagely glared at him. He felt his heart thumping in his chest.

Lieutenant Colonel Charles L. Pierson nearly scared him to death. He bounced down to the frightened sentry as if he were tripping about on a Sunday outing. He spoke pleasantly to Whittaker, then handed him his field glass and asked if he would like to see the abandoned guns with it. Whittaker looked long and hard at the silent field pieces. The colonel took the glasses back and quietly returned to the regiment. For some unexplainable reason, the private's fear left him for the evening. He spent the entire night on duty, unafraid and unmolested.[2]

In the woods north of Saunders Field, Company A of the 49th Pennsylvania drew picket duty. The occasional shots which whistled through the night into the trees around Sergeant Alfred Thompson (Company A, 49th Pennsylvania) did not disturb him. He went on duty, despite his leg wound, with a genuine enthusiasm. After the fighting subsided at dark and the regiment returned to its position in the woods, the sergeant limped toward the hospitals along the Germanna Road. He happened across Major General John Sedgwick, the VI Corps commander, who asked him about his wound. When Thompson told him it was minor, Sedgwick told him to return to his regiment to inspire his men. Thompson turned around and comforted himself with the thought that had the general known there were no surgeons on the battle line he would never have sent him back.[3]

Several hundred yards to the west, the Confederates nestled down behind their works and tried to sleep. The acrid smoke of burning brush and trees mingled with the gut wrenching smell of frying flesh. Flames crackled and snapped in the woods between the lines. Wounded men, unable to escape the fires, screamed piteously for help which would not come to them.

15th New Jersey
On the Hill, Northeastern Side of Saunders Field

The pleas of the wounded and the dying for water nearly drove the New Jersey men insane. Not long after dark, a long, thundering volley rolled from the right flank of the VI Corps to the front of the regiment. It took the greatest exertion from the officers and sergeants to keep the men and the troops massed behind them from responding to what they mistook for enemy rifle fire. The Confederates were too close to the 15th New Jersey's pickets. When they sniped at Captain Ellis Hamilton's skirmishers (Company F), Colonel William H. Penrose sent the captain a message to cease fire. Twice, Hamilton informed the colonel that the Rebels were doing the shooting, not his men.[4]

Brigadier General John Pegram's Brigade
In the Woods, North of Saunders Field

In front of Pegram's line, the wounded and the dying Yankees moaned continuously. Owls hooted ominously in the trees and the persistent whippoorwills serenaded them all night. "All firing had ceased." Captain Samuel Buck (Company H, 13th Virginia) noted, "The loneliness is of itself sufficient, and these birds seemed to mock our grief, and laugh at the groans of the dying." He hated the whippoorwill for the rest of his life and referred to its call as "the most hideous of all noises that I ever heard on a battle field."[5] Private George Peyton (Company A), having been under fire for the first time, had no appetite for looting the dead Union soldiers in front of the regiment's works. He watched his comrades slip over the headlogs into the woods but declined to go with them. "As I had more than I wanted to take, I did not try to get anything more," he entered in his diary.[6]

First Lieutenant Robert D. Funkhouser (Company D, 49th Virginia) tried to blot out the shrieks of the wounded between the lines. Unable to stay awake, the exhausted officer fell asleep while his men reinforced the earthworks around him. He awoke with a start when Captain John B. Updike jabbed him in the ribs. Updike remonstrated him sharply, "Here you are asleep when the men are all working to make the breastworks stronger. You ought to be up to superintend your part of the line." "Oh," Funkhouser groggily moaned. The captain walked away and the lieutenant dropped off again, not to be awakened for the rest of the evening.[7]

In the 13th Virginia, Buck found himself on picket duty despite his protests that it was not his turn to go out. Under orders to establish a picket line as close to the Federals as possible, he stumbled over the Yankee casualties, who lay too close together to avoid. He halted his men when they were within speaking distance of the Yankee outposts. Neither side wanted to engage in combat. Their mutual silence clearly indicated that they had seen enough killing for one day. The captain ordered his men not to fire unless they absolutely had to do so. He did not want to get caught between two fires because of a stupid mistake. He remembered seeing one incident during the night when the Confederates fired for fifteen minutes into their own pickets. He did not want to die that way. By 10:00 P.M. Buck had established contact with the pickets on both flanks. He then waited to be relieved as promised. But his relief never arrived. He kept himself awake by constantly walking from one end of his outpost to the other, knowing full well that in the morning, when an attack came, he would be the first one hit.[8]

An hour or two after sunset, a skirmisher darted into the 52nd Virginia blurting, "Boys, you just ought to see how the Yankees are momicked up out there in the brush." In the moonlight, Captain James Bumgardner, Jr. (Company F) stole into the thickets where the 110th Ohio and the 6th Maryland had so stubbornly tried to hold their own. The ghastliness of the area took the veteran captain aback. He had never seen the dead and the wounded so closely packed together. He suspected that the rear lines had stayed their ground and therefore created a massed front for the Confederate bullets. All things considered, the 52nd had fared well with only two or three men wounded. The captain returned to his regiment. That night, the men reinforced their earthworks. A working party cleared a field of fire fifty yards wide along the brigade's front. In addition, Captain Bumgardner had his men blaze the trees on the Yankee side of the clearing at the proper height to make their shots count. He then instructed his soldiers to aim below the blazes when the Federals again attacked.[9]

Near Lacy's

As night enveloped the woods, Captain James G. Grindlay (Company D, 146th New York), the senior surviving officer of the regiment, ordered his Zouaves to their feet for roll call. The men sullenly fell in around the tattered colors. Their powder blackened eyes and blank expressions reflected the soul draining effects of shock and fatigue. They muttered "Here" to the officer calling the roll. Of the twenty-four commissioned officers and 556 enlisted men who went into action at noon, only ten officers and 254 enlisted men responded to the call. In an estimated ten minutes of combat, the 146th New York had lost 55 percent of its personnel – approximately thirty-two men per minute. Over two hundred of the men were listed as missing or captured.[10] The 146th New York, as far as the fighting in the Wilderness was concerned, was *hors de combat*.

The 140th New York, which had led the assault of Ayres' brigade that morning had fared just as badly. Of the 529 officers and men who had marched onto the field that day only 49 percent mustered around the colors that evening in the regiment's bivouac north of Lacy's. The men grimly rounded up the knapsacks of those confirmed wounded and sent them back to the division hospital. The rest of the unclaimed knapsacks and haversacks they distributed among themselves. Colonel George Ryan, the major, Captains Porter Farley (Company B) and Allen McMullin (Company D), one other captain and five lieutenants remained on active duty. Porter Farley summed up the mood of the bloodied regiment when he wrote, "A terrible gloom spread like a black pall over the remnant which gathered together at our rallying place and looked upon those ten piles of unclaimed knapsacks, the only visible reminder of the lost."[11]

The North Side of Saunders Field

The 37th Virginia, having finally arrived from picket duty along the Rapidan, tottered into Steuart's brigade too late to get involved in any of the fighting. While the regiment stood in the Culpeper Mine Road awaiting orders to deploy to the far left to support Pegram's brigade, the footsore soldiers gazed at the pitifully distorted corpses which the stretcher crews had placed side by side along the road.[12] Private James Huffman (Company I, 10th Virginia), who had stumbled into his regiment after a strenuous trek of over twenty miles, momentarily forgot the discomfort of his growling stomach as he gaped at the graying corpses of several officers and men with whom he had served before this day. He noticed Colonel Edward T. H. Warren's stiffening body first, then that of his captain, Samuel A. Sellers (Company I). "All these men had stood together with us in so many hard-contested battles," he grieved, "but they would no more unsheathe their swords or raise their voices in battle-cry in defense of rights, home, and liberty." He hunkered down next to his dead friends to eat, undisturbed by their presence, fully aware of how calloused he had become. He was a veteran. While the 37th Virginia tramped farther north, Huffman moved on to rejoin his regiment.[13] Yankee casualties blanketed the ground in front of the 10th Virginia. The deteriorating condition of the corpses disturbed the allegedly "hardened" Huffman. In short order, they had bloated and turned black. The rank and file attributed the discoloration to intemperate whiskey guzzling. Huffman did not need to understand why they had discolored. He only knew that they had and their present state made him ill.[14]

Captain Emmett E. DePriest (Company H, 23rd Virginia) staggered into the brigade well after dark, bringing with him his inebriated soldiers and their equally drunken prisoners. Propping himself against a nearby tree to steady himself, DePriest garrulously reported his "separate operations" to a slightly bemused Captain McHenry Howard (Steuart's staff). Howard listened halfheartedly to DePriest.

The cries of the wounded and the dying between the lines eerily resonated through the blackened woods. It seemed to the ever sensitive Howard, that the injured, who normally bore their suffering in silence, could not restrain themselves. He remorsefully penned years later, "...their moans and cries were painful to listen to. In the still night air every groan could be heard and the calls for water and entreaties to brothers and comrades by name to come and help them..." went on throughout the night. Twice, Howard attempted to retrieve a couple of men. Hostile rifle fire thwarted his efforts. He laid himself down to sleep with their strained pleas for aid ringing in his head and he would awake the next morning with the moans still echoing overhead.[15]

The memory of a Confederate artillery piece nearly running over him that afternoon, seemed like an apparition to the exhausted First Sergeant Louis Dugal (Company F, 146th New York). When he awoke, after dark, it was to find a Rebel infantryman straddling him with the muzzle of a rifle pointed at his head. The Reb threatened to kill him if he gave the alarm. After robbing Dugal of his watch, pipe, and other personal effects, the brigand departed. Not long after, an officer who identified himself as Lieutenant John A. Morgan (Company A, 1st North Carolina) stumbled across the terribly wounded private and stayed by his side throughout the night.[16]

Lieutenant John A. Morgan (Company A, 1st North Carolina) spent the evening of May 5 with the badly wounded Sergeant Louis Dugal (Company F, 146th New York) to protect the sergeant from Confederate looters.

(Clark, I)

The Southeastern Edge of Saunders Field

Down near the southern end of Saunders Field, Sergeant "Jim" Stearns (Company K, 13th Massachusetts) patiently listened to the fires crackle and flare in the woods north of the regiment. In the distance, he heard a wounded man plead incessantly for help. Every time someone attempted to get to the fellow, they drew fire from the Confederate pickets.[17] While the regiment lay in its briar patch, the misplaced Company D and its tired first lieutenant, Edward F. Rollins, finally wandered into the ranks.

Having been abandoned on the northern side of the turnpike earlier that afternoon, he had kept his men on skirmish duty until relieved by some newly arrived troops. He returned his men to the pike only to be ordered back to Lacy's. When he arrived there, someone told him he could find the brigade in the woods where it had gone that afternoon. As the company wearily tramped west in the road through the scores of wounded who were returning from the front, one of them, a disheveled, panic stricken fellow attracted Rollins' attention. He was First Sergeant William Rawson (Company K). The lieutenant grabbed the terrified sergeant by the arm and jerked him around to face him. Where was the regiment? the frustrated lieutenant demanded. All cut up. Worst fight he had ever seen, the barely coherent Rawson gasped. Hardly any men left. Rollins released his grip, confused as to what he should do. He decided to lead his company into the field and assist the regiment with the evacuation of the wounded. Near the woods, he came across a brigade staff officer who directed him to the regiment's position. That officer relieved Rollins' mind about the severity of the engagement.[18] Eleven casualties did not indicate serious participation in a general engagement.[19]

Colonel Charles W. Tilden (16th Maine) sent First Lieutenant Abner Small back into the forest to locate stragglers. Not too far behind the line, he tripped over several of them, all of whom were frightened into nearly catatonic states. The adjutant understood their anguish and patiently reassured them they would feel more secure if they returned to their companies. They would thank him later on for going back. Each man feebly reassured Small they would return. He stayed momentarily to watch them stagger to their wobbly legs and stumble west. "I didn't blame them for dreading the return," he wrote.

Confederate shells arched through the night sky overhead like gigantic fireflies as he pushed his way through the undergrowth toward the northern side of the Orange Turnpike. Every now and then a projectile would burst among the trees and catch the leaves on fire. Each time the ground would briefly erupt into flame then the fire would die out and darkness would envelope him again. In the flare of a nearby explosion, the white blooms of a flowering dogwood tree distracted him, then it too disappeared in the foreboding darkness. The woods stank of burning leaves and smoldering branches. Small stumbled over an unseen obstacle and tumbled forward onto his hands, pushing a pile of glowing leaves into a spurt of flame. The quick fire ignited the beard of a dead sergeant who lay nearby. The corpse's hair immediately melted and singed, revealing a ghastly gray face whose wide open, cold eyes shocked the lieutenant to his feet.

Small did not stop running until he found the 16th Maine again. He felt secure with his men on that stinking, smoky night. In the endless darkness, between the armies, he distinctly heard the wounded pleading for help. No one dared go to their assistance. The Rebs were too edgy. Experience had taught the veterans not to risk their lives for someone who was probably going to die anyway.[20]

The 21st Virginia
Near the Orange Turnpike, West of Saunders Field

Shortly before nightfall, Steuart's Confederate brigade had slipped north of the Orange Turnpike to the earthworks along the Culpeper Mine Road. The men bedded down with their weapons and fell into a deep sleep. Shortly after midnight, an officer gently shook the exhausted Sergeant John Worsham

(Company F, 21st Virginia) awake. He wanted Worsham to deliver a directive to the officer in charge of the picket line. "Take no weapons, be extremely quiet, and take your time," the officer warned him.

Worsham nervously slipped east into the pine thicket where the fighting had begun that morning. No moon light filtered through the interlaced branches. "I could almost feel the darkness," he recalled. As he slithered through the low hanging branches, something snatched his footing from him and hurled him onto his face with a tremendous racket. Almost immediately, hundreds of rifles echoed into the darkness and minie balls snipped the pine needles off the trees above his head. Worsham froze as low to the ground as he could get. The shooting stopped as abruptly as it began. Worsham sat upright and cautiously probed the ground with his hands. He had tripped over a sword which was still attached to the corpse's belt. In falling, he had rattled the sword against the dead man's canteen.

Worsham quickly reported the incident to the officer of the skirmish line, a friend of his, who quietly chuckled at his story. With a warning not to start another ruckus, Worsham disappeared back into the trees, determined to retrace his steps back to the corpse. He found him. Removing the sword, he proceeded to methodically loot the man's pockets. He found a knife, a pipe, a length of string, and, more importantly, plenty of tobacco. The dead man had smoking tobacco in every pocket. Pleased with his "find," the happy noncom scurried back to his regiment.[21]

Brigadier General Truman Seymour's Brigade
The Woods North of Saunders Field

Lieutenant Colonel Thomas Hyde (7th Maine) of Sedgwick's staff spent the entire night wandering about in the briar patches of the Wilderness. Having delivered a message to Seymour after dark, he had turned to go back to headquarters and promptly got lost. Every now and then he stumbled upon isolated groups of soldiers and listened carefully to their dialects before approaching them. The night's adventure cost him his hat. Cut all over by thorns and soaking wet because he had fallen into a stream or two, he found his fellow officers at daylight sleeping in the Germanna Road.[22]

Somewhere along that same road, Captain Albert Nickerson (Company E, 7th Maine) awoke with the taste of warm medicinal whiskey burning his throat and equally warm water splashing his face. He opened his pained eyes to see Chaplain Norman Fox (77th New York) leaning over him with a canteen in each hand. Seconds later he found himself being hoisted up on his stretcher and slid onto the floor of an ambulance next to another wounded officer. To his surprise it was his own lieutenant, Webber, whom he had turned the company over to at the time he was shot through both legs.[23]

Sergeant John P. Beech and Private John Duncan (both from Company B) wandered a considerable distance from the left flank of the 6th Maryland before they came across the 4th New Jersey, which had gone prone behind the 43rd New York. The terribly absent-minded Duncan wandered along the rear rank looking for Private Jerome Cunningham (Company B). Whenever Duncan complained about losing something he had misplaced, Cunningham would confront him with, "What's the matter now, Duncan; lost your tin cup?" The untried Duncan found his antagonist hugging the ground as if he were molded into it. Nudging the veteran with his toe, Duncan quipped, "What's the matter, Cunningham; lookin' for your tin cup?" Cunningham said nothing in response.[24]

The Prisoner Pen Near Grant's Headquarters

Major Henry Handerson (Stafford's staff) and the courier bedded down for the night under the shelter half which the Yankee provost marshal, Brigadier General Marsena Patrick, had personally given to him shortly after his internment. Overlooking the catcalling and the indignity of having been searched by an enlisted man within sight of Grant's headquarters, he had resigned himself to his fate and had decided to make the best of a miserable situation.[25]

Brigadier General John B. Gordon's Brigade
In the Woods South of the Orange Turnpike

The humiliated men of the 7th Pennsylvania Reserves did not say anything to their captors until Major James D. Van Valkenburg (61st Georgia) turned them over to the provost guard in the Confederate rear lines. They talked freely. Having been sent into the open field to relieve their retreating troops, they believed that Gordon's brigade had actually cut them off. Only one man escaped, they insisted – the runner sent to inform their division headquarters that they could not find the troops which they were supposed to support. They felt even more humiliated when the Rebel major took a receipt for forty officers and 474 enlisted personnel, an exaggeration of 211 men.[26]

Colonel Clement A. Evans (31st Georgia) returned his twenty men back into the reassembled brigade after dark. "Boys, this beats Gettysburg," their comrades crowed, while standing on their toes, "We've captured twenty-five hundred Yankees, including a full Pennsylvania regiment, with their colonel." Private I. Gordon Bradwell (Company I), exhausted as he was, only half believed their overblown claims. He did not see any prisoners. His party had captured no one. Lee had been there himself, his comrades boasted, and had "shook hands with Gordon." They said that Lee promoted him to major general on the spot.[27] As a reward to the men, Gordon ordered rations to be brought up too. The food did not get there on time. A few minutes after it arrived, Gordon detached the 31st Georgia north to assist the Louisiana Tigers, who had entrenched near the Culpeper Mine Road.[28]

Near the Rail Road Bed (Federal Lines)

At 8:00 P.M., Company H of the 145th Pennsylvania (Brooke's brigade), Captain J. Boyd Espy commanding, advanced into the woods south of Barlow's division and promptly became lost after relieving the 125th New York. After walking for what seemed like hours in column on the Brock Road, the New York regiment finally arrived at the division's bivouac near the Plank Road. Throughout the entire march, the men anxiously listened to the sharp and continuous musketry northwest of their approach. When they attempted to bed down along the roadside, their comrades told them about the brigade's losses (26 men) for that day. They also received word to prepare for a 4:00 A.M. assault the next morning. With the order came the command to start digging. They spent the entire night constructing breastworks.[29]

The Plank Road (Federal Lines)

While the regiments prepared to protect themselves, Major General David B. Birney, whose division opened the fighting that afternoon for the II Corps, sent a detachment from the 2nd U. S. Sharpshooters into the ground between the lines to retrieve the two artillery pieces lost earlier that day. Captain S. M. Norton (Company E) led the expedition down the Plank Road. The intrepid raiders succeeded in bringing back one of the guns and all of the harnesses off the caissons' dead horses.[30]

It was dark before the shooting stopped, at which time, the soldiers started tabulating their losses. Private John Haley's Company I (17th Maine) had two more men dying and seven more wounded. He and three others found Private Frank Sweetser, who was gut shot, and Private Fred Loring, with a crushed hip, lying in the woods, bleeding to death. Their four comrades made stretchers from poles and blankets for them and hauled them back to the Brock Road field hospital. To the broken hearted Haley it seemed like ten miles.

He and Sweetser were dear friends. He loved the man like a brother. Sweetser writhed constantly upon the stretcher and begged continually for water, which he threw up every time he swallowed it. Fred Loring, Haley's messmate, a stoic, solemn teenager, earned Haley's abiding respect. Unlike all of the other injured, he neither screamed nor cried out. Not a curse nor a prayer came from his mouth. Every now and then he sighed or stopped the men to mutter a quiet request.

Haley spent the entire night in the field hospital where there lay hundreds of men who received no medical attention. The cries and the moans wearied the exhausted private, whose face was still encrusted with the dried blood from his persistent nose bleed. He was too tired to stand up and too weary to shut up a bothersome Irishman, who demanded constant attention. The fellow persistently raised himself up on his elbows and cried out, "Murther! Murther! MURTHER!" in a vain attempt to get medical assistance.[31]

The whippoorwills serenaded the 152nd New York (Owen's brigade) from the woods. Pretty soon, the New Yorkers joined them in their chorus with "Grant will whip," "Grant will whip."[32]

North of the Plank Road

While the Confederates annoyed Colonel Samuel Carroll's brigade, Captain John G. B. Adams (Company B, 19th Massachusetts) had retreated toward the Brock Road. His remaining eighteen men stayed close to their wiry captain, feeling quite certain that he was a safe man to follow. They were right. The company dove over the makeshift earthworks along the Brock Road without any further losses. Adams peered over the top logs of his section of the line but could see nothing but shadows darting through the woods. He could not distinguish friend from foe in the night. The pungent odor of smoldering leaves and pine needles drifted over the regiment. The nauseating smell of roasting flesh mingled with the wood smoke and permeated the area. The taste lingered in his mouth and sickened the captain at heart. He and his men knew where the wounded were between the lines, but they had no way to rescue them. He was smelling their funeral pyres.[33]

Nearby, Second Lieutenant Thomas Galwey (Company B, 8th Ohio) stared into the smoky woods. With visibility cut in most places to a little more than twenty feet and with night rapidly enveloping the foreboding woods, he sadly realized they would recover few of the wounded. He hated the Wilderness. He put himself to bed with the pickets' sporadic pot shots ringing out in the evening.[34] The shooting had ceased and the whippoorwills continued to sing out in the evening.[35]

South of the Plank Road

The 1st U.S. Sharpshooters counted their losses. Company F suffered the heaviest casualties in the regiment with six killed, five wounded, and two missing. Two of the wounded suffered particularly nasty wounds. The surgeons amputated Private Spafford Wright's arm above the elbow. Corporal Michael Cunningham had a large caliber hole from the center of his breast through his back, near the spine. The round miraculously struck no vital organs. Even more remarkably, he survived the operation at the field hospital where Assistant Surgeon B. Howard (United States Volunteers) hermetically sealed his wound.[36]

Private William Kent, believing himself among the wounded, cautiously wormed his hand up his back between his field pack and his blouse, all the while feeling for blood. The spent ball fell into his palm. Closer inspection revealed that the slug had bored through his rolled blanket (on the top of his knapsack), his rubber blanket, writing paper, tobacco pouch, and letters before stopping at his shirt. Much to his relief, it left him with an egg sized welt between his shoulder blades and nothing more.[37]

He settled down in the dark to eat his hard bread and sugar ration. Coffee fires were not allowed. The men ate the sugar despite the intense thirst it produced. Most of the men had drained their canteens during the approach march from Todd's Tavern and contented themselves to do without. A few comrades, slinging empty canteens, came into the regiment, with word from the Vermont Brigade, which was bivouacked north of the crossroads. Kent, who hoped to find his brother, Evarts, among them, snatched up a canteen and left his company. He found him and spent the most precious half hour he ever remembered recalling the old days with him.[38]

Along Wilderness Run, South of Lacy's

Brigadier General James S. Wadsworth's division of the V Corps, with Brigadier General Henry Baxter's brigade in tow, was supposed to leave Lacy's lower fields around 4:30 P.M. with orders to connect with Hancock's Corps along the Plank Road. Morale was not good among some of the rank and file in Colonel Roy Stone's brigade. Around 5:00 P.M. the 149th Pennsylvania received an estimated one hundred rounds of ammunition for each man. A number of them in Company D decided that the cartridges weighed too much to carry. Sergeant F. C. Dorrington and Corporal John W. Nesbit (both from Company D) decided to dump at least half of their ammunition in a nearby stream.[39]

The men of the 143rd Pennsylvania kicked out their coffee fires and stepped slowly into formation. Colonel Roy Stone, their brigade commander, used the opportunity to troop the regimental line and berate the men for having caused the brigade's rout earlier that day. First Sergeant "Orr" Harris (Company B) considered the colonel's behavior shameful and unjust. "I would like to have seen a Rebel shell come and [take] the [colonel's] drunken head clean from his shoulders after he got thro' with his abuse," he bitterly wrote.[40] Within an hour and a half, Wadsworth had deployed his division in column of brigades and began his advance into the brush between the middle and eastern branches of Wilderness Run which flowed south into the Plank Road. Stone's Pennsylvania brigade, which had behaved quite poorly earlier in the day near the Higgerson farm, covered the advance. The 149th Pennsylvania (on the left) with the 143rd Pennsylvania (on the right) went forward as skirmishers.[41] Baxter's brigade (Robinson's division) moved into line to its right rear with the 12th Massachusetts on its right flank.[42] Cutler's brigade, then Rice's brigade, finished out the column.[43]

The four brigades stepped out around 7:00 P.M. at the double quick, attempting an advance in the dark. Their skirmishers went headlong into the

Wilderness' cursed brush. Sporadic muzzle flashes burst almost immediately from the trees along the Federals' front. The Confederate skirmishers fell back quickly before the rapid fire of Stone's Pennsylvanians.[44] Swallowed up by the close set scrub pines which clawed at their bodies and disrupted their formations, the skirmishers found themselves stumbling around in a terrifying blackness. They slowed their pace, which, in turn, brought the rest of the division to a crawl. It took Wadsworth and his veterans almost an hour and a half to cover a mile of swamp and woodland.[45]

Along the entire route, Stone's Pennsylvanians responded vigorously to the Confederates who sniped at them in the darkness. Cutler's brigade in Wadsworth's third line overreacted to the incoming rounds and fired blindly into the trees to their front. The 6th Wisconsin could tell by the scattered Confederate casualties which they stumbled across that their shots had taken effect.[46] To their right front, however, on the extreme flank of Baxter's brigade, Company E of the 12th Massachusetts caught a glimpse of what appeared to be a column of troops moving by files through the pines, heading north past the regiment's right side. (Judging by the column's approximate distance from the Plank Road, the Federals stumbled across Orr's Rifles and the 5th Alabama Battalion.)[47] The company immediately wheeled right. The officers on that wing of the regiment yelled for their companies to change "front to the right." Defying the blackness of the pine forest, the separate companies individually halted, wheeled right, and successively marched west into a new line perpendicular to the left wing of the regiment. The veteran New Englanders leveled their weapons by command and volleyed into the darker shadows which crashed through the woods in their immediate front.

The Confederate regiments recoiled and fell back toward the creek which paralleled their route of march but quickly rallied and returned the fire.[48] The 149th Pennsylvania retreated from the left of Stone's skirmish line and dragged Companies C and I of the 143rd Pennsylvania with it, which left Company B unsupported. The 149th smashed the formation of the 150th Pennsylvania. The two regiments crashed rearward into the leveled weapons of Cutler's Iron Brigade. The Westerners herded the rattled Pennsylvanians back into some kind of formation but could not get them to advance any farther. Stone, bareheaded, his coat thrown open, galloped up to the two cowering regiments. Cursing and swearing at the top of his voice, he pushed them back to his skirmish line.

The incoming fire was hitting the 143rd. Privates Than Holly and Will Chandler (both Company B) shrieked and staggered from the line. Harris noticed two Confederates step from behind a turned up stump and fire simultaneously before ducking to cover. He feverishly tried to load his rifle to take out at least one of them. They fired first. One round carried the lockplate of his rifle away. The second minie burned a bluish streak across the toe of his right shoe and struck his leg with a numbing jolt. The impact whirled him completely around. Before he could regain his composure, Captain Jacob Lingfelter (Company B) cried for help.

Harris limped over to the downed officer. Lingfelter, who was shot in the foot, begged to be taken to the rear. The sergeant and another man pulled the captain's boot off. The ball, which had penetrated the thick sole of the captain's boot, had lodged in the heel of his foot. Not too long after Harris was hit, the Iron Brigade came up on the right of the 143rd Pennsylvania. At that point, the sergeant decided it was time for him to quit the field. He staggered rearward toward Lacy's without Lingfelter. On the way back, he managed to talk a slightly wounded man into getting an opiate for him. The drug felled him.[49]

Neither side remembered how long the exchange of musketry lasted. They only noted that it was brief and deadly. When it ended around 8:30 P.M., it had cost the 12th Massachusetts fifteen dead and forty-two wounded, seven of whom were officers.[50] The Confederates left many of their casualties behind. Their cries and moans kept Lieutenant Colonel Rufus Dawes (6th Wisconsin) awake for the better part of the night. He and his men groped around in the dark rendering whatever aid they could to the forlorn soldiers. Dawes described the pleas of the wounded as "harrowing," in particular, the ranting of one man who repeatedly screamed, "My God, why hast thou forsaken me!"[51] It was a question for which no one had any answers.

Wadsworth called off his flanking advance half a mile north of his objective – the Plank Road. The darkness, the pesky Confederate skirmishers, and the hard day's fighting had left his men exhausted and their cartridge boxes almost depleted. The sounds of battle, which he had used to guide his command south, ceased shortly after the 12th Massachusetts became engaged. Without any musketry to alert himself to the Rebels' approximate position, he halted his division for the night.

Wadsworth had an aide, Captain Robert Monteith (Company H, 7th Wisconsin), take two orderlies back to the division's ordnance wagon at Lacy's for ammunition. He instructed Monteith to report the division's situation to Major General Gouverneur K. Warren at corps headquarters and to receive any orders before returning.[52] Craning his neck skyward as they rode, the captain successfully guided his two orderlies out of the woods by the North Star and they eventually found themselves on the southern edge of Lacy's property.[53] While Monteith ventured north to safety, Colonel Edward S. Bragg (6th Wisconsin) sent Sergeant Lewis A. Kent on an unauthorized reconnaissance. The sergeant stole into the woods and brush beyond the skirmish line established by Stone's Pennsylvania brigade and crawled around the division's entire perimeter until he located the Confederate position along the branch of Wilderness Run which ran along the eastern side of the Widow Tapp's plateau. He scurried back to Bragg who in turn personally passed the information on to Wadsworth. The general silently received the information. Bragg came away from him feeling miffed. He spent some time complaining to his regimental officers about how he was not even congratulated for delivering what he considered to be militarily significant information.[54]

North of the Plank Road (Confederate Lines)

Lieutenant Robert Ward (Company B, 42nd Mississippi), whose very small regiment anchored the left of Stone's brigade line, suddenly realized that there were no more troops within his immediate vicinity. He was close enough to Wadsworth's division, however, to see the Federals' incoming rounds literally cut a path through the line formerly held by the 26th Mississippi of his brigade. The regiment was on the forward slope of the west bank of Wilderness Run. The lieutenant immediately faced the 42nd's left wing (five companies) north, behind the trunk of a dead tree which had conveniently fallen uphill.

He conferred with the regiment's four remaining officers about their options to escape. They whispered the command to cease fire along the short line. With bullets striking into the ground from the north, east, and southeast, they decided to bolt into the blackness to their right rear. The regiment slipped away through a gap which Ward estimated to be no more than ninety feet wide. The Mississippians did not stop running until they reached the Plank Road. Far to the south, Lane's men continued blazing away into the prone Federal lines.[55]

South of the Plank Road (Confederate Lines)

The 27th North Carolina, behind McGowan's brigade, used a temporary lull in the shooting to realign itself with its brigade, several hundred yards to the rear. The regiment quietly slipped onto a smaller back road about one hundred yards below the Plank Road and headed west. In the near total darkness, the wounded Captain John A. Sloan (Company B) noticed another group of men marching silently in the dirt track on the left of the regiment. As he glanced off to the side, Sloan noticed how similar the knapsacks of the other men were. Their uniforms also seemed to be in much better condition than those Sloan had seen in his brigade.

Unable to positively identify who occupied the other half of the road, he slipped closer to their column. They were Yankees. The captain hastily skittered to Lieutenant Colonel George F. Whitfield at the front of the column. "Impossible!" the colonel blurted. Unconvinced, Whitfield sidled over to the parallel column to get a closer look for himself. He panicked. Jerking his pistol from its holster, he foolishly screamed, "Yes, they are Yankees! Shoot them, boys! Shoot them!" A few shots reverberated loudly through the woods. Both regiments broke for cover along their side of the dirt track and did not

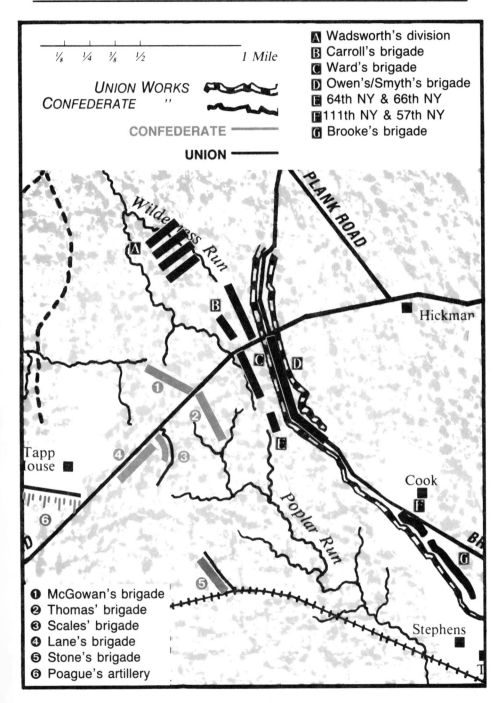

MAP 45: Situation along the Plank Road, evening, May 5, 1864.

stop running until they reached their "own" lines. The 27th North Carolina struck the Plank Road and solemnly marched farther to the rear. The Yankees, whoever they were, scurried back to their own line as well.[56]

Northern Side of the Plank Road (Wilderness Run)

Back at the Plank Road, Private Berry Benson (Company H) and his five remaining sharpshooters from the 1st South Carolina stumbled into one of McGowan's couriers, Center, who told them that the brigade was lying down along the ridge just to the north. The six men parted and searched out their own companies in the battered and smoldering woods.

Pickets from McGowan's brigade stood glumly in the creek bottom just yards from their counterparts from the 10th New York and the 12th New Jersey. Benson lost his bearings. Somewhere he expected to find his regiment lying awake but he did not know which direction to turn. "First South Carolina!" Benson nervously whispered. "Here! This way!" someone called softly from across from him. "Don't go that way; that's a Yankee," another voice warned from the opposite side.

Benson hesitated for a tense second or two, then instinctively turned in the direction of the second voice. Cocking his rifle, he cautiously took several steps, then found himself within his own lines. (In the excitement he completely forgot how he managed to identify his anonymous sentry.) He stumbled farther along the line until he found his own company only to learn that a comrade had been shot through both knees earlier in the day. Traveling farther south he found the entire company of sharpshooters lying down behind a fallen tree.

The South Carolinians were lowly bantering with the New Yorkers across from them for some time. Although it started as innocent teasing, it quickly escalated into verbal abuse. Then, one of the pickets from the 10th New York called one of the Sharpshooters a "son of a bitch." The angered Southerner fired an angry shot at the Yankee. The Yankees responded with a volley and the 1st South Carolina returned fire.[57] Within seconds the rest of the South Carolina Brigade cut loose with a long rolling fire into the 12th New Jersey at the other end of the line.[58] The musketry also struck the 1st Delaware which had just started to descend the slope toward the swampy ground behind the Jerseymen. The dense scrub oak and small pines snatched at the men's clothes as the bullets thunked and thudded into the regiment.[59] Large numbers of men dropped or were flung from both regiments. The 12th New Jersey loosed a single volley, then hurled itself down to the ground alongside the 10th New York, while the 1st Delaware, infuriated by the suddenness of the attack, returned the fire with equal viciousness. A bullet grazed Colonel Samuel Carroll's arm while he was riding near the line, but he refused to leave the field.[60] First Lieutenant George A. Bowen (Company C, 12th New

Jersey) listened intently to the heavy, continuous roar of the riflery which thudded and hammered into the woods on both flanks. It sounded to him like millions of men marching through a plank floored mill. It almost deafened him.[61]

Poplar Run (Federal Lines)

Satisfied with their twenty prisoners, the old hands of the 124th New York established their pickets in the low ground, on the eastern bank of Poplar Run, and maintained a vigorous musketry until 8:00 P.M. when it got too dark to fire any longer. All the while they listened to the brigades on their flanks take a fearful drubbing.[62] Very shortly after dark, Ward's brigade extended its line to the left and went to bed with its arms. Private Ashbury F. Haynes (Company F, 3rd Maine) groped around in the dark until he found a log to curl up against for the night, probably to protect himself from a stray bullet during the night. Draping his blanket over the log and himself, he fell asleep.[63]

South of the Brock Crossroads

Private William Kent (Company F, 1st U.S. Sharpshooters) returned to his company in time to have his knapsack handed to him. The regiment was going on picket. As he passed between the two abandoned guns in the Plank Road, he called a good-bye to his brother, who called back. The profound silence which prevailed as the company neared the crossroads made Kent shudder. Yankee soldiers lounged around the roadside as if nothing were going on to their front. Four bronze Napoleons sat in the center of the crossing. Four enlisted men, carrying a body on a blanket and accompanied by an officer, disrupted the flow of Company F around the field pieces. The captain recognized the dismounted officer as Major Darling on Hays' staff. The captain asked who was on the blanket. "It's the general," the major sadly answered.

An audible shudder billowed through the ranks. The men had admired the crusty old man. Kent gaped at the general's head, and the fresh blood which trickled over his right temple, as the stretcher bearers struggled by him. He compassionately recollected how the general used to praise the Berdans as "the damdest [sic] thieves and the damdest [sic] fighters in the old 3rd Corps."[64]

Captain Charles D. Merriman (Company F) took them almost to Wilderness Run before flanking them right into a relatively cleared space. The large trees scattered throughout the area provided the men better protection than they had used earlier in the day. In the blackness, they tripped over dead and wounded alike. Feet stretched into imaginary yards. Men fell on their faces and cursed as quietly as possible at themselves for making so much noise. Merriman eventually halted the column. The Sharpshooters counted off in squads of five, one of whom would stand sentry duty while the others slept.

No talking or smoking, the officer remonstrated them. While he departed, he mumbled something about a 4:00 A.M. assault the next day.

Standing alone in the eery woods, Kent found himself thinking, "...the stillness seems like that of death." When he walked back to the reserve post, he found the men chewing their tobacco. He tried to do likewise, but his empty stomach rejected it. Exhaustion eventually overpowered him and he slept better than he ever had.[65] Even in the darkness, Captain C. A. Stevens could see how closely the riflery had cropped the bushes and saplings to the ground.[66]

An hour and a half later (9:30 P.M.) the 5th Michigan crawled over the earthworks along the Brock Road and plopped down to eat dinner. Before long, Orderly Sergeant Harrison Caril (Company C) saw stretcher bearers lug in his lieutenant colonel, John Pulford. Simultaneously word rippled through the regiment about Hays' death.[67]

In the smokey darkness of the Wilderness, the two armies bedded down for an uncomfortable night. Stone's brigade threw itself down along the south side of the Plank Road not too far east of the Widow Tapp's.[68] Brigadier General Edward L. Thomas' Georgians were on the south side of the Plank Road, about three hundred fifty yards west of the easternmost branch of Poplar Run, with the line bent back at a southwesterly angle from the road.[69] McGowan's South Carolina brigade fell back from Wilderness Run until it came opposite Thomas' men. Its line stretched to the road from the north to form an inverse angle with Thomas' command.[70]

Scales' North Carolinians had fallen back to a ridge some four hundred forty yards west of Thomas's position with their left on the Plank Road. The 38th North Carolina held the left of the brigade line. The 16th North Carolina, to its right, unknowingly overlapped the front of the 33rd North Carolina from Lane's brigade which had gone into line behind and parallel to Scales' right rear.[71] In the dark it was impossible to tell where anyone was. Scales mistakenly believed that Lane and Thomas were in line across his front. Nevertheless he sent pickets from the 16th North Carolina to cover his front, while most of his regiments

Brigadier General Alfred M. Scales, in the darkness, overlapped the front of Lane's brigade, with his command. He did not realize that he was in the second Confederate defensive line and not the third line.

(Clark, I)

dragged in fallen trees and rotten logs from the surrounding woods to construct some kind of breastworks.[72] Second Lieutenant Octavius A. Wiggins (Company E, 37th North Carolina) watched the individual regiments lie down in the darkness.[73]

Stone patrolled the Plank Road on horseback until he stumbled into his lost 42nd Mississippi. Once the Mississippians rejoined his command, he moved them south to Poplar Run until the right flank nearly touched the railroad cut – a little over a mile below the Plank Road. The exhausted Lieutenant Robert Ward (Company B, 42nd Mississippi) drew picket detail. The small guard had gone a little under forty yards when one of the nervous pickets gingerly picked his way back to Ward. "The Yankees are right out there," the fellow whispered. When Stone learned of the Federals' proximity, he quietly recalled Ward and his men. The pickets stood their duty on top of their slumbering brigade. The men slept with their weapons snuggled close to their bodies and with their accoutrements strapped on.[74] No organized battle lines existed whatsoever.[75]

Adjutant William H. McLaurin (18th North Carolina), in vain, warned Wilcox that the Federals were too close to the Confederate lines.

(Clark, II)

The situation was not much better in the rest of Henry Heth's division. His battered regiments were scattered along both sides of the pike east of the Tapp farm. No one in the Confederate high command seemed to believe that the Army of the Potomac might renew the attack in the morning, despite alarming reports from men who straggled in from the front that Brigadier General Cadmus Wilcox's division was not properly deployed. It took Adjutant William H. McLaurin (18th North Carolina) about four hours to find his regiment. During that time he had inadvertently wandered into the II Corps pickets. Running as fast as his rugged surroundings permitted, he reached the Plank Road and Wilcox's lines around 11:00 P.M. In the darkness he thought he recognized the general's white horse. The tired lieutenant broke into a trot and, upon reaching the horse, recognized the general. There were no Confederates between his division and Hancock's Federals, McLaurin blurted. The general curtly dismissed the excited officer, just short of calling him a liar.

McLaurin continued west on the road until he found his own brigade. He immediately reported to Lane and his own colonel, John D. Barry, and several other officers who had gathered around him, what he had seen. (By then

Lane had moved his brigade into line paralleling the Plank Road.) Lane and Barry approached Wilcox together and implored him to deploy pickets to the front. The general refused. He insisted that there were no Yankees in front of his division and that Heth's division was between them and the enemy. Besides, he continued, Lane's soldiers needed a rest.[76] He told Lane to stay in his present position. Major General Richard H. Anderson's division would be there by daylight to relieve them.[77]

The IX Corps – Near the Rapidan River

Throughout the early afternoon and into the night, Major General Ambrose Burnside's IX Corps, which had spent the better part of May 4 straggling along a twenty-seven mile circuitous route from Rappahannock Station to Germanna Ford, crossed the Rapidan and filed into bivouacs behind the V Corps and the VI Corps.[78] Brigadier General Thomas G. Stevenson's First Division led the advance followed by Brigadier General Robert B. Potter's Second Division, then by Brigadier General Orlando Willcox's Third Division.[79] Brigadier General Edward Ferrero's Fourth Division, being composed almost entirely of United States' Colored Troops, had been stuck with the corps' wagons and were a day behind the rest of the divisions, north of the Rapidan.[80]

In the darkness, the men became more acutely aware of their environment and the behavior of the men around them. Captain Z. Boylston Adams (Company F, 56th Massachusetts) whose company had drawn picket duty for part of Stevenson's division during the early afternoon, had listened intently to the scattered rifle fire in the woods to the southwest. The shots sounded very close but he could see no smoke. By evening, when the temperature had dropped from 76 degrees to 61.5 degrees, he still sweltered in his poncho. He felt very alone.[81]

Farther to the rear, and closer to Germanna Ford, the IX Corps bands serenaded the troops with patriotic airs while the soldiers waited for their coffee to boil. The veterans did not want to hear the selections the musicians had chosen. The rank and file insisted on "Home, Sweet Home." The sight of so many playing cards strewn along the roadside had led many of the men in the 45th Pennsylvania (Potter's Division) to think of their souls. Private William A. Roberts (Company K) listened to the melancholy strains of the John H. Payne favorite and solemnly observed veterans, like himself, crying unashamedly. Others sputtered and coughed as they swallowed their sobs. The foreboding of the Wilderness had already taken hold of them.

As it grew silent, later in the night, the whippoorwills punctuated the quiet with their annoying calls. Other night birds added to the eeriness with their chirping. It strained the Pennsylvanians' nerves. At one point, an exasperated enlisted man blurted, half aloud, "Ah, birdie, if I had your wings I wouldn't be in these 'diggins' very long." No one felt like staying in that terrifying jungle. The Pennsylvanians spent the night with their knapsacks on and their weapons by their sides.[82]

Closer to the ford, the 27th Michigan (Willcox's Division) went prone in line of battle in the woods west of the Germanna Plank Road to wait out the evening. Sergeant C. F. Jeffers, one of the few veterans in the regiment, carefully watched the "green" troops who lay in front of him. The responsibility of taking care of so many untried soldiers worried him. They knew nothing of survival in the field. Throughout the afternoon, while they listened apprehensively to the firing in the woods to the south, he noticed how the recruits nervously eyed the "old hands," trying to discern what they should do from moment to moment. The veterans, who had seen too many friends die, did not readily share their expertise with the new men and as he listened apprehensively to the noises in the trees beyond the regimental line, Jeffers wondered just how far he was expected to carry his responsibility for them.[83]

ppendix

Order of Battle

(from *BATTLES AND LEADERS OF THE CIVIL WAR* VOLUME IV.)

THE UNION ARMY - Lt. Gen. Ulysses S. Grant, commanding
THE ARMY OF THE POTOMAC - Maj. Gen. George G. Meade,
    commanding
    Provost Guard - Brig. Gen. Marsena R. Patrick
        C and D, 1st. Mass. Cav.   80th N.Y. (20th militia)   3rd Pa. Cav.
        68th Pa.   114th Pa.
    Volunteer Engineer Brigade
        50th N.Y. Engineers

SECOND ARMY CORPS - Maj. Gen. Winfield Scott Hancock, commanding
    Escort - 1st Vt. Cav., Co. M
    FIRST DIVISION - Brig. Gen. Francis C. Barlow, commanding
    First Brigade - Col. Nelson A. Miles
        26th Mich.   61st N.Y.   81st Pa.   140th Pa.   183rd Pa.
    Second Brigade - Col. Thomas A. Smyth
        28th Mass.   63rd N.Y.   69th N.Y.   88th N.Y.   116th Pa.
    Third Brigade - Col. Paul Frank
        39th N.Y.   52nd N.Y.   57th N.Y.   111th N.Y.   125th N.Y.   126th N.Y.
    Fourth Brigade - Col. John R. Brooke
        2nd Del.   64th N.Y.   66th N.Y.   53rd Pa.   145th Pa.   148th Pa.

SECOND DIVISION - Brig. Gen. John Gibbon
    Provost Guard
        2nd Co. Minn. Sharpshooters
    First Brigade - Brig. Gen. Alexander S. Webb
        19th Me.   1st Co. Andrew Sharpshooters   15th Mass.   19th Mass.
        20th Mass.   7th Mich.   42nd N.Y.   59th N.Y.   82nd N.Y.
    Second Brigade - Brig. Gen. Joshua T. Owen
        152nd N.Y.   69th Pa.   71st Pa.   72nd Pa.   106th Pa.
    Third Brigade - Col. Samuel S. Carroll
        14th Conn.   1st Del.   14th Ind.   12th N.J.   10th N.Y.   108th N.Y.
        4th Ohio   8th Ohio   7th W.Va.
THIRD DIVISION - Maj. Gen. David B. Birney
    First Brigade - Brig. Gen. J. H. Hobart Ward
        20th Ind.   3rd Me.   40th N.Y.   86th N.Y.   124th N.Y.   99th Pa.
        110th Pa.   141st Pa.   2nd U.S. Sharpshooters
    Second Brigade - Brig. Gen. Alexander Hays (killed, May 5)
                          Col. John S. Crocker
        4th Me.   17th Me.   3rd Mich.   5th Mich.   93rd N.Y.   57th Pa.
        63rd Pa.   105th Pa.   1st U.S. Sharpshooters
FOURTH DIVISION - Brig. Gen. Gershom Mott
    First Brigade - Col. Robert McAllister
        1st Mass.   16th Mass.   5th N.J.   6th N.J.   7th N.J.   8th N.J.
        11th N.J.   26th Pa.   115th Pa.
    Second Brigade - Col. William R. Brewster
        11th Mass.   70th N.Y.   71st N.Y.   72nd N.Y.   73rd N.Y.
        74th N.Y.   120th N.Y.   84th Pa.
    Artillery Brigade - Col. John C. Tidball
        Me. Light, 6th Btty., (F)   Mass. Light, 10th Btty.
        N.H. Light, 1st Btty.   1st N.Y. Light, Co. G
        4th N.Y. Heavy, 3rd Bttn.   1st Pa. Light, Co. F   1st R.I. Light, Co. A
        1st R.I. Light, Co. B   4th U.S., Co. K   5th U.S., Cos. C & I

FIFTH ARMY CORPS - Maj. Gen. Gouverneur K. Warren, commanding
    Provost Guard
        12th N.Y. Bttn.
FIRST DIVISION - Brig. Gen. Charles Griffin
    First Brigade - Brig. Gen. Romeyn Ayres
        140th N.Y.   146th N.Y.   91st Pa.   155th Pa.   2nd U.S.   11th U.S.
        12th U.S.   14th U.S.   17th U.S.

Second Brigade - Col. Jacob B. Sweitzer
    9th Mass.   22nd Mass.   32nd Mass.   4th Mich.   62nd Pa.
Third Brigade - Brig. Joseph J. Bartlett
    20th Me.   18th Mass.   1st Mich.   16th Mich.   44th N.Y.   83rd Pa.
    118th Pa.
SECOND DIVISION - Brig. Gen. John C. Robinson
  First Brigade - Col. Samuel H. Leonard (May 5)
             Col. Peter Lyle (May 6)
    16th Me.   13th Mass.   39th Mass.   104th N.Y.
  Second Brigade - Brig. Gen. Henry Baxter (wounded, May 6)
             Col. Richard Coulter
    12th Mass.   83rd N.Y.   97th N.Y.   11th Pa.   88th Pa.   90th Pa.
  Third Brigade - Col. Andrew W. Denison
    1st Md.   4th Md.   7th Md.   8th Md.
THIRD DIVISION - Brig. Samuel W. Crawford
  First Brigade - Col. William McCandless
    1st Pa. Res.   2nd Pa. Res.   6th Pa. Res.   7th Pa. Res.   11th Pa. Res.
    13th Pa. Res.
  Third Brigade - Col. Joseph W. Fisher
    5th Pa. Res.   8th Pa. Res.   10th Pa. Res.   12th Pa. Res.
FOURTH DIVISION - Brig. James S. Wadsworth (m. wounded, May 6)
             Brig. Gen. Lysander Cutler
  First Brigade - Brig. Gen. Lysander Cutler
             Col. William W. Robinson
    7th Ind.   19th Ind.   24th Mich.   1st N.Y. Bttn. Sharpshooters
    2nd Wis.   6th Wis.   7th Wis.
  Second Brigade - Brig. Gen. James C. Rice
    76th N.Y.   84th N.Y.   95th N.Y.   147th N.Y.   56th Pa.
  Third Brigade - Col. Roy Stone (disabled, May 6)
             Col. Edward S. Bragg
    121st Pa.   142nd Pa.   143rd Pa.   149th Pa.   150th Pa.
  Artillery Brigade - Col. Charles S. Wainwright
    Mass. Light, 3rd Btty. (C)   Mass. Light, 5th Btty., (E)
    1st N.Y. Light, Co. D   1st N.Y. Light, Cos. E & L
    1st N.Y. Light, Co. H   4th N.Y. Heavy, 4th Bttn.
    1st Pa. Light, Co. B   4th U.S. Co. B   5th U.S. Co. D

SIXTH ARMY CORPS - Maj. Gen. John Sedgwick, commanding
  Escort - 8th Pa. Cav., Co. A

FIRST DIVISION - Brig. Gen. Horatio G. Wright
  First Brigade - Col. Henry W. Brown
    1st N.J. 2nd N.J. 3rd N.J. 4th N.J. 10th N.J. 15th N.J.
  Second Brigade - Col. Emory Upton
    5th Me. 121st N.Y. 95th Pa. 96th Pa.
  Third Brigade - Brig. Gen. David A. Russell
    6th Me. 49th Pa. 119th Pa. 5th Wis.
  Fourth Brigade - Brig. Gen. Alexander Shaler (CIA, May 6)
                Col. Nelson Cross
    65th N.Y. 67th N.Y. 122nd N.Y.
SECOND DIVISION - Brig. Gen. George W. Getty (wounded May 6)
                  Brig. Gen. Frank Wheaton (May 6)
                  Brig. Gen. Thomas H. Neill (May 7)
  First Brigade - Brig. Frank Wheaton
    62nd N.Y. 93rd Pa. 98th Pa. 102nd Pa. 139th Pa.
  Second Brigade - Col. Lewis A. Grant
    2nd Vt. 3rd Vt. 4th Vt. 5th Vt. 6th Vt.
  Third Brigade - Brig. Gen. Thomas H. Neill (Div. C.O., May 7)
                Col. Daniel D. Bidwell
    7th Me. 43rd N.Y. 49th N.Y. 77th N.Y. 61st Pa.
  Fourth Brigade - Brig. Gen. Henry L. Eustis
    7th Mass. 10th Mass. 37th Mass. 2nd R.I.
THIRD DIVISION - Brig. Gen. James B. Ricketts
  First Brigade - Brig. Gen. William H. Morris
    14th N.J. 106th N.Y. 151st N.Y. 87th Pa. 10th Vt.
  Second Brigade - Brig. Gen. Truman Seymour (CIA, May 6)
                Col. Benjamin F. Smith
    6th Md. 110th Ohio 122nd Ohio 126th Ohio 67th Pa. 138th Pa.
  Artillery Brigade - Col. Charles H. Tompkins
    Me. Light, 4th Btty., (D)   Mass. Light, 1st Btty., (A)
    N.Y. Light, 1st Btty. N.Y. Light, 3rd Btty. 4th N.Y. Heavy, 1st Bttn.
    1st R.I. Light, Co. C 1st R.I. Light, Co. E 1st R.I. Light, Co. G
    5th U.S., Co. M

NINTH ARMY CORPS (under direct command of U. S. Grant)
                Maj. Gen. Ambrose E. Burnside, commanding
  Provost Guard - 8th U.S. Infantry
FIRST DIVISION - Brig. Gen. Thomas G. Stevenson
  First Brigade - Col. Sumner Carruth (sunstruck, May 6)
                Col. Jacob P. Gould
    35th Mass. (not engaged) 56th Mass. 57th Mass. 4th U.S.
    10th U.S.

Second Brigade - Col. Daniel Leasure
  3rd Md.   21st Mass.   100th Pa.
Artillery
  Me. Light, 2nd Btty., (B)   Mass. Light, 14th Btty.
SECOND DIVISION - Brig. Gen. Robert B. Potter
  First Brigade - Col. Zenas R. Bliss (sunstruck, May 6)
                    Col. John I. Curtin
    36th Mass.   58th Mass.   51st N.Y.   45th Pa.   48th Pa.
    7th R.I. (train guard)
  Second Brigade - Col. Simon G. Griffin
    31st Me.   32nd Me.   6th N.H.   9th N.H.   11th N.H.   17th Vt.
  Artillery
    Mass. Light, 11th Btty.   N.Y. Light, 19th Btty.
THIRD DIVISION - Brig. Gen. Orlando B. Willcox
  First Brigade - Col. John F. Hartranft
    2nd Mich.   8th Mich.   17th Mich.   27th Mich.   109th N.Y.   51st Pa.
  Second Brigade - Col. Benjamin C. Christ
    1st Mich. Sharpshooters 20th Mich.   79th N.Y.   60th Ohio   50th Pa.
  Artillery
    Me. Light, 7th Btty., (G)   N.Y. Light, 34th Btty.
FOURTH DIVISION - (Not Engaged)
                    Brig. Gen. Edward Ferrero
              (All infantry units were African-American Troops)
  First Brigade - Col. Joshua K. Sigfried
    27th U.S.   30th U.S.   39th U.S.   43rd U.S.
  Second Brigade - Col. Henry G. Thomas
    30th Conn. (detachment)   19th U.S.   23rd U.S.
  Artillery
    Pa. Light, Co. D   3rd Vt.
  Cavalry
    3rd N.J.   22nd N.Y.   2nd Ohio   13th Pa.
  Reserve Artillery
    N.Y. Light, 27th Btty.   1st R.I. Light, Co. D
    1st R.I. Light, Co. H   2nd U.S., Co. E   3rd U.S., Co. G
    3rd U.S., Cos. L & M
  Provisional Brigade - Col. Elisha G. Marshall
                    (Served as Infantry)
    24th N.Y. Cav.   14th N.Y. Heavy Arty.
    2nd Pa. Provisional Heavy Arty.

CAVALRY CORPS - Maj. Gen. Philip H. Sheridan, commanding
  Escort - 6th U.S.
FIRST DIVISION - Brig. Alfred T. A. Torbert (sick, May 7)
               Brig. Gen. Wesley Merritt
  First Brigade - Brig. Gen. George A. Custer
    1st Mich.   5th Mich.   6th Mich.   7th Mich.
  Second Brigade - Col. Thomas C. Devin
    4th N.Y.   6th N.Y.   9th N.Y.   17th Pa.
  Reserve Brigade – Brig. Gen. Wesley Merritt (promoted, May 7)
               Col. Alfred Gibbs
    19th N.Y. (1st Dragoons) 6th Pa. 1st U.S. 2nd U.S. 5th U.S.
SECOND DIVISION - Brig. Gen. David McM. Gregg
  First Brigade - Brig. Gen. Henry E. Davies, Jr.
    1st Mass.   1st N.J.   6th Ohio   1st Pa.
  Second Brigade - Col. J. Irvin Gregg
    1st Me.   10th N.Y.   2nd Pa.   4th Pa.   8th Pa.   16th Pa.
THIRD DIVISION - Brig. Gen. James H. Wilson
  First Brigade - Col. Timothy M. Bryan, Jr. (acting C.O. w/Div.)
            Col. John B. McIntosh (C.O., May 5 w/5th N.Y.)
    1st Conn.   2nd N.Y.   5th N.Y.   18th Pa.
  Second Brigade - Col. Charles H. Chapman
    3rd Ind.   8th N.Y.   1st Vt.
  First Brigade Horse Artillery - Capt. James M. Robertson
    N.Y. Light, 6th Btty.   2nd U.S., Cos. B & L   2nd U.S., Co. D
    2nd U.S., Co. M   4th U.S., Co. A   4th U.S., Cos. C & E
ARTILLERY - Brig. Gen. Henry J. Hunt
  Artillery Reserve - Col. Henry S. Burton
  First Brigade - Col. J. Howard Kitching
    6th N.Y. Heavy   15th N.Y. Heavy (both served as infantry)
  Second Brigade - Maj. John A. Tompkins
    Me. Light, 5th Btty., (E)   1st N.J. Light, Co. A   1st N.J. Light, Co. B
    N.Y. Light, 5th Btty.   N.Y. Light, 12th Btty.   1st N.Y. Light, Co. B
  Third Brigade (Not Engaged) - Maj. Robert H. Fitzhugh
    Mass. Light, 9th Btty.   1st N.Y. Light, Co. C   N.Y. Light, 11th Btty.
    N.Y. Light, 15th Btty.   1st Ohio Light, Co. H   5th U.S., Co. E
HORSE ARTILLERY
  Second Brigade (Not Engaged) - Capt. Dunbar R. Ransom
    1st U.S., Cos. E & G   1st U.S., Cos. H & I   1st U.S., Co. K
    2nd U.S., Co. A   2nd U.S., Co. G   3rd U.S., Cos. C, F & K

THE CONFEDERATE ARMY
ARMY OF NORTHERN VIRGINIA - Gen. Robert E. Lee, commanding

FIRST ARMY CORPS - Lieut. Gen. James Longstreet, commanding
(wounded, May 6)
KERSHAW'S DIVISION - Brig. Gen. Joseph B. Kershaw
  Kershaw's (Henagan's) Brigade - Col. John W. Henagan
    2nd S.C. 3rd S.C. 7th S.C. 8th S.C. 15th S.C. 3rd S.C. Bttn.
  Humphreys' Brigade - Brig. Gen. Benjamin G. Humphreys
    13th Miss. 17th Miss. 18th Miss. 21st Miss.
  Wofford's Brigade - Brig. Gen. William T. Wofford
    16th Ga. 18th Ga. 24th Ga. Cobb's Ga. Leg. Phillips' Ga. Leg.
    3rd Ga. Bttn.
  Bryan's Brigade - Brig. Gen. Goode Bryan
    10th Ga. 50th Ga. 51st Ga. 53rd Ga.
FIELD'S DIVISION - Maj. Gen. Charles W. Field
  Jenkins' Brigade - Brig. Gen. Micah Jenkins (killed, May 6)
    1st S. C. 2nd S. C. (Rifles) 5th S. C. 6th S. C.
    Palmetto Sharpshooters
  Anderson's Brigade - Brig. Gen. George T. Anderson
    7th Ga. 8th Ga. 9th Ga. 11th Ga. 59th Ga.
  Law's Brigade - Brig. Gen. E. McIver Law (under arrest, May 6)
            Col. William F. Perry (May 6)
    4th Ala. 15th Ala. 44th Ala. 47th Ala. 48th Ala.
  Gregg's Brigade - Brig. Gen. John Gregg
    3rd Ark. 1st Tex. 4th Tex. 5th Tex.
  Benning's Brigade - Brig. Gen. Henry L. Benning
    2nd Ga. 15th Ga. 17th Ga. 20th Ga.
  Artillery - Brig. Gen. E. Porter Alexander
  Huger's Battalion - Lieut. Col. Frank Huger
    Fickling's Va. Btty. Moody's La. Btty. Parker's Va. Btty.
    J. D. Smith's Va. Btty. Taylor's Va. Btty. Woolfolk's Va. Btty.
  Haskell's Battalion - Maj. John C. Haskell
    Flanner's N.C. Btty. Garden's S. C. Btty. Lamkin's Va. Btty.
    Ramsay's N.C. Btty.
  Cabell's Battalion - Col. Henry C. Cabell
    Callaway's Ga. Btty. Carlton's Ga. Btty. McCarthy's Va. Btty.
    Manly's N.C. Btty.

SECOND ARMY CORPS - Lieut. Gen. Richard S. Ewell, commanding
EARLY'S DIVISION - Maj. Gen. Jubal A. Early
  Hays' Brigade - Brig. Gen. Harry T. Hays
    5th La.   6th La.   7th La.   8th La.   9th La.
  Pegram's Brigade - Brig. Gen. John Pegram (wounded, May 5)
    13th Va.   31st Va.   49th Va.   52nd Va.   58th Va.
  Gordon's Brigade - Brig. Gen. John B. Gordon
    13th Ga.   26th Ga.   31st Ga.   38th Ga.   60th Ga.   61st Ga.
JOHNSON'S DIVISION - Maj. Gen. Edward Johnson
  Stonewall Brigade - Brig. Gen. James A. Walker
    2nd Va.   4th Va.   5th Va.   27th Va.   33rd Va.
  Steuart's Brigade - Brig. Gen. George H. Steuart
    1st N.C.   3rd N.C.   10th Va.   23rd Va.   37th Va.
  Jones' Brigade - Brig. Gen. John M. Jones (killed, May 5)
    21st Va.   25th Va.   42nd Va.   44th Va.   48th Va.   50th Va.
  Stafford's Brigade - Brig. Gen. Leroy Stafford (killed, May 5)
    1st La.   2nd La.   10th La.   14th La.   15th La.
RODES' DIVISION - Maj. Gen. Robert E. Rodes
  Daniel's Brigade - Brig. Gen. Junius Daniel
    32nd N.C.   43rd N.C.   45th N.C.   53rd N.C.   2nd N.C. Bttn.
  Ramseur's Brigade - Brig. Gen. Stephen D. Ramseur
    2nd N.C.   4th N.C.   14th N.C.   30th N.C.
  Doles' Brigade - Brig. Gen. George Doles
    4th Ga.   12th Ga.   44th Ga.
  Battle's Brigade - Brig. Gen. Cullen A. Battle
    3rd Ala.   5th Ala.   6th Ala.   12th Ala.   26th Ala.
  Johnston's Brigade - Brig. Gen. Robert D. Johnston
    5th N.C.   12th N.C.   20th N.C.   23rd N.C.
  Artillery - Brig. Gen. Armistead L. Long
  Hardaway's Battalion - Col. J. T. Brown
    Graham's Va. Btty.   C. B. Griffin's Va. Btty.   Jones' Va. Btty.
    B. H. Smith's Va. Btty.
  Nelson's Battalion - Col. J. T. Brown
    Kirkpatrick's Va. Btty.   Massie's Va. Btty.   Milledge's Ga. Btty.
  Braxton's Battalion - Col. J. T. Brown
    Carpenter's Va. Btty.   Cooper's Va. Btty.   Hardwick's Va. Btty.
  Cutshaw's Battalion - Col. Thomas H. Carter
    Carrington's Va. Btty.   A. W. Garber's Va. Btty.   Tanner's Va. Btty.

Page's Battalion - Col. Thomas H. Carter
  W. P. Carter's Va. Btty.   Fry's Va. Btty.   Page's Va. Btty.
  Reese's Ala. Btty.

THIRD ARMY CORPS - Lieut. Gen. Ambrose P. Hill, commanding
ANDERSON'S DIVISION - Maj. Gen. Richard H. Anderson
  Perrin's Brigade - Brig. Gen. Abner Perrin
    8th Ala.   9th Ala.   10th Ala.   11th Ala.   14th Ala.
  Mahone's Brigade - Brig. Gen. William Mahone
    6th Va.   12th Va.   16th Va.   41st Va.   61st Va.
  Harris' Brigade - Brig. Gen. Nathaniel H. Harris
    12th Miss.   16th Miss.   19th Miss.   48th Miss.
  Wright's Brigade - Brig. Gen. Ambrose R. Wright
    3rd Ga.   22nd Ga.   48th Ga.   2nd Ga. Bttn.
  Perry's Brigade - Brig. Gen. E. A. Perry
    2nd Fla.   5th Fla.   8th Fla.
HETH'S DIVISION - Maj. Gen. Henry Heth
  Davis' (Stone's) Brigade - Col. John M. Stone
    2nd Miss.   11th Miss.   42nd Miss.   55th N.C.
  Cooke's (MacRae's) Brigade - Col. William MacRae
    15th N.C.   27th N.C.   46th N.C.   48th N.C.
  Kirkland's Brigade - Brig. Gen. William W. Kirkland
    11th N.C.   26th N.C.   44th N.C.   47th N.C.   52nd N.C.
  Walker's Brigade - Brig. Gen. Henry H. Walker
    40th Va.   47th Va.   55th Va.   22nd Va. Bttn.   13th Ala.
    1st Tenn. (Provisional Army)   7th Tenn.   14th Tenn.
WILCOX'S DIVISION - Maj. Gen. Cadmus Wilcox
  Lane's Brigade - Brig. Gen. James H. Lane
    7th N.C.   18th N.C.   28th N.C.   33rd N.C.   37th N.C.
  Scales' Brigade - Brig. Gen. Alfred M. Scales
    13th N.C.   16th N.C.   22nd N.C.   34th N.C.   38th N.C.
  McGowan's Brigade - Brig. Gen. Samuel McGowan
    1st S. C. (Provisional Army)   12th S. C.   13th S. C.   14th S. C.
    1st S. C. "Orr's" Rifles
  Thomas' Brigade - Brig. Gen. Edward L. Thomas
    14th Ga.   35th Ga.   45th Ga.   49th Ga.
  Artillery - Col. R. Lindsay Walker
  Poague's Battalion - Col. William T. Poague
    Richards' Miss. Btty.   Utterback's Va. Btty.   Williams' N.C. Btty.
    Wyatt's Va. Btty.

McIntosh's Battalion - Lieut. Col. D. G. McIntosh
    Clutter's Va. Btty.   Donald's Va. Btty.   Hurt's Ala. Btty.
    Price's Va. Btty.
Pegram's Battalion - Lieut. Col. W. J. Pegram
    Brander's Va. Btty.   Cayce's Va. Btty.   Ellett's Va. Btty.
    Marye's Va. Btty.   Zimmerman's S. C. Btty.
Cutts' Battalion - Col. A. S. Cutts
    Patterson's Ga. Btty.   Ross's Ga. Btty.   Wingfield's Ga. Btty.
Richardson's Battalion - Lieut. Col. Charles Richardson
    Grandy's Va. Btty.   Landry's La. Btty.   Moore's Va. Btty.
    Penick's Va. Btty.

CAVALRY CORPS - Maj. Gen James E. B. (Jeb) Stuart, commanding
HAMPTON'S DIVISION - Maj. Gen Wade Hampton (not present)
  Young's Brigade - Brig. Gen. Pierce M. B. Young
    7th Ga.   20th Ga. Bttn.   Cobb's Ga. Leg.   Phillips Ga. Leg.
    Jeff Davis Miss. Leg.
  Rosser's Brigade - Brig. Gen. Thomas L. Rosser
    7th Va.   11th Va.   12th Va.   35th Va. Bttn.
  Butler's Brigade - Brig. Gen. M. C. Butler (Not Engaged)
    4th S.C.   5th S.C.   6th S.C.
FITZHUGH LEE'S DIVISION - Maj. Gen. Fitzhugh Lee
  Lomax's Brigade - Brig. Gen. Lunsford L. Lomax
    5th Va.   6th Va.   15th Va.
  Wickham's Brigade - Brig. Gen. Williams C. Wickham
    1st Va.   2nd Va.   3rd Va.   4th Va.
W. H. F. LEE'S DIVISION - Maj. Gen. W. H. F. Lee
  Chambliss' Brigade - Brig. Gen. John R. Chambliss, Jr.
    9th Va.   10th Va.   13th Va. (Not engaged)
  Gordon's Brigade - Brig. Gen. James B. Gordon
    1st N.C.   2nd N.C.   5th N.C.
  Horse Artillery Maj. Robert P. Chew
  Breathed's Battalion - Maj. James Breathed
    Hart's S. C. Btty.   Johnston's Va. Btty.   McGregor's Va. Btty.
    Shoemaker's Va. Btty.   Thomson's Va. Btty.

Endnotes

Chapter One

1. Charles E. Davis, Jr., *Three Years in the Army, The Story of the Thirteenth Massachusetts Volunteers* (Boston: Estes and Laureat, 1894), 326.

2. (Ibid.)

3. Arthur Kent, ed., *Three Years With Company K* (Rutherford: Farleigh Dickinson University Press, 1976), 257-258.

4. Harold Adams Small, ed., *The Road to Richmond* (Berkeley: University of California Press, 1939), 130-131.

5. Amos M. Judson, *History of the Eighty-Third Regiment Pennsylvania Volunteers* (Dayton: Morningside Bookshop, 1986), 192.

6. John D. Vautier, *History of the 88th Pennsylvania Volunteers in the War for the Union 1861-1865* (Philadelphia: J. B. Lippincott Co., 1894), 173.

7. Alfred S. Roe, *The Thirty-Ninth Massachusetts Volunteers, 1862-1865* (Worchester: Regimental Veteran Association, 1914), 161.

8. O. B. Curtis, *History of the Twenty-Fourth Michigan of the Iron Brigade* (Detroit: Winn & Hammond, 1891), 230.

9. (Small 1939, 130-131)

10. William Todd, ed., *History of the Ninth Regiment N.Y.S.M.-N.G.S.N.Y. Eighty-Third N. Y. Volunteers* (New York: Veterans of the Regiment), 321-322.

11. (Davis, Jr. 1894, 326 and 327)

12. Frederick David Bidwell, comp., *History of the Forty-Ninth New York Volunteers* (Albany: J. B. Lyon Co., Printers, 1916), 43.

13. Alfred S. Roe, *The Tenth Regiment Massachusetts Volunteer Infantry 1861-1864* (Springfield, Mass.: Tenth Regiment Veteran Association, 1909), 253.

14. Nelson V. Hutchinson, *History of the Seventh Massachusetts Volunteer Infantry in the War of the Rebellion of the Southern States 1861-1865* (Taunton, Mass.: Regimental Association, 1890), 172.

15. Alfred Thompson, Diary, May 4, 1864, Jay Luvaas Collection, Manuscript Department, USAMHI, Carlisle Barracks, Pa. Hereafter cited as USAMHI.

16. Thomas W. Hyde, *Following the Greek Cross* (Boston: Houghton, Mifflin and Co., 1894), 182.

17. (Roe 1909, 254)

18. Mark De Wolfe Howe, ed., *Touched With Fire, Civil War Letters and Diary of Oliver Wendell Holmes, Jr., 1861-1864* (Cambridge: Harvard University Press, 1946), 103.

19. Scott, Robert N., comp., *The Official Records of the War of the Rebellion*, XXXVI, part 1 (Washington, D.C.: 1887), 305.

20. Ibid.

21. W. J. Clark, "At the Wilderness," *The National Tribune*, October 23, 1890, 4.

22. Charles Chapin, 1st Vt. Cav. Regt., Entry for May 4, 1864, Diary, January 1, 1864 - December 18, 1864, Civil War Miscellany Papers C-E, Manuscript Department, USAMHI.

23. (*OR*, XXXVI, part 1, 305, 306, 316)

24. James College, "The Wilderness, The Place Where the First Battle of the Campaign Was Fought," *The National Tribune*, April 30, 1891, 3.

    The historian of the 91st Pennsylvania said the regiment crossed the Rapidan at 6:00 A.M.

    Samuel P. Bates, *History of Pennsylvania Volunteers 1861-5*, III (Harrisburg: B. Singerly Printers, 1869), 190.

25. Robert Goldwaite Carter, *Four Brothers in Blue* (Austin: University of Texas Press, 1978), 390. Francis J. Parker, *The Story of the Thirty-Second Massachusetts Infantry* (Boston: C. W. Calkins & Co., 1880), 209.

26. (Small 1939, 131)

27. Gerrish made this entry for May 1. The weather was about the same on May 3-4.

    Theodore Gerrish, *A Private's Reminiscences of the Civil War* (Portland, Me.: Hoyt, Fogg & Donham, 1882), 156-157.

28. (Todd 1889, 322)

29. (Curtis 1891, 230)

    According to the historian of the 56th Pennsylvania, the regiment, which belonged to Wadsworth's division, crossed the Rapidan at 4:00 A.M.

    (Bates 1869, II:221)

30. (Bates 1869, I:261)

31. (Todd 1889, 322)

32. Benjamin F. Cook, *History of the Twelfth Massachusetts Volunteers (Webster Regiment)* (Boston: Twelfth (Webster) Regiment Association, 1882), 127.

33. (Todd 1889, 322)

34. (Gerrish 1882, 158)

35. Edwin C. Bennett, *Musket and Sword* (Boston: Coburn Publishing Co., 1900), 206.

36. *OR*, XXXVI, Part 1, 876. Report of Brig. Gen. James H. Wilson, commanding the Third Cavalry Division.

    "The Wilderness Campaign," *The National Tribune*, February 12, 1891, 3.

    The returns show Voorhies, Desmond and Follett as missing on May 5, 1864 and Case as missing on May 4, 1864. The Confederate reports, in conjunction with the *National Tribune* articles cited from the 3rd Indiana Cavalry and the 1st Vermont, and Chapin's diary of the 1st Vermont, with Wilson's report indicate a cavalry skirmish of some sort. The dates for the May 5 casualties are not correct.

"Nominal Casualties for the 3rd Division Cav. Corps from May 4th 60 June 20th 1864," RG 27, Box 28.

Edward A. Green, 12th Virginia Cavalry, while mistakenly recording the fight at Parker's Store, clearly stated that the 12th Virginia encountered Federal cavalry and captured several men on May 4, 1864. He erroneously remembered the fight occurring at dawn. He said the fighting lasted all day and that the cavalry fought dismounted. He further said the regiment built fires that night, then moved south to the vicinity of the Catharpin Road.

Edward A. Green Papers, Museum of the Confederacy, Richmond, Va.

37. Charles Chapin, 1st Vt. Cavalry Regiment, Diary, May 4, 1864, Civil War Miscellany Papers, C-E, Manuscript Department, USAMHI. W. J. Clark, "At the Wilderness," *The National Tribune*, October 23, 1890, 4.

38. (Ibid.)

39. Wilson said the detachment on the Orange Plank Road was to push as far as Robertson's, then rejoin the division at Parker's Store. He also mentioned that he interrogated prisoners captured on the Orange Turnpike.

(*OR*, XXXVI, Part 1, 876) Brig. James Wilson's report.

Chapin, after saying the company was skirmishing, noted they went back three miles, which would have placed them on the eastern side of Saunders Field and that they then retired one mile more which would have placed them at Wilderness Tavern, behind the V Corps bivouacs. He also said they skirmished until dark. The fighting began at 2:00 P.M. and ended at 7:00 P.M. That would have placed the cavalry on picket several hours before the V Corps relieved them.

I read into the action the part about the Confederates slowing down. They had to have done something to tip off the Federals that they had passed into safe territory.

The infantry encountered had to be from J. M. Jones' brigade.

Charles Chapin, 1st Vt. Cav., Diary, May 4, 1864, Civil War Miscellany Papers, C-E, Manuscript Department, USAMHI.

40. What was left of Young's and Gordon's brigades were at Guiney's Station. Lomax's and Wickham's brigades were at Fredericksburg and Chambliss' brigade was ordered to move across the Rapidan and destroy the abandoned Federal camps in the vicinity of Culpeper. This left him with Rosser's command as his only large and available cavalry force.

Theodore Garnett Memoirs, University of Virginia.

41. (Cook 1882, 127)

42. Company C of the 83rd New York was among them.
(Todd 1889, 322)

43. (Kent 1976, 257), (Cook 1882, 127)

44. (Roe 1914, 162), (Cook 1882, 127)

45. (Small 1939, 176)

46. (Todd 1889, 322-323)

47. (Cook 1882, 127)

48. (Vautier 1894, 173)

49. Louis Dugal, "Wounded At the Wilderness. Our Boys Had a Hard Time of It," *The National Tribune*, November 28, 1912, 7.

50. James College, "The Wilderness, The Place Where the First Battle of the Campaign Was Fought," *The National Tribune*, April 30, 1891, 3.

51. (Carter 1978, 390)

52. Survivors' Association, *History of the Corn Exchange Regiment, 118th Pennsylvania Volunteers* (Philadelphia: J. L. Smith, Publisher, 1888), 397.

53. Charles Chapin, 1st Vt. Cav., Diary, May 4, 1864, Civil War Miscellany Collection, Manuscript Department, USAMHI.

54. (*OR*, XXXVI, part 1, 579-580)

55. (Ibid., 580) Report of Lt. Col. William A. Throop, 1st Mich., commanding.

56. Ms. Brainard's footnote identified the stream as Wilderness Run. It seems to me that it was the northern branch of the Run, known as Caton Run.

    Mary Genevie Green Brainard, comp., *Campaigns of the One Hundred and Forty-Sixth Regiment New York State Volunteers* (N.Y.: G. P. Putnam's Sons, 1915), 176. (Survivors Assoc. 1888, 397)

57. (Bennett 1900, 207)

58. (Bates 1869, II: 459)

59. (Carter 1978, 390), (Parker 1880, 209)

60. (Brainard 1915, 177-178)

61. (Ibid., 178.)

62. (Roe 1909, 254)

63. (Hutchinson 1890, 172-173)

64. Alanson Haines, *History of the Fifteenth Regiment New Jersey Volunteers* (N.Y.: Jenkins & Thomas, Printers, 1883), 141.

65. James L. Bowen, *History of the Thirty-Seventh Regiment Mass. Volunteers in the Civil War of 1861-1865* (Holyhoke, Mass.: Clark W. Bryan & Co., 1884), 271.

66. Alfred Thompson, Diary May 4, 1864 and Letter to Mother, May 10, 1864, Jay Luvaas Collection, USAMHI.

67. George W. Bicknell, *History of the Fifth Regiment Maine Volunteers* (Portland: Hall L. Davis, 1871), 302.

68. George T. Stevens, *Three Years in the Sixth Corps* (Albany: S. R. Gray, Publishers, 1866), 303.

69. Robert S. Westbrook, *History of the 49th Pennsylvania Volunteers* (Altoona: 1898), 186.

70. J. Payne, "The Wilderness, The Turning of the Right Flank May 6, 1864," *The National Tribune*, July 18, 1889, 3.

71. (Howe 1946, 103-104)

72. Alexander R. Boteler, Diary, May 4, 1864, Manuscript Division, Library of Congress. Hereafter cited as LOC.

73. Louis N. Boudrye, *Historic Records of the Fifth New York Cavalry* (Albany: J. Munsell, Albany, 1868), 122. D. H. Robbins, "Thrice Distinguished. Who Opened the Fight in the Wilderness," *The National Tribune*, May 13, 1909, 7.

74. Henry R. Pyne, *Ride to War. The History of the First New Jersey Cavalry*, Earl Schenck Miers, ed. (New Brunswick: Rutgers University Press, 1961), 183 and 185.

75. (*OR*, XXXVI, part 1, 305 and 316)

76. (Pyne 1961, 185)

77. (*OR*, XXXVI, part 1, 869) Report of 16th Pennsylvania Cavalry.

78. (Ibid.), "Report of Major General Fitzhugh Lee of the Operations of His Cavalry Division A.N.V. From May 4th 1864 To September 19th 1864, (both inclusive)," Eleanor S. Brockenbrough Library, The Museum of the Confederacy, Richmond, VA, 1866, 3. Henry P. Turner, 1st Massachusetts Cavalry, Diary, May 4, Civil War Miscellaneous Collection, Tuffman - Walker, Manuscript Department, USAMHI.

79. Thomas Francis, *The Valiant Hours*, Wilbur S. Nye, ed. (Harrisburg: Stackpole, 1961), 195. Charles D. Page, *History of the Fourteenth Regiment, Connecticut Vol. Infantry* (Meriden: Horton Printing Co., 1906), 233.

80. (Galwey 1961, 195), (Page 1906, 233)

81. (Page 1906, 233)

82. Captain Favill (Co. A) said the regiment crossed the river at 10:00 A.M.

   Josiah Marshall Favill, *The Diary of a Young Officer* (Chicago: Donnelly and Sons, 1909), 287.

   The lieutenant (Co. B) remembered that the regiment reached Ely's Ford at daylight.

   Gilbert Frederick, *The Story of a Regiment, Being a Record of the Military Services of the Fifty-Seventh New York State Volunteer Infantry in the War of the Rebellion 1861-1865* (Chicago: The Fifty-Seventh Veteran Association, 1895), 219. Ezra D. Simons, *A Regimental History, The One Hundred Twenty-Fifth New York Volunteers* (NY: Ezra D. Simons, 1888), 197.

83. Ruth L. Silliker, ed., *The Rebel Yell & the Yankee Hurrah, The Civil War Journal of a Maine Volunteer* (Camden, Me.: Down East Books, 1985), 142.

84. Andrew E. Ford, *The Story of the Fifteenth Regiment Massachusetts Volunteer Infantry in the Civil War 1861-1864* (Clinton: W. J. Coulter, 1898), 322.

85. (Page 1906, 233)

86. (Ibid., 233 and 277)

87. (Galwey 1961, 195), (Page 1906, 233)

88. George A. Bowen, (1st Lt., Co. C, 12th N.J.), Diary, May 4, 1864.

89. (Frederick 1895, 219)

90. (Silliker 1985, 142)

91. Heinz K. Meier, ed., *Memoirs of a Swiss Army Officer in the American Civil War* (Bern: Herbert Lang, 1972), 147.

92. George W. Kilmer, "With Grant in the Wilderness," *The National Tribune*, July 17, 1924, 7.

93. Minard McDonald, "March and Battler," *The National Tribune*, March 26, 1896, 3.

94. (Silliker 1985, 142)

95. Daniel G. Grotty, *Four Years Campaigning in the Army of the Potomac* (Grand Rapids, Mich.: Dygert Bros. & Co., 1874), 126.

96. (Silliker 1985, 142)

97. A Committee of the Regimental Association, *History of the Thirty-Fifth Regiment Massachusetts Volunteers, 1862-1865* (Boston: Mills, Knight & Co., 1884), 223.

98. Ernst Linden Waitt, comp., *History of the Nineteenth Regiment Massachusetts Volunteer Infantry 1861-1865* (Salem: The Salem Press, 1906), 367.

99. Charles F. Walcott, *History of the Twenty-First Regiment Massachusetts Volunteers in the War for the Preservation of the Union 1861-1865* (Boston: Houghton, Mifflin and Company, 1882), 312.

100. Amos Hadley, ed., *History of the Sixth New Hampshire Regiment in the War for the Union* (Concord: Republican Press Association, 1891), 213.

101. Committee for the Regiment, *History of the Thirty-Sixth Regiment Massachusetts Volunteers 1862-1865* (Boston: Rockwell and Churchill, 1884), 146.

102. (Walcott 1882, 312) James Madison Stone, *Personal Recollections of the Civil War* (Boston: by the Author, 1918), 159. Stephen M. Weld, *Civil War Diary and Letters of Stephen Minot Weld* (Boston: Massachusetts Historical Society, 1979), 284.

103. Z. Boylston Adams, "In the Wilderness," *Civil War Papers, Read Before the Commandery of Massachusetts, Military Order of the Loyal Legion of the United States,* II (Boston: 1900), 373.

104. Leander W. Cogswell, *A History of the Eleventh New Hampshire Regiment Volunteer Infantry in the Rebellion War, 1861-1865* (Concord: Republican Press Association, 1891), 340.

105. Lyman Jackman, *History of the Sixth New Hampshire Regiment in the War for the Union* (Concord: Republican Press Association, 1891), 213.

106. (Waitt 1906, 367)

107. George Quintus Peyton, "A Civil War Record For 1864-1865," (1906), Fredericksburg and Spotsylvania National; Battlefield Park, Chatham, 21-22.

108. Major J. D. Ferguson, "Memoranda of the Itinerary and Operations of Major General Fitz. Lee's Cavalry Division of the Army of Northern Virginia from May 4th 1864 to October 15th 1864, inclusive," Thomas T. Munford Papers, Special Collections Department, William R. Perkins Library, Duke University, Durham, N.C., 1.

109. Luther W. Hopkins, *From Bull Run to Appomattox, a Boy's View* (Baltimore: Fleet-McGinley Co., 1914), 144-145.

110. J. F. J. Caldwell, *The History of a Brigade of South Carolinians* (Philadelphia: King & Baird, Printers, Philadelphia, 1866), 126. (Reprint, Continental Book Company, Marietta, Ga., 1951).

Chapter Two

1. Pocket Diary, William G. Perry, Stationer, Philadelphia, from the Fredericksburg and Spotsylvania National Battlefield Parks. Captain William B. Cary, "The Wilderness Fight. Opening the Fight of the 5th N.Y. Cav. and the First Man to Fall There," *The National Tribune,* February 1, 1912, 11.

2. William B. Cary, "The Wilderness Fight," *The National Tribune,* February 1, 1912, 11.

3. (*OR,* XXXVI, part 1, 876) Report of Brig. Gen. James H. Wilson.

4. "Report of Major General Fitzhugh Lee of the Operations of His Cavalry Division, A. N. V. From May 4th 1864 to September 19th 1864 (both inclusive)," Eleanor S. Brockenbrough Library, The Museum of the Confederacy, Richmond, Va., 1866, 3.

5. This is based upon the known position of Rosser's brigade on May 5, 1864. Portions of Brigadier General P. M. B. Young's five regiments (the 7th and 20th Georgia Battalion, Cobb's and Phillips' Legions, and the Jeff Davis Legion) and Millen's Georgia Artillery and Louis' Alabama Artillery had not reached the Army of Northern Virginia yet.

   Report from Headquarters, Hampton's Cavalry Division, May 5, 1864, The South Carolinia Library, University of South Carolina, 30.

6. The captain did not describe what he saw in this much detail. He did not see the skirmish line at first but he knew that one was advancing toward him. He had to have heard it.

7. Report of Henry Heth, Spring 1864 to October 1864, unpublished, Army of Northern Virginia, Leaders, Volume 178, Fredericksburg and Spotsylvania National Battlefield Parks.

8. William B. Cary, "The Wilderness Fight," *The National Tribune*, February 1, 1912, 11.

9. The *Tribune* recorded Barker as "Baker" and Cary, in the article, reported the lieutenant at his later rank in the regiment.

   (Ibid.)

10. D. Robbins, "Thrice Distinguished," *The National Tribune*, May 13, 1909, 7.

11. Captain John Thorp said that the 47th North Carolina did not lose many men until he encountered the dismounted cavalry. Captain Cary in his story for the *National Tribune* reported that he was outnumbered and that he had to continually admonish the recruits in his company not to fire wildly. The Confederates did not attempt to charge the Federals at any time in the fighting along the creek. They tried to outflank them instead.

   Walter Clark, ed., *Histories of Several Regiments and Battalions From North Carolina in the Great War*, III (Raleigh: E. M. Uzzell, 1901), 94. Report of Capt. John H. Thorp, 47th N.C.

12. (Clark 1901, III:110) Report of 2nd Lt. J. Rowan Rogers, Co. I, 44th N.C.

13. William B. Cary, "The Wilderness Fight," *The National Tribune*, February 1, 1912, 11.

14. (*OR*, XXXVI, part 1, 580) Report of Lt. Col. William Throop, 1st Mich., commanding.

15. Thomas G. Jones, Letter to John W. Daniel, July 3, 1904, John Warwick Daniel Papers, 1849-1904, Special Collections Department, William R. Perkins Library, Duke University, Durham, N.C., 2. "Barringer's N. C. Brigade of Cavalry," North Carolina *Daily Confederate*, February 22, 1865, 2, col. 1.

16. (Brainard 1915, 179)

17. (*OR*, XXXVI, part 1, 580) Thomas G. Jones, Letter to John W. Daniel, July 3, 1904, John Warwick Daniel Papers, 1849-1904, Special Collections Department, William R. Perkins Library, Duke University, Durham, N.C., 2-3.

18. (Brainard 1915, 179)

19. (Ibid., 181)

20. (Ibid., 180, 182)

21. (Ibid., 181)

22. (Ibid., 181-182)

23. (Ibid., 178-179)

24. (Kent 1976, 258-259)

25. John Worsham, *One of Jackson's Foot Cavalry* (N.Y.: The Neale Publishing Co., 1912), 201.

26. This is at best an estimate. At a walk, averaging 4 miles per hour, Massaponax Church - 6 miles from Spotsylvania Court House - was about an hour and a half away. Luther Hopkins (6th Virginia Cavalry) said the regiment left early in the morning. One can assume it was around 5:00 A.M. - several minutes after dawn.

27. (*OR*, XXVI, part 1, 867) Report of Brig. Gen. Henry E. Davies, Jr., 1st Brig., 2nd Div., commanding.

28. The Richmond paper said the Confederates encountered a small party of 60-70 Federals.

   "Skirmish on the Right Wing," Richmond *Daily Dispatch*, May 7, 1864, 1, col. 1.

29. (*OR*, XXXVI, part 1, 876) Report of Brig. Gen. James Wilson.

30. The 3rd Indiana and the 8th New York suffered nominal casualties during the Wilderness Campaign. The 8th New York lost its four men at Saunders Field the day before. The 3rd Indiana lost seven men during the engagement while the 1st Vermont lost forty-six troopers. Wilson said that Chapman's brigade held the meeting house until it was repulsed. Based upon the casualty returns, it appears that the 1st Vermont did most of the fighting.

31. Dennis E. Frye, *12th Virginia Cavalry* (Lynchburg, Va.: H. E. Howard, Inc., 1988), 64.

32. (*OR*, XXXVI, part 1, 897) Report of Col. George H. Chapman, commanding 2nd Brig., 3rd Div., Cavalry Corps, Army of the Potomac.

33. "Diary of W. H. Arehart," *The Rockingham Recorder*, Vol. II, #3, October 1959, 150-151.

34. (Frye 1988, 64)

35. Chapman indicated that the Confederates dismounted and fought a stubborn withdrawal action with his better armed Federal cavalry. Dennis Frye, in his regimental of the 12th Virginia, said that the Federals chased the Confederates back upon the rest of Rosser's brigade but McDonald's account in *The Laurel Brigade* does not corroborate that statement.

   (*OR*, XXXVI, part 1, 897)

36. (*OR*, XXXVI, part 1, 897)

37. Charles Chapin, 1st Vt. Cav., Diary, May 5, 1864, Civil War Miscellany Papers, C - E, Manuscripts Department, USAMHI.

38. Rev. Joseph T. Durkin, S.J., *Confederate Chaplain, A War Journal of Rev. James B. Sheeran, c.s.s.r., 14th Louisiana, C.S.A.* (Milwaukee: The Bruce Publishing Co., 1960), 86.

39. Armstrong said the regiment advanced at 11:00 A.M.

   Richard L. Armstrong, *25th Virginia Infantry and 9th Battalion Virginia Infantry* (Lynchburg, Va.: H. E. Howard, Inc., 1990), 75.

   Colonel S. D. Thurston (3rd N.C.) said the fighting began at 10:30 A.M.

   S. D. Thurston, "Report of the Conduct of General George H. Steuart's Brigade from the 5th to the 12th of May, 1864," *Southern Historical Society Papers*, XIV, 147. Hereafter cited as *SHSP*.

40. (Worsham 1912, 200)

41. (Armstrong 1990, 75)

42. (Ibid.)

The Federals claimed the victory in the skirmish and went so far as to insist that they drove the Confederates from Saunders Field.

(*OR*, XXXVI, part 1, 575) Report of Lt. Col. Colonel William B. White, 18th Massachusetts, commanding.

43. (*OR*, XXXVI, part 1, 575) Report of Lieut. Col. Colonel William B. White, 18th Massachusetts, commanding.

44. (Worsham 1912, 200)

45. John Chapla, *48th Virginia Infantry* (Lynchburg: H. E. Howard, Inc., 1989), 70.

46. (Armstrong 1990, 75)

47. (*OR*, XXXVI, part 1, 575) Report of Lt. Col. William B. White, 18th Massachusetts, commanding.

48. (Brainard 1915, 182-183)

49. George R. Agassis, ed., *Meade's Headquarters 1863-1865, Letters of Colonel Theodore Lyman From the Wilderness to Appomattox* (Freeport, N.Y.: Libraries Press, 1970), 100.

50. McHenry Howard, *Recollections of a Maryland Confederate Soldier and Staff Officer* (Dayton: Morningside Bookshop, 1975), 270.

51. The 5th Virginia held the right of the brigade line that afternoon. When the regiment broke, it fell back on the 27th Virginia.

Lee A. Wallace, Jr., *5th Virginia Infantry*. (Lynchburg: H. E. Howard, Inc., 1988), 56.

According to Mr. Reidenbaugh, the 4th, 5th, and part of the 27th Virginia regiments broke in battle that afternoon. The 4th formed at right angles to allow the rest of the brigade to reform. The 33rd Virginia held the left of the brigade line. The 2nd Virginia had no other place to form than between the 4th and the 33rd Virginia. The setting fits together this way: the 5th Virginia was on the right, followed by the 27th, the 4th, the 2nd and the 33rd Virginia.

Lowell Reidenbaugh, *33rd Virginia Infantry*. (Lynchburg: H. E. Howard, Inc., 1987), 82.

52. If the firing was heard to the right rear and the skirmishers did reach the Germanna Plank Road, the brigade had to have been operating as flank cover for the Army of Northern Virginia.

(Reidenbaugh 1987, 81-83)

53. Colonel S. D. Thurston of the 3rd North Carolina shows the Louisianans on line with Steuart's men by 11:40 A.M.

(Howard 1975, 277) Henry E. Handerson, *Yankee in Gray* (Western Reserve, Oh.: The Press of Western Reserve University, 1962), 69.

54. (Handerson 1962, 69-70)

55. S. D. Thurston, "Report of the Conduct of General George H. Steuart's Brigade from the 5th to the 12th of May 1864, inclusive," *SHSP*, XIV, 148.

56. Battle's brigade went in with its left on the Orange Turnpike. When Cutler's Federal brigade engaged the 48th Virginia, it broke through the Confederate line between Doles and Jones' without overrunning Doles' line. If Doles had been in contact with the 48th Virginia it would have been hit on the front.

57. The map shows Rodes' division in the Orange Turnpike from east to west as follows: Doles, Daniel and Gordon.

Edward Steere, *The Wilderness Campaign* (Harrisburg, Pa.: The Stackpole Co., 1960), 126. (Clark 1901, III:43)

58. (Brainard 1915, 183)

59. (Ibid.)

60. James College, "The Wilderness," *The National Tribune*, April 30, 1891, 3.

61. (Brainard 1915, 185-186)

62. The regimental strengths are from RG 94, OAG, Volunteer Organizations, Civil War, Returns, 5th Army Corps, Army of the Potomac, April 1864, Box 19, National Archives. Hereafter cited as NA.

63. (Brainard 1915, 185-186)

"I am uncertain whether it was a single line which so advanced or whether we were followed by a second one."

Porter Farley, *The 140th N.Y. Vols.: Wilderness, May 5, 1864* (Gettysburg: The Conflict, 1990), 21.

The Regulars formed in two lines.

Louis Dugal, "Wounded at the Wilderness," *The National Tribune*, November 28, 1912, 7.

The field was too small to accommodate so many regiments in a two line formation. One way to explain the light casualties of the 2nd and 17th Regulars is to place them behind preceding lines of battle. They could not have literally been in the field if they were in a single line. They would have been hundreds of feet into the woods. McHenry Howard said the Federals attacked their position in four lines.

Lieutenant George Head (D/1/11th U.S.) wrote that the 12th U.S. was behind his regiment and that his regiment's flank was exposed during the charge. That would have placed the 11th U.S. on the right of the 140th N.Y. and the 12th U.S. in the second line. The 14th and the 12th U.S. were in the same line.

Timothy J. Reese, *Sykes' Regular Infantry Division, 1861-1865* (Jefferson, N.C.: McFarland & Co., Inc., 1990), 309. (Howard 1975, 210)

The returns for Ayres' brigade on April 30, 1864 were recorded as follows: 2nd U.S. 173 officers and men (6 companies)

>   11th U.S. 277 o & m (6 cos.)
>
>   12th U.S. 394 o & m (10 cos.)
>
>   14th U.S. 448 o & m (8 cos.)
>
>   17th U.S. 242 o & m (8 cos.)
>
>   140th N.Y. 627 o & m (10 cos.)
>
>   146th N.Y. 589 o & m (10 cos.)
>
>   91st Pa. 401 o & m (10 cos.)
>
>   155th Pa. 488 o & m (10 cos.)

RG 94, OAG, Volunteer Organizations, Civil War Returns, V Corps, Box 19, April 30, 1864, NA.

64. (Reese 1990, 301)

65. John R. King, *My Experience in the Confederate Army and in Northern Prisons* (Clarksburg, West Virginia: Stonewall Jackson Chapter, No. 1333, United Daughters of the Confederacy, 1917), 22.

66. (Brainard 1915, 185-186)

67. (Ibid., 186-187)

68. (Ibid., 194)

69. (Ibid., 186-187)

70. (Carter 1978, 390)

71. (Bennett 1900, 208-209)

72. (Gerrish 1882, 158)

Chapter Three

1. He described the position of 44th and the 26th North Carolina regiments.

   (Clark 1901, III:27) Report of Maj. Charles M. Stedman, 44th.

   Foster said the Yankees made a stand at the south end of an old field with woods to protect them. This fits the southern end of the field south of Parker's Store below the Plank Road. The 52nd had to have been on the extreme right of the brigade to see that.

   Diary, 1st Sergeant John A. Foster, Company A, 52nd , John A. Foster Papers, 1862-65, Reminiscences, Special Collections Department, William R. Perkins Library, Duke University, Durham, N.C.

2. D. H. Robbins, "Thrice Distinguished," *The National Tribune*, May 13, 1909, 7.

3. William B. Cary, "The Wilderness Fight," *The National Tribune*, February 1, 1912, 11.

4. (*OR*, XXXVI, Part 1, 885) Report of Col. McIntosh, 3rd Pa. Cav.

5. William B. Cary, "The Wilderness Fight," *The National Tribune*, February 1, 1912, 11.

6. Louis N. Boudrye, *Historical Records of the Fifth New York Cavalry* (Albany: J. Munsel, 1868), 123.

7. D. H. Robbins, "Thrice Distinguished," *The National Tribune*, May 13, 1909, 7.

8. William B. Cary, "The Wilderness Fight," *The National Tribune*, February 2, 1912, 11.

9. (*OR*, XXXVI, Part 1, 129)

   The regimental historian reported 13 killed, 22 wounded, 22-24 known missing, and 15-20 missing and presumed dead for an estimated total of 72-79 casualties.

   (Boudrye 1868, 122)

10. Allan Nevins, ed., *A Diary of Battle, The Personal Journals of Colonel Charles S. Wainwright, 1861-1865* (Gettysburg: Stan Clark Books, 1962), 349 -350.

11. (*OR*, XXXVI, part 1, 418.)

12. Alexander R. Boteler Diary, LOC.

13. Theodore Garnett Memoirs, Special Collections Department, University of Virginia. J. R. Sypher, *History of the Pennsylvania Reserves* (Lancaster, Pa.: Elias Barr & Co., 1865), 510.

14. Alexander R. Boteler Diary, LOC.

15. (Steere 1960, 115) Theodore Garnett Memoirs, Special Collections Department, University of Virginia.

16. John A. Sloan, *Reminiscences of the Guilford Grays, Co. B, 27th N.C. Regiment* (Washington, D.C.: R. O. Polkinhorn, Printer, 1883), 81.

Lieutenant Graham said his brigade moved into the front line to relieve Kirkland's men around 11:00 A.M. In this particular battle the Confederate watches seemed to agree with the Northern times to within half an hour. Both sides agree that the counterattack by the VI Corps came sometime between 2:30 P.M. to 3:00 P.M. He places the 15th and the 46th North Carolina on the south side of the road and the 48th and the 27th North Carolina on the north side of the road.

Letter, James A. Graham, (2nd Lt., Co. G, 27th N.C.), to his mother, May 9, 1864, Special Collections Department, William R. Perkins Library, Duke University, Durham, N.C. (Clark 1901, II: 446) Report of Lt. James A. Graham, Co. G, 27th N.C.

Wadill said Company B (which would have been the left company in a regimental line) was in the Plank Road.

(Ibid., III:75) Report of Q.M. Sgt. John M. Wadill, 46th N.C.

17. William Thomas Poague, *Gunner With Stonewall*, Monroe F. Cockrell, ed.. (Jackson, Tenn.: McCowat-Mercer Press, Inc., 1957), 87-88.

18. Alexander R. Boteler Diary, LOC.

19. (Clark 1901, III:304) Report of Adj. Charles M. Cooke, 55th N.C.

20. (*OR*, XXXVI, Part 1, 676) Report of Brig. Gen. George W. Getty, 2nd Div., VI Corps, commanding.

21. (Ibid., 665) Report of Col. Emory Upton, 2nd Brig., 1st Div., VI Corps, commanding.

22. (Ibid., 659) Report of Brig. Gen. Horatio G. Wright, 1st Div., VI Corps, commanding.

23. (Ibid., 665) Col. Emory Upton's report. (Ibid,, 659) Brig. Gen. Horatio G. Wright's report.

Bicknell places the regiment in an open field bordered by woods just a short distance from the Germanna Plank Road. It had to be Mrs. Spotswood's farm. It was the only open spot in the vicinity of the Culpeper Mine Road.

(Bicknell 1871, 302)

24. (Bicknell 1871, 302)

25. (Ibid., 303) Thomas G. Jones to John W. Daniel, Letter, July 3, 1904, John Warwick Daniel Papers, Special Collections Department, William R. Perkins Library, Duke University, Durham, NC, 1.

26. Maurus Oesterich, Diary, May 5, 1864, Harrisburg Civil War Round Table Collection, Box M - Z, Manuscript Department, USAMHI, 44. Henry Keiser, Diary, May 5, 1864, Harrisburg Civil War Round Table Collection, Box FR - HE, Manuscript Department, USAMHI, 107.

27. Upton in his report did not place the New Jersey Brigade upon his right. He did say that Russell's brigade was on his right. Horatio G. Wright, in the *Official Records*, said that the division formed from left to right as follows: Upton, Brown, Russell. This seems like it occurred prior to advancing into the Wilderness. If that is the case, the New Jersey Brigade was completely out of touch with its division and Upton. Beech noted that the time was 10:00 A.M.

John P. Beech, "Gallantry of the 4th New Jersey in the Wilderness: The Break in the Lines of the Sixth Corps," *Grand Army Scout and Soldiers' Mail,* October 25, 1884, 1.

28.　Private Westbrook said the 49th Pennsylvania led the advance. The 119th Pennsylvania had to be immediately behind it, because it volleyed into the 49th later during the attack. The 6th Maine, the only regiment, which I cannot place in the brigade, probably came next. Logically, the 5th Wisconsin was behind it. It makes sense that the 5th Wisconsin was at the end of the column. By being at the rear, it would have been easier to detach five companies forward and to the flank as skirmishers than from the center of the brigade.

(Westbrook 1898, 187) (*OR,* XXXVI, Part 1, 672) Report of Col. Oliver Edwards, 37th Massachusetts, 3rd Brig., 1st Div., VI Corps, commanding.

29.　(Ibid., 676) Report of Brig. Gen. George W. Getty, 2nd Div., VI Corps, commanding. John P. Beech, "Gallantry of the 4th New Jersey in the Wilderness," *Grand Army Scout and Soldiers' Mail,* October 25, 1884, 1.

30.　(Haines 1883, 145)

31.　(*OR,* XXXVI, Part 1, 676) Report of Brig. Gen. George W. Getty, 2nd Div., VI Corps, commanding.

32.　The regiment would have marched with its weapons at the "shoulder shift" because it was the standard means of carrying a weapon into action.

George H. Uhler, "The Wilderness. A Pennsylvania Comrade Gives His Experience in the Big Battle," *The National Tribune,* May 21, 1891, 3.

33.　(Bates 1870, III:290) George H. Uhler, "The Wilderness. A Pennsylvania Comrade Gives His Experience in the Big Battle," *The National Tribune,* May 21, 1891, 3.

34.　(*OR,* XXXVI, Part 1, 681) Report of Brig. Gen. Frank Wheaton, 1st Brig., 2nd Div., VI Corps, commanding.

35.　(Bates 1870, III:290) George H. Uhler, "The Wilderness. A Pennsylvania Comrade Gives His Experience in the Big Battle," *The National Tribune,* May 21, 1891, 3.

36.　(*OR,* XXXVI, Part 1, 696) Report of Col. Lewis A. Grant, 2nd Brig., 2nd Div., VI Corps, commanding.

37.　(Ibid., 709) Report of Col. Thomas L. Seaver, 3rd Vt., commanding.

38.　(Ibid., 696) Report of Col. L. A. Grant.

39.　(Ibid., 711) Report of Lt. Col. Stephen M. Pingree, 4th Vt., commanding.

40.　Pingree said his regiment relieved the 1st Brigade. To have done that, at least one regiment of that brigade had to have been south of the Plank Road. I believe the 93rd Pennsylvania was that regiment.

(Bates 1870, IV:380), (*OR,* XXXVI, Part 1, 681) Brig. Gen. Frank Wheaton's Report. (Ibid., 691) Report of Maj. Thomas McLaughlin, 102nd Pa. (Ibid., 711) Report of Lieut. Col. Stephen M. Pingree, 4th Vt., commanding.

41.　Robert Hunt Rhodes, ed., *All for the Union* (Lincoln, R.I.: Andrew Mowbray Inc., 1985), 144. (Hutchinson 1890, 176), (Roe 1909, 257)

42.　(Roe 1909, 257)

43.　(*OR,* XXXVI, Part 1, 897) Col. George Chapman's Report.

44.　(Ibid., 877) Brig. Gen. James Wilson's report.

45.　Pennington said he followed the cavalry onto the field and went into position at the meeting house. It is safe to assume that the cavalry were behind the guns and not in front of them.

(Ibid., 902-903) Report of 1st Lt. Alexander Pennington, Btty. M, 2nd U.S. Arty., commanding.

46.   (Ibid., 877) Brig. Gen. James Wilson's report.

47.   (Frye 1988, 64)

48.   Frank M. Myers, *The Comanches: A History of White's Battalion of Virginia Cavalry* (Marietta, Ga.: Continental Book Co., 1956), 258-259.

49.   (*OR*, XXXVI, part 1, 877, 869) Reports of Brig. Gen. James Wilson and Col. George Chapman, respectively.

50.   (Ibid., 555) Report of Maj. John D. Lentz, 91st Pa., commanding.

51.   The 1st New York Sharpshooters are not mentioned in the brigade formation yet the regiment suffered over thirty casualties, which is indicative of having been in combat. The logical place to put the sharpshooters was on the skirmish line and therefore, the regiment would not have been in the formation.

52.   Curtis erred when he placed the brigade on the left of the division. He also erred when he lined up the brigade.

      (Curtis 1891, 230-231)

      Dawes, who was in the Wilderness, where Curtis was not, said his regiment was 100 paces behind the 7th Indiana.

      Rufus R. Dawes, *Service With the Sixth Wisconsin Volunteers* (Dayton: Morningside Bookshop, 1984), 259.

      Welsh says his regiment was on the right of the brigade.

      (*OR*, XXXVI, part 1, 617) Report of Major Merit Welsh, 7th Ind., commanding.

53.   Avery Harris, "Personal Reminiscences of the Author from August 1862 to June 1865, War of the Rebellion," Avery Harris Papers, USAMHI, 156.

54.   (Brainard 1915, 184)

55.   (Carter 1978, 391)

56.   (Curtis 1891, 232)

57.   L. Allison Wilmer, J. H. Jarret, and George W. F. Vernon, *History and Roster of Maryland Volunteers, War of 1861-5*, I (Baltimore: Press of Guggenheimer, Weil & Co., 1898), 265.

58.   Avery Harris, "Personal Reminiscences of the Author from August 1862 to June 1865, War of the Rebellion," Avery Harris Papers, USAMHI, 157.

59.   Thomas Chamberlin, *History of the One Hundred and Fiftieth Regiment Pennsylvania Volunteers* (Baltimore: Butternut and Blue, 1986), 206 and 209.

60.   Avery Harris, "Personal Reminiscences of the Author from August 1862 to June 1865, War of the Rebellion," Avery Harris Papers, USAMHI, 158.

61.   (Bates 1869, II:221-222)

62.   Abram P. Smith, *History of the 76th Regiment New York Volunteers* (Courtland, N.Y.: 1867), 284.

63.   (*OR*, XXXVI, part 1, 631)

64.   (Chamberlin 1986, 207)

65.   (Dawes 1984, 259)

66.   W. F. Beyer and O. F. Keydel, (eds.), *Deeds of Valor*, I (Detroit: Keydel Co., 1907), 316.

67. John W. Nesbit, *General History of Company D, 149th Pennsylvania Volunteers and Personal Sketches of the Members* (Oakdale, Cal.: Oakdale Print & Publishing Co., 1908), 25-26.

68. Avery Harris, "Personal Reminiscences of the Author from August 1862 to June 1865, War of the Rebellion," Avery Harris Papers, USAMHI, 158.

69. (Wilmer 1898, I:265)

70. (Dawes 1984, 259-260)

71. This is based upon Avery Harris' description of the terrain in his recollections.

72. (Westbrook 1898, 187)

73. (*OR*, XXXVI, Part 1, 665) Report of Col. Emory Upton. W. J. Hardee, *Rifle and Light Infantry Tactics, School of the Battalion*, Vol. II. (Westport, Conn.: Greenwoods Press, Publishers, 1971), 27-29.

74. (Bicknell 1871, 303)

Chapter Four

1. (*OR*, XXXVI, part 1, 897) Col. George Chapman's report.

2. Charles Chapin, 1st Vt. Cav., Diary, May 5, 1864, Civil War Miscellany Papers, C - E, Manuscripts Department, USAMHI.

3. (Myers 1956, 259)

4. William N. McDonald, *A History of the Laurel Brigade*, Bushrod C. Washington, ed. (Kate S. McDonald, 1907), 226.

5. (Ibid.)

6. (*OR*, XXXVI, part 1, 897) Col. George Chapman's report.

7. (McDonald 1907, 226)

8. Charles Chapin, 1st Vt. Cav., Diary, May 5, 1864, Civil War Miscellany Collections, C - E, Manuscripts Department, USAMHI.

9. This is my interpretation.

10. (*OR*, XXXVI, part 1, 877) Brig. Gen. James Wilson's report.

11. Chapman's report implied a panic much like the one described here. Casualty reports of the Army of the Potomac.

    (Ibid., 129) Charles Chapin, 1st Vt. Cav., Diary, May 5, 1864, Civil War Miscellany Collection, C - E, Manuscripts Department, USAMHI.

12. (*OR*, XXXVI, part 1, 129)

13. Pennington said he fired upon the Rebels' flank as soon as the 2nd brigade fell back and cleared his field of fire. McDonald said the Confederates came under severe artillery fire. He said that the Federals yielded to the Confederate advance then came under the fire of an annoying Federal battery on a hill. Wilson said that the 8th Illinois, with the assistance of the two Federal batteries, saved his life while the rest of the First Brigade retreated from the field.

    (Ibid., 877, 903) Lt. A. Pennington's report.

    The casualties are based upon Mr. Frye's research.

    (Frye 1988, 64-65)

Captain McDonald's exciting account would have the reader believe that the 12th Virginia did not stop herding the Federals back until they were swept past the Po River. On the next page, however, he asserted that the Federal retreat was orderly and well conducted. He also said the charge of the 12th Virginia occurred immediately after the Federals' First Brigade broke to the rear.

Wilson's and Pennington's reports clearly refute that as do the casualty figures reported in the *Official Records*. While it seems more dramatic to portray the Southern cavalier as the ever charging gallant, it is evident from Colonel Chapman's report that the Rebels attacked in strong force, which could not have been effected by dismounted cavalry in the woods. They would not have had enough punch to achieve their objective if they had remained dismounted. Chapman's skirmishers reported that the Rebels reinforced their line and were preparing to advance in force which implies a charge in column.

Pennington's account does not provide any evidence of a rout from Craig's Meeting House but rather an orderly, slow withdrawal which McDonald supported on p.227.

(McDonald 1907, 226)

Myers definitely stated that the brigade took casualties in the charge which he believed occurred around 2:00 P.M.

(Myers 1956, 260)

14.   (Ibid.), (Frye 1988, 65)

15.   Report of Captain P. P. Pendleton, Headquarters, Horse Artillery, November 19, 1864, 2, Archives, Virginia Military Institute.

16.   Paul Chiles, chief historian for Antietam National Battlefield, explained to me that Federal arsenals did use pine pitch to hold the musket balls in a case shot in place as well as packed sulphur. He explained that pine pitch burned black and sulphur burned yellow or white. He also showed me a cut away view of a case shot from a 10 Pounder Parrott to explain how the shells were constructed. He said that the bursting charges could have blasted away the casing around the balls which would cause the shells to glow red and to burn black.

George M. Neese, *Three Years in the Confederate Horse Artillery* (Dayton: Morningside Bookshop, 1983), 259-260.

17.   (*OR*, XXXVI, part 1, 557) Report of Col. Alfred L. Pearson, 155th Pa., commanding.

18.   (King 1917, 22)

19.   (Reese 1990, 309)

20.   (Farley 1990, 22)

21.   (Ibid., 23, 24, 27)

22.   (Reese 1990, 302)

23.   Handerson did not say that the men were relieving themselves but it can be inferred. It naturally occurs after long marches and hastily eaten meals.

(Handerson 1962, 70)

24.   (Brainard 1915, 188-190)

25.   (Reese 1990, 303)

26.   (Brainard 1915, 188-190)

27.   As it originally started, Ayres' brigade consisted of three lines, all of which had their left flank anchored on the Orange Turnpike. The 140th New York, with the four

companies of the 11th U.S., held a front of about 772 feet which would have placed
most of the 11th U.S. in the woods until the 140th New York veered left and crossed
the pike. The 12th and the 14th U.S. would have created a line about 811 feet long
with the 2nd and the 17th U.S. extending it about 393 feet further into the woods.
The 146th New York, 155th Pennsylvania and the 91st Pennsylvania occupied a
front of about 1423 feet with the two Pennsylvania regiments extending some 862
feet into the woods.

The 1st line = 772'

The 2nd line = 1210'

The 3rd line = 1423'

When the 2nd U.S. and the 17th U.S. moved in behind the 12th and the 14th Regulars, they uncovered the fronts of the 155th Pennsylvania and the 91st Pennsylvania.
The movement was completed without the knowledge of either of the Pennsylvania
regiments.

(Reese 1990, 303), T. F. Walter, "Another Account of the 91st P.V.," *Grand Army Scout
and Soldiers' Mail,* October 18, 1884, 2. The 155th Regimental Association, *Under the
Maltese Cross: Antietam to Appomattox, The Loyal Uprising in Western Pennsylvania 1861-
1865* (Pittsburgh: The 155th Regimental Association, 1910), 247-248.

28. (Handerson 1962, 70)

29. (*OR,* XXXVI, part 1, 580-581) Report of Lt. Col. William Throop, 1st Mich., com-
    manding.

30. *Medical and Surgical History of the Civil War,* VIII (Wilmington, N.C.: Broadfoot Pub-
    lishing Co., 1991), 574.

31. (*OR,* XXXVI, part 1, 580-581) Report of Lieut. Col. William Throop, 1st Mich.,
    commanding.

32. There was no mention of the 16th Michigan's place in the formation. It was not on
    the skirmish line and not in the direct assault. Like the 44th New York, I believe it
    was in the rear line and not heavily engaged.

    (Ibid., 587) Report of Maj. Edward Knox, 44th N.Y., commanding.

33. Eugene A. Nash, *A History of the 44th Regiment, New York Volunteer Infantry in the Civil
    War* (Chicago: R. R. & Sons, Co., 1911), 184. (Judson 1986, 193)

34. (Nash 1911, 286)

35. (Judson 1986, 193-194)

36. (Gerrish 1882, 161)

37. (*OR,* XXXVI, part 1, 589) Report of Lt. Col. DeWitt McCoy, 83rd Pa., commanding.

38. John J. Pullen, *The 20th Maine* (Greenwich, Conn.: Fawcett Publications, Inc., 1962),
    193.

39. (Survivors Assoc. 1888, 399)

40. William Shaw Stewart, "Experiences of an Army Surgeon, 1863-1864," The Marjory
    G. Blubaugh Collection, 14. Used with permission. (Howard 1975, 272), W. S. Dunlop,
    Lee's Sharpshooters (Dayton: Morningside Bookshop, 1988), 387-388.

    The attack was so sudden that Daniel, who was in the pike, and Moore insisted that
    Early and Jones fell in the same fire.

    Major Samuel J. G. Moore to Major John W. Daniel, June 30, 1905, and Statement by
    John W. Daniel, May 5, 1864, John Warwick Daniel Papers, Civil War Materials,

Wilderness 5 May, 1864, Special Collections Department, Accession # 158 5383 A-E, Box 24, Alderman Library, University of Virginia.

41. (Judson 1986, 193-194)

42. The 83rd Pennsylvania and the 18th Massachusetts had to have stayed together because Lieutenant Colonel McCoy (83rd Pennsylvania) and Colonel Hayes (18th Massachusetts) conferred with one another prior to the retreat.

   (*OR*, XXXVI, part 1, 589) Report of Lt. Col. DeWitt McCoy, 83rd Pa., commanding.

43. (Ibid., 575-576) Report of Lieut. Col. William White, 18th Massachusetts, commanding.

44. (Survivors Assoc. 1888, 399 and 401)

45. (Gerrish 1882, 161)

46. Major John W. Daniel stated that Junius Daniel was in position near John M. Jones' brigade.

   Statement by John Warwick Daniel, John Warwick Daniel Papers, Civil War Material, Wilderness 5 May, 1864, Special Collections Department, Accession # 158 5383 AE, Box 24, Alderman Library, University of Virginia.

47. (Judson 1986, 193-194)

48. Statement by John W. Daniel, May 5, 1864, Civil War Materials, Wilderness 5 May, 1864, Accession # 158 5383 A-E, Box 24, Special Collections Department, Alderman Library, University of Virginia.

49. (Armstrong 1990, 75)

50. Statement by John W. Daniel, May 5, 1864, Civil War Materials, Wilderness 5 May, 1864, Accession # 158 5383 A-E, Box 24, Special Collections Department, Alderman Library, University of Virginia.

51. (Clark 1901, III:43-44)

52. (Judson 1986, 193-194), (Clark 1901, III:44)

53. (*OR*, XXXVI, part 1, 589) Report of Lt. Col. DeWitt McCoy, 83rd Pa., commanding.

54. (Judson 1986, 193-194)

55. (Clark 1901, III:44)

56. (Gerrish 1882, 161)

57. (Pullen 1962, 194)

58. (Survivors Assoc. 1888, 400)

59. (Judson 1986, 193-194)

60. (Survivors Assoc. 1888, 400)

61. The 20th Maine, based upon my research, advanced without making contact with the 118th Pennsylvania after the two regiments got into the woods.

62. (Judson 1986, 193-194), (*OR*, XXXVI, part 1, 576) Report of Lt. Col. William White, 18th Massachusetts, commanding.

63. (Ibid., 573) Report of Maj. Ellis Spear, 20th Me., commanding.

64. (Pullen 1962, 195), (*OR*, XXXVI, part 1, 573) Report of Maj. Ellis Spear, 20th Me., commanding.

65. (Gerrish 1882, 166)

66. (Brainard 1915, 188-190)

67. (Worsham 1912, 201)

68. (*Medical and Surgical History* 1991, VIII:311)

69. (Ibid., 377)

70. (Farley 1990, 26-28)

71. (Worsham 1912, 202)

72. (Brainard 1915, 188-190), S. D. Thurston, "Report of the Conduct of General George H. Steuart's Brigade from the 5th to the 12th of May, inclusive," *SHSP*, XIV, 148. (Clark 1901, I:150-151) Col. Hamilton A. Brown, 1st N.C., "The Wilderness Campaign."

73. (Farley 1990, 36-37)

74. John H. Worsham, *One of Jackson's Foot Cavalry*, James I. Robertson, Jr., ed.. (Jackson, Tenn.: McCowat-Mercer Press, Inc., 1964) fn, 129. (Worsham 1912, 202)

75. (*OR*, XXXVI, part 1, 640) Report of Col. Charles S. Wainwright, 1st N.Y. Lgt. Arty., commanding Arty. Brig.

76. (Worsham 1912, 202), (Farley 1990, 37)

77. (Durkin 1960, 86-87), Statement by John W. Daniel, May 5, 1864, Civil War Materials, Wilderness 5 May, 1864, Accession # 158 5383 A-E, Box 24, Special Collections Department, Alderman Library, University of Virginia.

78. (Howard 1975, 271)

79. (Worsham 1912, 202)

80. (Howard 1975, 271)

81. (*OR*, XXXVI, part 1, 640) Report of Col. Charles S. Wainwright, 1st N.Y. Lgt. Arty., commanding Arty. Brig.

82. (Howard 1975, 272)

83. (Brainard 1915, 188-190)

84. (Ibid., 190-192)

85. (Ibid.)

86. Louis Dugal, "Wounded at the Wilderness," *The National Tribune*, November 28, 1912, 7.

87. (Reese 1990, 306 and 309)

88. (Brainard 1915, 190-192)

89. (Ibid.)

90. (Ibid. 188-190), S. D. Thurston, "Report of the Conduct of General George H. Steuart's Brigade from the 5th to the 12th of May, inclusive," *SHSP*, XIV, 148.

    Brown said two of the guns escaped capture. Evidence does not support this assertion. Only two were deployed in Saunders Field.

    (Clark 1901, I:150-151.), Col. Hamilton A. Brown, 1st N.C., "The Wilderness Campaign."

91. (Farley 1990, 28-29)

92. (Brainard 1915, 190-192)

93. (Steere 1960, 160)

94. (Brainard 1915, 190-192)

95. (Bates 1870, III:190)

96. T. F. Walter, "Another Account of the 91st P.V.," *Grand Army Scout and Soldiers' Mail*, October 18, 1884, 2. (Bates 1870, III:190)

97. (Brainard 1915, 192-193)

98. *(OR*, XXXVI, part 1, 557) Report of Col. Alfred L. Pearson, 155th Pa., commanding. Terrence V. Murphy, *10th Virginia Infantry*, (1st Ed.). (Lynchburg, Va.: H. E. Howard, Inc., 1989), 93. (Regimental Assoc. 1910, 247-248)

99. (Brainard 1915, 193-194)

100. (Ibid., 192-193)

101. (Ibid., 197-198)

102. (Ibid., 192-193)

103. (Ibid., 194)

104. (Ibid., 198-199)

105. (*Medical and Surgical History* 1991, VIII:119)

106. (Brainard 1915, 192-193)

107. Louis Dugal, "Wounded at the Wilderness," *The National Tribune*, November 28, 1912, 7.

108. (Brainard 1915, 194)

109. (Ibid., 196-197)

110. (Steere 1960, 160)

111. S. D. Thurston, "Report of the Conduct of General George H. Steuart's Brigade from the 5th to the 12th of May, inclusive," *SHSP*, XIV, 149.

112. (*Medical and Surgical History* 1991, VII:44)

113. S. D. Thurston, "Report of the Conduct of General George H. Steuart's Brigade from the 5th to the 12th of May, inclusive," *SHSP*, XIV, 149.

114. (Curtis 1891, 232)

115. (Dawes 1984, 259-260)

116. (Wilmer 1898, I:265)

117. (Beyer and Keydel 1901, I:317)

118. (Ibid.)

119. (Chamberlin 1986, 207)

120. (Beyer and Keydel 1901, I:317)

121. (Curtis 1891, 231)

122. (Chapla 1989, 70)

123. (Curtis 1891, 231)

124. U. S. Department of the Army, Public Information Division, *The Medal of Honor of the United States of America* (Washington, DC: U.S. Government Printing Office, 1948), 151.

125. (*OR*, XXXVI, part 1, 617) Report of Maj. Merit Welsh, 7th Ind., commanding.

126. (Curtis 1891, 231)

127. Henry W. Thomas, *History of the Doles-Cook Brigade Army of Northern Virginia, C.S.A.* (Atlanta, Ga.: The Franklin Printing and Publishing Co., 1903), 477.

128. A. Harshberger, Surgeon, 149th Pennsylvania, "Notes," Milroy, Mifflin County, Pa., March 25, 1867, Civil War Times Illustrated Collection, Manuscripts Department, USAMHI, Carlisle Barracks, Pa., 7.

129. Letter, Ashbury Hull Jackson to Mrs. Luticia Jackson, May 11, 1864, Edward Harden Papers, Special Collections Department, Duke University Library, Durham, N.C.

130. I. G. Bradwell, "Battle of the Wilderness," *Confederate Veteran*, XXVII, 1919, 458. Statement by John W. Daniel, May 5, 1864, Civil War Materials, Wilderness 5 May, 1864, Accession # 158 5383 A - E, Box 24, Special Collections Department, Alderman Library, University of Virginia.

131. F. L. Hudgins, "38th Ga. Regiment at the *Wilderness* 5th 6th 7th of May 1864," Confederate Veteran Papers - Battles 1861-1932 & n. d., Box 1, Special Collections Department, William R. Perkins Library, Duke University, Durham, N.C., 2.

132. (Ibid.)

Gordon stated in the *OR*'s and in his reminiscences that he met Ewell who directed him onto the field. The enlisted men also recorded Robert E. Lee as being present.

John B. Gordon, *Reminiscences of the Civil War*, (Memorial Edition) (Dayton, Oh.: Morningside Press, 1985), 238-239.

133. George W. Nichols asserted that Lee was present and urged Gordon forward. Neither Gordon nor anyone else recalled the commanding general's presence there. Therefore, I did not use Nichols' account in this scenario.

F. L. Hudgins, "38th Ga. Regiment at the *Wilderness* 5th 6th 7th of May 1864," Confederate Veteran Papers - Battles 1861-1932 & n. d., Box 1, Special Collections Department, William R. Perkins Library, Duke University, Durham, N.C., 2. Statement by John W. Daniel, May 5, 1864, Civil War Materials, Wilderness 5 May, 1864, Accession # 158 5383 A - E, Box 24, Special Collections Department, Alderman Library, University of Virginia.

134. G. W. Nichols, *A Soldier's Story of His Regiment (61st Georgia)* (Dayton: Morningside Bookshop, 1961), 146-147.

135. In his official report, Gordon left a good description of his brigade formation. It was left to right, respectively: 26th Ga. - 31st Ga. - 38th Ga. - 13th Ga. - 60th Ga. - 61st Ga. (*OR*, XXXVI, part 1, 1077) Report of Brig. Gen. John B. Gordon, Gordon's brig., commanding.

136. Statement by John W. Daniel, May 5, 1864, Civil War Materials, Wilderness 5 May, 1864, Accession # 158 5383 A - E, Box 24, Special Collections Department, Alderman Library, University of Virginia.

137. I. G. Bradwell, "Battle of the Wilderness," *Confederate Veteran*, XXVII, 1919, 458.

138. (Nichols 1961, 142)

Mr. Murray positively identified James Spivey as Irvin Spivy.

Alton J. Murray, *South Georgia Rebels* (St. Mary's, Ga.: Alton J. Murray, 1976), 149.

139. I. G. Bradwell, "Battle of the Wilderness," *Confederate Veteran*, XXVII, 1919, 458.

140. (Ibid.)

141. F. L. Hudgins, "38th Ga. Regiment at the *Wilderness* 5th 6th 7th of May 1864," Confederate Veteran Papers - Battles 1861-1932 & n. d., Box 1, Special Collections Department, William R. Perkins Library, Duke University, Durham, N.C., 3.

142. I. G. Bradwell, "Battle of the Wilderness," *Confederate Veteran*, XXVII, 1919, 458.

143. Avery Harris, "Personal Reminiscences of the Author from August 1862 to June 1865, War of the Rebellion," Avery Harris Papers, USAMHI, 158.

144. I. G. Bradwell, "Battle of the Wilderness," *Confederate Veteran*, XXVII, 1919, 458.

145. Edward Steere in his book on the Wilderness established that Gordon struck Stone's brigade first. The 121st Pennsylvania lost 29 men total for three days' action, which indicates that it was not heavily involved. The 150th Pennsylvania was on the skirmish line and took 92 casualties. The 142nd Pennsylvania lost only 52 men, which leaves the 143rd Pennsylvania (220 casualties) and the 149th Pennsylvania (215 casualties) to have borne the brunt of Gordon's assault.

146. Avery Harris, "Personal Reminiscences of the Author from August 1862 to June 1865, War of the Rebellion," Avery Harris Papers, USAMHI, 159.

147. I. G. Bradwell, "Battle of the Wilderness," *Confederate Veteran*, XXVII, 1919, 458.

148. (Ibid., 459), (Nichols 1961, 142)

149. A. Harshberger, Surgeon, 149th Pennsylvania, "Notes," Milroy, Mifflin County, Pa., March 25, 1867, Civil War Times Illustrated Collection, Manuscripts Department, USAMHI, 7.

150. Avery Harris, "Personal Reminiscences of the Author from August 1862 to June 1865, War of the Rebellion," Avery Harris Papers, USAMHI, 159.

151. I. G. Bradwell, "Battle of the Wilderness," *Confederate Veteran*, XXVII, 1919, 459. (Nichols 1961, 142)

152. (*OR*, XXXVI, part 1, 1077) Report of Brig. Gen. John B. Gordon, Gordon's brig., commanding. (Thomas 1903, 478)

153. I. G. Bradwell, "Battle of the Wilderness," *Confederate Veteran*, XXVII, 1919, 459.

154. A. Harshberger, Surgeon, 149th Pennsylvania, "Notes," Milroy, Mifflin County, Pa., March 25, 1867, Civil War Times Illustrated Collection, Manuscripts Department, USAMHI, 7-8.

155. (Smith 1867, 284)

156. (Bates 1869, II:221-222), (Smith 1867, 284)

157. (Smith 1867, 290)

158. (Bates 1869, II:222)

159. (Smith 1867, 289-290)

160. (*OR*, XXXVI, part 1, 623) Report of Col. William J. Hofmann, 56th Pa., commanding.

Chapter Five

1. (Clark 1901, III:44)

2. (Ibid., I:150-151, 200-201) Reports of Col. Hamilton Brown (1st N.C.) and Capt. John Cowan (Co. D, 3rd N.C.).

3. (Brainard 1915, 198-199)

4. (Survivors Association 1888, 401)

5. (*OR*, XXXVI, part 1, 125)

6. The author of this regimental was prone to be "flowery" when trying to explain combat.

   (Survivors Association 1888, 401)

7. (Nevins 1962, 350)

8. (Howard 1975, 272), (Clark 1901, I:150-151, 200) Reports of Col. Hamilton Brown (1st N.C.) and Capt. John Cowan (Co. D, 3rd N.C.).

   Shelton wrote his account for the "Century Magazine" in October 1890 and Colonel S. D. Thurston (3rd North Carolina), who related the Confederate view of the capture in Vol. XIV, *SHSP*, May 1886, rendered a more colorful account. Shelton credited the colonel of the 61st Alabama with his capture. (The 61st Alabama was at the Wilderness.) The North Carolinians said they captured Shelton and that the 6th Alabama claimed to have captured the guns. I tend to believe the North Carolinians' story. Their account of the fighting is more consistent than any of those which I have found from the 6th Alabama.

   (Farley 1990, 37-38)

9. (Clark 1901, I:200-201) Report of Capt. John Cowan (Co. D, 3rd N.C.).

10. (Pullen 1961, 198), (Gerrish 1882, 161)

11. (Clark 1901, III:44)

12. (Ibid.)

13. (Nash 1911, 286)

14. (Ibid., 185)

15. (Ibid., 264 and 265)

16. (Clark 1901, III:44)

17. This is implied but not directly stated in the account of the 1st North Carolina which is found in Clark's *North Carolina Regiments.*

18. The quote from Colonel Brown reads, "We in turn rose up from the now famous gully and, to his astonishment and disappointment, proved to him that the prize and the honor were ours."

   (Clark 1901, I:151) Account of Col. Hamilton A. Brown, 1st N.C.

19. The regiment was in action for thirty minutes.

   (*OR*, XXXVI, part 1, 587) Report of Maj. Edward Knox, 44th N.Y., commanding.

20. (Judson 1986, 193-194)

21. (*OR*, XXXVI, part 1, 576) Report of Lt. Col. William White, 18th Massachusetts, commanding.

22. (Judson 1986, 193-194), (Bates 1869, II:1256)

23. (Nash 1911, 286)

24. (Worsham 1912, 202-203)

25. (Ibid.)

26. (*OR*, XXXVI, part 1, 665) Report of Col. Emory Upton.

   (Bicknell 1871, 304)

27. (*OR*, XXXVI, part 1, 665) Report of Col. Emory Upton.

28. In recollecting the story, Worsham referred to the "east" as the "west" and to the "west" as the "east," which I took the liberty of correcting.

   (Worsham 1912, 202-203)

29. (Clark 1901, I:151) Account of Col. Hamilton A. Brown, 1st N.C.

30. The author believes this to be the approximate position of Upton's brigade. Upton advanced his regiments in parallel files. The 95th Pennsylvania eventually moved forward to become the skirmishing regiment. It lost 25 men in the two day action at the Wilderness. Other accounts placed the 121st New York behind the 15th New Jersey which relieved the 95th Pennsylvania.

    The trench system which the Federals constructed before May 6, covered about 1925 feet to the point held by the 7th Maine.

    The 96th Pennsylvania (385 men) covered about 465 feet. It is known that the 119th Pennsylvania (502) and 1/2 of the 5th Wisconsin (251 men) occupied that same line to the left of the 49th New York (406 men) and the 7th Maine (446 men), both of which anchored the Federal right where John Gordon's brigade turned the Federal right on May 6. Allowing 1 foot of coverage per man in each regiment it would have stretched 1990 feet. Such frontage would have restricted the front of all three Federal brigades which deployed along that line and would have forced Upton to commit only one regiment at a time to the field. His regiments, with the exception of the 121st New York which became engaged on the 6th against Gordon, all suffered relatively minor casualties.

31. Brevet Major Holman S. Melcher, "An Experience in the Battle of the Wilderness," *War Papers Read Before the Commandery of the State of Maine, M.O.L.L.U.S.*, Vol. I (Portland: The Thurston Print, 1898), 78.

32. For the road to be on Westbrook's left, his company was probably in the elbow of the road where it turns from a southerly to a more westerly direction.

    (Westbrook 1898, 187)

33. The 61st Pennsylvania, in the second line, relieved the 49th at 7:00 P.M. (Bidwell 1916, 44)

    Both of these men placed the 7th Maine on the right of the line.

    A. L. Syphers, (Co. A, 7th Me.), "In the Wilderness, Was the Right Flank Turned May 6?", *The National Tribune*, June 13, 1889, 3. Albert A. Nickerson, "Experience of a Line Officer," unpublished M.O.L.L.U.S. Papers, Manuscripts Department, USAMHI, Carlisle Barracks, Pa., 26.

    Bidwell placed the 49th New York and the 7th Maine on the right of the brigade.

    (*OR*, XXXVI, part 1, 719) Report of Brig. Gen. Daniel D. Bidwell, 3rd Brig., 2nd Div., VI Corps, commanding.

    During the second day's fight, the 43rd New York, standing back to back on the 7th Maine, held off Gordon's counterattack. To do that, the two regiments had to have been parallel to each other.

    (Hyde 1894, 187 and 188)

34. Again, this formation is based in part upon Steere's research, upon the known strength (frontage) of each regiment, and statements by survivors concerning the positions of the front line regiments during that day.

    (Bidwell 1916, 43)

35. A. T. Brewer, *Sixty-first Regiment Pennsylvania Volunteers, 1861-1865.* (Regimental Association 1911), 82. (*Medical and Surgical History* 1991, VII:95 and 137)

36. (Handerson 1962, 70)

37. Thomas S. Doyle, "Memoir of Thomas S. Doyle," Manuscript Division, Library of Congress, from typed transcript, Virginia Infantry 31st - 60th, Vol. 67, Fredericksburg and Spotsylvania National Battlefield Park, 2.

38. (Wallace 1988, 56)

39. Thomas S. Doyle, "Memoir of Thomas S. Doyle," Manuscript Division, Library of Congress, from typed transcript, Virginia Infantry 31st - 60th, Vol. 67, Fredericksburg and Spotsylvania National Battlefield Park, 2.

40. (Nash 1911, 286)

41. (Ibid., 285)

42. (Ibid., 265)

43. William Shaw Stewart, "Experiences of an Army Surgeon, 1863-1864," 14, The Marjory G. Blubaugh Collection.

    Used with permission.

44. The Union troops had to have left the left flank unmolested. Had there been a serious threat to the brigade, he would not have left the 1st Louisiana in such a confused state before returning to Stafford. When Handerson wrote "the skirmishers of the hostile line [were] advancing steadily in our rear and almost upon us," he did not mention in which direction they were advancing.

    Had he said they were advancing "on" the regiment's rear it would make the account more clear. As I see it, the Federal skirmishers slipped into the woods behind the left rear of Stafford without seeing or hearing his line in the fight which was raging to the east.

    (Handerson 1962, 70-71)

45. Thomas S. Doyle, "Memoir of Thomas S. Doyle," Manuscript Division, Library of Congress, from typed transcript, Virginia Infantry 31st - 60th, Vol. 67, Fredericksburg and Spotsylvania National Battlefield Park, 3.

46. (Hyde 1894, 184-185)

47. In his account of the Wilderness Sergeant John Beech (Company B, 4th New Jersey) mentioned the fight against the 25th Virginia in which his regiment captured about 100 Confederates. He said that the regiment attacked the Confederates before they could face their line from front to rear. For that to have happened, the regiment had to have been north of the Culpeper Mine Road. He also said that later the 6th Maryland came on line to the right of the regiment, which confirms that the regiment had been to the right of Neill's brigade.

    Camille Baquet, *History of the First Brigade, New Jersey Volunteers from 1861-1865* (State of New Jersey, 1910) (Reprint by Stan Clark Books: Gettysburg, Pa.), 114. John P. Beech, "Gallantry of the 4th New Jersey in the Wilderness," *Grand Army Scout and Soldiers' Mail,* October 25, 1884, 1.

48. (Hyde 1894, 184-185)

49. (Baquet 1910, 114-115)

50. (Brewer 1911, 82)

51. Terry L. Jones, *Lee's Tigers, The Louisiana Infantry in the Army of Northern Virginia* (Baton Rouge: Louisiana State University Press, 1987), 197.

52. (Handerson 1962, 70-71)

53. (Westbrook 1898, 187)

54. (Handerson 1962, 71)

55. (Westbrook 1898, 187)

56. (Handerson 1962, 71), (Westbrook 1898, 187)

57. (Westbrook 1898, 187)

58. (Brainard 1915, 195)

59. (Carter 1978, 391)

60. (Bennett 1900, 209)

61. It is known that the 32nd Massachusetts, the 22nd Massachusetts, and the 9th Massachusetts went into action as described. The 62nd Pennsylvania was on the extreme right of the brigade and I assume the 4th Michigan was between it and the Massachusetts regiments.

Daniel G. Macnamara, *History of the Ninth Regiment Massachusetts Volunteer Infantry June 1861-June 1864* (Boston: E. B. Stillings & Co., Printers, 1899), 371-372. (Carter 1978, 390), (Bates 1869, II:459)

62. (Bennett 1900, 209-210)

63. (*OR*, XXXVI, part 1, 559) Report of Col. William S. Tilton, 22nd Massachusetts, commanding.

64. (Bennett 1900, 210)

65. (Parker 1880, 21)

66. (*OR*, XXXVI, part 1, 123)

67. (Bates 1869, II:459)

68. (*Medical and Surgical History* 1991, VIII:330)

69. (Macnamara 1899, 372)

70. (Ibid., 372)

71. (Bennett 1900, 210-211)

72. Bowerman said the 1st Maryland was on his right and that his regiment, the 4th Maryland, was the right of the brigade. In the *Md. Vols.*, Col. Charles Phelps, 7th Maryland, commanding, puts his regiment partly in Higgerson's field with the 8th Maryland on his right and the other two regiments to its right.

(Wilmer 1898, I:265), (*OR*, XXXVI, part 1, 604) Report of Col. Richard Bowerman, 4th Md., commanding.

73. (Dawes 1984, 260-261)

74. (Wilmer 1898, I:266)

75. (Nichols 1961, 143)

76. I. G. Bradwell, "Battle of the Wilderness," *Confederate Veteran*, XXVII, 1919, 459.

77. (Wilmer 1898, I:266)

78. I. G. Bradwell, "Battle of the Wilderness," *Confederate Veteran* XXVII, 1919, 459.

79. (Wilmer 1898, I:266)

80. I. G. Bradwell, "Battle of the Wilderness," *Confederate Veteran*, XXVII, 1919, 459.

81. (Ibid.)

82. (Wilmer 1898, I:265), Charles Camper and J. W. Kirkley, *Historical Record of the First Regiment Maryland Infantry* (Baltimore: Butternut and Blue, 1990), 128.

83. (*OR*, XXXVI, part 1, 604) Report of Col. George Bowerman, 4th Md., commanding.

84. (Camper 1990, 128)

85. I. G. Bradwell, "Battle of the Wilderness," *Confederate Veteran*, XXVII, 1919, 459.

86. (Wilmer 1898, I:266)

87. (Ibid.)

88. I. G. Bradwell, "Battle of the Wilderness," *Confederate Veteran*, XXVII, 1919, 459.

89. (Wilmer 1898, I:265-266)

90. I. G. Bradwell, "Battle of the Wilderness," *Confederate Veteran*, XXVII, 1919, 459.

91. (Ibid.)

92. Bish's account is the only account from the Reserves regarding the Wilderness which I have been able to locate to date. His description of the "far field" has to refer to Chewning's. There is no evidence that the brigade fought in Jones' field. Bish did not identify the regiment, but it had to have been part of the badly fragmented 61st Georgia. Crawford's men were the ones who prompted Lee to send Cadmus Wilcox's division onto Chewning's plateau.

    Elijah Bish, (Co. K, 11th Pennsylvania Res.), "Which Division Was Broken?" *The National Tribune*, January 9, 1990, 3.

93. (Nichols 1961, 143-144)

94. Jacob Heffelfinger, Diary, May 5, 1864, CWTI Collection, Manuscript Department, USAMHI.

95. (Nichols 1961, 143-144)

96. (Steere 1960, 172)

97. (Nichols 1961, 144)

98. (*OR*, XXXVI, part 1, 124)

99. (Dawes 1984, 261)

100. (Ibid.)

101. Small, the adjutant of the 16th Maine, recorded that his brigade went on line with other troops which were already engaged in combat along the eastern side of Saunders Field.

    (Small 1939, 132)

    The 90th Pennsylvania was officially transferred with its colonel, Peter Lyle, on May 7, 1864.

    (*OR*, XXXVI, part 1, 124)

    Robinson clearly stated that the 90th Pennsylvania was in the fight with Leonard's brigade.

    (Ibid., 593) Report of Brig. Gen. John Robinson, 2nd Division, V Corps, commanding.

102. (Kent 1976, 259-260)

103. (Carter 1978, 391)

104. The regiment picked up 5 men from a 100 day regiment. It was probably one of those men who fired prematurely.

    (Roe 1914, 173)

105. Carter said the regiment which fired was a new regiment. It sounds a great deal like the 39th Massachusetts which had a number of trigger happy men in it.

    (Carter 1978, 391)

106. (*OR*, XXXVI, part 1, 123)

107. Diary, Henry Keiser, Co. G, 96th Pennsylvania, Diary, May 5, 1864, Harrisburg Civil War Round Table Collection, USAMHI, 107.

108. (Roe 1914, 173)

109. (Macnamara 1899, 372)

110. (Handerson 1962, 71-72)

111. (Kent 1976, 259)

112. (Ibid., 259-260)

113. (Small 1939, 132)

114. (Stearns 1976, 259)

115. (Ibid., 259-260)

116. (Roe 1914, 174)

117. (King 1917, 23)

118. (Armstrong 1990, 75)

119. (Frye 1988, 61), (Wallace, Jr. 1988, 56), (Reidenbaugh 1987, 82), Thomas S. Doyle, "Memoir of Thomas S. Doyle," Manuscript Division, Library of Congress, from typed transcript, Virginia Infantry 31st - 60th, Vol. 67, Fredericksburg and Spotsylvania National Battlefield Park, 2.

120. Dennis E. Frye, *2nd Virginia Infantry*, (1st ed.). (Lynchburg, Va.: H. E. Howard, Inc., 1984), 61-62.

121. (Jones 1987, 197)

122. Pegram's brigade formed in support of the other two brigades in the division. He said that the division received a volley and went forward and then came back and re-formed. That did not happen on the Orange Turnpike, but after the brigade turned north with some of Johnson's division in tow.

    Samuel D. Buck, "With the Old Confeds," Manuscript, Samuel D. Buck Papers, Ca. 1890, Special Collections Department, William R. Perkins Library, Duke University, Durham, N.C., 93.

123. William W. Smith, "The Wilderness and Spotsylvania," John Warwick Daniel Papers, 1905-1910, 22 - G, Special Collections Department, William R. Perkins Library, Duke University, Durham, N.C., 1.

124. Captain James Bumgardner, "The Fifty-Second Virginia," Richmond *Dispatch*, October 8, 1905, Manuscripts Department, University of Virginia Library, Charlottesville, Va.

125. (Jones 1987, 197)

    The NPS map shows the lines at this juncture being approximately 200 yards apart.

    "Gordon Flank Attack Trail, A Walking Tour," National Park Service Pamphlet, Fredericksburg & Spotsylvania National Military Park, U.S. Department of the Interior, Map.

    William E. S. Whitman and Charles H. True, *Maine in the War for the Union: A History of the Part Borne By Maine Troops in the Suppression of the American Rebellion* (Lewiston, Me.: Nelson Dingley Jr. & Co., Publishers, 1865), 186.

126. (Bidwell 1916, 44)

    (Whitman and True 1865, 186)

127. (Whitman and True 1865, 186)

128. The 15th New Jersey and the 3rd New Jersey were not heavily engaged on either day, losing only 22 men between them which indicates they were in a quiet sector of the field. The 15th New Jersey did move into Saunders Field, therefore it is safe to assume both regiments were in the vicinity of Upton's brigade.

     The 1st and 4th New Jersey were hardest hit and the 2nd and the 10th New Jersey regiments lost the next heaviest casualties. The 1st and 4th were closest to the firing line and the other two regiments were probably in a second line behind the 1st New Jersey. There was not enough room to allow the brigade to form in a single line as shown on Steere's maps.

     Albert A. Nickerson, "Experiences of a Line Officer," 7th Maine, Read May 3, 1911, unpublished M.O.L.L.U.S. papers, Manuscript Division, USAMHI, 26.

129. Thomas S. Doyle, "Memoir of Thomas S. Doyle," Manuscript Division, Library of Congress, from typed transcript, Virginia Infantry 31st - 60th, Vol. 67, Fredericksburg and Spotsylvania National Battlefield Park, 2.

130. (Jones 1987, 198)

131. (Whitman and True 1865, 186)

132. John P. Beech, "Gallantry of the 4th New Jersey in the Wilderness," *Grand Army Scout and Soldiers' Mail*, October 25, 1884, 1.

133. It is safe to assume that the 6th Louisiana was part of the command to confront the 7th Maine. The 5th Wisconsin captured an estimated 300 prisoners. The 25th Virginia had only 50 men present with it. The balance had to come from another regiment.

     (Jones 1987, 198)

134. Albert A. Nickerson, "Experiences of a Line Officer," 7th Maine, Read May 3, 1911, no publisher, M.O.L.L.U.S. Papers, Manuscript Department, USAMHI, Carlisle Barracks, Pa., 26.

135. (Whitman and True 1865, 186)

136. Albert A. Nickerson, "Experiences of a Line Officer," 7th Maine, Read May 3, 1911, unpublished, M.O.L.L.U.S. Papers, Manuscript Department, USAMHI, 26.

137. Sergeant John P. Beech, 4th N.J., "Getting Even," *The National Tribune*, January 25, 1912, 8.

138. (Westbrook 1898, 187)

     The casualties on the part of the 119th Pennsylvania and the 5th Wisconsin indicate severe fighting that day.

     (*OR*, XXXVI, part 1, 126)

139. (Peyton 1929, 22)

     Neither of these regimentals indicate that these 4 regiments participated in the firing during Hays' attack. The 49th Virginia did respond to the shooting, however.

     Robert J. Driver, Jr., *58th Virginia Infantry*, (1st ed.) (Lynchburg: H.E. Howard, Inc., 1990), 58. John M. Ashcraft, *31st Virginia Infantry*, (1st ed.) (Lynchburg: H. E. Howard, Inc., 1988), 63. Captain James Bumgardner, "The Fifty-Second Virginia," Richmond *Dispatch*, October 8, 1905, Manuscripts Department, University of Virginia Library, Charlottesville, Va.

140. Samuel D. Buck Papers, 1890, Special Collections Department, William R. Perkins Library, Duke University, Durham, N.C., 94.

141. William W. Smith, "The Wilderness and Spotsylvania," John Warwick Daniel Papers, 1905-1910, 22 G, special Collections Department, William R. Perkins Library, Duke University, Durham, NC, 1. Laura Virginia Hale and Stanley S. Phillips, *History of the Forty-Ninth Virginia Infantry C.S.A. "Extra Billy Smith's Boys"* (Lynchburg, Va., H. E. Howard Inc., 1981), 105.

142. (Jones 1987, 198)

143. Louis Bronz, in the roster, appears as Bruns.

Maurus Oesterich, 96th Pennsylvania Infantry Regiment, Diary, May 5, 1864, Harrisburg Civil War Round Table Collection, Manuscript Department, USAMHI, 44–45.

144. (*OR*, XXXVI, part 1, 672) Col. Oliver Edwards' report. (Ibid. 719) Report of Brig. Gen. Daniel D. Bidwell, 3rd Brig., 2nd Div., VI Corps, commanding.

145. (Whitman and True 1865, 186), John P. Beech, "Gallantry of the 4th New Jersey in the Wilderness," *Grand Army Scout and Soldiers' Mail*, October 25, 1884, 1.

146. (King 1917, 23)

147. (*Medical and Surgical History* 1991, VII:132)

148. In his account Beech merely said that some of the men "stopped" the captain from murdering the Confederate. Polite requests would not have prevented a man who was as worked up as Captain Johnston from carrying out his order to show no quarter. In reading Beech's account, I sensed that he disapproved of wanton murder.

John P. Beech, "Gallantry of the 4th New Jersey in the Wilderness," *Grand Army Scout and Soldiers' Mail*, October 25, 1884, 1.

149. (Jones 1987, 198)

150. (Whitman and True 1865, 186)

151. This is a rough estimate based on information in the regimental history of the 49th New York.

Chapter Six

1. (Howard 1975, 278)

2. (Worsham 1912, 203-204)

3. (Bates 1870, III:1313)

4. (Survivors Association 1888, 403)

5. (Bates 1870, III:1313)

6. (Durkin 1960, 87)

7. Samuel Buck, Manuscript, Samuel Buck Papers, 1890, Special Collections Department, William R. Perkins Library, Duke University, Durham, N.C., 94.

8. (Hale and Phillips 1981, 105)

9. William W. Smith, "The Wilderness and Spotsylvania," John W. Daniel Papers, 1905-1910, 22 - G, Special Collections Department, William R. Perkins Library, Duke University, Durham, N.C., 1.

10. Captain James A. Bumgardner, Jr., "The Fifty-Second Virginia," Richmond *Dispatch*, October 8, 1905, Manuscripts Department, University of Virginia Library, Charlottesville, Va.

11. (Driver 1990, 58)

12. William W. Smith, "The Wilderness and Spotsylvania," John W. Daniel Papers, 1905-1910, 22 - G, Special Collections Department, William R. Perkins Library, Duke University, Durham, N.C., 1.

13. The Confederates reported that the Federals attacked on brigade front and in a depth of at least 5 lines. The troops, massed as described earlier, would have formed a column of that depth.

14. (Haines 1883, 145)

15. Though not listed as such, it had to have been an accidental wound. The 121st New York did not get close enough to the Confederates that day to get into hand-to-hand combat.

    (*Medical and Surgical History* 1991, VIII:400)

16. (Haines 1883, 145-146)

17. Thomas S. Berry, "In the Wilderness; Second Brigade, Second Division, Sixth Corps, May 6, 1864," *The National Tribune*, October 17, 1889, 5.

18. John P. Beech, "Gallantry of the 4th New Jersey in the Wilderness," *Grand Army Scout and Soldiers' Mail*, October 25, 1884, 1.

19. 1st Sergeant Grayson M. Eichelberger, Company D, 6th Maryland, "Memoirs," October 1912, Civil War Miscellaneous Collection, USAMHI, 18.

20. William W. Smith, "The Wilderness and Spotsylvania," John W. Daniel Papers, 1905-1910, 22 - G, Special Collections Department, William R. Perkins Library, Duke University, Durham, N.C., 1.

21. 1st Sergeant Grayson M. Eichelberger, Company D, 6th Maryland, "Memoirs," October 1912, Civil War Miscellaneous Collection, USAMHI, 18.

22. Samuel D. Buck, Memoirs, Samuel Buck Papers, 1890, Special Collections Department, William R. Perkins Library, Duke University, Durham, N.C., 94.

23. (Driver 1990, 59) William W. Smith, Letter to John W. Daniel, October 24, 1904, John W. Daniel Papers, Special Collections Department, William R. Perkins Library, Duke University, Durham, N.C., 1.

24. (*Medical and Surgical History* 1991, VIII:292)

25. (Ibid., VII:95 and 137)

26. (Brewer 1911, 82)

27. The Confederate accounts say that at least five Federal lines attacked them. This is my reconstruction of what happened.

28. (Baquet 1910, 115)

29. Samuel D. Buck, Memoirs, Samuel Buck Papers, 1890, Special Collections Department, William R. Perkins Library, Duke University, Durham, N.C., 94.

30. Alfred Thompson, Diary, May 5, 1864, Jay Luvaas Collection, Manuscript Department, USAMHI, Carlisle Barracks, Pa.

31. (*Medical and Surgical History* 1991, VII:195)

32. C. E. Garlinger, "Another Account," *The National Tribune*, October 3, 1889, 3.

33. James Davis, Company A, 138th Pennsylvania, Diary, May 5, 1864, Civil War Miscellaneous Collection, DA - DE, Manuscripts Department, USAMHI.

34. 1st Sergeant Grayson M. Eichelberger, Company D, 6th Maryland, "Memoirs," October 1912, Civil War Miscellaneous Collection, USAMHI, 17-18.

35. Cooper was captured and his wound was left untreated. The 126th Ohio did not get overrun until the evening of May 6. For him to have been captured, as stated in the *Medical History*, he would have to have been in the field hospital which was overrun at that time. If his wounds were not treated by the Confederates, this also implies that his wounds went untreated by his own doctors prior to his capture.

     (*Medical and Surgical History* 1991, VIII:348)

36. (Stearns 1976, 260)

37. (Roe 1914, 174)

38. (Small 1886, 132)

     Henry Keiser, Diary, May 5, 1864, Harrisburg Civil War Round Table Collection, Manuscript Department, USAMHI, Carlisle Barracks, Pa., 107.

39. (Howard 1975, 274)

40. (*OR*, XXXVI, part 1, 593) Report of Brig. Gen. John Robinson, 2nd Division, V Corps, commanding.

41. (Small 1886, 132)

42. (Kent 1976, 258 and 260)

43. (Ibid.)

44. Holman S. Melcher, "An Experience in the Battle of the Wilderness," *War Papers*, M.O.L.L.U.S. Commandery of the State of Maine, Vol. 1 (Portland, Me.: The Thurston Print, 1898), 79-81.

     (Gerrish 1882, 163-164)

Chapter Seven

1. William Kent, "A Wilderness Memory," *Civil War Times Illustrated*, March 1989, 35-36.

2. (Galwey 1961, 196)

    Gibbon said his men were under way at 5:00 A.M., which is not contradictory to Galwey. They were probably told to pack up at that time and got under way at 6:30 A.M. as stated. According to Galwey it took the regiment three hours to get to Todd's Tavern - a distance of about 6.0 miles. The regiment averaged 2.0 miles per hour, which was not an overly taxing march.

    John Gibbon, *Personal Recollections of the Civil War* (N.Y.: G. P. Putnam's Sons, 1928), 211-212.

3. Apparently Gibbon took the Furnace Road, because Birney followed right behind him. The 17th Maine belonged to Birney's division. Barlow, however, from the description, was taking a flank movement farther south on the Catharpin Road.

    (Silliker 1985, 143)

    Weygant was mistaken when he said the regiment took the Catharpin Road.

Charles H. Weygant, *History of the One Hundred Twenty-Fourth Regiment, N. Y. S. V.* (New Burgh, N.Y.: Journal Printing House, 1877), 285.

4. (Ibid.)

5. Based upon Colonel Robert McAllister's account in the *OR's* it appears that Mott's Division took the Catharpin Road and not the Catharine Furnace Road. This is definitely different from the line of march shown in Steere's book on the Wilderness.

   Samuel Dunham, (Co. K, 63rd Pennsylvania), "Death of General Hays, Where and How He Fell at the Battle of the Wilderness," *The National Tribune*, November 12, 1885, 3.

6. This is the order of march as gathered from the *Official Records.*

7. (*OR*, XXXVI, part 1, 406) Report of Brig. Gen. John R. Brooke, 4th Brig., 1st Div., II Corps, commanding.

8. Brooke definitely used the Catharine Furnace Road which he and other officers mistakenly called the "Catharpin" Furnace Road. Favill (57th N.Y.), Frederick (57th N.Y.), and Simons (125th N.Y.) from Frank's brigade clearly stated that the division was at Todd's Tavern and got there by the Catharpin Road.

   (Ibid.)

9. (Galwey 1961, 196), (*OR*, XXXVI, part 1, 350)

10. (Ibid., 467) Itinerary of Maj. Gen. David B. Birney's division.

11. (Silliker 1985, 143), (Meier 1972, 147)

12. Lieutenant Gilbert Frederick, Co. B, 57th New York, reported the regiment's position at a point about three miles below Todd's Tavern on the Brock Road. The Piney Branch Church Road intersects the Brock Road almost exactly at that distance. (Frederick 1895, 220)

13. Frederick 1895, 220), (Favill 1909, 287)

14. (Ibid.)

15. (Silliker 1985, 143)

16. (Weygant 1877, 285)

17. (Ibid.)

18. (King 1895, 60)

19. (Steere 1960, 106, fn 8)

20. (Gibbon 1978, 211)

    Galwey said they received the order to move at 10:00 A.M., and Gibbon said the division had to wait for Birney to move first which took until noon. This conforms to most of the other accounts which I found.

    When one considers that Gibbon did not attack until 4:30 P.M. and had 4.5 miles to cover between the Tavern and the crossroads, it becomes evident he did not move very quickly. Either the road was clogged with troops, as many of the accounts say, or the division "doublequicked" at the exceedingly slow pace of 1 mile per hour.

    (Galwey 1961, 196)

21. (*OR*, XXXVI, part 1, 318) Report of Maj. Gen. Winfield S. Hancock, II Corps, commanding.

22. McAllister did not say who ordered his advance, but one can assume that Hancock did.

    (Ibid., 487) Report of Col. Robert McAllister, 1st Brig., 4th Div., II Corps, commanding.

23. (Ibid.)

24. (Gibbon 1978, 211), (Galwey 1961, 196)

25. (Gibbon 1978, 211), (Galwey 1961, 196)

26. (Favill 1909, 287)

27. (Weygant 1877, 286)

28. Mott's division came from the Second Division of the III Corps and had kept its white diamond division insignia when it transferred to the II Corps after Gettysburg.

    (Silliker 1985, 143)

29. (Ibid.)

30. William Kent, "A Wilderness Memoir," *Civil War Times Illustrated*, March 1989, 36-37)

31. (Ibid.)

32. (*OR*, XXXVI, part 1, 318) Report of Maj. Gen. Winfield S. Hancock, II Corps, commanding.

33. (Ibid. 877) Brig. Gen. James H. Wilson's report.

34. (Ibid., 903) 1st Lt. Alexander Pennington's report.

35. He also said the guns remained upon the field an hour after the fighting ceased which contradicted any Rebel cavalrymen's claims about a frantic race toward the Po River.

    (Neese 1983, 258)

36. At a walk of four miles an hour it would take the column about an hour and fifteen minutes to get to Corbin's Bridge.

37. McConihe said he went into action at 3:00 P.M. Wilson said his men went into action at 5:00 P.M., which I believe to be an error.

    (*OR*, XXXVI, part 1, 318, 350, 481, 485) Reports of Maj. Gen. Winfield S. Hancock, II Corps, commanding; Maj. Samuel McConihe, 93rd N.Y.; Capt. John Wilson, 1st U.S.S.S., and the itinerary of the II Corps.

38. (Ibid., 350, 483) Reports of Lt. Col. William B. Neeper, 57th Pennsylvania and the itinerary of the II Corps.

39. (Bates 1870, III:786)

40. Hospital steward Sergeant Judson Gibbs of the 93rd New York placed the regiment on the right of the brigade line and he says that Hays was killed behind his regiment, which put it near the flank, on the left of the 63rd Pennsylvania.

    (King 1895, 63)

    Caril placed the 5th Michigan with the 1st Sharpshooters at the beginning of the day's march, which in counter marching, would place it near the rear of the column and probably at the position stated. The 3rd Michigan left no record of its position, but Federal forces tended to form dual lines of approximately equal length. It makes sense that the 3rd Michigan would cover the 4th Maine.

    Harrison, Caril, "Campaigning With Grant Through Virginia," *The National Tribune*, April 9, 1925, 5.

41. Harrison Caril, "Campaigning With Grant Through the Wilderness," *The National Tribune*, April 9, 1925, 5.

42. (Weygant 1877, 286)

43. (Ibid.)

44. Ward had to advance up the Brock Road and then move by the left flank into the woods behind Mott's troops, which were already engaged.

45. (A. P. Smith 1867, 286)

46. (Ibid.)

47. Birney arrived on the scene about 2:00 P.M. and did not advance until 4:15 P.M.

    (*OR*, XXXVI, part 1, 318, 350) Itinerary of the II Corps. Report of Maj. Gen. Winfield S. Hancock, II Corps, commanding.

48. The only occupied structure nearby was the Higgerson farm. Smith said the regiment was led to a main track which the regiment had been on during the Mine Run Campaign of 1863. This probably was the road to Parker's Store which the V Corps had taken earlier in the day.

    (A. P. Smith 1867, 287-289)

49. (A. P. Smith 1867, 287-289), J. H. Lane, "History of Lane's North Carolina Brigade," *SHSP*, Vol. IX, 124.

50. (A. P. Smith 1867, 287-289)

51. Wilber F. Swaringen, Company K, 28th North Carolina, "Record of the War Service of W. F. Swaringen, Confederate Veteran," Reminiscences 1861-1932, Box 6, Confederate Veteran Papers, Special Collections Department, William R. Perkins Library, Duke University, Durham, N.C., 3.

52. Wilber F. Swaringen, Company K, 28th North Carolina, "Record of the War Service of W. F. Swaringen, Confederate Veteran," Reminiscences 1861-1932, Box 6, Confederate Veteran Papers, Special Collections Department, William R. Perkins Library, Duke University, Durham, N.C., 3. George W. Hall, 14th Georgia, Diary, May 5, 1864, Georgia Room, University of Georgia.

53. (A. P. Smith 1867, 287-289), (*OR*, XXXVI, part 1, 631) Report of Maj. Robert Bard, 95th N.Y.

54. (Clark 1901, II:665) Account of 1st Lt. Octavius A. Wiggins, Co. E., 37th N.C., (*OR*, XXXVI, part 1, 125), George W. Hall, 14th Georgia, Diary, May 5, 1864, Georgia Room, University of Georgia.

    The 76th New York lost two captains and six lieutenants to the Confederates which agrees with Lane's report on the number of officers captured.

    (A. P. Smith 1867, 289)

55. (Caldwell 1951, 127-128)

56. Kent erred when he said that the Sharpshooters were the first of Hays' men to reach the crossroads. They were the first of his men to be fully deployed.

    William Kent, "A Wilderness Memory," *Civil War Times Illustrated*, March 1989, 36-37. (Silliker 1985, 143)

    Wilson said the regiment left Todd's Tavern about 3:00 P.M. and arrived at the crossroads about 5:00 P.M., which makes sense because the regiment was at the tail of the column. The regiment probably arrived closer to 4:00 P.M., which is the time stated by most of the participants.

    (*OR*, XXXVI, part 1, 485) Report of Capt. John Wilson, 1st U.S.S.S.

57. C. A. Stevens, *Berdan's United States Sharpshooters in the Army of the Potomac 1861-1865* (Dayton: Morningside Bookshop, 1984), 401.

Seaver said the II Corps formed immediately on his left.

(*OR*, XXXVI, part 1, 709) Report of Col. Thomas O. Seaver, 3rd Vt. (Meier 1972, 146)

58. William Kent, "A Wilderness Memory," *Civil War Times Illustrated*, March 1989, 37.

59. (Ibid.)

60. (Ibid.)

61. (Ibid., 38)

62. (Hutchinson 1890, 176)

63. (Bowen 1884, 275)

64. (*OR*, XXXVI, part 1, 681) Brig. Gen. Frank Wheaton's report.

65. The implication from Graham's report is that his regiment was on the flank of the brigade. It was posted several hundred yards north of the Plank Road.

W. M. Graham, "Twenty-Sixth Mississippi Regiment," *Confederate Veteran*, Vol. XV, 1907, 169.

Lieutenant Robert Ward indicated that the 42nd Mississippi was alone on the extreme left of the brigade during the later part of the day. This would have occurred after the rest of the brigade had abandoned the line. It is, therefore, my assumption that the 26th Mississippi had been on its left during the better part of the day.

Stone's brigade had 1200 officers and men. It was on the left of Cooke's right wing (approximately 800 officers and men). By allowing about 2 feet of line per each man in the first rank of the two brigades, this would give the two commands a total front of, at the least, 2,000 feet. The left flank of the 26th Mississippi would have been about 669 yards north of the Plank Road.

(Dunlop 1988, 374-375)

66. (Clark 1901, III:304) Charles M. Cooke, Adj., 55th N.C.

67. (Dunlop 1988, 367-369)

68. These positions are listed previously in the book.

69. James A. Graham, Letter to Mother, May 9, 1864, Special Collections Department, William R. Perkins Library, Duke University, Durham, N.C.

70. (Clark 1901, III:75) Q.M. Sgt. J. M. Wadill, 46th N.C.

71. (Dunlop 1988, 368-369, 372)

72. Most of the Federal accounts later stated that the shooting started on the right of the division before becoming a general engagement.

73. (Dunlop 1988, 369)

74. (Roe 1909, 257)

75. The 37th Massachusetts lost thirteen officers and men that day from indirect fire. The regiments that day, once the firing started, generally did not stand up to fight.

(Bowen 1884, 275)

76. (Roe 1909, 257)

77. (Dunlop 1988, 370)

78. (Roe 1909, 257)

79. (Clark 1901, III:75) Statement of Q.M. Sgt. J. M. Wadill, 46th N.C.

80. (*OR*, XXXVI, part 1, 711) Report of Lt. Col. Stephen Pingree, 4th Vt. (Bates 1870, III:290)

81. (*OR*, XXXVI, part 1, 697) Report of Col. Lewis A. Grant.

82. (Ibid., 710) Report of Col. Thomas O. Seaver, 3rd Vt.

83. William Kent, "A Wilderness Memory," *Civil War Times Illustrated*, March 1989, 38.

84. (*OR*, XXXVI, part 1, 711) Report of Lt. Col. Stephen Pingree, 4th Vt.

85. (Caldwell 1951, 128)

86. (Meier 1972, 148)

87. William Kent, "A Wilderness Memory," *Civil War Times Illustrated*, March 1989, 38.

88. (*OR*, XXXVI, part 1, 711) Report of Lt. Col. Colonel Stephen M. Pingree, 4th Vt.

89. (*Medical and Surgical History* 1991, VIII:503)

90. (*OR*, XXXVI, part 1, 710) Report of Col. Thomas O. Seaver, 3rd Vt.

91. Charles H. Myerhoff, 14th Indiana, "The Wilderness, The Charge of Carroll's Celebrated Brigade," *The National Tribune*, October 23, 1890, 4.

92. (Caldwell 1951, 128)

93. Poague, an experienced artilleryman, would have known how dangerous it was in the low terrain of the Wilderness to have fired over the heads of his own men.

94. Dudley, who helped retrieve the gun later in the day, did not say that the gun fired. In all likelihood, it did not. No Federals mention receiving any incoming rounds that day. In the *OR*s, Lewis A. Grant mentions when the Federal artillery did open fire and it would be hard to argue that Poague, whose guns were so close, did not attempt to provide some kind of help to neutralize the Federal guns.

    C. R. Dudley, "What I Know About the Wilderness," unpublished article, *Confederate Veteran* Papers, Special Collections, William R. Perkins Library, Duke University, Durham, N.C., 2. (Poague 1957, 87-88)

95. (Silliker 1985, 144)

96. (Ibid.)

97. (Ibid., 144-145)

98. (*OR*, XXXVI, part 1, 710) Report of Col. Thomas O. Seaver, 3rd Vt.

99. Richard O'Sullivan, *55th Virginia Infantry*, 1st Ed. (Lynchburg, Va.: H. E. Howard Co., 1989), 68.

100. (*OR*, XXXVI, part 1, 710) Report of Col. Thomas O. Seaver, 3rd Vt.

101. Robert E. L. Krick, *40th Virginia Infantry*, 1st Ed. (Lynchburg, Va.: H. E. Howard, 1985), 40.

102. (Bowen 1884, 275)

103. Kenneth Raynor Jones, Diary, Captain, Company I, 27th North Carolina, Kenneth Raynor Jones Papers, Southern Historical Collection, The Library of the University of North Carolina, at Chapel Hill, N.C., 27-28.

104. James A. Graham, Letter to Mother, May 9, 1864, James A. Graham Papers, 1861-1901, Special Collections Department, William R. Perkins Library, Duke University, Durham, N.C.

105. (Dunlop 1988, 371)

106. Daniel Seltzer, Company K, 46th North Carolina, Letter to Wife, May 7, 1864, Daniel Seltzer Papers, 1858-1865, Rowan County, N.C., Special Collections Department, William R. Perkins Library, Duke University, Durham, N.C.

107. (*Medical and Surgical History* 1991, VII:113)

108. (*OR*, XXXVI, part 1, 697) Report of Col. Lewis A. Grant.

109. (*OR*, XXXVI, part 1, 714) Report of Capt. Eugene A. Hamilton, 5th Vt.

110. Diary of Wilbur Fisk, 2nd Vermont, Manuscript Division, LOC.

111. (*Medical and Surgical History* 1991, VII:81 and VIII:339)

112. Diary of Wilbur Fisk, 2nd Vermont, Manuscript Division, LOC.

113. (McDonald 1907, 227)

114. (Myers 1956, 260)

115. Seibert said that parts of the Third Division were engaged with Gregg's brigade until dark. The casualties of the 1st Connecticut and the 2nd New York indicate severe action on their part.

      (*OR*, XXXVI, part 1, 877 and 885) Reports of Brig. Gen. James H. Wilson and Capt. Lewis Seibert, Wilson's assistant adjutant general.

116. (McDonald 1907, 227)

117. This is based upon Myers' account in *The Comanches.*

118. Diary of Private James F. Wood, Company F, 7th Virginia Cavalry, Virginia State Archives, Richmond, 1.

119. Report of Capt. P. P. Pendleton, Headquarters, Horse Artillery, Army of Northern Virginia, November 19, 1864, VMI Archives, 2.

120. Diary of Private James F. Wood, Company F, 7th Virginia Cavalry, Virginia States Archives, Richmond, 2.

121. (Ibid.)

122. (*OR*, XXXVI, part 1, 129), (McDonald 1907, 27), Diary of Private James F. Wood, Company F, 7th Virginia Cavalry, Virginia State Archives, Richmond, 2.

123. 1st Sergeant W. A. Rodgers, (Co. K, 18th Pennsylvania Cav.), "Mid Bullet and Shell. The 18th Pennsylvania Cav. Had A Lively Work in the Mine Run Fight," *The National Tribune*, May 27, 1897, 3.

124. (Myers 1956, 260-261)

      It is safe to assume that the 18th Pennsylvania got involved in hand-to-hand combat with the "Comanches." Wilson, in his report, credited the Pennsylvanians with three successive charges. Had they used their small arms more effectively, they would have turned back the Confederates without a need to charge.

      Committee of the Regimental Association, *History of the Eighteenth Regiment of Cavalry, Pennsylvania Volunteers (163d Regiment of the Line), 1862-1865* (New York: Wynkoop Hallenback Crawford Co., 1909), 21.

125. (Ibid., 261)

126. The 1st Pennsylvania Cavalry did move out on another road, according to Chaplain Pyne of the 1st New Jersey Cavalry. It was the Brock Road.

William Penn Lloyd, *History of the First Regiment Pennsylvania Reserve Cavalry* (Philadelphia: King & Baird, Printers, 1864), 90. (Pyne 1961, 189)

127. (Pyne 1961, 186)

128. (Ibid.)

129. Diary of Private James F. Wood, Company F, 7th Virginia Cavalry, Virginia State Archives, Richmond, 1.

130. (Pyne 1961, 186)

131. (Myers 1956, 261)

132. Pyne placed the Confederate artillery behind a barricade across the road.

   (Pyne 1961, 187)

   Myers said the Comanches rallied on the hill from which the fight first started.

   (Myers 1956, 261)

   The horse artillery fought under Rosser that day and did not state where the guns were specifically.

   (Neese 1983, 260)

133. (Myers 1956, 261)

134. (Favill 1909, 287)

135. (Ibid.)

136. (Simons 1888, 197)

137. (Favill 1909, 288)

138. (Ibid. 287), (*OR*, XXXVI, part 1, 318) Report of Maj. Gen. Winfield S. Hancock, II Corps, commanding.

139. (*OR*, XXXVI, part 1, 407) Report of Brig. Gen. John R. Brooke, 4th Brig., 1st Div., II Corps, commanding.

140. (Favill 1909, 287), (Simons 1888, 197)

Chapter Eight

1. The colonel said the fighting occurred near Alsop's Gate.

   Diary of Colonel William R. Carter, 3rd Virginia Cavalry, Confederate Miscellaneous, Fredericksburg and Spotsylvania National Military Park, Vol. 18. The original diary is in the Eggleston Library, Hampden-Sydney College.

2. There are no clear accounts of what actually transpired. The *Enquirer* said the 15th Virginia rode into an ambush and fell back in good order. This account pretty much agrees with Luther Hopkins' account which indicates that the Confederates fell back and then rallied.

   "The Wounded," *Richmond Whig*, May 7, 1864, p. 2, col. 1. "Skirmish on the Right Wing," Richmond *Daily Dispatch*, May 7, 1864, p. 1, col. 1. "The Wounded," *Richmond Enquirer*, May 10, 1864, p. 4, col. 4. Major, A.A.G., J. D. Ferguson, "Memoranda of the Itinerary and Operations of Major General Fitz Lee's Cavalry Division of the Army of Northern Virginia from May 4th 1864 to October 15th 1864, inclusive," Thomas

T. Munford Papers, Special Collections Department, William R. Perkins Library, Duke University, Durham, N.C., 1.

3. Rucker, who was 85 at the time he wrote his recollections, erred in recalling seeing the dead and wounded along the route of march.

    Samuel Burns Rucker, St., "Recollections of My War Record During the Confederacy," January 5, 1930, Jones Memorial Library, Lynchburg, Va., 2. (Hopkins 1914, 145-146)

4. Gregg, the division commander, in his report said that Company A, 4th U.S. and the 6th New York Light Artillery served in the action around Todd's Tavern. The Regular artillery lost two men wounded on May 7. There are no dates available for the casualty returns of the New York Artillery. It is the author's assumption that it saw service with the 1st Pennsylvania.

    May 5, Diary, Henry P. Turner, 1st Massachusetts Cavalry, Civil War Miscellaneous Collection, USAMHI, 2.

5. Samuel Burns Rucker, "Recollections," Civil War Miscellaneous Collection, USAMHI, 2. "The Wounded," *Richmond Whig*, May 7, 1864, p. 2, col. 1.

6. Samuel Rucker, "Recollections," Civil War Miscellaneous Collection, USAMHI, Carlisle Barracks, Pa., 2.

7. (Hopkins 1914, 146-147)

8. (Hopkins 1914, 147-148), May 5, 1864, Diary of William R. Carter, 3rd Virginia Cavalry, Special Collections Department, Eggleston Library, Hamden-Sydney College.

9. Mr. Suderow's footnotes indicate that the 1st Pennsylvania Cavalry picketed the Brock Road that night.

    Bryce Suderow, "Todd's Tavern, Va., May 5-8, 1864: Sheridan vs. Stuart: the Opening Round," unpublished monograph, 2-3.

10. (*OR*, XXXVI, part 1, 318, 350, 387) Itinerary of the II Corps. Report of Maj. Gen. Winfield S. Hancock, II Corps, commanding. Itinerary of the 1st Brig., 1st Div, II Corps.

11. Caril mistook the rolling, broken terrain as an earthwork. I have seen the same thing happen while hiking the unbelievably rough terrain of South Mountain (Md.) with the U.S. Army War College. The Confederates had not had the time to build earthworks so close to the Brock Road. No other accounts, which I have seen, indicate that formal works were constructed so close to the road at that time.

    (King 1895, 63), Harrison Caril, "Campaigning With Grant Through Virginia," *The National Tribune*, April 9, 1925, 5.

12. (Krick, 1985, 40)

13. (*OR*, XXXVI, part 1, 710) Report of Col. Thomas O. Seaver, 3rd Vt.

14. (Ibid., 701, 714) Reports of Col. Lewis A. Grant and Capt. Eugene A. Hamilton, 5th Vt. L. A. Grant, "In the Wilderness," *The National Tribune*, January 28, 1897, 1.

15. (Ibid., 697) Report of Col. Lewis A. Grant, Vt. Brig., commanding.

16. (Ibid., 711) Report of Lt. Col. Stephen Pingree, 4th Vt.

17. (Bates 1870, III:290)

18. (*OR*, XXXVI, part 1, 691) Report of Maj. Thomas McLaughlin, 102nd Pa.

19. (*Medical and Surgical History* 1991, VIII:222 and 336)

20. (Rhodes 1985, 144)

21. (Ibid., 146)

22. (Hutchinson 1890, 176)

23. (*Medical and Surgical History* 1991, VIII:240)

24. (Hutchinson 1890, 176)

25. (Roe 1909, 258)

26. (*Medical and Surgical History* 1991, VII:240)

27. (Bowen 1884, 275)

28. Samuel Dunham, "Death of General Hays, Where and How He Fell at the Battle of the Wilderness," *The National Tribune*, November 12, 1885, 3.

29. Elder died on May 30, 1864, probably from the head injury. (*Medical and Surgical History* 1991, VIII:335)

30. (Ibid., VIII:225)

31. Samuel Dunham, "Death of General Hays, Where and How He Fell at the Battle of the Wilderness," *The National Tribune*, November 12, 1885, 3.

32. (*OR*, XXXVI, part 1, 122 and 483) Report of Lt. Col. William B. Neeper, 57th Pennsylvania

    (Bates 1869, II:252)

33. For Hays to have been shot while riding behind the 93rd New York and the 63rd Pennsylvania, the two regiments had to have been on the line at the same time. The 57th Pennsylvania had to have retired from the firing to allow the 93rd New York to occupy the same space.

    (King 1895, 60)

34. (*OR*, XXXVI, part 1, 487) Report of Col. Robert McAllister, 1st Brig., 4th Div., II Corps, commanding.

35. (Marbaker 1898, 162)

36. (*OR*, XXXVI, part 1, 487) Report of Col. Robert McAllister, 1st Brig., 4th Div., II Corps, commanding.

37. (Ibid., 487, 492, 496, 498) Reports of Capt. Thomas C. Godfrey, 5th N.J.; Col. Robert McAllister, 1st Brig., 4th Div., II Corps, commanding; Lt. Col. John Schoonover, 11th N.J.; Capt. Thomas C. Thompson, 7th N.J.

38. These two regiments had to have been in the rear line. The report of the 7th New Jersey mentions the brigade's second line, and these two regiments were the only ones not in the front line.

39. Cornelius Van Santvoord, *The One Hundred and Twentieth Regiment New York State Volunteers* (Rondout, N.Y.: Kingston and Freeman, 1894), 114.

40. (*OR*, XXXVI, part 1, 697) Report of Col. Lewis A. Grant, Vt. Brig., commanding.

41. (Van Santvoord 1894, 114)

42. (*OR*, XXXVI, part 1, 697) Report of Col. Lewis A. Grant, Vt. Brig., commanding.

43. Harrison Caril, "Campaigning With Grant Through Virginia," *The National Tribune*, April 9, 1925, 5.

44. (Ibid.)

45. Harrison Caril, "Campaigning With Grant Through Virginia," *The National Tribune*, April 9, 1925, 5.

46. *(OR*, XXXVI, part 1, 697) Report of Col. Lewis A. Grant, Vt. Brig., commanding.

47. (Ibid., 487) Report of Col. Robert McAllister, 1st Brig., 4th Div., II Corps, commanding.

48. (Ibid., 492) Report of Lt. Col. John Schoonover, 11th N.J.

49. (Ibid., 498) Report of Capt. Thomas C. Thompson, 7th N.J.

50. (Ibid., 487) Report of Col. Robert McAllister, 1st Brig., 4th Div., II Corps, commanding.

51. (Ibid., 488)

52. (Ibid., 711) Report of Lt. Col. Stephen Pingree, 4th Vt. Wilbur Fisk, Diary, 2nd Vermont, Manuscript Division, LOC.

53. Wilbur Fisk, Diary, 2nd Vermont, Manuscript Division, LOC.

54. (Clark 1901, III:27) Account of Major Charles Stedman, 44th N.C.

55. (Ibid., I:595 and II:111) Accounts of Col. W. J. Martin and Capt. E. R. Outlaw, Co. C, 11th N.C., and 2nd Lt. Rowan Rogers, Co. I, 47th N.C.

56. *(OR*, XXXVI, part 1, 701) Report of Col. Lewis A. Grant, Vt. Brig.

57. (Clark 1901, III:304–305) Report of Charles M. Cooke, Adj., 55th N.C.

58. W. M. Graham, "Twenty-sixth Mississippi Regiment," *Confederate Veteran*, XV, 1907, 169.

59. This is based upon information established earlier.

60. Bert Berry, "General Alex. Hays," *The National Tribune*, October 29, 1885, 4. Samuel Dunham, "Death of General Hays, Where and How He Fell at the Battle of the Wilderness," *The National Tribune*, November 12, 1885, 3. (Silliker 1985, 146), (King 1895, 60)

61. Samuel Dunham, "Death of General Hays, Where and How He Fell at the Battle of the Wilderness," *The National Tribune*, November 12, 1885, 3. (Bates 1870, III:786)

62. James A. Graham, Letter to Mother, May 9, 1864, James A. Graham Papers, 1861-1901, Special Collections Department, William R. Perkins Library, Duke University, Durham, N.C.

63. C. R. Dudley, "What I Know About the Wilderness," Confederate Veteran Papers, Special Collections Department, William R. Perkins Library, Duke University, Durham, N.C., 2 and 3.

64. (Clark 1901, III:27-28) Account of Major Charles M. Stedman, 44th N.C.

65. (Ibid.)

66. (Ibid., 111)

67. (Ibid., 3)

68. *(OR*, XXXVI, part 1, 488) Report of Col. Robert McAllister, 1st Brig., 4th Div., II Corps, commanding.

69. (Ibid., 701) Report of Col. Lewis A. Grant, Vt. Brig.

70. W. M. Graham, "Twenty-Sixth Mississippi Regiment," *Confederate Veteran*, XV, 1907, 169.

71. (*OR*, XXXVI, part 1, 697, 701) Report of Col. Lewis A. Grant, Vt. Brig.

   (Clark 1901, I:596) Account of Capt. E. R. Outlaw, Company C, 11th N.C.

72. Besides the colonel, who was wounded, the Confederates killed three line officers, wounded six more, and killed, wounded or captured 187 enlisted men before the 5th Vermont quit the field.

   (*OR*, XXXVI, part 1, 714) Report of Capt. Eugene A. Hamilton, 5th Vt.

73. (Ibid.) Report of Lt. Col. John Schoonover, 11th N.J.

   (Van Santvoord 1894, 113)

74. (Ibid., 697, 701) Report of Col. Lewis A. Grant, Vt. Brig.

75. (Ibid., 492) Report of Lt. Col. John Schoonover, 11th N.J.

76. (Ibid.)

77. (Ibid., 488) Report of Col. Robert McAllister, 1st Brig., 4th Div., II Corps, commanding.

78. (Ibid., 697, 701) Report of Lewis A. Grant, Vt. Brig.

   (Clark, 1901, I:596) Account of Capt. E. R. Outlaw, Co. C, 11th N.C.

79. (Ibid.)

80. (Steere 1960, 228)

81. Berry Greenwood Benson, "Reminiscences of Berry Greenwood Benson, C.S.A.," Berry G. Benson Miscellaneous Writings, Typed Manuscript, Vol. I, Southern Historical Collection, University of North Carolina, Chapel Hill, N.C., 252.

82. (Caldwell 1951, 128)

83. (Ibid.)

84. (Ibid.)

85. (Clark 1901, IV:191) Account of 1st Lt. George H. Mills, Co. G, 16th N.C.

86. (Ibid.)

87. The exact position of the 13th North Carolina is not known, but if Lane's brigade relieved the 13th as stated, it had to have been on the right of the line, probably the extreme right. Lane struck the southern most part of the Federal line near the Brock Road.

   (Ibid., 675-676) Account of Lt. R. S. Williams, Co. I, 13th N.C.

88. Dudley did not mention that three infantrymen helped him bring in the gun. Dudley's letter to *Confederate Veteran* predates Poague's manuscript by seven years. Poague said the piece was a 3 inch rifle and he credited a lieutenant of the 44th North Carolina with saving it. Dudley, whose account is the only one consistent with Poague's in regard to the number of guns rescued, said the gun was a 12 Pounder Napoleon. I took Dudley's word over Poague's because Dudley was among the men who saved the field piece.

   C. R. Dudley, "What I know about the Wilderness," June 12, 1896, *Confederate Veteran* Papers, Special Collections Department, William R. Perkins Library, Duke University, Durham, N.C., 3. (Clark 1901, III:28) Account of Maj. Charles M. Stedman, 44th N.C. (Poague 1957, 88)

Chapter Nine

1. (Gibbon 1978, 212)

2. John G. B. Adams, *Reminiscences of the Nineteenth Massachusetts Regiment* (Boston: Wright & Potter Printing Co., 1899), 87-88.

3. (Ford 1898, 323-324)

4. (*OR*, XXXVI, part 1, 350) Itinerary of the II Corps.

5. (Gibbon 1978, 211-212)

6. William P. Seville, *History of the First Regiment, Delaware Volunteers* (Longstreet House, reprint, 1986), 106.

7. Seville described the terrain and Bowen the time of the advance.

   (Ibid.), Diary, George A. Bowen, (Co. C, 12th New Jersey), Diary, May 5, 1864.

8. The 26th North Carolina was the only regiment on line directly in front of the 16th North Carolina.

   (Clark 1901, IV:191) Account of 1st Lt. George H. Mills, Co. G, 16th N.C.

9. (Ibid., I:596) Account of Maj. W. J. Martin, and Capt. Edward R. Outlaw, Co. C, 11th N.C.

10. Russell C. White, ed., *The Civil War Diary of Wyman S. White* (Baltimore: Butternut and Blue, 1991), 360-361.

11. (Weygant 1877, 286-287), George W. Kilmer, (Cpt., Co. C, 141st Pennsylvania), "With Grant in the Wilderness," *The National Tribune*, July 17, 1924, 7. David Craft, *History of the One Hundred Forty-First Pennsylvania Volunteers, 1862-1865* (Towanda, Pa.: Reporter-Journal Printing Co., 1885), 178.

12. (*OR*, XXXVI, part 1, 487, 492) Reports of Col. Robert McAllister, 11th N.J., 1st Brig., 4th Div., II Corps, commanding, and Lt. Col. John Schoonover, 11th N.J.

13. (Weygant 1877, 287)

14. (Ibid.)

15. (Ibid.)

16. (Adams 1899, 87-88)

17. (Seville 1986, 106)

18. (Page 1906, 234, 235, 277, 281)

19. (*Medical and Surgical History* 1991, VIII:342)

20. (Page 1906, 234, 235, 277, 281)

21. At Chancellorsville, a bullet permanently dislocated Crinyan's left thumb. One month later, at Gettysburg, a second round struck him above the left knee and gave him a permanent limp. This wound left him with dizzy spells and a constant headache.

    (*Medical and Surgical History* 1991, VII:103)

22. (Ibid., 504)

23. (Page 1906, 234, 235, 277, 281)

24. Berry Greenwood Benson, "Reminiscences of Berry Greenwood Benson, C.S.A.," Berry Benson Miscellaneous Writings, Typed Manuscript, Vol. 1, Southern Historical Collection, University of North Carolina, Chapel Hill, N.C., 252.

25. Caldwell said that the brigade guided left which would have accounted for it losing contact with Scales' brigade on its right and which would concur with Berry Benson who said that he and the sharpshooters formed the extreme right of the brigade whose flank was on the north side of the Plank Road.

    (Caldwell 1951, 128)

26. Berry Greenwood Benson, "Reminiscences of Berry Greenwood Benson, C.S.A.," Berry Benson Miscellaneous Writings, Typed Manuscript, Vol. 1, Southern Historical Collection, University of North Carolina, Chapel Hill, N.C., 252, 256.

27. "Monument to Nine Confederate Brothers," *Confederate Veteran*, XX, 1913, 225.

28. Berry Greenwood Benson, "Reminiscences of Berry Greenwood Benson, C.S.A.," Berry Benson Miscellaneous Writings, Typed Manuscript, Vol. 1, Southern Historical Collection, University of North Carolina, Chapel Hill, N.C., 252, 256.

29. Berry Greenwood Benson, "Reminiscences of Berry Greenwood Benson, C.S.A.," Berry Benson Miscellaneous Writings, Typed Manuscript, Vol. 1, Southern Historical Collection, University of North Carolina, Chapel Hill, N.C., 252-253.

30. (Craft 1885, 178)

31. (Weygant 1877, 288)

32. Ashbury F. Haynes, "How Haynes Won His Medal of Honor," *The National Tribune*, October 21, 1926, 3.

33. Sergeant Moore suffered from giddiness, headaches, and impaired vision for the rest of his life.

    (*Medical and Surgical History* 1991, VIII:286 and VII:116)

34. (Weygant 1877, 288)

35. The historian of the 141st Pennsylvania placed the time of the lull at around 5:30 P.M. which makes sense. He then went on to claim that the 20th Indiana flanked and destroyed the 7th North Carolina around dusk. Evidence indicates that the 20th Indiana did capture a large part of the 55th Virginia and its colors. The 66th New York took out the 7th North Carolina.

    (Craft 1885, 178)

36. Kilmer mistakenly believed the Indianans took the colors of the 7th North Carolina.

    George W. Kilmer, "With Grant in the Wilderness," *The National Tribune*, July 17, 1924, 7. (*The Medal of Honor* 1948, 152), (Sullivan 1989, 68)

37. Berry Greenwood Benson, "Reminiscences of Berry Greenwood Benson, C.S.A.," Berry Benson Miscellaneous Writings, Typed Manuscript, Vol. 1, Southern Historical Collection, University of North Carolina, Chapel Hill, N.C., 253.

38. (Caldwell 1951, 129)

39. (*OR*, XXXVI, part 1, 351) Itinerary of the II Corps.

40. Henry Roback, comp., *The Veteran Volunteers of Herkimer and Ostego Counties in the War of the Rebellion: Being a History of the 152nd N.Y.V.* (Little Falls: L. C. Childs and Son, 1888), 67-68.

41. Galwey cited the time as 4:30 P.M.

    (Galwey 1961, 197)

    Bowen said the regiment, Carroll's front right, received one volley and were hurt badly by the Confederates.

George A. Bowen, (Lt., Co. C, 12th N.J.), Diary, May 5, 1864.

He remembered his regiment received several volleys.

(Seville 1986, 106)

42. He described McGowan's brigade as getting fired on from the rear. It seems that this had to have been the 12th South Carolina which had advanced too far forward ahead of its brigade.

(Dunlop 1988, 397)

43. His watch might not have been accurate. It had to have been after 4:40 P.M. to fit the time established in the *OR* by the II Corps Itinerary.

(Galwey 1961, 196-197)

44. The 4th Ohio regiment was not present on May 5. It had train guard until May 6.

(Seville 1986, 105), Owen T. Wright, "Liked Gen. Grant's Story," *The National Tribune*, February 25, 1897, 3. William Kepler, *History of the Three Months' and Three Years' Service From April 16th, 1861, to June 22d, 1864, of the Fourth Regiment Ohio Volunteer Infantry in the War for the Union* (Cleveland: Leader Printing Co., 1886), 164.

45. (Roback 1888, 67-68)

46. Charles H. Myerhoff, "The Wilderness, The Charge of Carroll's Celebrated Brigade," *The National Tribune*, October 23, 1890, 4. Owen T. Wright, "Liked Gen. Grant's Story 'One Who Was There' Tells How He Was Taken in by the Johnnies," *The National Tribune*, February 25, 1897, 3. (Steere 1960, 231)

47. (Steere 1960, 229)

48. (Caldwell 1951, 132)

49. (Dunlop 1988, 375), (Clark 1901, III:303) Report of Adj. Charles M. Cooke, 55th N.C.

50. (Seville 1986, 106), Diary, George A. Bowen, (Co. C, 12th N.J.), Diary, May 5, 1864.

51. Diary, George A. Bowen, (Co. C, 12th N.J.), Diary, May 5, 1864.

52. (Favill 1909, 288)

53. (*OR*, XXXVI, part 1, 388) Report of Capt. James Fleming, 28th Massachusetts

54. (Ibid., 395) Report of Capt. Robert Milliken, 69th N.Y.

55. (*Medical and Surgical History* 1991, VIII:289, 353, 359)

56. J. H. Lane, "History of Lane's North Carolina Brigade," *SHSP,* IX, 1881, 124.

57. (Clark 1901, I:676) Account of 1st Lt. Rowland S. Williams, Co. I, 13th N.C.

58. (Steere 1960, 235)

59. (Clark 1901, II:47)

60. (*OR*, XXXVI, part 1, 372) Report of Maj. Nathan Church, 26th Mich.

61. (Ibid., 378, 381, 383, 385) Reports of Maj. George W. Scott, 61st N.Y.; Lt. James Deno, 81st Pennsylvania; Capt. Thomas Henry, 140th Pennsylvania; and Lt. Col. George Egbert, 183rd Pennsylvania

62. (Ibid., 407) Report of Brig. Gen. John R. Brooke, 4th Brig., 1st Div., II Corps, commanding.

63. (Ibid., 399) Itinerary of the 3rd Brig., 1st Div., II Corps.

64. (Favill 1909, 287)

65. This is based upon Favill's statement that Frank, who was on the extreme left of the division, did not incline far enough to the right to cover the railroad bed, which cut southeasterly across, and almost parallel to the division's front. Smyth, whose command lost 349 men in two days of fighting, had to have been severely engaged on the left where the heavy firing was reported. Brooke, on the other hand, suffered only 26 losses in two days.

(OR, XXXVI, part 1, 121)

The 148th Pennsylvania acted as brigade skirmishers and flankers. It appears that Brooke, in advancing 600 yards, stumbled upon A. P. Hill's division and started the action. Frank's brigade then came to its support as it fell back.

(Bates 1870, IV:579)

66. (Pyne 1961, 187)

67. (Myers 1956, 262)

68. (OR, XXXVI, part 1, 407) Report of Brig. Gen. John R. Brooke, 4th Brig., 1st Div., II Corps, commanding.

69. (Ibid., 420) Report of Lt. Simon Pincus, 66th N.Y.

70. This is based upon the report of the 66th New York (Brooke) which said the regiment was on the right of Frank's Brigade.

71. (OR, XXXVI, part 1, 420) Report of Lt. Simon Pincus, 66th N.Y.

72. James C. Mohr, ed., *The Cormany Diaries: A Northern Family in the Civil War* (Pittsburgh: University of Pittsburgh Press, 1982), 419.

73. (Pyne 1961, 189), (Myers 1956, 262), (Neese 1983, 260)

74. (OR, XXXVI, part 1, 867) Itinerary of the 8th Pennsylvania Cav., May 1-June 30.

75. Major J. D. Ferguson, "Memoranda of the Itinerary and Operations of Major General Fitz. Lee's Cavalry Division of the Army of Northern Virginia from May 4th 1864 to October 15th 1864, inclusive," Thomas T. Munford Papers, Special Collections Department, William R. Perkins Library, Duke University, Durham, N.C., 1. "Report of Major General Fitzhugh Lee," Eleanor S. Brockenbrough Library, The Museum of the Confederacy, 4.

Hopkins did not see the fighting on May 5. He described the fighting on May 6, 7, and 8. He wrote, quite correctly, "The first day we did not see the enemy, but we knew he was there, for the woods were ringing with the sound of his guns, and bullets were hissing about our ears."

(Hopkins 1914, 145)

76. Annette Tapert, ed., *The Brothers' War* (N.Y.: *Time* Books, 1988), 190.

77. Diary of Private James F. Wood, Company F, 7th Virginia Cavalry, Virginia State Archives, Richmond, 1. (OR, XXXVI, part 1, 129)

78. "Report of Major General Fitzhugh Lee," Eleanor S. Brockenbrough Library, The Museum of the Confederacy, 4.

79. (OR, XXXVI, part 1, 407) Report of Brig. Gen. John R. Brooke, 4th Brig., 1st Div., II Corps, commanding.

80. (Favill 1909, 288)

81. (Ibid.)

82. (Ibid.), (Frederick 1895, 220)

83. (Ibid.)

84. (*OR*, XXXVI, part 1, 420) Report of Lt. Simon Pincus, 66th N.Y.

85. (Clark 1901, I:383)

86. (Clark 1901, I:383)

87. (*OR*, XXXVI, part 1, 420) Report of Lt. Simon Pincus, 66th N.Y.

88. (Steere 1960, 235)

89. (Favill 1909, 289)

90. (Frederick 1895, 220)

91. (Favill 1909, 289)

92. This is based upon the approximate location of the two regiments as stated in Clark's *North Carolina Regiments.*

    (Frederick 1895, 220)

93. M. McDonald, "March and Battle," *The National Tribune*, April 2, 1896, 3.

94. (Frederick 1895, 220)

95. (*Medical and Surgical History* 1991, VIII:341)

96. (Frederick 1895, 221)

97. (*Medical and Surgical History* 1991, VIII:422)

98. Thomas Alfred Martin Memoir, Wilmer D. Martin Collection, 10. Used with permission.

99. (Clark 1901, II:569) Account of Maj. J. A. Weston, 33rd N.C.

100. Berry Greenwood Benson, "Reminiscences of Berry Greenwood Benson, C.S.A.," Berry G. Benson Miscellaneous Writings, Typed Mss., Vol. 1, Southern Historical Collection, University of North Carolina, Chapel Hill, N.C., 254-255.

Chapter Ten

1. The *OR's* show one man missing in the 13th Massachusetts. It is safe to assume that those men did return to the regiment after the Wilderness and before Laurel Hill.

   (*OR*, XXXVI, part 1, 123)

2. (Roe 1914, 174-175)

3. Alfred Thompson, Diary, May 5, 1864, Jay Luvaas Collection, Manuscript Department, USAMHI.

4. (Haines 1897, 146)

5. Samuel Buck, Memoirs, Samuel Buck Papers, 1890, Special Collections Department, William R. Perkins Library, Duke University, Durham, N.C., 94-95.

6. George Q. Peyton, "A Civil War Record for 1864-1865," FSNBP, Chatham, 22.

7. (Hale and Phillips 1981, 105-106)

8. Samuel Buck, Memoirs, Samuel Buck Papers, 1890, Special Collections Department, William R. Perkins Library, Duke University, Durham, N.C., 96-97.

9. Captain James Bumgardner, Jr., "The Fifty-second Virginia," Richmond *Dispatch*, October 8, 1905, Manuscripts Department, University of Virginia Library, Charlottesville, Va.

10. (Brainard 1915, 196-197)

    The *OR's* reported 312 casualties.

    (*OR*, XXXVI, part 1, 123)

11. (Farley 1990, 33-34)

12. (Howard 1975, 274, 275)

13. James Huffman, *Ups And Downs Of A Confederate Soldier* (N.Y.: William E. Rudge's Sons, 1940), 85.

14. (Ibid., 85-86)

15. (Howard 1975, 278)

16. W. H. Morgan does not appear on that regiment's roster. The man had to have been John A. Morgan.

    Louis Dugal, "Wounded at the Wilderness," *The National Tribune*, November 18, 1912, 7.

17. (Kent 1976, 260)

18. (Ibid.)

19. (*OR*, XXXVI, part 1, 123)

20. (Small 1939, 133)

21. (Worsham 1912, 204-205)

22. (Hyde 1894, 185)

23. Brevet Major Albert A. Nickerson, 7th Maine, "Experiences of a Line Officer," Read May 3, 1911, MOLLUS Papers, unpublished, Manuscripts Department, USAMHI, 26.

24. John Duncan was reported as missing in action on May 12, 1864.

    John P. Beech, "Getting Even," *The National Tribune*, January 25, 1912, 8. John P. Beech, "Gallantry of the 4th New Jersey in the Wilderness," *Grand Army Scout and Soldiers' Mail*, October 25, 1884, 1.

25. (Handerson 1962, 72)

26. (Nichols 1961, 144)

27. I. G. Bradwell, "Battle of the Wilderness," *Confederate Veteran*, XXVII, 1919, 459.

28. (Ibid.)

    Nichols, at this point, got his facts confused. He recalled the 31st Georgia leaving around 9:00 A.M. This is contrary to Bradwell's account, which makes more sense.

    (G. W. Nichols 1961, 147)

29. (Simons 1888, 197-198)

    Company H was sent out on the 5th of May to join the division's outposts (125th N.Y.) and was forgotten about and assumed captured for two days.

    (Bates 1870, IV:522)

30. (Stevens 1866, 401)

31. (Silliker 1985, 145)

32. (Roback 1888, 67-68)

33. (Adams 1899, 87-88)

34. (Galwey 1961, 197)

35. Diary, George A. Bowen (Co. C, 12th N.J.), May 5, 1864.

36. (*Medical and Surgical History* 1991, VIII:500)

37. William Kent, "A Wilderness Memory," *Civil War Times Illustrated*, March 1989, 38.

38. (Ibid., 38-39)

39. (Nesbitt 1908, 348)

40. Avery Harris, "Personal Reminiscences of the Author from August 1862 to June 1865, War of the Rebellion," Avery Harris Papers, Manuscript Department, USAMHI, 161.

41. (Curtis 1891, 233, 234), Avery Harris, "Personal Reminiscences of the Author from August 1862 to June 1865, War of the Rebellion," Avery Harris Papers, Manuscript Department, USAMHI, 161.

42. (Todd 1889, 324)

43. (Steere 1960, 223, map 14)

44. (Cook 1882, 127), Earl M. Rogers, A.D.C., "How Wadsworth Fell, His Death in the Battle of the Wilderness," *The National Tribune*, December 24, 1885, 1. Avery Harris, "Personal Reminiscences of the Author from August 1862 to June 1865, War of the Rebellion," Avery Harris Papers, Manuscript Department, USAMHI, 162-163.

45. Lieutenant Colonel Cook said the regiment made a "tiresome march" around night-fall, which would have placed the time at 7:00 P.M. and that the regiment became engaged after an advance of one mile. The firing stopped around 8:30 P.M.

    (Cook 1882, 127-128)

46. (Dawes 1984, 261)

47. According to Steere in *The Wilderness Campaign*, Wadsworth's men ran into the 5th Alabama Sharpshooters but the brigade to which that regiment belonged had remained quite cohesive and was engaged in Saunders Field. More than likely it was the 5th Alabama Battalion which was attached as A. P. Hill's provost guard.

48. (Cook 1882, 127-128), (Todd 1889, 324)

49. Avery Harris, "Personal Reminiscences of the Author from August 1862 to June 1865, War of the Rebellion," Avery Harris Papers, Manuscript Department, USAMHI, 162-163.

50. (Cook 1882, 127-128), (Todd 1889, 324)

51. (Dawes 1984, 261)

52. Earl M. Rogers, ADC, "How Wadsworth Fell, His Death at the Battle of the Wilderness," *The National Tribune*, December 24, 1885, 1.

53. Captain Robert Monteith, "Battle of the Wilderness, And Death of General Wadsworth," *War Papers Read Before the Commandery of the State of Wisconsin, Military Order of the Loyal Legion of the United States*, I (Milwaukee: Burdick, Armitage & Allen, 1891), 412-413.

54. (Dawes 1984, 261)

55. (Dunlop 1988, 375)

56. (Sloan 1883, 82)

57. Berry Greenwood Benson, "Reminiscences of Berry Greenwood Benson," Berry G. Benson Miscellaneous Writings, Typed Manuscript, Vol. 1, Southern Historical Collection, University of North Carolina, Chapel Hill, N.C., 255-256.

58. Diary, George A. Bowen (Co. C, 12th N.J.), May 5, 1864.

59. (Seville 1986, 106)

60. (Cowtan 1882, 246), (Seville 1986, 106)

61. Diary, George A. Bowen (Co. C, 12th N.J.), May 5, 1864. (Seville 1986, 106)

62. (Weygant 1877, 288)

63. Ashbury F. Haynes, "How Haynes Won His Medal of Honor," *The National Tribune,* October 21, 1926, 3.

64. William Kent, "A Wilderness Memory," *Civil War Times Illustrated,* March 1989, 37.

65. (Ibid.)

66. (Stevens 1866, 402)

67. Harrison Caril, "Campaigning With Grant Through Virginia," *The National Tribune,* April 9, 1925, 5.

68. (Clark 1901, III:305)

69. Diary, George W. Hall, 14th Georgia Volunteers, May 5 and 6, 1864, Georgia Room, University of Georgia. (Caldwell 1951, 181)

70. (Ibid., 131-132)

71. J. H. Lane, "History of Lane's North Carolina Brigade," *SHSP,* IX, 1881, 126. (Clark 1901, IV:191) Report of 1st Lt. George H. Mills, Co. G, 16th N.C.

72. (Ibid., I:676, and IV:191)

73. (Ibid., II:569, 665)

74. (Dunlop 1988, 375-376)

75. (Clark 1901, II:569, 665)

76. (Ibid., II:47)

77. J. H. Lane, "History of Lane's North Carolina Brigade," *SHSP,* IX, 1881, 126.

78. (Weld 1979, 285)

79. John Anderson, *The Fifty-Seventh Regiment of Massachusetts Volunteers in the War of the Rebellion, Army of the Potomac* (Boston: E. B. Stillings & Co., Printers, 1896), 34. Byron M. Cutcheon, *The Story of the Twentieth Michigan Infantry July 15th, 1862, to May 30th, 1865* (Lansing: Robert Smith Printing Co., 1904), 103.

80. "Memoirs of William Baird," 1911, Michigan Historical Collections, Bentley Historical Library, University of Michigan, 15.

81. (Adams 1900, 374-375), Weather report from Georgetown, May 4-June 1864, Fredericksburg and Spotsylvania National Battlefield Park.

82. Allen D. Albert, *History of the Forty-Fifth Regiment Pennsylvania Veteran Volunteer Infantry 1861-1865* (Williamsport, Pa.: Grit Publishing Co. 1912), 114.

83. C. F. Jeffers, "What The Ninth Corps Did," *The National Tribune,* July 2, 1896, 2.

Bibliography

Published Primary Sources

Adams, John G. B. *Reminiscences of the Nineteenth Massachusetts Regiment.* Boston: Wright & Potter Printing Co., 1899.

Adams, Z. Boylston. "In the Wilderness," *Civil War Papers Read Before the Commandery of Massachusetts, Military Order of the Loyal Legion of the United States.* II. Boston: 1900.

Agassis, George R. ed. *Meade's Headquarters 1863-1865, Letters of Col. Theodore Lyman From the Wilderness to Appomattox.* Freeport, N.Y.: Libraries Press, 1970.

Albert, Allen D. ed. *History of the Forty-Fifth Regiment Pennsylvania Veteran Volunteer Infantry 1861-1865.* Williamsport, Pa.: Grit Publishing Co., 1912.

Anderson, John. *The Fifty-Seventh Regiment of Massachusetts Volunteers in the War of the Rebellion.* Boston: E. B. Stillings & Co., 1896.

Baquet, Camille. *History of the First Brigade, New Jersey Volunteers From 1861-1865.* Gettysburg: Stan Clark Military Books.

Bates, Samuel P. *History of Pennsylvania Volunteers 1861-5.* 4 volumes. Harrisburg: S. Singerly Printers, 1869-70.

Bennett, Edwin C. *Musket and Sword.* Boston: Coburn Publishing Co., 1900.

Bicknell, George W. *History of the Fifth Regiment Maine Volunteers.* Portland, Me.: Hall L. Davis, 1871.

Bidwell, Frederick David. comp. *History of the Forty-Ninth New York Volunteers.* Albany: J. B. Lyon Co., 1916.

Boudrye, Louis N. *Historic Records of the Fifth New York Cavalry.* Albany: J. Munsel, 1868.

Bowen, James L. *History of the Thirty-Seventh Regiment Mass. Volunteers in the Civil War of 1861-1865.* Holyhoke, Mass.: Clark W. Bryan & Co., 1894.

Brainard, Mary Genevie Green, comp. *Campaigns of the One Hundred and Forty-Sixth Regiment New York State Volunteers.* New York: G. P. Putnam's Sons, 1915.

Brewer, A. T. *History of the Sixty-first Regiment Pennsylvania Volunteers 1861-1865.* 1911.

Caldwell, J. F. J. *History of a Brigade of South Carolinians Known First as "Gregg's:" and Subsequently as "McGowan's Brigade."* Marietta, Ga.: Continental Book Co., 1851.

Camper, Charles and J. W. Kirkley. *Historical Record of the First Regiment Maryland Infantry.* Baltimore: Butternut & Blue, 1990.

Carter, Robert Goldthwaite. *Four Brothers in Blue.* Austin: University of Texas, 1978.

Chamberlin, Thomas. *History of the One Hundred and Fiftieth Regiment Pennsylvania Volunteers, Second Regiment, Bucktail Brigade.* Baltimore: Butternut & Blue, 1986.

Clark, Walter, ed. *Histories of Several Regiments and Battalions From North Carolina in the Great War.* 5 volumes. Raleigh: E. M. Uzzell, 1901.

Cogswell, Leander W. *A History of the Eleventh New Hampshire Regiment Volunteer Infantry in the Rebellion War, 1861-1865.* Concord: Republican Press Association, 1891.

Committee of the Regiment. *History of the Thirty-Sixth Regiment, Massachusetts Volunteers 1862 - 1865.* Boston: Rockwell and Churchill, 1884.

Committee of the Regimental Association. *History of the Eighteenth Regiment of Cavalry, Pennsylvania Volunteers (163rd Regiment of the Line) 1862-1865.* New York, Wynkoop Hallenback Crawford Co., 1909.

Committee of the Regimental Association. *History of the Thirty-Fifth Regiment, Massachusetts Volunteers, 1862-1865.* Boston: Mills, Knight & Co., 1884.

Cook, Benjamin F. *History of the Twelfth Massachusetts Volunteers (Webster Regiment).* Boston: Twelfth (Webster) Regiment Association, 1882.

Cowtan, Charles W. *Services of the Tenth New York Volunteers (National Zouaves) in the War of the Rebellion.* New York: Charles H. Ludwig, 1882.

Craft, David. *History of the One Hundred Forty-First Pennsylvania Volunteers.* Towanda, Pa.: Reporter-Journal Printing Co., 1885.

Curtis, O. B. *History of the Twenty-Fourth Michigan of the Iron Brigade.* Detroit: Winn & Hammond, 1891.

Cutcheon, Byron M. *The Story of the Twentieth Michigan Infantry.* Lansing: Robert Smith Printing, 1904.

Davis, Charles E., Jr. *Three Years in the Army: The Story of the Thirteenth Massachusetts Volunteers.* Boston: Estes and Lauriat, 1894.

Dawes, Rufus R. *Service With the Sixth Wisconsin Volunteers.* Dayton, Ohio: Morningside Bookshop, 1984.

Dickert, D. Augustus. *History of Kershaw's Brigade.* Dayton, Ohio: Morningside Bookshop, 1976.

Dunlop, W. S. *Lee's Sharpshooters.* Dayton, Ohio: Morningside Bookshop, 1988.

Durkin, Joseph T., ed. *Confederate Chaplain, A War Journal of Rev. James B. Sheeran, c.s.s.r., 14th Louisiana, C.S.A..* Milwaukee: The Bruce Publishing Co., 1960.

Farley, Porter. *The 140th New York Volunteers: Wilderness, May 5, 1864.* Gettysburg: The Conflict, 1990.

Favill, Josiah Marshall. *Diary of a Young Officer.* Chicago: Donnelley & Sons, 1909.

Ford, Andrew E. *The Story of the Fifteenth Regiment Massachusetts Volunteer Infantry in the Civil War 1861-1864.* Clinton: W. J. Coulter, 1898.

Frederick, Gilbert. *The Story of a Regiment, Being a Record of the Military Services of the Fifty-Seventh New York State Volunteer Infantry in the War of the Rebellion 1861-1865.* Chicago: The Fifty-Seventh Veteran Association, 1895.

Galwey, Thomas Francis. *The Valiant Hours,* Wilbur S. Nye, ed. Harrisburg: Stackpole, 1961.

Gerrish, Theodore. *A Private's Reminiscences in the Civil War.* Portland, Me.: Hoyt, Fogg & Donham, 1882.

Gibbon, John. *Personal Recollections of the Civil War.* New York: G. P. Putnam's Sons, 1928.

Gordon, John B. *Reminiscences of the Civil War.* Dayton, Ohio: Morningside Bookshop, 1985.

Grotty, Daniel G. *Four Years Campaigning in the Army of the Potomac.* Grand Rapids, Mich.: Dygert Brothers & Co., 1874.

Hadley, Amos, ed., *History of the Sixth New Hampshire Regiment in the War for the Union.* Concord: Republican Press Association, 1891.

Haines, Alanson A. *History of the Fifteenth Regiment New Jersey Volunteers.* New York: Jenkins & Thomas Printers, 1883.

Hale, Laura Virginia and Stanley S. Phillips. *History of the Forty-Ninth Virginia Infantry, C.S.A., "Extra Billy Smith's Boys."* Lynchburg: H. E. Howard, Inc., 1981.

Handerson, Henry E. *Yankee in Gray: The Civil War Memoirs of Henry E. Handerson.* Western Reserve, Ohio: Western Reserve University, 1962.

Hopkins, Luther W. *From Bull Run to Appomattox.* Baltimore: Fleet-McGinley Co., 1914.

Howard, McHenry. *Recollections of a Maryland Confederate Soldier and Staff Officer.* Dayton, Ohio: Morningside Bookshop, 1975.

Howe, Mark DeWolfe, ed. *Touched With Fire, Civil War Letters and Diary of Oliver Wendell Holmes, Jr. 1861-1864.* Cambridge: Harvard University Press, 1946.

Huffman, James. *Ups and Downs of a Confederate Soldier.* New York: William E. Rudge's Sons, 1940.

Hutchinson, Nelson V. *History of the Seventh Massachusetts Volunteer Infantry in the War of the Rebellion of the Southern States 1861-1865.* Taunton, Mass.: Regimental Association, 1890.

Hyde, Thomas W. *Following the Greek Cross or Memories of the Sixth Army Corps.* Boston: Houghton, Mifflin and Co., 1894.

Jackman, Lyman. *History of the Sixth New Hampshire Regiment in the War for the Union.* Concord: Republican Press Association, 1891.

Jones, Terry L., ed. *The Civil War Memoirs of Captain William J. Seymour.* Baton Rouge: Louisiana State University Press.

Judson, Amos M. *History of the Eighty-Third Regiment Pennsylvania Volunteers.* Dayton, Ohio: Morningside Bookshop, 1986.

Kent, Arthur A., ed. *Three Years With Company K.* Rutherford: Farleigh Dickinson University Press, 1976.

Kepler, William. *History of the Three Months' and Three Years' Service of the Fourth Ohio Volunteer Infantry in the War for the Union.* Cleveland: Leader Printing Co., 1886.

King, David H., et al., comp. *History of the Ninety-Third Regiment, New York Volunteer Infantry, 1861-1865.* Milwaukee: Swain & Tate Co., 1895.

King, John R. *My Experience in the Confederate Army and in Northern Prisons.* Clarksburg: U.D.C., 1917.

Lloyd, William Penn. *History of the First Reg't Pennsylvania Reserve Cavalry.* Philadelphia: King & Baird, Printers, 1864.

Macnamara, Daniel George. *The History of the Ninth Regiment Massachusetts Volunteer Infantry June 1861-June 1864.* Boston: E. B. Stillings & Co., 1899.

Marbaker, Thomas D. *History of the Eleventh New Jersey Volunteers From Its Organization to Appomattox.* Trenton: MacCrellish & Quigley, 1898.

McDonald, William N. *A History of the Laurel Brigade,* Bushrod C. Washington, ed., Kate S. McDonald, 1907.

Meier, Heinz K., ed. *Memoirs of a Swiss Officer in the American Civil War*. Bern: Herbert Lang, 1972.

Melcher, Holman S. "An Experience in the Battle of the Wilderness," *War Papers Read Before the Commandery of the State of Maine, Military Order of the Loyal Legion of the United States*. I. Portland: The Thurston Print, 1898.

Mohr, James C., ed. *The Cormany Diaries, A Northern Family in the Civil War*. Pittsburgh: University of Pittsburgh Press, 1982.

Monteith, Robert. "Battle of the Wilderness and Death of General Wadsworth," *War Papers Read Before the Commandery of the State of Wisconsin, Military Order of the Loyal Legion of the United States*. I. Milwaukee: Burdick, Armitage & Allen, 1891.

Myers, Frank. *The Comanches: A History of White's Battalion, Virginia Cavalry*. Marietta, Ga.: The Continental Book Co., 1956.

Nash, Eugene A. *A History of the 44th Regiment, New York Volunteer Infantry in the Civil War*. Chicago: R. R. & Sons, Co., 1911.

Neese, George M. *Three Years in the Confederate Horse Artillery*. Dayton, Ohio: Morningside Bookshop, 1983.

Nesbit, John W. *General History of Company D, 149th Pennsylvania Volunteers and Personal Sketches of the Members*. Oakdale, Cal.: Oakdale Print and Publishing Co., 1908.

Nevins, Allan, ed. *A Diary of Battle, The Personal Journals of Colonel Charles S. Wainwright 1861-1865*. Gettysburg: Stan Clark Military Books,1962.

Nichols, G. W. *A Soldier's Story of His Regiment (61st Georgia)*. Kennesaw, Ga.: Continental Book Co., 1961.

155th Regimental Association. *Under the Maltese Cross: Antietam to Appomattox, The Loyal Uprising in Western Pennsylvania, 1861-1865*. Pittsburgh: the 155th Regimental Association, 1910.

Page, Charles D. *History of the Fourteenth Regiment, Connecticut Vol. Infantry*. Meriden: Horton Printing Co., 1906.

Parker, Francis J. *The Story of the Thirty-Second Massachusetts Infantry*. Boston: C. W. Calkins & Co., 1880.

Perry, William G. Pocket Diary, FSNBP.

Poague, William Thomas. *Gunner With Stonewall, Monroe F. Cockrell, ed.* Jackson, Tenn.: McCowat-Mercer Press, Inc. 1957.

Pyne, Henry R. *Ride to War, The History of the First New Jersey Cavalry*. New Brunswick: Rutgers University Press, 1961.

Rhodes, Robert Hunt, ed. *All for the Union*. Lincoln, R.I.: Andrew Mowbray, Inc., 1985.

Roback, Henry, comp. *The Veteran Volunteers of Herkimer and Ostego Counties in the War of the Rebellion: Being a History of the 152nd N.Y.V.* Little Falls: L. C. Childs and Son, 1888.

Roe, Alfred S. *The Tenth Regiment Massachusetts Volunteer Infantry 1861-1864*. Springfield, Mass.: Tenth Regiment Veteran Association, 1909.

Roe, Alfred S. *The Thirty-Ninth Regiment Massachusetts Volunteers 1862-1865*. Worcester: Regimental Veteran Association, 1914.

Scott, Robert N. comp. *The Official Records of the War of the Rebellion*. Vol. XXXVI, part 1. Washington, D.C.: U.S. Government Printing Office, 1887.

Seville, William P. *History of the First Regiment, Delaware Volunteers.* Longstreet House: reprint, 1986.

Silliker, Ruth L., ed. *The Rebel Yell & the Yankee Hurrah, The Civil War Journal of a Maine Volunteer.* Camden, Me.: Down East Books, 1985.

Simons, Ezra D. *A Regimental History of the One Hundred Twenty-Fifth New York Volunteers.* New York: Ezra D. Simons, 1888.

Sloan, John A. *Reminiscences of the Guilford Grays, Co. B, 27th N.C. Regiment.* Washington, D.C.: R. O. Polkinhorn, 1883.

Small, Harold Adams, ed. *The Road to Richmond.* Berkeley: University of California Press, 1939.

Smith, A. P. *History of the Seventy-Sixth Regiment New York Volunteers.* Cortland: 1867.

Stevens, C. A. *Berdan's Sharpshooters in the Army of the Potomac, 1861-1865.* Dayton, Ohio: Morningside Bookshop, 1984.

Stevens, George T. *Three Years in the Sixth Corps.* Albany: R. S. Gray, 1866.

Stone, James Madison *Personal Recollections of the Civil War.* Boston: 1918.

Styple, William B. and John J. Fitzpatrick. *The Andersonville Diary & Memoirs of Charles Hopkins.* Kearny, N.J.: Belle Grove Publishing Co., 1988.

Survivors' Association. *History of the Corn Exchange Regiment, 118th Pennsylvania Volunteers.* Philadelphia: J. L. Smith, Publisher, 1888.

Sypher, J. R. *History of the Pennsylvania Reserves.* Lancaster, Pa.: Elias Barr & Co., 1865.

Tapert, Annette, ed. *The Brothers' War.* N.Y.: Time Books, 1988.

Thomas, Henry W. *History of the Doles-Cook Brigade, Army of Northern Virginia.* Atlanta: The Franklin Printing and Publishing Co., 1903.

Todd, William, ed. *History of the Ninth Regiment N.Y.S.M.-N.G.S.N.Y. (Eighty-Third New York Volunteers).* New York: Veterans of the Regiment, 1889.

Van Santvoord, Cornelius. *The One Hundred and Twentieth New York State Volunteers.* Rondout, N.Y.: Kingston and Freeman, 1894.

Vautier, John D. *History of the 88th Pennsylvania Volunteers in the War for the Union, 1861-1865.* Philadelphia: J. B. Lippincott, 1894.

Waitt, Ernest Linden, comp. *History of the Nineteenth Regiment Massachusetts Volunteer Infantry 1861-1865.* Salem: The Salem Press, 1906.

Walcott, Charles F. *History of the 21st Massachusetts Volunteers in the War for the Preservation of the Union, 1861-1865.* Boston: 1882.

Weld, Stephen M. *Civil War Diary and Letters of Stephen Minot Weld 1861-1865.* Boston: Massachusetts Historical Society, 1979.

Westbrook, Robert S. *History of the 49th Pennsylvania Volunteers.* Altoona, 1898.

Weygant, Charles H. *History of the One Hundred Twenty-Fourth Regiment, N.Y.S.V.* Newburgh: Journal Printing House, 1877.

White, Russell C., ed. *The Civil War Diary of Wyman S. White.* Baltimore: Butternut & Blue, 1991.

Whitman, William E. S. and Charles H. True. *Maine in the War for the Union: A History of the Part Borne by Maine Troops.* Lewiston: Nelson Dingley, Jr. & Co., 1865.

Wilmer, L. Allison and George W. F. Vernon. *History and Roster of Maryland Volunteers, War of 1861-5.* I. Baltimore: Press of Guggenheimer, Weil & Co., 1898.

Worsham, John H. *One of Jackson's Foot Cavalry.* N.Y.: The Neale Publishing Co., 1912.

Regimentals - Secondary Sources

H. E. Howard, Inc.: Lynchburg, Va.

Armstrong, Richard L. *25th Virginia Infantry and 9th Battalion Virginia Infantry.* 1990.

Ashcraft, John M. *31st Virginia Infantry.* 1988.

Chapla, John. *48th Virginia Infantry.* 1989.

Driver, Robert J, Jr. *58th Virginia Infantry.* 1990.

Frye, Dennis E. *2nd Virginia Infantry.* 1984.

Frye, Dennis E. *12th Virginia Cavalry.* 1988.

Krick, Robert E. L. *40th Virginia Infantry.* 1985.

Murphy, Terrence V. *10th Virginia Infantry.* 1989.

O'Sullivan, Richard. *55th Virginia Infantry.* 1989.

Reidenbaugh, Lowell. *33rd Virginia Infantry.* 1987.

Robertson, James I. *4th Virginia Infantry.* 1982.

Wallace, Lee A. *5th Virginia Infantry.* 1988.

Other Regimentals

Jones, Terry L. *Lee's Tigers.* Baton Rouge: Louisiana State University Press, 1987.

Pullen, John J. *The 20th Maine.* Greenwich, Conn: Fawcett Publications, Inc., 1962.

Reese, Timothy J. *Sykes' Regular Infantry Division, 1861-1864.* Jefferson, N.C.: McFarland & Co., 1990.

Suderow, Bryce. "Todd's Tavern, Va., May 5-8, 1864: Sheridan vs. Stuart: The Opening Round," unpublished monograph.

Periodicals, Newspapers - Primary Sources

Civil War Times Illustrated

Kent, William. "A Wilderness Memory," XXVIII, #1, March 1989, 34-39.

Confederate Veteran

Bradwell, I. G. "Battle of the Wilderness," XVII, 1919, 458-459.

Graham, W. M. "Twenty-Sixth Mississippi Regiment," XV, 1907, 169.

"Monument to Nine Confederate Veterans," XX, 1913, 225.

Rockingham Recorder

"Diary of W. H. Arehart," II, #3, October 1959, 148-155.

Southern Historical Society Papers

Lane, J. H. "History of Lane's North Carolina Brigade," IX, 1881, 124-129.

Thurston, S. D. "Report of the Conduct of General George H. Steuart's Brigade From the 5th to the 12th of May, inclusive," XIV, 1886, 146-151.

The National Tribune

Beech, John P. "Getting Even," January 25, 1912, 8.

Berry, Bert. "General Alex. Hays," October 29, 1885, 4.

Bish, Elijah. "Which Division Was Broken?" January 9, 1990, 3.

Caril, Harrison. "Campaigning With Grant Through Virginia," April 9, 1925, 5.

Cary, William B. "The Wilderness Fight. Opening the Fight by the 5th N.Y. Cav. and the First Man to Fall There," February 1, 1912, 11.

College, James. "The Wilderness. The Place Where the First Battle of the Campaign Was Fought," April 30, 1891, 3.

Dugal, Louis. "Wounded at the Wilderness. Our Boys Had a Hard Time of It Before They Finally Landed at Annapolis," November 28, 1912, 7.

Dunham, Samuel. "Death of General Hays. Where and How He Fell at the Battle of the Wilderness," November 12, 1885, 3.

Garlinger, C. E. "Another Account," October 3, 1889, 3.

Grant, L. A. "In the Wilderness," January 28, 1897, 1.

Haynes, Ashbury F. "How Haynes Won His Medal of Honor," October 21, 1926, 2.

Jeffers, C. T. "What the Gallant Ninth Corps Did," July 9, 1896, 1.

Kilmer, George W. "With Grant in the Wilderness," July 17, 1924, 7.

McDonald, M. "March and Battle," April 2, 1896, 3.

Myerhoff, Charles H. "The Wilderness. The Charge of Carroll's Celebrated Brigade," October 23, 1890, 4.

Robbins, D. H. "A Good Battalion. The 5th N.Y.'s Service at the Wilderness Battle," July 21, 1898, 2.

Robbins, D. H. "Thrice Distinguished. Who Opened the Fight in the Wilderness," May 13, 1909.

Rodgers, Earl M. "How Wadsworth Fell. His Death at the Battle of the Wilderness," December 24, 1885, 1.

Rodgers, W. A. "Mid Bullet and Shell. The 18th Pa. Cav. Had Lively Work in the Mine Run Fight," May 27, 1897, 3.

Syphers, A. L. "In the Wilderness. Was the Right Flank Turned May 6?" June 13, 1889, 3.

Uhler, George H. "The Wilderness. A Pennsylvania Comrade Gives His Experience in the Big Battle," May 21, 1891, 3.

Walley, J. J. "In the Wilderness. Another Account of the Fight at the Angle," December 18, 1890, 4.

Wright, Owen T. "Liked Gen. Grant's Story. One Who Was There Tells How He Was Taken in by the Johnnies," February 25, 1897, 3.

Grand Army Scout and Soldiers' Mail

Beech, John P. "Gallantry of the 4th New Jersey in the Wilderness: The Break in the Lines of the Sixth Corps," October 25, 1884, 1.

Walker, T. F. "Another Account of the 91st P.V.," October 18, 1884, 2.

Newspapers

The Daily Confederate (Richmond, Va.) "Barringer's N.C. Brigade of Cavalry," February 22, 1865.

Daily Dispatch (Richmond, Va.) "Skirmish on the Right Wing," May 7, 1864.

The Richmond Enquirer, "The Wounded," May 10, 1864.

The Richmond Whig, "The Wounded," May 7, 1864.

Manuscript Collections

Alabama State Archives, Montgomery, Alabama

> Battle, Andrew Cullen. "The Third Alabama Regiment."

Marjory G. Blubaugh Collection.

> Stewart, William Shaw. "Experiences of an Army Surgeon, 1863-1864. With Permission.

Duke University, Special Collections Department, William R. Perkins Library, Durham, North Carolina.

> Buck, Samuel. "Recollections of an Old Confed," Samuel Buck Papers, ca. 1890.

> Dudley, C. R. "What I Know About the Wilderness," Confederate Veteran Papers.

> Ferguson, J. D. "Memoranda of the Itinerary and Operations of Major General Fitz Lee's Cavalry Division of the Army of Northern Virginia from May 4th to October 15th, inclusive," Munford-Ellis Family Papers, Thomas T. Munford Div. 1, Miscellany - Box 1, Civil War Mss., 1861-1865.

> Foster, John A. Reminiscences, John A. Foster Papers, 1862- 865.

> Graham, James A. Letter to his mother, May 9, 1864, James A. Graham Papers, 1861-1901.

> Hudgins, Francis L., "38th Georgia Regiment at the Wilderness," Confederate Veteran Papers, Battles 1861-1932 & n.d., Box 1.

> Jackson, Ashbury H. Letter to mother, May 11, 1864, Edward Hardin Papers, 1772-1940.

> Jones, Thomas G. Letters to John W. Daniel, February 29, June 20, and July 3, 1904, John Warwick Daniels Papers, 1849-1904, 22-G.

> Jones, Kenneth Raynor. Diary, 1864.

> Seltzer, Daniel. Letter to his wife, May 7, 1864, Daniel Seltzer Papers, 1858-1865, Rowan Co., N.C.

> Smith, W. W. Letter to John W. Daniel, October 24, 1904, John Warwick Daniel Papers, 1849-1904, 22-G.

> Smith, William W., "The Wilderness and Spotsylvania," John Daniel Warwick Papers, 1905-1910, 22-G.

> Swaringen, Wilber F., "Record of the War Service of W. F. Swaringen, Confederte Veteran," Confederate Veteran Reminiscences 1861-1932, Box 6.

Fredericksburg and Spotsylvania National Battlefield Park, Chatham Hall, Fredericksburg, Virginia.

> Peyton, George Quintus. "A Civil War Record for 1864-1865," 1906.

> "Report of Henry Heth, Spring 1864 to October 1864," Mss., ANV, Leaders, Vol. 178.

Hampden-Sydney College, Eggleston Library.

    Carter, William. Diary.

Wilmer D. Martin Collection, Tuscon, Arizona.

    Martin, Alfred Thomas, Memoir, 38th North Carolina. With Permission.

Library of Congress, Manuscript Division, Washington, D.C.

    Boteler, Alexander R. Diary.

    Doyle, Thomas S. "Memoir of Thomas S. Doyle, Lt., Co. E, 33rd Virginia Infantry."

    Fisk, Wilbur. Co. E, 2nd Vermont, Diary.

Museum of the Confederacy, Eleanor S. Brockenbrough Library, Richmond, Va.

    "Report of Major General Fitzhugh Lee of the Operations of His Cavalry Division, A.N.V., From May 4th 1864 to September 19th 1864 (both inclusive).

National Archives, Washington, D.C.

    RG 94, OAG, Volunteer Organizations, Civil War Returns, Grand Army of the Potomac.

John M. Priest Collection, Boonsboro, Md.

    Bowen, George A. Diary, 12th New Jersey.

The South Carolinia Library, University of South Carolina, Columbia, S.C.

    Hagood, J. R. "Memoirs of the First South Carolina Regiment of Volunteer Infantry in the Confederate War for Independence from April 12, 1861 to April 10, 1865.

    "Reports of Operations of Wade Hampton's Cavalry Division."

United States Army Military History Institute, Manuscripts Department, Carlisle Barracks, Pa.

    Chapin, Charles. Diary, January 1, 1864–December 18, 1864, 1st Vermont Cavalry, Civil War Miscellany Papers, C-E.

    Davis, James. Co. A, 138th Pa., Diary, Civil War Miscellaneous Collection, DA-DE.

    Eichelberger, Grayson M., "Memoirs," October, 1912, Civil War Miscellaneous Collection.

    Harris, Avery. "Personal Reminiscences of the Author From August 1862 to June 1865, War of the Rebellion," Avery Harris Papers.

    Harshberger, A. Surgeon, 149th Pa., "Notes," Milroy, Mifflin Co., Pa., March 25, 1867, Civil War Times Illustrated Collection.

    Heffelfinger, Jacob. Diary, Civil War Times Illustrated Collection.

    Keiser, Henry. Diary, September 21, 1861-July 20, 1865, Harrisburg Civil War Round Table Collection.

    Nickerson, Albert A. "Experiences of a Line Officer," unpublished, M.O.L.L.U.S. Papers.

    Oesterich, Maurus, Diary, Harrisburg Civil War Round Table Collection, Box M-Z, Mss. Dept. 44.

    Rucker, Samuel Burns. "Recollections of My War Record During the Confederacy," January 5, 1930, Civil War Miscellaneous Collection.

    Thompson, Alfred. Letters and Diary, Jay Luvaas Collection.

    Turner, Henry P. Diary, January 1-December 29, 1864, Civil War Miscellaneous Collection.

University of Georgia, Athens, Ga.

> Hall, George W. Diary, 14th Georgia Volunteers, Georgia Room.

University of Michigan, Bentley Historical Library, Ann Arbor, Michigan.

> "Memoirs of William Baird," Michigan Historical Collections.

University of North Carolina at Chapel Hill, Special Collections Department, Chapel Hill, North Carolina.

> Benson, Berry G. "Reminiscences of Berry Greenwood Benson, C.S.A." I, Berry G. Benson Miscellaneous Writings.

University of Virginia, Manuscripts Department, Alderman Library, Charlottesville, Virginia.

> Bumgardner, James. "The Fifty-Second Virginia," *Richmond Dispatch*, October 8, 1905, James Bumgardner Papers.

> Theodore Garnett Memoirs. Garnett Family Papers (#38-45-D)

Virginia Military Institute, Archives Department, Lexington, Virginia.

> Black, William. Diary, 1864.

> "Reports of John J. Shoemaker and P. P. Pendleton, HQ, Horse Artillery, A.N.V."

Virginia State Archives, Richmond, Virginia.

> Wood, James F. Diary, Company F, 7th Virginia Cavalry.

References

Beyer, W. F. and O. F. Keydel, ed. *Deeds of Valor*. I. Detroit: Perin-Keydel Co., 1907.

Hardee, W. J. *Rifle and Light Infantry Tactics, School of the Battalion*. II. Westport, Conn.: Greenwood Press, Reprint, 1971.

Harrison, Noel G. *Gazeteer of Historical Sites Related to the Fredericksburg and Spotsylvania National Military Park*. I, Fredericksburg and Spotsylvania National Military Park, 1986.

Medical and Surgical History of the Civil War. VIII. Wilmington, N.C.: Broadfoot Publishing Co., 1991.

Steere, Edward. *The Wilderness Campaign*. Harrisburg, Pa.: The Stackpole Co., 1960.

U. S. Department of the Army, *The Medal of Honor of the United States*. Washington, D.C.: U. S. Government Printing Office, 1948.

Index

A

Adams, John G. B. (Capt., Co. B, 19th Mass.), 189, 216

Adams, Z. Boylston (Capt., Co F, 56th Mass.), 226

Aldrich farm, 16, 31, 135

Allison, Joseph J. (Sgt., Co. B, 39th Mass.), 115, 116

Alsop's Gate, 31, 163, 168, 169, 170, 201

Amidon, Henry A. (Pvt., Co. K, 4th Vt.), 152

Arehart, William H. (Sgt., Co. H, 12th Va. Cav.), 32

Armstrong, Orlando W. (Asst. Surg., 5th N.Y. Cav.), 43

Army of Northern Virginia
A. P. Hill's Corps, 10, 21, 23
Ewell's Corps, 10, 32
Longstreet's Corps, 10

Army of the Potomac
II Corps, 17-18, 135-138, 161, 164, 176, 199, 215
V Corps, 3-4, 6, 10-12, 13, 26, 28, 29, 31, 37, 43, 46, 47, 53, 98, 126, 136, 142, 143, 217, 226
VI Corps, 4-6, 12-13, 46-47, 97, 100, 121, 126, 136, 137, 147, 173, 207-208, 226
IX Corps, 6, 19-20, 226-227

Arnold, George A. (Pvt., Co. G, 2nd Vt.), 156

Aschmann, Rudolf (Capt., Co. A, 1st U.S. S.S.), 18, 136, 151

Ayres, Romeyn (Brig. Gen., U.S.A.), 28, 37, 38
brigade of: 6, 11, 39, 53, 67, 68, 74, 77, 209

B

Bain, John W., Jr. (2nd Lt., Co. C, 2nd Vt.), 183

Baker, Jacob (Pvt., Co. F, 7th Va. Cav.), 163

Ballentine, John W. (2nd Lt., Co. E, 7th N.C.), 203

Barbour, William M. (Col., 37th N.C.), 196

Bard, Robert (Maj., 95th N.Y.), 56

Barger, Robert B. (Capt., Co. H, 56th Pa.), 56, 89

Barker, Elmer J. (1st Lt., Co. H, 5th N.Y. Cav.), 25

Barlow, Francis (Brig. Gen., U.S.A.), 199, 203
division of: 17, 135, 137, 161, 164, 196, 200, 215

Bartlett, Joseph J. (Brig. Gen., U.S.A.), 32, 34, 70, 94, 96
brigade of: 11, 29, 39, 53, 72, 74, 83, 96, 106, 124

Battle, Cullen (Brig. Gen., C.S.A.)
brigade of: 37, 71, 72, 73, 86, 96, 125, 131

Baxter, Henry (Brig. Gen., U.S.A.)
brigade of: 3, 11, 217-218

299